Praise for *Ancient Persia and the Book of Esther*

'In this accessible and well-illustrated volume, Llewellyn-Jones provides a detailed cultural and iconographic companion to the biblical book of Esther, one which helpfully illuminates for historians and biblical scholars alike the broader Achaemenid context of the narrative.'

Matthew A. Collins, University of Chester, UK

'Biblical scholars know that the Persian context is relevant and significant for understanding the rich narrative of Esther, but most are not trained in the art and archaeology of the Achaemenid world. Llewellyn-Jones, who is so well at home in the Persian cultural context, makes a major contribution to scholarship on Esther, and to the Persian period in biblical studies more generally, with this book. This is indispensable for anyone working on Esther.'

Aaron Koller, Yeshiva University, USA

'Lloyd Llewellyn Jones uses his profound knowledge of ancient Persian culture to shine new light on the book of Esther, highlighting the rich iconography of the Persian court that flavours the Judaeo-Christian text, and setting the Biblical story within the context of the region to provide deeper understanding of this fascinating book.'

Lisa Maurice, Bar-Ilan University, Israel

Ancient Persia and the Book of Esther

Achaemenid Court Culture in the Hebrew Bible

Lloyd Llewellyn-Jones

I.B.TAURIS
LONDON • NEW YORK • OXFORD • NEW DELHI • SYDNEY

I.B. TAURIS
Bloomsbury Publishing Plc
50 Bedford Square, London, WC1B 3DP, UK
1385 Broadway, New York, NY 10018, USA
29 Earlsfort Terrace, Dublin 2, Ireland

BLOOMSBURY, I.B. TAURIS and the I.B. Tauris logo
are trademarks of Bloomsbury Publishing Plc

First published in Great Britain 2023

Copyright © Lloyd Llewellyn-Jones, 2023

Lloyd Llewellyn-Jones has asserted his right under the Copyright, Designs and
Patents Act, 1988, to be identified as Author of this work.

For legal purposes the Acknowledgements on p. xix constitute
an extension of this copyright page.

Cover design by www.paulsmithdesign.com
Cover image: *Haman and Mordecai*, 1884, by Paul Leroy (1860–1942).
Odessa Museum of Western and Eastern Art.

All rights reserved. No part of this publication may be reproduced or transmitted
in any form or by any means, electronic or mechanical, including photocopying,
recording, or any information storage or retrieval system, without prior
permission in writing from the publishers.

Bloomsbury Publishing Plc does not have any control over, or responsibility for,
any third-party websites referred to or in this book. All internet addresses given
in this book were correct at the time of going to press. The author and publisher
regret any inconvenience caused if addresses have changed or sites have ceased
to exist, but can accept no responsibility for any such changes.

A catalogue record for this book is available from the British Library.

A catalog record for this book is available from the Library of Congress.

ISBN:	HB:	978-1-7883-1737-5
	PB:	978-0-7556-0302-2
	ePDF:	978-1-7867-3635-2
	eBook:	978-1-7867-2629-2

Typeset by Integra Software Services Pvt. Ltd.
Printed and bound in Great Britain

To find out more about our authors and books visit www.bloomsbury.com
and sign up for our newsletters.

To Carol Thomas – 'Mrs T' – my teacher.
'Her price is far above rubies'
Proverbs 31:10

Contents

List of Figures	viii
Acknowledgements	xix
Abbreviations	xx
Introduction	1
Commentary	13
Concluding Thoughts	227
Bibliography	230
Index	257

Figures

1.1	Calcite or alabaster jar bearing the names and titles of Xerxes; from Egypt	17
1.2	An Achaemenid king girds his loins and fights with a mythical beast. Doorjamb from the Hall of a Hundred Columns, Persepolis	18
1.3	Stamp seal with a scene of heroic combat. From Persepolis	18
1.4	Cylinder seal with a scene of heroic combat. From Persepolis	19
1.5	Cylinder seal with a scene of heroic combat. From Persepolis	19
1.6	Seal impression showing a Neo-Assyrian king slaying a lion. From Nineveh	19
1.7	Egyptian relief showing a soldier grabbing a prisoner by the hair as he delivers a death blow	19
1.8	Achaemenid seal impression (unknown provenance) of a double hunt scene	20
1.9	A Persian Great King slays a Greek hoplite in combat. Stamp seal from Achaemenid-occupied Anatolia	20
1.10	Delegation of Medes; east staircase of the Apadana at Persepolis	25
1.11	Delegation of Elamites; east staircase of the Apadana at Persepolis	26
1.12	Delegation of Nubians (Kushites); east staircase of the Apadana at Persepolis	26
1.13	Representatives of the Persian empire lift up the king on a huge 'throne'; doorjamb from the Hall of a Hundred Columns, Persepolis	26
1.14	Adopting the so-called 'Atlas pose', representatives of all the lands of the Persian empire lift up the king on a huge bench-throne (*takht*). Façade of the tomb of Darius I, Naqš-i Rustam	27
1.15	The Persian Great King sits upon his throne beneath a woven canopy. The god Ahuramazda hovers overhead. Doorjamb from the Hall of a Hundred Columns, Persepolis	33
1.16	King or prince from North Syria sits upon an ornamental throne with a matching footstool	34
1.17	Seal impression found on a bulla from the City of David showing the presence of YHWH on his throne	34
1.18	Late Period Egyptian schist statue of the goddess Isis sitting on a throne, holding the infant Horus	34

1.19	Detail of a Late Bronze Age ivory (the Megiddo Ivory) from Canaan depicting a local king or prince on his elaborate throne	35
1.20	The ruler of Byblos, Ahiram, depicted on his sarcophagus, sitting on a throne with winged sphinx details	36
1.21	Assyrian king seated on his high throne and footstool; Til Barsip, northern Syria	36
1.22	Assyrian goddess enthroned; Nimrud	37
1.23	Sennacherib seated on his high throne and footstool; Lachish Reliefs, South-West Palace of Sennacherib in Nineveh	37
1.24	Assyrian eunuchs carrying a portable throne; wall relief from Khorsabad	37
1.25	Fragmentary relief showing an Assyrian throne; probably from Nimrud	37
1.26	Achaemenid Great King seated on a throne; detail originally from the east staircase of the Apadana at Persepolis	38
1.27	Remains of an Achaemenid-style throne discovered at Samaria, north Israel	38
1.28	Patterned textiles on an Achaemenid throne; detail originally from the east staircase of the Apadana at Persepolis	38
1.29	The 'Pazyrik Carpet' – actually an Achaemenid-era felt saddlecloth – perfectly preserved in the ice of the Crimea and housed in the State Hermitage Museum, St Petersburg	39
1.30	Detail of the 'Pazyrik Carpet'	39
1.31	Detail from an Uratrian bronze plaque depicting intricately woven textile designs. From near Lake Van	39
1.32	Funerary stele of Djedherbes, showing the deceased sitting on a Persian-style throne. From Persian-occupied Egypt	40
1.33	Persian nobles perform ignoble tasks at court: a royal groom carrying a saddle cloth and whip and an attendant carrying a footstool with which the Great King will mount his horse. East staircase of the Apadana, Persepolis	40
1.34	Early dynastic representation of a pharaoh defeating a foreign (Libyan) enemy	41
1.35	Tiglath-pileser III of Assyria brandishes his weapons of war and stamps on the neck of an enemy prisoner	42
1.36	Anubanini, king of the Lullubi, humiliates his enemies in the presence of the goddess Ištar; Sar-i Pol-i Zahab relief, western Iran	42
1.37	A victorious King Darius I stands on the belly of the would-be usurper Gaumāta; Bisitun Relief, north-west Iran	42
1.38	Pharaoh Thutmose IV rests his feet on a footstool bearing images of the so-called 'Nine Bows', the traditional foreign enemies of Egypt	43

1.39	Adopting the so-called 'Atlas pose', but in the presence of the Persian military, representatives of the Persian empire lift up the king on a huge bench-throne (*takht*). Detail from the façade of the tomb of Darius I, Naqš-i Rustam	43
1.40	Pharaoh Ramses III is carried on his throne as a kind of palanquin; wall relief, Medinet Habu, Thebes	44
1.41	Assyrian soldiers transport cult images, each sitting on their palanquin-thrones, away from Babylon to Assyria. Relief sculpture, Nineveh	44
1.42	Ivory furniture inlay depicting a Persian satrap or noble reclining on a couch (*takht*) in the presence of a woman (a wife?) and servants; from Persian-occupied Asia Minor	44
1.43	Silver dish representing a Sasanian Shah, in the company of courtiers, seated on a bench-throne (*takht*). From Iran	45
1.44	Plan of the Elamite city of Susa at the time of the Achaemenids	46
1.45	Silver siglos, minted by the Achaemenid kings in the western satrapies of the empire. Discovered in Athens	58
1.46	Profile of two Persian soldiers. Detail from the east staircase of the Apadana at Persepolis	61
1.47	Detail of the head of Darius I from the Bisitun Relief, north-west Iran	61
1.48	Detail of Darius' crenellated crown from the Bisitun Relief	62
1.49	Detail of a plain *polos*-style crown; from the east staircase of the Apadana at Persepolis	63
1.50	Stamp seal from Anatolia; a crowned Persian winged sphinx	63
1.51	Persian riding habit or cavalry dress; from the Apadana at Persepolis	63
1.52	Persian court robe; from the palace of Xerxes, Persepolis	64
1.53	Gold disks, used to decorate Persian court garments. Discovered at Susa	64
1.54	Ivory relief of a Persian nobleman in court dress, embellished with appliqué gold disks	64
1.55	The god Aššur; relief carving from Nineveh	65
1.56	Mughal miniature depicting Jahangir embracing the Safavid king Shah Abbas; late sixteenth century	66
1.57	Iranian deity, possibly a war god, from Taq-i Bustan, Kermanshah, Iran; Sasanian carved stone capital	67
1.58	Persian cylinder seal impression; Ahuramazda, depicted twice. From Persepolis	67
1.59	Persian cylinder seal impression from Persepolis. The king in combat with a beast is accompanied by the *farr* – radiance of rulership	68

Figures   xi

1.60	Gold earring with semi-precious stone inlays; Achaemenid. Possibly from Susa	69
1.61	Egyptian-made over-life-size statue of Darius I, found at Susa	71
1.62	Possible reconstructions of the statues of Darius once located at the royal gateway into the Susa palace compound	71
1.63	Coloured glazed brick relief of a snarling lion; from the main thoroughfare leading to the Ištar Gate, Babylon. Neo-Babylonian period	72
1.64	Ground plan of the Achaemenid palace at Susa	72
1.65	Reconstruction of the appearance of the Apadana at Susa	73
1.66	Double bull protome column capital from the Apadana at Susa	73
1.67	Stone relief depicting an Assyrian royal garden at Nineveh, including a pavilion with a standing sculpture of a king	77
1.68	Garden banqueting scene from the palace of Ashurbanipal at Nineveh	77
1.69	Tree of Life guarded by *apkallu*; stone relief from Nimrud	78
1.70	Persian cylinder seal impression; Xerxes offers gold decorations to a sacred tree	79
1.71	Detail from the Hellenistic-era Palestrina Mosaic depicting Nilotic scenes, including a palace façade with textile awnings	80
1.72	Banqueting scene. A nobleman reclines on a couch while his wife, seated beside him, proffers a fruit. Funerary stele from Achaemenid-occupied Anatolia	82
1.73	Neo-Assyrian stone relief which once decorated Ashurbanipal's palace at Nineveh. It represents a woven carpet	83
1.74	Delegation I (Medes) from the east staircase of the Apadana at Persepolis	85
1.75	Delegation III (Armenians) from the east staircase of the Apadana at Persepolis	85
1.76	Delegation VI (Lydians) from the east staircase of the Apadana at Persepolis	85
1.77	Delegation XII (Ionians? Greeks?) from the east staircase of the Apadana at Persepolis	85
1.78	Delegation XV (Parthians?) from the east staircase of the Apadana at Persepolis	86
1.79	Delegation IV (Arians?) from the east staircase of the Apadana at Persepolis	86
1.80	Delegation VII (Drangians) from the east staircase of the Apadana at Persepolis	86
1.81	Delegation XIII (Bactrians?) from the east staircase of the Apadana at Persepolis	86

1.82	Delegation XVIII (Indians?) from the east staircase of the Apadana at Persepolis	86
1.83	Delegation XXIII (Nubians) from the east staircase of the Apadana at Persepolis	86
1.84	Delegation V (Babylonians) from the east staircase of the Apadana at Persepolis	87
1.85	Delegation VIII (Assyrians) from the east staircase of the Apadana at Persepolis	87
1.86	Silver dish inscribed with the name and titles of King Artaxerxes I	87
1.87	Silver Achaemenid animal rhyton in the form of a stag	87
1.88	Gold Achaemenid rhyton in the form of a mythical beast	87
1.89	Silver Achaemenid animal rhyton in the form of a ram or ibex	87
1.90	Silver and gold figurative Achaemenid bowl	87
1.91	Gold Achaemenid dish decorated with rampant lions	88
1.92	Satrap or nobleman reclines on a couch in the presence of slaves, including a fan-bearer and a cup-bearer. Painted tomb fresco from Achaemenid-occupied western Asia Minor	89
1.93	Women preparing a banquet; detail from an incised bronze belt from Urartu	92
1.94	New Kingdom Egyptian all-female banquet scene; wall painting from Thebes	92
1.95	New Kingdom Egyptian all-female banquet scene; wall painting from Thebes	92
1.96	North Syrian ivory relief furniture inlay depicting a woman drinking and accompanied by servants and a pet rabbit	92
1.97	Enthroned woman (queen? goddess?) receives food and drink from slaves. Incised bronze plaque, Urartu	93
1.98	Noblewoman holding a flower and wreath and wearing a linen gown sits on a high-backed throne or chair. Ring impression; Achaemenid-occupied Anatolia	93
1.99	Semi-nude women recline under a grape vine to enjoy a feast. Sasanian silver dish	93
1.100	Elamite seal impression from a seal belonging to Rašda, Steward of Lady Irdabama, mother of Darius I	93
1.101	Group of female harpists. Late Sasanian period, from Taq-i Bustan, Kermanshah, Iran	93
1.102	Group of all female singers, musicians, and entertainers. Detail from an incised bronze belt, Urartu	93

1.103	Stone relief sculpture of a eunuch; palace of Darius, Persepolis	95
1.104	Fragmentary Neo-Assyrian relief depicting a queen wearing a mural crown. From Nineveh	98
1.105	Detail of the head of the wife of Ashurbanipal, showing her wearing a mural crown. From Nineveh	98
1.106	Egyptian-blue miniature head of a Persian woman, boy or eunuch wearing a crenellated crown. From Persepolis	98
1.107	Flat gold metal sheet in the form of a crowned woman; Achaemenid period, discovered close to the Oxus River	99
1.108	Detail of a textile fragment representing Achaemenid women; from the Crimea	99
1.109	Ring seal depicting a seated, crowned, lady with a bird. Achaemenid-occupied Asia Minor	100
1.110	Bulla depicting a woman in a linen court robe. Achaemenid-occupied Anatolia	101
1.111	Neo-Assyrian ivory furniture inlay depicting a female face. From Nimrud	102
1.112	Neo-Assyrian ivory furniture inlay depicting a seated female. From Nimrud	103
1.113	Limestone plaque depicting an Achaemenid woman in a court gown	103
1.114	Limestone plaque depicting an Achaemenid woman in a court gown	103
1.115	Detail of a bronze caryatid figure of an Achaemenid woman in a court gown and jewellery. From Jordan	104
1.116	Ivory figurine of a woman in Achaemenid dress lifting her breasts; from Phoenicia	104
1.117	Ivory figurine of a woman in Achaemenid dress lifting her breasts; from Phoenicia	104
1.118	Bone figurine of a woman in Achaemenid dress lifting her breasts; from the Levant	105
1.119	North Syrian ivory figurine of a fertility goddess	105
1.120	Egyptian First Intermediate Period wall relief depicting an emaciated woman	105
1.121	Clay mould figurine of an Elamite fertility goddess; from Susa	106
1.122	Stone relief of a woman in Achaemenid dress with a flower; from Phoenicia	106
1.123	Clay plaque of a woman in Achaemenid dress lifting a breast; from Phoenicia	106
1.124	Clay plaque of a woman in Achaemenid dress holding a flower; from Phoenicia	106

1.125	Bronze cosmetic container in the shape of a woman in Achaemenid dress	107
1.126	Terracotta cosmetic container in the shape of a woman in Achaemenid dress	107
2.1	Series of rooms making up the 'harem wing' of Xerxes' palace at Persepolis	134
2.2	A room and antichamber; part of the 'harem wing' of Xerxes' palace at Persepolis	135
2.3	Staircases connecting Xerxes' palace with the 'harem wing' at Persepolis	136
2.4	Schematic view of a New Kingdom Egyptian 'harem wing' from the tomb of Aye, Amarna	137
2.5	Schematic view of a New Kingdom Egyptian 'harem wing' from the tomb of Tutu, Amarna	138
2.6	Scene of Queen Kawit with her hairdresser and page; sarcophagus from Deir el-Bahri	140
2.7	Egyptian prostitute applies make-up; New Kingdom erotic papyrus from Deir el-Medinah	140
2.8	Ramesside wall painting of a young Egyptian woman with an elaborate hairstyle and heavy eye make-up	140
2.9	Female party-goers in elaborate wigs have perfume cones applied to their heads by a naked slave girl. New Kingdom, from Thebes	141
2.10	Neo-Assyrian limestone relief depicting the head of a male courtier wearing kohl around his eyes. From Nineveh	141
2.11	Silver perfume flask representing a woman in Achaemenid court dress and a crown. Provenance unknown	141
2.12	Silver perfume flask representing a woman in Achaemenid court dress and a crown. Provenance unknown	141
2.13	Achaemenid-period bronze incense burner; possibly from the Levant	144
2.14	Achaemenid-period silver incense burner from Asia Minor with a stone relief showing incense burners from Persepolis	144
2.15	Achaemenid-period bronze incense burner with caryatid figure; from Jordan	144
2.16	Stone relief from the 'Syrian' gatehouse at Medinet Habu, Thebes. Pharaoh Ramses III and concubines. New Kingdom	147
2.17	Stone relief from the 'Syrian' gatehouse at Medinet Habu, Thebes. Pharaoh Ramses III and concubines. New Kingdom	147
2.18	Stone relief from the 'Syrian' gatehouse at Medinet Habu, Thebes. Pharaoh Ramses III and concubines. New Kingdom	148
2.19	Female musician; painted ostraca from Deir el-Medinah, Thebes; New Kingdom	148

2.20	Group of Egyptian female musicians, possibly concubines. From Thebes, New Kingdom	148
2.21	Female musician at a Canaanite court. Detail from the 'Megiddo Ivory'; late Bronze Age	149
2.22	Queen Ankhesenamun shares an intimate moment with her husband, Tutankhamun. New Kingdom, from Thebes	152
2.23	Ivory plaque depicting a kissing couple; north Syria	152
2.24	Plan of the royal gateway into the palace compound at Susa; Achaemenid period	156
2.25	Relief sculpture of a guardian figure from a surviving doorjamb at the entrance gate to Pasargadae, Iran. Late Teispid–early Achaemenid period	156
2.26	Cross-section of Xerxes' Gate of All Lands at Persepolis	157
2.27	Human-headed winged bull guardian figure, part of Xerxes' Gate of All Lands at Persepolis	157
2.28	Neo-Assyrian stone relief depicting the sack of a city; prisoners are impaled before the city walls. From Nineveh	161
2.29	Neo-Assyrian stone relief depicting impaled prisoners. From Nineveh	161
2.30	Neo-Assyrian bronze relief depicting impaled and mutilated prisoners. From Balawat	161
2.31	Assyrian impalement scene from the Balawat Gates	161
3.1	Detail of a limestone relief depicting a royal audience scene. Originally from the east staircase of the Apadana, Persepolis	167
3.2	Egyptian tomb wall painting from Memphis showing foreign petitioners or prisoners in front of Egyptian officials; New Kingdom	167
3.3	Elamite captives kowtow to Assyrian soldiers. Stone relief from Nineveh	167
3.4	Jehu, king of Israel, kisses the ground before Sennacherib, king of Assyria; 'Black Obelisk' from Nimrud	169
3.5	Foreign tribute bearers present themselves to an Egyptian vizier; tomb painting from Thebes; New Kingdom	169
3.6	Woman performs a full prostration before the image of a god. Egyptian papyrus painting; New Kingdom	170
3.7	Assyrian dice recovered at Tepe Gawra	170
3.8	Clay cube lot belonging to Iahali; Neo-Babylonian	171
3.9	Hellenistic wall painting depicting a girl playing with gaming lots	171
3.10	Detail from a south Italian red-figure vase (The Darius Vase) showing a 'Persian' tax collector recording payments	172
3.11	Ring with seal impression; from Achaemenid-occupied Anatolia	173
3.12	Battle scene of Persians fighting nomadic peoples; cylinder seal impression	173

3.13	Gold ring with incised image of a Persian archer; inscribed with the owner's name – Athenades	173
3.14	Example of a cylinder seal in its setting	174
3.15	Seal impression of Parnaka (PFS 9) from Persepolis	174
3.16	Seal impression of Ziššawiš (PFS 83*) from Persepolis	174
3.17	Second seal impression of Parnaka (PFS 16*) from Persepolis	175
3.18	Second seal impression of Ziššawiš (PFS 11) from Persepolis	175
4.1	Professional mourners accompany the deceased on a barge; wall painting from a tomb at Thebes; New Kingdom	178
4.2	Mourning women, stripped to the waist, on the sarcophagus of King Ahiram of Byblos	178
4.3	Fragmentary relief sculpture of Egyptian mourning women. Late Period, from Thebes	178
4.4	Mourning women squat close to the ground. Egyptian tomb painting, Thebes	179
4.5	Mourning women squat close to the ground. Egyptian tomb painting, Thebes	179
4.6	Large group of professional mourners; Egyptian tomb painting; New Kingdom	179
4.7	Funerary stele of a Persian nobleman from Persian-occupied Egypt (The Memphis Stela)	180
4.8	Ostracon showing a grieving Ramesside pharaoh. From Deir el-Medinah; late New Kingdom	180
4.9	Achaemenid royal audience scene; seal impression from Persian-occupied Anatolia	183
4.10	Persian soldier with shield raised; from the Alexander Sarcophagus; early Hellenistic period from Sidon	183
4.11	Achaemenid royal audience scene painted inside the shield depicted in Figure 4.10	183
4.12	Achaemenid royal audience scene; originally attached to the north staircase of the Apadana at Persepolis	184
4.13	Achaemenid royal audience scene; originally attached to the east staircase of the Apadana at Persepolis	185
4.14	The Greek god Zeus; red-figure vase painting; early Classical period; from Athens	186
4.15	Great King in procession; doorjamb at the palace of Xerxes, Persepolis	186
4.16	Detail from a south Italian red-figure vase (The Darius Vase) showing a 'Persian' monarch in audience	186

4.17	A Persian 'king' shown with his bow and sceptre; from a red-figure drinking cup; early Classical period from Athens	187
4.18	Neo-Assyrian king with sceptre stands with his designated heir; stone relief sculpture from Nineveh	187
4.19	Tiglath-pileser III uses his sceptre to humiliate a foreign suppliant. Stone relief sculpture from Kalhu	187
5.1	Achaemenid seal impression of a female audience scene (De Clerq Seal); possibly from Susa	191
5.2	Achaemenid cylinder seal impression of seated woman spinning and flywhisk-bearing attendant. Unknown provenance	192
5.3	Reconstruction of the façade of the Apadana at Susa	193
5.4	Representation of the sons of Ramses II; Ramesseum, Thebes; New Kingdom	194
5.5	Representation of the sons of Ramses III; Medinet Habu, Thebes; New Kingdom	194
6.1	Miniature painting from the *Jami'al-Tawrikh* of Rashid al-Din, c. 1307 CE; from Baghdad	201
6.2	Detail from a fragmentary Egyptian statue of the Achaemenid period; an official is depicted wearing a golden Persian-style torc	201
6.3	A Persian magus depicted on a stone stela from northern Anatolia	203
6.4	A Persian nobleman and his wife (?); from Persian-occupied Asia Minor	203
6.5	Bronze statuette of a Persian nobleman in a riding outfit; from the area of the Oxus River	203
6.6	Persian nobleman wearing the riding habit; from a sculpted relief panel at Persepolis	203
6.7	Cylinder seal impression from Persian-occupied Egypt depicting a Persian warrior and his horse; official seal of the Egyptian satrap Aršama	205
6.8	Achaemenid cylinder seal showing a mare suckling her foal	205
6.9	Achaemenid stamp seal impression depicting a seated Persian wearing the riding habit in the company of his horse	205
6.10	Silver coin from Tyre depicting the Persian Great King riding in a chariot	205
6.11	Miniature gold model of a royal chariot with four horses, a driver, and a seated dignitary. Found near the River Oxus	206
6.12	Cylinder seal impression of the Great King's camel-drawn chariot. From Persepolis	206
6.13	The royal chariot pulled by Nisaean horses, controlled by a charioteer; wall relief from the east staircase at Persepolis	206

6.14	Small Achaemenid bronze figurine of a horse and its rider	207
6.15	Detail taken from the 'Pazyrik Carpet' – a Persian horseman; from the Crimea	207
6.16	Women horse-riding; fragment of a relief sculpture from Persian-occupied Asia Minor	208
6.17	Neo-Assyrian horse bridles and bits	208
6.18	Parthian mounted warrior and his horse with rich trappings; from Persepolis	208
6.19	Central Asian Late Antique wall painting depicting a horse with elaborate trappings. From Panjikent	209
6.20	Brass figurine of a crowned man riding an elaborately canopied war horse; Late Sasanian or Early Islamic Iran	209
6.21	Wall relief showing a Sasanian nobleman riding a richly decorated horse. From Taq-i Bustan, north-west Iran	209
7.1	Clay plaque depicting love making on a couch; Sumerian	216
7.2	Clay moulded figurine representing a couple lying together on a couch; from Babylonia	216
8.1	Seal of the steward Šalamana (PFS 535) from Persepolis	222

Acknowledgements

My thanks go to Timur Khan for creating the following drawings: 1.86; 1.91; 1.101; 2.11; 2.12; 6.11. Sophie Rudland, Yasmin Garcha, and the team at I.B. Tauris have been exemplary colleagues and have my sincere gratitude. I want to thank the anonymous Reader of the draft manuscript for the encouraging words and for the thoughtful comments. As ever, huge thanks to David Pineau for keeping things real and making the tea.

Abbreviations

Persian

A¹	Artaxerxes I
A²	Artaxerxes II
A³	Artaxerxes III
Am	Ariaramnes
As	Arsames
C	Cyrus
D	Darius I
D²	Darius II
X	Xerxes
B	Babylon (for the Cyrus Cylinder)
B	Bisitun (for the inscription of Darius I)
E	Elvend
H	Hamadan
M	Parsagade
N	Naqš-i Rustam
P	Persepolis
S	Susa
V	Van (Lake Van, Armenia)
Z	Suez
SC	Seal
VS	Vase
W	Weight
§	indicates a paragraph/section number

Languages

Akkad.	Akkadian
Arab.	Arabic
Av.	Avestan
Bab.	Babylonian
Elam.	Elamite
Heb.	Hebrew
Gk.	Greek
Lat.	Latin
OI	Old Iranian
OP	Old Persian
Med.	Median
MP	Middle Persian (Pahlavi)
NP	New Persian (Farsi)
Turk.	Turkish

Near Eastern sources

SAA	State Archives of Assyria

Classical authors

Ael.	Aelian
VH	*Varia Historia*
Ar.	Aristophanes
Ach.	*Acharnians*
Arr.	Arrian
Anab.	*Anabasis*
Ath.	Athenaeus, *Deipnosophistae*
Curt.	Q. Curtius Rufus, *Historiae Alexandri Magni*

Diod. Sic.	Diodorus Siculus, *Bibliotheca Historica*
Hdt.	Herodotus, *Histories*
Joseph.	Josephus
AJ	*Antiquities of the Jews*
Pl.	Plato
Alc.	*Alcibiades*
Plin.	Pliny the Elder, *Naturalis Historia*
Plut.	Plutarch
Alex.	*Alexander*
Arta.	*Artaxerxes*
Hell.	*Hellenica*
Mor.	*Moralia*
Oec.	*Oecononicos*
Per.	*Pericles*
Them.	*Themistocles*
Polyaenus	Polyaenus, *Strategemata*
Ps.Arist.	Pseudo-Aristotle, *De Mundo*
Xen.	Xenophon
An.	*Anabasis*
Cyr.	*Cyropaedeia*
Hel.	*Hellenica*

Introduction

(i) The purpose of this book

I have been familiar with the Book of Esther ever since my childhood in Wales, where, from Sunday School lessons in chapel, I learned about 'the queen who saved her people'. I started to write about Esther in 2002 when I used it to think about the function of eunuchs at the ancient Persian court. I have been writing about ancient Persia ever since, and Esther has appeared, in some shape or form, in almost all of my research on the Achaemenid period. I have found the biblical text to be a fruitful one, containing much of value on the life of the royal court of Persia as well as the bigger theme of outsider perceptions of the Persians and their vast empire. For me, Esther has been, and remains, good to think with; it raises questions, provides models for analysis, and always, always, fascinates. So, on one level, this study is the result of my high regard for the Book of Esther – for its historical setting, its period flavour, and for what it means to the living faith of Jews and Christians today. I will not be assessing this latter aspect of Esther's appeal, however, and I leave that task to scholars far more qualified to approach that theme (although I will say that I am drawn especially to the theological readings provided by Kandy Queen-Sutherland 2016 and Marion Ann Taylor 2020).

This book takes the form of a commentary on the Hebrew book of Esther. I found it the best and most compact way to tackle the ancient text, but I write it from the point of view which I know best – that of an ancient historian active in researching the world of ancient Persia. The commentary that follows is not a linguistic one (although philology lifts its head, certainly), nor is it a literary study (although some comment on the storytelling motifs is expressed). The commentary is certainly not theological in tone, nor is it written for a specifically Jewish readership – nor for a Christian one for that matter. It is a commentary primarily aimed at two groups of people: bible students (of all sorts and at all levels) who want to put Esther secularly into its historical and cultural milieu, and ancient historians (again of all types and ranges) who want to know more about the hows and whys of approaching the Hebrew bible as resource for research. I hope that both groups will locate something in the commentary which they find useful.

My contention is simple: the book of Esther is a genuine Persian-period source. Therefore, it should be incorporated into the sources which historians employ in the study of Persia on a more routine basis than it currently enjoys. For a historian of ancient Persia to overlook Esther is a mistake, for the book tells us much about the realia of court life at Susa and even more about the perceptions of the Persians through the lens of a subject people – the Jews. For a biblical scholar, approaching Esther and getting the maximum out of it requires an understanding of the world in which Esther was created. The Persian period is currently recognized as a pivotal moment in the construction of the Hebrew scriptures (see especially Gerstenberger 2011 and Silverman 2012 and 2020), but it is one of the least known eras of Near Eastern history among bible scholars. The book of Esther is also one of the most visual books of the bible; it is filled with descriptions of physical places and things and with rich visual metaphors and similes. Therefore, I have punctuated the commentary with numerous line drawings in the hope of exposing the visual world of Esther and the rich artistic heritage of Persia and the Near East. I principally follow the methodology of 'iconographic exegesis' established by Othmar Keel (1978, 1994, 2012) and his school (Keel and Uehlinger 1998; de Hulster and Lemon 2014; de Hulster, Strawn and Bonfiglio 2015) and I hope to show that an understanding of the realia of the book of Esther, together with its visual code, is best understood when we combine text and image in a holistic study of the Near Eastern world which sits alongside the Hebrew bible.

The commentary follows my own translation of the Hebrew text, based on the NIV translation and I take the opportunity to remark on key words, passages and themes as they are encountered in the text. I cross-reference later appearances of any given subject, but I do not expand on the commentary when the theme is next encountered. Therefore, the opening three chapters of Esther seem to be given all the attention, but this is only because many of the main subjects which are worthy of comment are first located in these rich opening chapters.

(ii) Author, date and genre

The textual history of Esther is complex (Clines 1984; Day 1995; Grossman 2011). The question of its canonicity is still debated, and its theological content is much questioned. It is the only book of the Hebrew bible that was not found among the Dead Sea Scrolls, suggesting that the Essenes did not recognize the text, probably because of the absence of any mention of God. In fact, Esther did not find a secure place in the Hebrew and Christian scriptures until the fourth century CE, perhaps as a result of the Greek recension of the Hebrew text (known as the 'Alpha Text') and the book's appearance in the Septuagint (Greek) translation of the Hebrew *Megillat Esther* (Heb. 'scroll of Esther'), with its many additions, in which God was inserted into the story, alongside a conspicuous use of prayer and divine petition. Certainly, from a Jewish perspective, the Hebrew version of Esther is disconcerting given that there are no references to Jewish ritual, the covenant, Moses, Torah, Jerusalem or the Temple. Moreover, the Jewish heroine of the book is married to a pagan king whilst concealing her Jewish identity. Given the life-threatening situation confronting both Esther (4:8, 11, 16) and her people (3:13-14), one might reasonably have expected a passing mention of prayer. Even Jewish dietary laws are broken when Esther shares food with gentiles at a series of opulent banquets. One writing found in the Babylonian Talmud (*Meg.* 7a) therefore notes that Esther 'savours of irreverence'.

However, some Jewish authorities embraced the book. Simon ben Lakish (c. CE 300) believed that although all scriptures would fade away with the coming of the Messiah, the Torah and the scroll of Esther would endure (see Bickerman 1967: 211). At Dura-Europos in Syria, a third-century CE mural painted on the walls of a synagogue depicts Esther, Mordecai and the Persian king in a place of honour, immediately opposite an image of the Tabernacle (Bickerman 1967: 74–5). After all, Esther claims to give the historical origins for Purim, a wildly popular Jewish festival celebrated on the 14th and 15th of the month of Adar (i.e. the 12th month of the Babylonian calendar, corresponding to March–April) and as it stands in the MT (Hebrew Masoretic Text), the book is primarily concerned with telling a story which would provide the historical setting for the festival of Purim, both days of it (9:16-19, 20-2, 26-8, 31). No doubt the mass appeal of the spring festival consolidated the story's popularity. Even today, Jews recite the entire book twice during Purim and the ritual is accompanied by plays, musical entertainments and games. This has helped make Esther a cornerstone of Jewish faith and identity. In contrast, Christians tend not to know Esther; in the three-year liturgical cycle, it receives only one reading (Est. 7:1-6, 9-10; 9:20-2). The Protestant disregard for Esther no doubt originates from Martin Luther who declared, 'I am so hostile to this book [2 Maccabees] and Esther that I could wish that they did not exist at all; for they Judaize too greatly and have much pagan impropriety' (although see Holt 2021: 4–8 for a more nuanced understanding of Luther's approach to Esther). To complicate matters further, in the Jewish canon, Esther is included amongst the *Ketuvim* ('Writings') as part of a subset of five festival scrolls (*Megilloth*), while in the Christian bible Esther comes after Ezra and Nehemiah, thereby recognizing its historical setting in the post-exilic Persian-period Jewish diaspora. The version of Esther used in this book is found in the NIV Bible and is based on the Hebrew Masoretic Text (MT). By and large, the other early versions of Esther, each preserved in Greek (the Old Greek or B-text which is found in the Septuagint (LXX; see Kahana 2005), the A-text and the retelling of Esther in Josephus' *Antiquities of the Jews* (11.184–296), are ignored in this study. The MT Esther is the shortest extant version, lacking, as has been noted, any reference to God or to religious practices.

The author of MT Esther is unknown. There are no clues to his identity (he was undoubtedly male) and no tradition, Jewish or Christian, survives to link him to any named individual. The author writes in a third-person voice and takes on no 'character' *per se*. Yet the storytelling is vivid and moves at a good pace; it is written in standard late biblical Hebrew and has a playful tone (it is at times quite funny), subtly alluding to other biblical texts, especially the story of Joseph (Gen. 37–48), which probably received its final written version in the period in which Esther was composed (e.g. compare Gen. 40:22 and Est. 1:3; Gen. 39:10 and Est. 3:4; Gen. 41:37 and Est. 1:21; Gen. 41:35 and Est. 2:3; Gen. 41:42 and Est. 3:10; 8:2). Berlin (2001: 7) suggests that the author's attempt to 'sound biblical' might explain the style of the language of the book. The text is littered with Persian words (and playfully fake Persian names; Young and Rezetko 2008: I. 289–309) suggesting that the author had a very good knowledge of the Persian world. He was certainly *au fait* with the workings of the royal court at Susa which suggests, perhaps, that the author was an elite diaspora Jew, possibly

Susa-born, who had a knowledge of Persia's nobility and was completely untroubled and unbothered by his ancestral homeland and its religious traditions.

Esther dates to the period 400–350 BCE, that is to say, the book was composed during the High Empire period of Persia's history (see further Baldwin 1984: 48–9; Beal 1997: 112; Levenson 1997: 26; Harvey 2003: 4–5; Alter 2015: 85; Middlemas 2019). Talmon (1963: 420) suggests that 'the author of the Esther-story shows an intimate knowledge of Persian court etiquette and public administration' and notes that 'If his tale does not mirror historical reality, it is indeed well imagined'. Esther is so *au fait* with Persian law, custom and language precisely because it is a product of the Achaemenid era. Its author was very familiar with royal Persian institutions. Robert Gordis (1974: 8) argues that 'The style [of the book] indicates a date of composition of approximately 400 BCE, only a few decades after the reign of Xerxes … There is a considerable number of Persian and Aramaic words and idioms. There are, however, no Greek words, a fact which clearly points to a pre-Hellenistic date.' For Berg (1979: 2), 'The number of Persian words in Esther and its numerous Aramaisms suggest the story's composition during a period not far from the events it describes.'

But Esther is not a history book and it does not contain history *per se* (in spite of the valiant effort by Gérard Gertoux (2015) to fix Esther's narrative precisely in time). It is a playful narrative based on Mesopotamian and Iranian myths and legends, as well as a heavy dose of folklore. Gordis (1981: 375) explained the absence of any reference to God or Judaic beliefs and practices by his hypothesizing that Esther represents a heretofore unrecognized biblical genre:

> A Jewish author undertook to write his book in the form of a chronicle of the Persian court, written by a gentile scribe. A Jew of the eastern diaspora … writes the book as if it were an excerpt from the official chronicles of – the kings of Media and Persia (10:2).

At best, Esther is a romanticized Persian history, a pseudo-historical narrative which contains much palace intrigue that frequently shades into romance. A form of historical fiction was certainly taking shape in the literary climate of fourth-century Persia, exemplified by the *Persica* ('Persian Things') of Ctesias of Cindus, a Greek resident at the court of Artaxerxes II who wrote a mammoth 24-book-long treatment of Persia's past and present. Surviving today only in fragments, it is nonetheless clear that the *Persica* was composed of many dozens of short stories, a compendium of tales or an assortment of 'novellas' (for further discussion see Stevenson 1997; Stronk 2004–5; Llewellyn-Jones and Robson 2010).

A novella is a story of limited length, intended to entertain, and with a plot which, typically, operates around the reversal in fortunes of a central character. A novella is concerned with ostensibly 'real-life' characters (although not all necessarily drawn from history) in 'real-life' settings. Ostensibly Ctesias' *Persica* was made up of a string of short (and longer) novellas interspersed into a historical framework to form a continuous narrative. The novella was a growing hallmark of literature during Ctesias' lifetime (the works of Herodotus and Thucydides certainly contain characteristics of the novella) and Xenophon, Ctesias' contemporary, certainly used the novella form within his historical works. His *Cyropaedia* ('Education of Cyrus'), a didactic semi-fictionalized biography of Cyrus the Great (which is in fact a fawning panegyric about Cyrus the Younger) contains no fewer than four novellas interwoven into the main historical narrative. These are the stories of Panthea the Lady of Susa (5.1.1–30; 6.1.30–55; 6.4.1–20; 7.3.3–17), King Croesus (7.2.1–29), Prince Gobryas (4.6.1–12; 5.2.1–14; 5.4.41–51) and Gadatas the Chieftain (5.3.15–4.51) – all four either royal or noble Asiatics. Xenophon uses the novellas carefully throughout the main body of the historical work and each of the four stories share several important, and overlapping, features: (1) All four stories are presented episodically and are fitted into the wider picture of the *Cyropaedia*. (2) The stories are no mere digressions but are linked into the *Cyropaedia*'s main narrative framework. (3) While the tales are narrated with brevity, nonetheless they often contain scenes of emotional intensity and grandiloquence. (4) Most importantly, perhaps, the novellas are frequently interspersed with dialogues, which form an important aspect of the way in which the stories are told.

The MT Esther has all the hallmarks a historical novella. The story is set in a precise location (Susa in Persia), at a specific time (the third year of the reign of Xerxes) and follows two classic reversal of fortune scenarios: as Esther and Mordecai rise from obscurity to their exalted positions at court, so the wicked Haman, the king's chief minister, falls from grace and is executed. Here the unknown author has chosen to set his story at a precise moment in time and in an exact locale and has to face his critics on the thoroughness of his research and his use of historical data. To look at the historical accuracy of his work is a legitimate act (and many biblical scholars have attempted to do just this), but that does not prejudge the question of literary genre. Indeed, there are several marks of history writing in Esther – the book actually opens with the phrase, 'This is what happened during the time of Xerxes' (Est. 1:1) – and the author presents his work as if it were history, although the story itself is much more at home in the genre of the historical novella. It is clear that, on all levels, the author of Esther was deliberately blending historical details, fantasy and novella-style storytelling to create a rich, fluid and gripping historical romance.

However, there is a further aspect to the composition of Esther that is often overlooked. Esther is connected to a historiographic tradition that was blossoming in the Near East in the period between the mid-seventh and late fourth centuries BCE: the 'Court Tale' (Wills 1990 and 1995; Chyutin 2011). The *Tale of Ahiqar*, about an Assyrian courtier who has to contend with the plots and schemes of his wicked nephew in order to win back his place at the royal court, was well known. It incorporates many famous names and figures from Assyria's history and weaves them into a gripping narrative. The biblical stories of Daniel and Joseph are good examples of the genre too (Holm 2013). Indeed, Meinhold (1976) viewed the Daniel, Joseph and Esther stories as 'diaspora novellas', which provided models for a general lifestyle, or mode of living, for Jews living in the pagan environment of the Diaspora. The 1994 publication of Aramaic fragments (4Q550) from Qumran revealed the presence of more cycles of tales about the Persian court, similar to Esther, and in circulation in the middle Second Temple period (White Crawford 1996 and 2002). The plot(s) seem to follow the exploits of Patireza, a servant of King Darius I, and is set in the reign of his successor, Xerxes.

Like Ahiqar, Patireza suffers some kind of injustice, uncovered in the royal archives and the king attempts to rectify the misdemeanour. A female character, a 'princess', is somehow involved:

1. 'person, yet the king kno[ws] whether there is [...]
2. and his good name shall not perish, [nor his] loyal[ty [...]'
3. the king [said], 'Does Patireza have a son?' And [...]
4. the terror of the house of [the] scri[be ...] fell upon him [...]
5. messenger of the kin[g], "Comma[nd] and it shall be given [...]
6. my house and my belongings for all that which may be [given ...]
7. if you are able you shall receive the office of your father [...]'
8. [...] the m[ess]enger of the king, 'Say to the princess [...]
9. [...] Patireza [your] father since the day that he took up [his] office before the king [...]
10. [...] he served in honesty and in [...] before him
11. [...' ...] and the messenger of [the king ...] said ['...]
12. [...]
13. [...]
14. ['... and who used to o]bey Patireza your father [...]
15. among the servants of the royal wardrobe, in [every]thing [... to un]dertake
16. the king's service according to all that he recei[ved ...' ...] in that same year
17. the king had trouble sleeping [... boo]ks of [h]is father [would b]e read before him, and among
18. the books was found a cer[tain] scroll [sea]led with seven stamp[s] of the signet-ring of Darius his father, whose heading
19. [... 'Dar]ius the king to the servants of the Empire <of a[ll] the[e]arth>: greetings!' It was opened, read, and found written therein: 'Darius the king
20. [... who shall] reign after me and to the servants of the Empire: gre[et]ings! Let it be known to you that every oppressor or deceiver ...'

(Wechsler 2000)

Another story centres on a Jewish courtier named Bagasaro (also transliterated as Bagasraw, Bagasro and Bagasrava) and a conflict he had with Bagoshi, another courtier, out of which Bagasaro emerges triumphant:

1. Behold, yo[u] know [...] my [faults] and the faults of my fathers
2. who sinned before you. And [...] to [...] and I stretched out [...] you, a man of
3. Judah from among the princes of the k[ing ...] standing in front of him and [...] goo[d ...]
4. the good man served [...] What shall I do for you? For you kno[w that] it is possib[le]
5. for a man like [me] to recompense [a man] l[i]ke you, standing in the place where you stand
6. [...] demand of me whatever you de[si]re, and when [you d]ie I will bury you in [...]

7. dwells in all, 'Is it possible that my ascension into office be[fore … a]ll that […]'
8. […] the decree of [… and] the sec[ond ones] passed […]
9. [… and] the [th]ir[d ones] pass[ed …] in the garments […]
10. […] crown of go[ld …] and the fi[t]h ones pass[ed …]
11. […] by himself [… and] the sixth ones passed […]
12. […] <all >si]lver and <[a]ll >gold [and <all >possess]ions which[bel]ong to Bagasaro are yours in doub[l]e […]
13. and […] Bagasraw [al]so entered the court of the king, in pe[ac]e, […]
14. Bagasar[o was put to d]eath, whereupon [B]agasraw entered the co[ur]t of the king […]
15. and Baga[sraw] to[ok] it […] upon [his] head […] and kissed him, answering and saying, 'Bagasraw, Ba[ga]sraw, from […]'
16. […] 'The Most High whom you fear [and wo]rship rules over [all] the[ea]rth. All that he desires is within his ha[nd] to d[o].
17. [And] every person who utters an [ev]il word against [B]agasraw […shall] be put to death, for there i[s] no […]
18. [and] <to him> his good for[ev]er […]' which he s<a>w […]two. And the king said, 'Let him wri[te …]
19. […] them in the great court of the roya[l] palace
20. [… shall] rise [u]p after Bagas[raw] (and) read in thi[s] book
21. [… e]vil, his evil shall return upon his [head], all […]'

(Wechsler 2000)

The Aramaic fragments, as scrappy as they certainly are, nonetheless attest to the presence of the genre of Court Tales circulating in the Levant in the period of Persian domination and its aftermath.

The best-known Court Tale cycle centres on King David. These stories were originally composed as a factual Court History in the post-Solomonic era, and certainly in the time before the Israelites were deported to Babylon, was reworked as a kind of historical novella cum Court Tale and put into the canon of the Hebrew bible in the post-exilic age, that is to say in the Persian period, c. 550–400 BCE. The original text of the Court Tale is believed to incorporate most of 2 Samuel, except for the first few chapters (and a few more minor parts), and the opening chapters of 1 Kings. The Court Tale concentrates for much of the time on the scandalous affairs of David's family and retainers – his wives and their offspring, his ministers and priests. It reveals the tensions within the Davidic court and plays up stories of intrigue, rebellion and sexual adventure. David's lust for Bathsheba and the murder of her husband Uriah the Hittite, Amnon's rape of his half-sister Tamar, and Absalom's revenge and rebellion are all contained in 2 Samuel, whilst 1 Kings reveals the political and sexual shenanigans surrounding the death of David as Bathsheba fights for the succession rights of her son Solomon over the claims of his elder half-brother Adonijah (the so-called 'Throne Succession Narrative'). The book of Esther shares many themes with the novella-like Davidic Court Tale. Set in the Achaemenid court, the story follows the exploits of a Jewish girl who enters the harem of the Great King, whom she eventually marries. She later uses her exalted rank to secure the safety of her people from persecution by

Haman, a hateful high official who has access to the royal seal. Court intrigues and the machinations of prominent courtiers form the background to the story which is packed with incidental detail about Persian court life, palace protocol, the topography of Susa, and the like.

The 'Davidic Court History' and Esther share numerous similarities with the themes of Ctesias' *Persica* too, although this is not to say that Ctesias was aware of the Court History or of Esther, nor that the Jewish scribes knew of Ctesias' work either. However, it does point to a genre of romantic 'history'-writing that was perhaps emergent in Iran, Babylonia and the Levant in the Achaemenid High Empire period which centred on the affairs at the heart of government and, specifically, at the royal court. Nevertheless, Maria Brosius (2003: 144 and 2015: 199–200) thinks that Esther (or parts of Esther) was based on stories found in Herodotus and she notes that there is a 'compelling argument' to be made for regarding Herodotus' Persian court scenes (especially in *Histories* Book 9) as 'a template for the story of Esther'. But it is unnecessary to privilege the Greek historian (or any Greek) in this way; the Persians were quite capable of coming up with their own folktales and histories, as Stephanie Dalley (2007) has demonstrated in her illuminating study of the Near Eastern motifs in the Esther story. As Berlin (2001: xlii–xliii) stresses,

> The Greeks did not pretend to have invented the stories they told about the Persians; they collected them from informants who had first-hand knowledge. So, there is every reason to think that these stories and motifs were commonly known throughout the Near East. And that the author of Esther could have drawn on them easily. The fact that they were preserved primarily by the Greeks (who gave them their own distinctive twist) is an accident of literary history, for we do not have an extensive narrative literature from elsewhere during the Persian period.

Finally, a word about the presence of Persia in the Hebrew bible and in Jewish memory (for which see especially Silverman 2012 and 2020; Edelman and Ben Zvi 2013; Silverman and Waerzeggers 2015). There are essentially two ways to think about the way in which Persia can be located in the Hebrew bible – first, those books (or sections of books) written during the Achaemenid era (even though Persia might not be explicitly mentioned in them). Second, those books (or sections of them) composed after the fall of the Achaemenids, but nevertheless set in the Persian empire.

(a) Achaemenid-period texts: These include the historical narratives in 2 Chronicles, Ezra, Nehemiah, 1 Esdras, Second-Isaiah, Heggai and Zechariah which all in all cover some two hundred years of Persian rule over Judah and Samaria. The historical novella of Esther can be added to the list as can, I think, can the novella-like moments in 2 Samuel and 1 Kings, where monarchs, such as Solomon, masquerade in the shadow of an Achaemenid Great King and the novellas of Ruth and Jonah. Ecclesiastes is largely a product of the Persian period too and sections of the Pentateuch (much debated by scholars; Carr 2011; Edelman 2015) might be Achaemenid-era creations too. The chief focus of the historical-facing texts rests on the end of the Babylonian exile and the beginning of the rebuilding of the Jerusalem temple (2 Chron. 36; Ezra 1-6; 1 Esd.; Isa. 44:28–45:13; Hag.; Zech. 1-8), the missions to Jerusalem authorized by Artaxerxes (Ezra 7-10; Neh. 1-13; Esd.), and the presence of a Jewish community in the reign of Xerxes (Est.).

(b) Post-Achaemenid texts: Daniel is set in the courts of Babylonian, Median and Persian monarchs, although Chapters 7-12 contain detailed historical allusions to the Hellenistic era, focusing especially on the politico-religious tensions of the reign of the Seleucid king Antiochus IV. The origins of Daniel might well be found in the Babylonian exile period, but its final form is a product of the Hellenistic period, looking back to a Persian heyday. Daniel too contains element of the novella.

The unknown author of MT Esther might be classified as a novelist working within the framework of history. History is present in Esther, but not in the form we have come to expect history writing. Even if we are prepared to accept Esther as a 'history', then we must concede that the narrow line of vision of historical enquiry is pinpointed down to the court and the court alone. That is because Esther is a well-constructed Court Tale, written along the lines of other court stories created at the time, and as such it records the kind of machinations, plots, tensions and cruelties that are present at the courts of all absolute rulers. Esther's author transmitted a rich mixture of authentic Persian and other Near Eastern stories of kings, queens, and courtiers in a unique mélange of history, gossip, fantasy and frivolity.

(iii) The troublesome Chapter 9

There is not much frivolity to be had in Chapter 9 of Esther though. In fact, the entire chapter has a very different feel from the rest of the book; its tone is starkly different as it becomes increasingly bloodthirsty. Scholarly efforts (see Harvey 2003) to soften or rationalize away such things as Esther's requests both for an additional day to kill more of her enemies in Susa (9:13) and for permission to expose to public view the corpses of the ten sons of Haman who had been killed the day before (9:13-14) are not satisfactory. The narrator's approving report that the Jews had defeated all their enemies, slaughtering and annihilating them (500 in Susa and 75,000 elsewhere) and were treating their enemies as they pleased (9:5) is equally unsettling. Chapter 9 of Esther seems to exist in the cruel world of Judges and Nahum. True, in Esther, intrigue, deceit, hatred, murder and revenge abound, regardless of whether the spotlight is on Haman, Esther or Mordecai (Ruiz-Ortiz 2017), but the violence (and the language of violence) encountered in Chapter 9 is totally disjointed from the rest of the book. As Tsaurayi Mapfeka (2020) perceptively recognizes,

> Chapter 9 opens with no indication of any awareness of the resolution of the crisis which is presupposed in the previous chapter. The chapter goes on to provide detailed accounts of a two-day murderous spree that resulted in the deaths of

about 75,000 people who were identified as enemies of the Jews. There is nothing outside of this chapter to suggest that the community of the Jews identified in the story had identifiable enemies they intended to harm in such a dramatic manner. The narrative of a wanton massacre and inexplicable bloodbath in Esther 9 presents several exegetical challenges in the first instance, and also serious ethical dilemmas when it comes to the book's reception. The narrative inconsistencies and the author's tendency to exaggerate are characteristic traits of the entire story, which Esther 9 simply brings to a grand finale. The problems associated with this chapter include both those inherent within the chapter itself and those that stand out when read against the rest of the book's storyline and the world it purports to capture.

It is my contention that Chapter 9 was a later addition to MT Esther, inserted into the story around the time that the Greek Additions to Esther were being composed. Chapter 9 is not a product of the Persian period, but of the Hellenistic – and more specifically, of the Maccabean (or Hasmonean) – era. The period of the Maccabees saw the expansive employment of collective violence, guerrilla warfare and an increasing glorification of fighting. The accounts of the origins of the festivals of Hanukkah and Nicanor's Day in 1 and 2 Maccabees reinforce the close connection between violence against the community and the apocalyptic memories of the Maccabean rebellion that the authors of these books promoted.

Meinhold (1976) maintained that the festival legend of Purim was not originally a part of the Esther story and Clines (1984) too argued for a late addition for the Purim motif. Clines suggests that there were two originally distinct and separate stories – one, a court conflict/deliverance tale concerning a 'Mordecai'-character, and another a success/deliverance tale concerning an 'Esther'-character that were successfully combined in what he refers to as a Pre-Masoretic Story. Then, another separate tale, the 'Vashti' story was added to the mix (Clines 1984: 151). The text of this Pre-Masoretic Esther is best reflected in the Hebrew Vorlage of the Greek A-Text, ending at 8:17 (= 8:2 of MT Esther). A third stage of composition (a Proto-Masoretic Story, according to Clines) introduced the concept of the irrevocability of Persian law (= 1:19 and 8:8 of the MT), with all that that involved, and the discovery of the conspiracy of the two eunuchs (= 2:21-3 of MT), with its elaborate ramifications. A subsequent addition of three distinct 'Appendices', as Clines (1984: 167) terms them, followed:

(1) Est. 9: 1-19, which introduced a bloody narrative to the plot.
(2) Est. 9:20-32, which linked the celebration of the story's events with the traditional festivals of the Jewish year. It was at this stage of the story's evolution that the name of Purim [9:26] first entered the story.
(3) Est. 10:1-3, a final coda.

In my opinion, Clines' Appendixes (1) and (2) were formed in the violent atmosphere of the Maccabean age, perhaps sometime between 168 and 130 BCE when religious and national identity was being forged through oppression and conflict and the future of the Jewish people needed to be fought for. Esther 9 freely recounts that

Jews kill non-Jews. The Jewish author felt secure enough in his environment to portray Jews killing their non-Jewish enemies – this, surely, is the world of the Maccabees' struggle against the Seleucids and their pagan allies (see Grabbe, Boccaccini and Zurawski 2016 and Sissom 2019: 131–202).

It is probable that the additions to Chapter 9 (and the short Chapter 10 – Clines' Appendix (3)) were finalized and codified in the 103-year Hasmonean period, though, when a stable and successful Jewish ruling dynasty had emerged out of the bloodshed. It is possible – likely, even – that the Hasmonean queen Shlomtzion (aka Salome Alexandra, 141–67 BCE) promoted the Esther story amongst her subjects and found obvious propagandistic opportunities in linking herself with the Jewish heroine of the old tale. Esther sits very well in a Hasmonean context and the support of Purim, like the festivals of Hanukkah and Nicanor's Day, which was fostered by the Hasmoneans, helped give support to an increasingly powerful Jewish national identity.

Effectively, then, in keeping with the tone of the rest of the novella, the MT Esther ends at 8:17, with the triumph of Mordecai and with a general feeling of 'joy and gladness among the Jews'.

Commentary

Chapter 1

1 Once upon a time, during the reign of **Xerxes, the Xerxes who ruled** over **one hundred and twenty-seven provinces** stretching from **India to Cush**: 2 At that time King Xerxes **reigned from his royal throne** in the **citadel of Susa**, 3 and in the **third year of his reign** he gave a **banquet for all his nobles and officials**. The **military leaders** of **Persia and Media**, the **princes**, and the **nobles of the provinces** were there.

4 For **a full 180 days** he displayed the vast **wealth of his kingdom** and **the splendour and glory of his majesty**. 5 When these days ended, **the king gave a banquet**, lasting **seven days**, in the walled garden of the **king's palace**, for all the people from the poorest to the wealthiest who were in the **citadel of Susa**. 6 The **garden** had **hangings of white and blue linen, fastened with cords of white linen and purple material to silver rings on marble pillars**. There were **couches of gold and silver** on a mosaic pavement of porphyry, marble, mother-of-pearl and other costly stones. 7 **Wine was served in goblets of gold, each one different from the other**, and the **royal wine** was abundant, in keeping with the king's generosity. 8 By the king's command each guest was permitted to drink with no limits, for the king instructed all the **wine stewards** to serve each man what he desired.

9 **Queen Vashti** also gave a **banquet for the women** in the royal palace of King Xerxes.

10 On the seventh day, when King Xerxes was drunk from wine, he commanded the seven **eunuchs** who served him – **Mehuman, Biztha, Harbona, Bigtha, Abagtha, Zethar and Karkas** – 11 to bring before him Queen Vashti, wearing her **royal crown**, in order to parade **her beauty** to the people and nobles, **for she was lovely to look at**. 12 But when the attendants delivered the king's command, Queen **Vashti refused to come**. Then **the king became furious and burned with anger**.

13 Since **it was customary for the king to consult experts in matters of law and justice**, he spoke with the wise men who understood the times 14 and were closest to the king – **Karshena, Shethar, Admatha, Tarshish, Meres, Marsena and Memukan**, the **seven nobles of Persia and Media who had special access to the king** and were highest in the kingdom. 15 'According to law, **what must be done to Queen Vashti?**' he asked. 'She has not observed the command of King Xerxes that the eunuchs have taken to her.' 16 Then Memukan replied in the presence of the king and the nobles, 'Queen Vashti has done wrong, not only against the king but also against all the nobles and the peoples of all the provinces of King Xerxes. 17 For the queen's behaviour will become known to all the women, and so they will scorn their husbands and say, "King Xerxes

commanded Queen Vashti to be brought before him, but she would not come." 18 This very day the Persian and Median women of the aristocracy who have heard about the queen's conduct will respond to all the king's nobles in the same way. **There will be no end of disrespect and discord.**

19 Therefore, **if it pleases the king**, let him issue a royal decree and let it be written in the laws of Persia and Media, **which cannot be repealed**, that Vashti is never again to **enter the presence of King Xerxes**. Also let the king **give her royal position to someone else** who is better than she. 20 Then when the king's edict is proclaimed throughout all his vast realm, all the women will revere their husbands, from the poorest to the richest.'

21 The king and his nobles were pleased with this advice, so the king did as Memukan proposed. 22 He sent **dispatches to all parts of the kingdom**, to each province in its **own script** and to each people **in their own language**, decreeing that every man should be ruler over his own household, using his **native tongue**.

Commentary

1:1 Xerxes, the Xerxes who ruled …

(i) The name

Xerxes is name of two Achaemenid kings and of some later, post-Achaemenid, princes. *Xerxes* is the Gk. (Ξέρξης) and Lat. form (*Xerxes* or *Xerses*) of the Achaemenid name which in OP is rendered *x-š-y-a-r-š-a* (*Xšaya-ṛšā*, or perhaps **Xšayaṛšā*). In Bab. it is found rendered as *Ḫi-ši-'-ar-šá*, with other variations. The OP *Xšaya-ṛšā* is a compound of the *xšaya-* 'ruling' and **ṛšan-* 'hero, man', and therefore the name means 'ruling over heroes', 'ruling over heroic men' or 'hero among rulers (kings)'. Less championed, but certainly feasible and attractive, is 'the mighty prince' (How and Wells 1912: 105; Tavernier 2007: 23).

In the Heb. text of Esther, the name 'Aḥašvērōš is given to the Persian king. It occurs also in Ezra 4:6 and Dan. 9:1, as well as in the apocryphal Tob. 14:15. In Tobit, Nebuchadnezzar and Ahasuerus (Gk. *Asuēros*) are said to have captured and destroyed Nineveh (612 BCE); therefore, Ahasuerus must equate with Cyaxares (OI **huvaxštra*), the ruler of the Medes in the north of Iran (Hdt. 1.103). In the Greek text of Esther, the Persian king's name is *Artaxerxes* (see (iv) below). However, it is impossible to equate the OP for Artaxerxes (*Artaxšaçā*) with the Heb. 'Aḥašvērōš. The name 'Aḥašvērōš should therefore be read as an attempted transliteration of the Iranian name *Xšaya-ṛšā*: Xerxes (contra Hughes 2016, who inexplicably links 'Aḥašvērōš to Darius I).

Xerxes' name is found on a calcite or alabaster jar in a quadrilingual (in Old Persian, Egyptian, Babylonian and Elamite) signature. It was discovered in the ruins of the

Mausoleum at Halicarnassus, in Caria, and reads, 'Xerxes the Great King' (**Figure 1.1**). It may have contained water drawn from the Nile, received by Xerxes as a symbol of Egypt's submission to Persian rule. Other examples of broadly similar jars are known throughout the Achaemenid Empire, including one jar dating to the reign of Darius I.

(ii) Royal Achaemenid naming practices

Evidence of personal names in the Achaemenid period is considerable, and numerous sources written in the most varied languages and writing systems from within and outside the empire provide a good database of names and naming practices. Elamite, Akkadian/Babylonian, Aramaic, Hebrew, hieroglyphic and demotic Egyptian, Lycian, Lydian, Greek and other languages of the Persian empire preserve a rich onomastic tradition. However, in the indigenous Iranian sources, principally the monumental OP inscriptions of the Achaemenid monarchs themselves, less than fifty authentic names are documented. Among these are the names of kings (or eponymous ancestors) from the period before Darius I: Haxāmaniš (Achaemenes), then Tišpiš (Teispes), Ariyāramna (Ariamnes), Aršāma (Arsames), Kuruš (Cyrus), and Kambūjiya/Kambūjiya (Cambyses). From Darius I onwards, the Achaemenid monarchs are known by throne names, rather than birth names, a practice very well attested among Egypt's pharaohs.

Figure 1.1 Calcite or alabaster jar bearing the names and titles of Xerxes; from Egypt.

It is probable that at the royal investiture, when a Persian Great King first ascended to the throne, he adopted an official throne name and stopped using the familial name by which he had previously been known. Before his accession, for example, Darius II was called *Va(h)uš (Gk. *Ochus*), and Artaxerxes II had been called Arses or Arsaces (according to the Greek author Ctesias F15 §47, 55). While we cannot be sure that every Achaemenid monarch utilized this policy, the concept of a throne name would help explain the preponderance of a particularly strong onomastic tradition throughout the dynasty's history where certain royal names appear with regularity: *Dāraya-vauš* (Darius) 'Holding Firm the Good', *Xšaya-ṛša* (Xerxes) 'Hero Among Rulers' and *Ṛta-xšaça* (Artaxerxes) 'Whose Reign is Through Truth'. With their rich symbolic meanings, these were the Achaemenid dynastic names *par excellence*. Interestingly the Teispid dynastic name *Kuruš* (Cyrus) – 'Humiliator of the Enemy' – was sparingly used by the Achaemenids and is attested only once more in the dynasty's history as the name of the second son of Darius II, Prince Cyrus the Younger.

The Achaemenid kings adopted throne names to express religious-political programmes or dictums. The OP throne names evoke a subtle and sophisticated use of imagery which seems to address different ideologies regarding the conquest, maintenance and scale of the empire. For instance, the name Darius in OP, *Dāraya-vauš*, is related to the verb *dar-*, 'to hold'. It literally means 'Holding Firm the Good', a message that is too politically loaded to be overlooked. Darius the Great's empire was *held* together because of his rulership. Darius uses *dar-* to refer to the land which he holds under the auspices of Ahuramazda. As he states, 'By the will of Ahuramazda, this is the kingdom [which] *I hold*' (OP: *vašnā Auramazdāha ima xšaçam dārayāmiy*; DB I.26) and 'By the will of Ahuramazda, these are the lands which I *hold* in addition to this Persian people' (OP *vašnā Auramazdāha imā dahyāva tyā adam adaršiy hadā anā Pārsā kārā*; DPe 6–9); Darius even maintains that his empire was 'held' together by his law: 'My law thus *held* them' (OP *dātam tya manā avadiš adāraya*; DSe and DNa 21–2). The verb 'to hold' was used by Darius describe his control over the Persian empire and it was a fitting component of his throne name.

(iii) What's in a name? Xšaya-ṛša: 'Hero Among Rulers'

It is the *ṛšan-* compound of Xerxes' name, *Xšaya-ṛša*, which offers scope for interpretation. Meaning 'hero', *ṛšan-* has built into it an important Achaemenid concept of rulership which Xerxes was clearly keen to project, for it was the Persian king's duty, under the auspices of the deity Ahuramazda, to maintain the status quo of his empire, to act as shepherd and judge, and to bring order out of potential chaos. It was his obligation to uphold Truth (OP *arta*) and dispel the Lie (OP *drauga*) which was best represented by the chaos of rebellion and insurgence against the throne. In purely visual terms, this was reflected through the king's guise as a 'Persian Hero', an Everyman-figure, depicted slaughtering a lion or hybrid monster that represents the essence of chaos, as seen in **Figure 1.2**. Several doorjambs in the so-called Hall of a Hundred Columns at Persepolis, built under Xerxes, show this important motif, and in the case of **Figure 1.2**, the composite creature facing to the left has the foreparts of a lion, the horns of a bull, the crest, wings and hindlegs of an eagle and a scorpion's tail (see further Uehlinger 1999). The Persian royal hero grasps the monster by its horn and plunges a short dagger into its belly. For maximum mobility, the hero-figure has rolled back the overhanging fabric of his garment to free his arm and girded his long robe so as to expose his bare legs, unencumbered by the drapery of his garment. The large-scale scenes of mythological combat were rendered in miniature on seals too. In fact, the motif forms a substantial corpus in the seal imagery of the Persepolis Fortification Tablets and the Persepolis Treasury Tablets (**Figure 1.3**,

Figure 1.2 An Achaemenid king girds his loins and fights with a mythical beast. Doorjamb from the Hall of a Hundred Columns, Persepolis.

Figure 1.3 Stamp seal with a scene of heroic combat. From Persepolis.

Figure 1.4 and **Figure 1.5**). Scenes of heroic encounter can be classified as representations in which a protagonist exerts power and control over animals or creatures in a manner that explicitly transcends the plausible. Xerxes' throne name, 'Hero Among Rulers', does come close to elucidating the notion of Persian royal heroism and must be somehow connected to this important iconographic motif which, after all, was already in use in Sumerian culture and

Figure 1.4 Cylinder seal with a scene of heroic combat. From Persepolis.

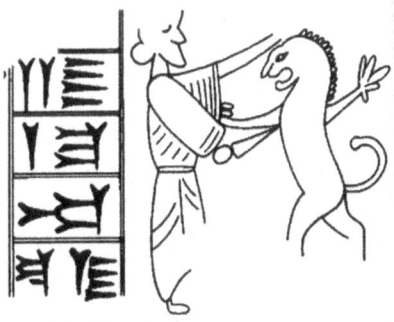

Figure 1.5 Cylinder seal with a scene of heroic combat. From Persepolis.

flourished in the Neo-Assyrian period (**Figure 1.6**). In itself, the lion/monster-slaughter is a riff on a much-used image of military conquest employed throughout the ancient Near East (**Figure 1.7**).

A more unusual imagining of the heroic combat theme is found in **Figure 1.8**, where the royal hero is depicted twice, once wielding a spear and once a bow and arrows. Aided by hunting dogs, he brings down a lion and, it seems from the small fragments that can be made out, human enemies too. The nexus between warfare and the hunt is always prevalent in Near Eastern art, but is not blatantly found in Achaemenid iconography. Its employment in heroic conflict seal-imagery, as seen here, is very rare. The heroic combat between animals or monsters was clearly an alternative to literal representations of actual warfare,

Figure 1.7 Egyptian relief showing a soldier grabbing a prisoner by the hair as he delivers a death blow.

Figure 1.6 Seal impression showing a Neo-Assyrian king slaying a lion. From Nineveh.

Figure 1.8 Achaemenid seal impression (unknown provenance) of a double hunt scene.

such as the Achaemenid seal-impression (**Figure 1.9**) depicting a spear-wielding Persian monarch delivering the death-blow to a fallen Greek. But it is clear from the standard composition of the heroic combat scenes (for instance the correlation which exists between the hero's grip on the creature's horn and the warrior's grip of the enemy's hair) that there was a blurred boundary between actuality and reality.

(iv) Imperial titles

The Persian monarch's pre-eminent titles, found time and again in official rhetoric, were:

Figure 1.9 A Persian Great King slays a Greek hoplite in combat. Stamp seal from Achaemenid-occupied Anatolia.

- 'King of Kings' (OP *Xšayaθiya xšayaθiyanam*; Akkad. *šar šarrani*), which was derived from Urartian usage although originally of Mesopotamian origin. It was used by the Achaemenids to claim their legitimacy as the heirs of the Babylonian, Assyrian, Urartian and Median kings.
- 'Great King' (OP *Xšāyaθiya vazraka*; Akkad. *šar rabû*), a title first encountered in Mesopotamia but readily adopted by the Achaemenids.
- 'King of the Countries' (OP *Xšāyaθiya dahyūnām*) or its variations: 'King of the Countries Containing All Races' (OP *Xšāyaθiya dahyūnām vispazanānām*)

and 'King of the Countries Containing Many Races' (OP *Xšāyaθiya dahyūnām paruzanānām*). To which can be added another, lesser-used but nonetheless instructive title:
- 'King on this (Great) Earth (Even Far Off)' (OP *Xšāyaθiya ahyāyā būmiyā* (*vazrkāyā*) (*dūraiy apiy*)), suggesting a development in the Achaemenid conception of their own territorial expansions.

Surprisingly, the author of Esther makes no reference to these lofty and imposing royal titles, and throughout the book, Xerxes is simply referred to as 'the king'. Given the author's keen interest in royal protocol and court functioning, the absence of any imperial titles for Xerxes is striking, especially as the ruler's grandeur and power is so well reflected in the genuine Achaemenid terminology of rulership.

(v) Why 'Artaxerxes' in the Septuagint?

If we are confident in asserting that the king in the book of Esther is Xerxes, then why in the Septuagint Esther, as well as Josephus' rendering of the story, is the Hebrew name '*Aḥašvērōš* rendered as *Artaxerxes*? This might be because, as Thamar Gindin (2016: 38–9) suggests, for translators who had no knowledge of OP phonology, 'the name Ahasuerus sounded to them more similar to *Artaxerxes* or (MP) *Ardeshir* than *Xerxes* or *Khashayar*'. There may be some truth in that, although there is a bigger picture to take into account. There was a tendency, which first developed in BCE, for Greek literary endeavours to create a standardized 'Great King' – a depersonalized description that allowed for an open identification of any (or all) Persian kings as a single entity (Llewellyn-Jones 2012). The Attic orator Isocrates, for instance, routinely equated Xerxes with Artaxerxes II (5.42; 12.157–8), while Lysias (2.27), another courtroom lawyer, attributes the Battle of Marathon to the campaigns of Xerxes, not Darius I.

(vi) Xerxes: a literary construction

Esther's Xerxes is not the Xerxes of history (Moore 1971; Shea 1987; see also the Introduction to this volume). That is to say, Esther's Xerxes is a literary creation, very loosely based on the Xerxes of 'historical memory'. Any attempt to find the real Xerxes in Esther is futile, for he is not there (contra Gertoux 2015). Looking for the historical Xerxes in Esther is akin to looking for *Iliad*'s Helen, or *Moby Dick*'s Captain Ahab. The historical Xerxes, who reigned as Great King of Persia from 486 to 465 BCE, the son and successor of Darius the Great, can only be located in the genuine Achaemenid corpus of texts, images and archaeology, otherwise his portrayal in Greek history-writing and tragedy, and in the biblical canon, is largely fantasy, not fact (Bridges 2014; Stoneman 2015; on the Greek fantasy of the Great King in art and literature see Sánchez 2009).

Xerxes' campaign against the Greeks in 480 BCE was the focus of Aeschylus' great tragic drama *Persai* (*Persians*) of 472 BCE, in which the Great King was characterized as a monstrous but inept tyrant who attempted to crush the freedoms enjoyed by Athens and the Greek city-states (Ambrose 2008; Garvie 2009). The subsequent fortuitous repulsion of the overwhelming forces of the Achaemenid despots became something to celebrate in poetry, drama, art and new narrative histories, such as that which was crafted by Herodotus, hailed (inaccurately) as the 'Father of History'. Herodotus' Xerxes is a character of intense complexity whose blustering brutality alternates with childlike sulkiness and unexpected, mawkish explosions of tears. One of the most momentous and unanticipated incidents in Herodotus' *Histories* (7.8), which has the emotional subtlety of truly great fiction writing, comes when Xerxes, reviewing the armada of ships he has amassed for the invasion of Greece, breaks down and weeps genuine tears. He is 'overcome', as he explains to his courtiers, 'by pity'. Why? Because, out of the blue, he 'considered the brevity of human life.' For a despot whose casual indifference to humanity is highlighted throughout the *Histories* to have such a such a profound empathy towards the inevitability of death is a remarkable psychological detail. Herodotus effectively embroidered it into the Xerxes story. The nightmare of a psychopathic leader (one minute up, the next down) at the head of a brutally centralized authoritarian state has become an image that has unsettled liberal democrats ever since Herodotus first created it, but it has very little to do with the *real* Xerxes.

In the same vein, the Xerxes of the Book of Esther is a fabrication. Adele Berlin (2001: 5) explains that 'The Jewish experience with Xerxes was quite different from the Greek but to the extent that the literary motif of Xerxes circulated widely throughout the Mediterranean world, the Jews could have adopted it for their own purpose, as they did so many other motifs'. In Esther, the Persian king is an emblem of both great power and great ineptitude. In his literary incarnation, the biblical Xerxes is a somewhat pathetic character, exercising no leadership and little authority. It is little wonder that some commentators have regarded him as a rather comic figure (Samuel 1955; Brenner 1994; Portnoy Marshall 1989; Dickson and Botha 2000). Later rabbinic tradition regarded him as both a capricious fool and a cruel villain (Hakohen 1961).

1:1 one hundred and twenty-seven provinces stretching from India to Cush

The hyperbolic claim for the presence of 127 imperial provinces is historically unfounded. The Heb. used in the MT for 'province' is *medînôt* which (as in modern Heb.) means something like 'state', 'territory' or 'district' (see Lam. 1:1; the Arabic cognate, *medinah*, means 'city'). Perhaps 'city state' (Gk. *polis*) or 'urban centre' might be a better term, although in a Persian historical context this is still problematic. In Est. 3:12, 8:9, and elsewhere, the satraps are distinguished from governors (Heb. *pahôt*), and it is possible that the 127 'provinces' referred to in Esther (repeated also in 1 Esd. 3:1) refer to smaller administrative districts of the empire which had their own governors, as was the case with Judah and Samaria. Of course, it is possible that the biblical author deliberately exaggerated the number of 'provinces' to signify the vastness and power of the Persian empire as well as to chime with 'the tone of exaggeration' (Berlin 2001: 6) that permeates the book as a whole.

In historical terms, the numbering of the satrapies of the Persian empire varies slightly according to the source. But the author of Esther is correct in emphasizing that the Achaemenid empire stretched from Ethiopia (Kush) to India (incorporating Sind and Punjab); it extended from southern Russia to the Indian Ocean, making it, at its height, in the reign of Xerxes, the biggest Empire the ancient world had ever seen (on the variations in the number of provinces articulated in the royal inscriptions, see Briant 2002: 173). The administration of the Achaemenid empire was in the hands of a group of men drawn exclusively from the highest echelons of the Persian aristocracy, very often from the royal family itself. These men were known as satraps (OP *xshaçapāvan* – 'Protector of the Province' or 'Guardian of the Kingdom'; Heb. *ăḥašdarpån*, see Dan 6:2, where the number of satraps is given as 120). The title which had existed under the Medes (**xšaθrapāwan*) from at least 600 BCE, was given a more imperial flavour by Darius I. The satraps enjoyed the privilege of being the Great King's representatives within the empire at large and they were responsible for the collection of taxes and tribute, for raising armed forces when occasion required, and for the administration of local justice. At a regional level, satraps were also required to make all governmental decisions. For matters of international importance, however, satraps were compelled to consult the king and his chief ministers and, as a representative of the king, satraps were obliged to keep court and maintain court ceremony based on that of the king's court at the heart of the empire.

It was Darius I, a truly outstanding bureaucrat, who first divided the empire's territories into administrative satrapies in order to maintain the regular levy of tribute required from each region (this information is provided by Herodotus (3.98) but needs to be treated with caution; see Kleber 2021). It is his Bisitun Inscription which provides us with the oldest extant list of the territories of the empire, numbered at 23:

> These are the lands which obey me, by the favour of Ahuramazda. I was their king: Persia, Elam, Babylonia, Assyria, Arabia, Egypt, those of the sea, Lydia, Ionia, Media, Armenia, Cappadocia, Parthia, Drangiana, Areia, Chorasmia, Bactria, Sogdiana, Gandara, Scythia, Sattagydia, Arachosia, Maka: in all twenty-three lands.
>
> (DB I §6)

Here Darius lays claim to an empire that extended to India and to central Asia beyond the Oxus, into modern Uzbekistan as far as the Saca lands, west to Ethiopia and to the shores of the Mediterranean. The Bisitun inscription is the earliest surviving document to offer a self-consciously 'Persian' perspective on its empire – and it is addressed to the empire as a whole as opposed to a very specific part of it. But in addition to Darius' Bisitun catalogue of conquered lands, there are five more surviving OP 'Empire Lists' which project a parallel image of world-order functioning under the rulership of the Achaemenid king, although the number of the satrapies fluctuate:

1. DPe = 24 territories

By the favour of Ahuramazda these are the countries which I got into my possession along with this Persian people, which felt fear of me and bore me tribute: Elam, Media, Babylonia, Arabia, Assyria, Egypt, Armenia, Cappadocia, Lydia, the Greeks who are of the mainland and those who are by the sea, and countries which are across the sea, Sagartia, Parthia, Drangiana, Aria, Bactria, Sogdia, Chorasmia, Sattagydia, Arachosia, Hinduš, Gandara, the Sacae, Maka.

2. DSe = 27 territories

King Darius says: By the grace of Ahuramazda, these are the nations that I subdued outside Persia. I ruled them. They brought me tribute. What I ordered them, they did. They kept my law: the Mede, the Elamite, the Parthian, the Arian, the Bactrian, the Sogdian, the Chorasmian, the Drangian, the Arachosian, the Sattagydian, the Macian, the Gandaran, the Indian, the *haoma*-drinking Saca, the Saca with pointed caps, the Babylonian, the Syrian, the Arab, the Egyptian, the Armenian, the Cappadocian, the Lydian, the Greeks near and across the sea, the Thracian, the Libyan, the Kushite, the Carian.

3. DNa = 29 territories

King Darius says: By the favour of Ahuramazda these are the countries which I seized outside of Persia; I ruled over them; they bore tribute to me; they did what was said to them by me; they held my law firmly; Media, Elam, Parthia, Aria, Bactria, Sogdia, Chorasmia, Drangiana, Arachosia, Sattagydia, Gandara, India, the *haoma*-drinking Scythians, the Scythians with pointed caps, Babylonia, Assyria, Arabia, Egypt, Armenia, Cappadocia, Lydia, the Greeks, the Scythians across the sea, Thrace, the sun hat-wearing Greeks, the Libyans, the Nubians, the men of Maka and the Carians.

4. DSaa (an abridged variant of DSf) = 23 territories

These are the countries that brought building materials for the decoration of this palace: Persia, Elam, Media, Babylonia, Assyria, Arabia, Egypt, the countries of the sea (= the Greeks overseas [?]), Lydia, the Ionian Greeks, Armenia, Cappadocia, Parthia, Drangiana, Aria, Chorasmia, Bactria, Sogdia, Gandara, Scythia, Sattagydia, Arachosia, Maka.

5. XPh = 31 territories

Xerxes the King says: By the favour of Ahuramazda, these are the countries whose king I am, over and above Persia [...]: Media, Elam, Arachosia, Urartu, Drangiana, Parthia, Aria, Bactria, Sogdia, Chorasmia, Babylonia, Assyria, Sattagydia, Sardis, Egypt, the Greeks (lit. 'Ionians') who dwell in/by the Bitter River and who dwell on the far side of the Bitter River, Maka, Arabians, Gandara, India, Cappadocia, Dahai, Amyrgian Scythians (lit. 'Cimmerians'), Pointed-Cap Scythians (lit. 'Cimmerians'), Skudra, Akaufaka, Libya, Caria, Ethiopia.

The Persian monarch stressed his own centrality within the orbit of the conquered peoples. Xerxes is therefore not only 'Great King' and 'King of Kings' (see above for a discussion of royal titles), but also 'King of countries containing all kinds of men' and the 'King of many countries', as well as 'King in this great earth far and wide'. The Greek treaties on the Persians often refer to 'the land of the king', suggesting that they conceived of the Persian empire as the monarch's own territory. Interestingly, in OP terminology, Xerxes is the king of 'this land/people' (*dahyu* = people, i.e., Persia/Persians) and of all lands/people of the empire (*dahyāva*).

The diversity of the empire was an ideological tool, which the Achaemenid kings used to craft an image of a universal empire. Each inscription begins with a reference to Persia itself, the imperial core, and next in the list comes either (a) Media or Elam or (b) Elam and Media. Both are marked out for their proximity (in terms of both geography and culture and even linguistics, it is to be supposed) to the Achaemenid centre. From there on, the order in which the territories are catalogued in each Empire List roughly follows the map of the empire in a clockwise fashion, first referring to the western satrapies, then those in the northern part, followed by the lands in the east of the empire. But the ordering of the provinces always privileges those lands/peoples lying closest to the imperial centre (Elam, Media, Babylonia, Armenia). Those lands/peoples at the periphery of empire (Ionia, Libya, Ethiopia) are always enumerated at the end of each east-west provincial listing, clearly suggesting an Achaemenid ideology of ethnic hierarchy. Physical proximity to Persia, it appears, signified a higher level of regard on the part of the Achaemenids towards their neighbours and, no doubt, judgements on the levels of their civility and abilities were made in that regard too. This widely dispersed Achaemenid ideology was understood and clearly articulated by Herodotus (1.134):

> They honour most of all those who live nearest them, next those who are next nearest, and so on, going ever onwards they assign honour by this rule: those who dwell farthest off they hold least in esteem; for they think that they are themselves in all regards by far the best of all men, that the rest have only a proportionate claim to merit, until those who live farthest away have least merit of all.

This idiosyncratic aspect of Persian imperial ideology is so deep-set in the Achaemenid psyche that it is formatted in stone in the sculpted reliefs on the north and east staircases of the Apadana (throne hall) at Persepolis. The well-preserved east staircase shows twenty-three delegations of foreign peoples bringing tribute gifts to the Great King. Each delegation is carefully placed into the staircase's design and the composition is used to reflect its proximity to Persia. Although there is no overall consensus as to the identity of each foreign delegation, we can be certain that, with Media and Elam heading up the lines at the top of the staircase **(Figures 1.10, 1.11)** and the Kushite group

Figure 1.10 Delegation of Medes; east staircase of the Apadana at Persepolis.

Figure 1.11 Delegation of Elamites; east staircase of the Apadana at Persepolis.

Figure 1.12 Delegation of Nubians (Kushites); east staircase of the Apadana at Persepolis.

bringing up the rear at the far bottom of the structure (**Figure 1.12**), the ideology of imperial proximity is being clearly articulated (see further Bonfiglio 2021).

Royal texts constantly emphasize the size and the ethnic diversity of the empire but always privilege Persia at its heart. A series of four trilingual texts on gold and silver tablets found at Persepolis and two further trilingual texts on a silver and gold tablet from Hamadan (DPh; DH) are important in this regard:

> Darius the Great King, King of Kings, King of Countries. Son of Hystaspes, an Achaemenid. King Darius says: This is the kingdom which I hold, from the Saka who live beyond Sogdiana, from there all the way as far as Kush, from Sind, from there all the way as far as Sparda, which Ahuramazda the greatest of the gods bestowed on me. May Ahuramazda protect me and my house.

It has been noted that the OP word *dahyu* (pl. *daheyawa*) means both 'land' and 'people'. In official Achaemenid art the structure of the empire as well as its ethnic diversity is given physical form through the representation of the *daheyawa* – the peoples who inhabited the Great King's lands. We have already noted the depictions of foreign gift-bearers on the great Apadana staircases at Persepolis and the collaborative role they might have played in state ceremonials, but other representations of foreign peoples exist too. On doorjambs at Persepolis' Hall of a Hundred Columns, the enthroned king is lifted high (in what Cool Root 1979: 47–61 calls the 'Atlas pose'; see also Schmidt 1970: 108–19 and pl. 66) on a throne-platform by representative of his empire (**Figures 1.13, 1.14**) and on the façades of the royal tombs at Naqš-i

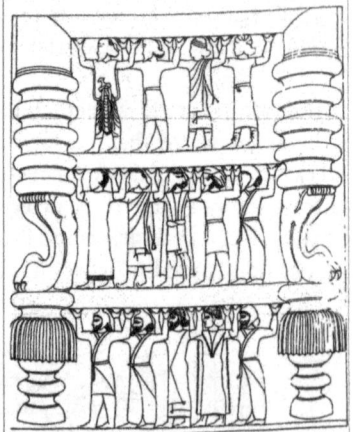

Figure 1.13 Representatives of the Persian empire lift up the king on a huge 'throne'; doorjamb from the Hall of a Hundred Columns, Persepolis.

Figure 1.14 Adopting the so-called 'Atlas pose', representatives of all the lands of the Persian empire lift up the king on a huge bench-throne (*takht*). Façade of the tomb of Darius I, Naqš-i Rustam.

Rustam and Persepolis, throne-bearers work together to lift high the image of the Great King who rules over them. This might be interpreted as a joyous act of reciprocal collaboration – the peoples of the empire exalting their monarch – but it is more probable that the emphasis is not so much on willing togetherness but on political subjugation. Lori Khatchadourian (2016: 9) sees things differently, and argues that the pose represents not only the easy support of the subject peoples, but also the dependency the king has on his people. Through this human agency, there is a 'looming metaphorical possibility' that the subject peoples would drop their arms at any time, undermining the entire imperial apparatus.

An inscription accompanying such a scene on the tomb of Darius I (DNa) invites the viewer to contemplate the meaning of the relief and suggests this domineering agenda:

> If you shall now think, 'How many are the lands which king Darius held?', then look at the sculptures of those who bear [i.e. carry] the throne, and then you shall know, then will it become known to you: the spear of a Persian man has gone far; then shall it become known to you: a Persian man has delivered battle far indeed from Persia.

Here the geographic centrality of Persia is stressed, as is the military prowess of the Persians themselves. However, each constituency of the empire is afforded its place in both the textual and visual details of the tomb façade. Each individual throne-bearer is dressed in 'national costume' (and the artist has taken care and delight in carefully rendering the details of the different forms of ethic dress and physiognomy) and each is named:

> This is the Persian; this is the Mede; this the Elamite; this is the Parthian; this is the Areian; this is the Bactrian; this is the Sogdian; this is the Chorasmian; [...]; this is the Drangianian; this is the Arachosian; this is the Sattagydian; this is the Gandaran; this is the Indian; this is the *homa*-drinking Saca [...] This is the Pointed Hat Saca; this is the Babylonian; this is the Assyrian; this is the Arab; this is the Egyptian; this is the Armenian; this is the Cappadocian; this is the Sardian; this is the Ionian; this is the Scythian across the sea; this is the Thracian; this is the *petasos*-wearing Ionian; this is the Libyan; this is the Nubian. This is the man from Maka. This is the Carian.

1:2 King

OP *xšāyaθiya*, 'king', 'royal', from the Indo-European root *ghedh*, 'to get', 'to seize'. The word is attested 281 times in OP royal inscriptions. It is also commonly written in a short-hand form as *XŠ*, with the same meaning. The NP equivalent is *shah*. The Heb.-Aram. word for 'king' (*melek*) is one of the most commonly used words in the Hebrew bible, occurring almost 2,700 times.

(i) Gaining the throne

What qualified a man to be king of Persia? What role did lineage play in the royal succession? Persian kingship was hereditary and the right to rule was strictly kept within the Achaemenid family and thereby a king's possession of the blood-royal was the very basis of the monarchy; this is why, from the reign of Darius I onwards, the OP title *Haxāmanišiya*, 'an Achaemenid' is reiterated time and again in the official texts of successive kings.

While there is little doubt that the birth of a king's first son was a cause for celebration and that this prince continued to hold a position of prestige throughout his life (Pl. *Alc.* 121c; Ath. 12.515a), it does not mean to say that he was automatically destined to follow his father to the throne. Primogeniture did not operate at the Persian court. In this respect, the Achaemenids followed a practice witnessed in the courts of Egypt, Assyria and Israel where on several occasions we learn that kings chose younger (more favoured or more able) sons to succeed them. For instance, David was succeeded by Solomon, his youngest (known) son (1 Kgs 1) and Sennacherib selected his youngest son Esarhaddon for the kingship (Kwasman and Parpola 1991: xxix–xxxiv). Each of these succession-decisions triggered fierce rebellions at court (which suggests that there was perhaps an expectation that the first-born or elder son might succeed his father). Sennacherib's choice of heir resulted in his assassination, prompting Esarhaddon, when his own time came to appoint a successor, to take steps to secure a smooth succession for his chosen relative, his grandson Ashurbanipal, who ascended the throne backed by powerful nobles who had been forced to swear an oath of loyalty to him (Llewellyn-Jones 2019).

Some Persian monarchs named their heirs in a timely fashion, but many did not. When Xerxes left for his military expedition against the Greeks in 480 BCE, he had not designated an heir and consequently his uncle, Artabanus, was left in charge of the court (but was not appointed as regent). This begs the question, what would have happened had Xerxes died on campaign? Pierre Briant (2002: 567) provides a frank answer: 'Dynastic wars, already frequent during anticipated successions, would have raged'.

To avoid this chaos, a king usually appointed his successor while he was still strong enough to defend his decision and provide the heir-designate with the support and instruction he needed. We know for instance that upon his appointment to office, an Assyrian Crown Prince subsequently moved into the so-called 'succession palace' (a distinct physical space separated from the main royal residence) and began his grooming for power. He acquired a harem and a wife (or wives – the 'ladies of the house'; see Svärd and Luukko 2009) and proceeded to take on royal duties both at the seat of government and in active military service in the provinces (Montero Fenollòs 2006). A similar situation might have existed for the Achaemenid Crown Prince too, as we know that he could acquire his own household of wives, ministers and servants (although there is no direct evidence for a Persian 'succession house'), and was provided with appropriate robes, a crown, and a chariot and horses (which are depicted on the walls of Persepolis; see generally Sánchez 2006) befitting his exalted status. He also received expert tuition in government from the Magi and other royal tutors (although he shared this privileged education with his brothers and the sons of aristocracy; see further Xen. *An.* 1.9.2). Briant (2002: 522) makes the important observation that given the high infant mortality rate, it would be unwise of a king not to educate all of his sons to a high standard – so any one of them had the potential to become king.

It is possible that the Achaemenid Crown Prince was known by a specific title: OP *visa-puthra ('son of the clan'), which set him above the other 'princes of the (royal) house' (Ar. *bny byt*'; see Samet 2021), although in a text recalling his succession to the throne (XPf §4–5) Xerxes allies himself to his father's memory and designates himself *maθišta* (lit. 'the greatest [after him]'):

Darius had other sons, but – thus was Ahuramazda's desire – my father Darius made me the greatest [*maθišta*] after him. When my father Darius went away from the throne, by the grace of Ahuramazda I became king on my father's throne.

In the visual programme of Persia, the Crown Prince is sometimes represented at the side of the Great King wearing similar garments, crowns and hair-styles to his father. Xerxes' statement that he was made the 'greatest' of Darius' sons is full of confidence and bravado, but is perhaps more hyperbole than reality, at least if we choose to follow the story of Darius' succession as told by Herodotus (7.2–3) who reports of a 'violent struggle' which erupted between Darius' many sons. Xerxes emerges victorious because he pulls rank over his brothers, the sons born to Darius while he was still a private man, but also because, as Herodotus insists, his mother Atossa, the eldest daughter of Cyrus the Great and one of Darius' six wives, 'had all the power'. Female intervention into the politics of succession is not at all infeasible. In fact, it was commonplace throughout the courts of the ancient Near East (see Llewellyn-Jones 2019).

Enticing (if somewhat tentative) evidence has recently emerged from the Persepolis Fortification archive which opens up the possibility of a new reading for a co-regency between Darius and Xerxes:

7 litres of flour, allocation from Mirizza, a Parthian named Tamšakama, spearbearer, assigned by Xerxes, together with his three companions, sent from the king [Darius] to Parthia: they received (it as) ration (for) one day. Third month, 24th year [of Darius]. Their ration (was) 1.5 litres, one servant received 1 litre. He (Tamšakama) carried a sealed document from the king.

(PF-NN1657)

This is the earliest known document to attest to the presence of Xerxes in the historical record. It can be dated to May/June 498 BCE. The text suggests that he was serving as a military commander in Parthia a full twelve years before his mention in Herodotus as Darius' heir. While PF-NN1657 does not categorically state that he was a joint-ruler, the document shows Xerxes taking full responsibility for the chain of command in Parthia, and as Wouter Henkelman notes,

> Since the Parthian men were travelling from the king to Parthia, and were carrying a sealed authorisation from the king, they may have been initially dispatched by Xerxes to report to his father. Having done so, they were now heading back with the king's response. The context makes the scribe's silence on Xerxes' title (or the fact that he was Darius' son) eloquent: his position was apparently well-known.
> (Henkelman 2010b: 31)

Text PF-NN1657 perhaps confirms Calmeyer's once controversial thesis that Xerxes was 'king and co-regent' for twelve years before Darius' death and that his reign began in 498 BCE (Calmeyer 1976: 83). Briant (2002: 522), however, suggests that the sacred office of kingship could not accommodate the notion of co-regency and that 'the official recognition of a crown prince in no way signified a sharing of power: the king was One'. The evidence for co-regency is scant and contradictory, and the question of whether the Achaemenid monarchs ever employed the co-regency system must remain open.

(ii) The Great King and the divine

There is no god in MT Esther. There is no Hebrew deity, nor is there any (overt) mention of pagan gods either. The divine is curiously omitted from the story, at least as it comes down to us in the textual tradition (see Dalley 2007 for a discussion of the presence of Mesopotamian gods woven into the (earlier) story of Esther; see also the Introduction to this volume). There are no references to Jewish, Persian or any other religious institutions or practices; there are no prayers, hymns, sacrifices and offerings, cult statues, temples or shrines. The world of Esther is entirely devoid of the divine. The absence of any religious motif in the book is hard to fathom, since the author also could easily have mentioned the Jewish God as being behind any of the numerous 'coincidences' in the story. In Esther, we are far removed from the world of Daniel, that other great diaspora drama, with its idols of gold, its ceremonies, dreams, omens and apparitions. The court of Nebuchadnezzar is rich in Mesopotamian-style ritual and belief, and the king himself, the most complicated character in the book, is made all the more believable because of his adherence to his gods and his belief in his own semi-divine nature. Without his absolute devotion to his pagan gods and an awareness of his own place in the divine order, Nebuchadnezzar's eventual recognition of the supremacy of Daniel's God (Dan. 4:1-37) would be much weakened. In Esther, however, Xerxes is given no religious context in which to operate his kingship. The original audience of the book would have known that the Achaemenid kings constructed themselves as piously reverential to the gods (foreign deities included; Isa. 44:23-8; 45:1-8) and that they held the achievements of their empire-building to divine favour. Without the acknowledgement of the divine presence (Jewish or pagan), the story of Esther is not only weakened, but it fails to resonate with the basic premises of Near Eastern kingship.

In the biblical tradition, Cyrus the Great was presented as YHWH's chosen instrument, and gained his kingship in order to redeem the Jews from exile (Ezra 1:1-4). God called him 'my shepherd' and bestowed on him the coveted title of *meshiach*, 'anointed one' (Isa. 44:28; 45:1). A similarly bespoke relationship is fostered between Cyrus and Babylon's supreme god, Marduk, as recorded in the highly propagandistic 'Cyrus Cylinder': 'Marduk took [Cyrus] by the hand, he called, for dominion over the totality of the world and he named his name – Cyrus of Anshan; he protected in justice and righteousness; Marduk, the great lord, who cares for his people, looked with pleasure at his good deeds and his righteous heart' (CB §43–5). Similarly, hymns intoned by priests at Neo-Assyrian coronation ceremonies laud a king's virtues and the blessings of the gods, and stress the confidence that deities place in the king's rulership (Livingstone 1989: 26–7):

> May Šamaš, king of heaven and earth, elevate you to the shepherdship over the four regions! May Aššur, who gave you the sceptre, lengthen your days and years! Spread your land wide at your feet! ... May the greater speak and the lesser listen! May concord and peace be established in Assyria! Aššur is king – indeed Aššur is king! Ashurbanipal is the representative of Aššur, the creation of his hands. May the great gods make firm his reign, may they protect the life of Ashurbanipal, king of Assyria! May they give him a straight sceptre to extend the land of his peoples! May his reign be rewarded, and may they consolidate his royal throne for ever! May they bless him day by day, month by month and year by year and guard his reign! In his years may there constantly be rain from the heavens and flood from the (underground) source!

Such sentiments resonated with monarchs throughout antiquity, for a king was not a law unto himself, but was subject to the favour of the gods. A good king needed to adhere to their commands. Things were no different in ancient Israel, where the king needed to heed the laws of YHWH, as stipulated in Deut. 17:14-20, he was to be chosen by God and had to be a Jew; he was required to restrain from accumulating horses (i.e., not build up or trust in military power) and wives (lest they should lure him towards pagan gods); he should not make himself personally wealthy. He must, however, write a copy of the law for himself; and, most importantly, obey it. The dangers of contravening the divine order could result in disaster, as the Israelite king Saul, cursed with bad dreams, failing mental health and a string of military defeats, experienced first-hand (1 Sam. 19–20). An eighth-century BCE Babylonian text admonishes an earlier monarch (probably Merodach Baladin) for his abuse of royal privileges, the misdeeds he committed to the peoples of Sippar, Nimrud and Babylon, and the fact that he turned his back on the will of the gods. Composed as an omen of warning, the text (Foster 2005, IV.13) lists the monarch's misdemeanours and warns all future kings of the consequences of acting in an un-godly manner:

> If the king has no regard for the gods or due process, his people will be thrown to chaos, his land will be devastated ... misfortunes will hound him. If he has no regard for his princes, his lifetime will be cut short. If he has no regard for scholarly council, his land will rebel against him. If he has regard for a scoundrel, the mentality of his country will change; if he values the clever trick, the great gods will hound him in right council in the cause of justice ... Marduk the lord of Heaven will establish his enemies over him and grant his possessions to the foe ...

We have seen that Xerxes attributed his success in the succession struggle which followed the death of Darius I directly to the divine favour and celestial support of Ahuramazda: 'by the grace of Ahuramazda, I became king on my father's throne', he proclaimed (XPf §4–5). But who exactly was Xerxes' helpful deity? The earliest reference to Ahuramazda ('the Wise Lord') is actually found in an eighth-century BCE Assyrian text, where *as-sa-ra ma-za-aš* is named as one god in a list of many deities. But he was lauded by the Achaemenids as the single god of creation: 'A great god is Ahuramazda, who created this earth, who created yonder sky, who created man, who created happiness for man' (DNb §1–3). The Persian kings envisaged the Wise Lord as a Creator only of what is good and through his auspices, working through the kings, that divine goodness was maintained: 'When Ahuramazda saw this earth turbulent, then he bestowed it on me ... By the will of Ahuramazda I set it again in its place' (DNa §31–6) and, 'After Ahuramazda made me king in this earth, by the will of Ahuramazda all (that) I did was good' (DSi §2–4).

Three key features underpinned the ideology of kingship in the ancient Near East. First and foremost was the fact that monarchy belonged to heaven and that earthly kingship was vested in the gods so that the men who ruled on earth did so as mediators and intercessors of a divine agency. Second, but as an extension of this god-given gift, kings had a judicial responsibility to guard and protect their subjects from war, want and terror. Third, kingship was sacred. Henri Frankfort (1944: 3, 12) summarized the centrality of the king's position in ancient life:

> The ancient Near East considered kingship the very basis of civilization. Only savages could live without a king. Security, peace, and justice could not prevail without a ruler to champion them. Whatever was significant was embedded in the life of the cosmos, and it was precisely the king's function to maintain the harmony of that integration ... For the truth about their king affected the lives in every (even the most personal) aspect, since through the king the harmony between human existence and the supernatural order was maintained.

In the Achaemenid mind, the universe was divinely ordered, and kings were formed by Ahuramazda for the purpose of serving him as his earthly viceroys. The reality was, of course, that Persia's kings were frequently confronted by all sorts of political upheavals, ranging from succession challenges to international rebellions and foreign wars, but the ideological picture of kingship created and promoted by the

Achaemenids was one of cosmic harmony maintained only through the centralized position of the throne. Rituals of Persian monarchy and the royal ideologies from which they emerged were designed to articulate the complex interconnection between the cosmological and earthly aspects of rulership. The Persian royal body was generally perceived to have taken on a new form of semi-divinity at the time of a king's investiture, and, certainly, in Achaemenid iconography, the Great King shares his appearance with that of the supreme Iranian deity, Ahuramazda. In this the Achaemenids echoed a *Hofstil* which was already identifiable in a proverb of the Neo-Assyrian period: 'Man is a shadow of God [but] the King is the perfect likeness of God' (Parpola 1970: 112–13, no. 145; on the physical relationship between the body of God and the king of Israel, see Hamilton 2005). It is clear from Achaemenid royal iconography that the king and his god share a physical form (**Figure 1.15**). The Great King encodes in his appearance the best physical attributes of the anthropomorphic Ahuramazda. He is the deity's *doppelgänger*. They adopt the same hair-style and beard-shape, the same crown, the same garment-type, and they 'emit' the same *xvarnah* or 'brilliance' (in terms of luminosity or glory; Battesti 2011; see comment on **1:4 glory of his majesty**). The iconography stresses that a reciprocity between king and god is guaranteed, and thus, in an inscription from Susa, Darius can state with confidence that 'Ahuramazda is mine; I am Ahuramazda's' (DSk). Even if Persian kings were not gods, they could be understood only in their intimate relationships with the divine.

Figure 1.15 The Persian Great King sits upon his throne beneath a woven canopy. The god Ahuramazda hovers overhead. Doorjamb from the Hall of a Hundred Columns, Persepolis.

1:2 reigned from his royal throne

That is to say, Xerxes 'sat on the throne', 'ruled'. The term 'ruled' or 'reign' occurs four times in the first three verses of Esther, a fact which emphasizes that the notion of kingship (Heb. *malkhut*) is central to the story. Its importance is highlighted by the frequency with which the Heb. root *mlk* appears in the book: of its 167 verses, *mlk* occurs 225 times (Berg 1979: 59 mistakenly counts 250 occurrences). The image of Xerxes seated on his throne therefore sets the theme of the book by endorsing the image of the king's command over his empire and its people. The irony is, however, that, throughout the book, the inexperienced king is manipulated, controlled and, ultimately, ruled by others, although James Kugel (2007: 645) is too cruel in calling him a 'pompous windbag, whose main concern in life is the endless stream of all-night drunken revels that he enjoys in the company of various members of his immense harem'. Xerxes comes across more as inexperienced than uncaring.

(i) Symbolism and appearance

Figure 1.16 King or prince from North Syria sits upon an ornamental throne with a matching footstool.

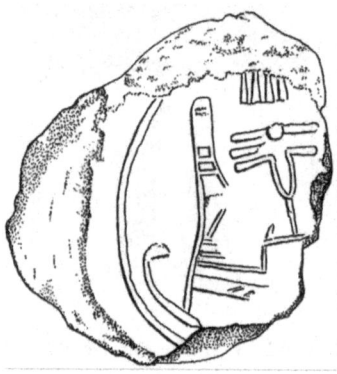

Figure 1.17 Seal impression found on a bulla from the City of David showing the presence of YHWH on his throne.

The royal throne was a significant icon of kingship in the Near East. Both monarchs and gods were frequently portrayed enthroned (**Figure 1.16**; Salvesen 1998: 132; Brettler 1989: 81–5; Levit-Tawil 1983). The throne was a powerfully evocative image, conjuring up thoughts of splendour and majesty. The Hebrew bible encodes the common Near Eastern motif of the throne as a seat of power for both kings and deities alike, and emphasizes that YHWH reigns as a universal king; the imagery of the throne is of central importance to that theme, garnishing, as it does, no less than 135 mentions. A unique seal impression found on a bulla from the City of David (**Figure 1.17**), depicting a throne – an elaborate seat with a high backrest – and two winged discs, may corroborate the assumption that the conceived image of Yahweh in Iron Age II Jerusalem was of a human-like form, capable of sitting and holding court (Ornan 2019). It is an 'empty seat' that was suitable for divine figures. Keel (2012: 332) has suggested that the elaborate throne on the Jerusalem bulla may have depicted an actual throne kept in the Holy of Holies in the Temple in Jerusalem. Therefore, the throne is to be considered as the seat of YHWH, indicating that although the god's figure is not shown on the bulla, he was conceived of as a human-shaped deity, undertaking human actions such as standing and sitting.

Kingship is made manifest when the monarch sits upon a throne. 'To sit on the throne' means 'to be king'. In pharaonic Egypt, the goddess Isis was a personification of the throne (she was depicted with a symbol for the throne on her head), and when the pharaoh sat upon the throne he was effectively sitting in the lap of the goddess, a theme that is meaningfully exploited in Egyptian iconography from the predynastic era through to the Roman period (**Figure 1.18**). The throne is the 'mother of the king' (see Charles-Gaffiot 2011 for an overview of the symbolism of thrones in world civilizations). When the Hebrew bible references royal thrones, readers

Figure 1.18 Late Period Egyptian schist statue of the goddess Isis sitting on a throne, holding the infant Horus.

are drawn to the image of monarchic power which resides in them, and the notion of the authority of rulership which projects from them (see, for instance, the focus on the thrones and rulership of the Egyptian pharaoh – Gen. 41:40; Exod. 11:5; 12:29; kings of Israel and Judah, such as Elah – 1 Kgs 16:11, Ahab – 2 Kgs 10:3, Jehu – 2 Kgs 10:30, Joash – 2 Kgs 11:19, 2 Chron. 23:20 and Jeroboam – 2 Kgs 11:19; the Babylonian kings Nebuchadnezzar – Jer. 43:10; the Ninevite king – Jon. 3:6 and Belshazzar – Dan. 5:20. Thrones are meant to be places of judgement, where kings dispense righteousness and justice (Prov. 16:12; 20:8; 25:5; 29:14). It was the symbolism of the throne, not necessarily the physical artefact itself, that shifted from one king to another and the image of the throne was therefore used in the ancient Near East to describe the transfer of rule: 'as YHWH was with my lord the king, so may he be with Solomon to make his throne even greater than the throne of my lord, King David' (1 Kgs 1:37). When a king ruled with integrity and justice and courted the goodwill of the gods, then he had no fear of being deposed from his occupancy of the throne: 'If a king judges the poor with fairness, his throne [ie., rule] will always be secure' (Prov. 29:14).

Subsequently, Solomon's throne becomes a centre of descriptive focus. Housed in the great Hall of Justice, which was panelled with cedar wood from floor to ceiling, the

> great throne [was] covered with ivory and overlaid with fine gold. The throne had six steps, and its back had a rounded top. On both sides of the seat were armrests, with a lion standing beside each of them. Twelve lions stood on the six steps, one at either end of each step. Nothing like it had ever been made for any other kingdom.
> (1 Kgs 10:18-20)

The biblical chronicler fails to convince since a series of images show Levantine kings seated on comparable thrones. The Megiddo Ivory of 1200 BCE (**Figure 1.19**) depicts a Canaanite ruler seated on a cherubim (or winged sphinx) throne, with clear Egyptianizing features. He sits in audience and receives his queen and a series of prisoners and on a stone sarcophagus from Phoenicia, Ahiram, king of Byblos, is seated on a bulkier

Figure 1.19 Detail of a Late Bronze Age ivory (the Megiddo Ivory) from Canaan depicting a local king or prince on his elaborate throne.

Figure 1.20 The ruler of Byblos, Ahiram, depicted on his sarcophagus, sitting on a throne with winged sphinx details.

cherubim throne with a high back, draped with a textile (**Figure 1.20**). Interestingly, an Akkad. term, *lā bēl kussî*, was applied to some foreign rulers in early Neo-Assyrian royal inscriptions by means of denigrating their power. The derogatory phrase is literally translated 'non-lord of a throne', suggesting a non-royal person who aspired to rulership (see Karlsson n.d.; the epithet corresponds with the term 'son of a nobody' – *mār lā mamman* – which was also applied to some foreign rulers in Neo-Assyrian texts). The Assyrian monarchs employed it to refer to usurpers, defeated kings whose thrones had been taken from them – in both a figurative and literal sense – and to aspirants to power. Shalmaneser III, for instance, recalled that in his twenty-eighth regnal year,

> while I was residing in Calah, a report was sent back to me that the people of the land Patinu had killed Lubarna, their lord, (and) appointed Surri, a non-royal person (lit. 'a non-lord of a throne'), as sovereign over them. I issued orders and sent out Daiiān-Aššur, the field marshal, chief of my extensive army, at the head of my army (and) camp. He crossed the Euphrates in flood and pitched camp at Kinalua, his royal city. Overwhelmed by fear of the radiance of Aššur, my lord, Surri, a non-royal person, departed this life.
>
> (Grayson 1996: 69, 81–2)

An ambitious foreign potentate 'who had placed himself for the kingship (of GN)' (*ša ramānšu iškunu ana šarrūti* GN) or 'who sat on his throne without my (Sennacherib's) permission' (*balum ṭēmeja ina kussîšu ūšibu*) is a rebel and an outlaw, a direct challenge to the world order established by the gods and administered by the Assyrian king. The Assyrian monarch himself could, without the help of any other human being, seize the throne alone, since he was the only (earthly) legitimate ruler (Karlsson 2016: 147–58).

Assyrian kings rejected the design of the cherubim-flanked seat of the Levant and opted instead for high-backed thrones with arm rests and conical feet (Curtis 1996). At Til Barsip (**Figure 1.21**), a king (probably Sargon) sits upon a high throne decorated with supporting caryatid figures or 'Stützfiguren' at the sides of the arm rest. These are representations of gods or genies whose role is to protect the king. They adopt

Figure 1.21 Assyrian king seated on his high throne and footstool; Til Barsip, northern Syria.

Chapter 1

the 'Atlas pose' as if they are lifting up or supporting the king. Similar figures are found on a throne without armrests upon which sits the goddess Ninlil (**Figure 1.22**) and again on the throne of Sennacherib on which he sits while he surveys the sack of Lachish (**Figure 1.23**). It has three rows of 'Atlas figures', all deities wearing horned headdresses. A throne carried by two eunuchs on a relief of Sargon at Khorsabad has pine-cone feet and an extra crossbar with large Atlas figures between it and the seat, and an arm rest with smaller figures; a large figure of a protective deity decorates the uprights (**Figure 1.24**). Occasionally, the decoration of the Assyrian throne is augmented with equine figures (**Figure 1.25**).

Figure 1.22 Assyrian goddess enthroned; Nimrud.

Figure 1.23 Sennacherib seated on his high throne and footstool; Lachish Reliefs, South-West Palace of Sennacherib in Nineveh.

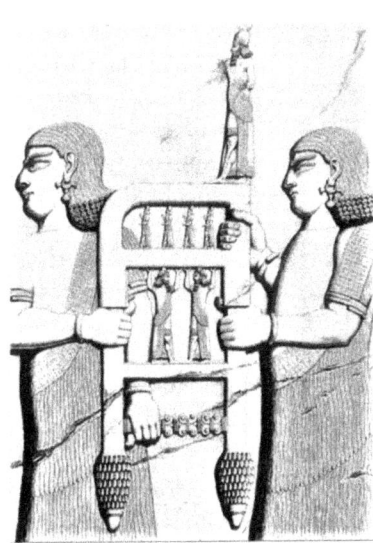

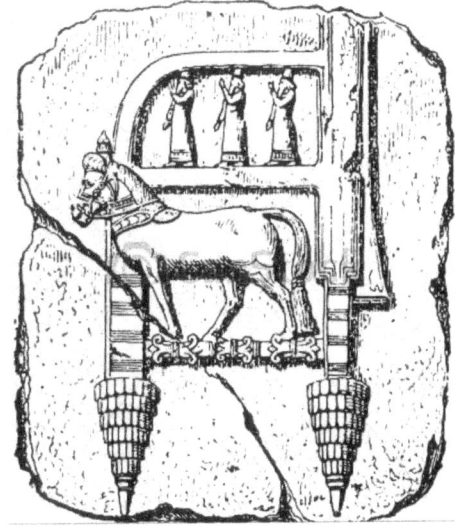

Figure 1.24 Assyrian eunuchs carrying a portable throne; wall relief from Khorsabad.

Figure 1.25 Fragmentary relief showing an Assyrian throne; probably from Nimrud.

The design and symbolism of the Achaemenid throne is, by and large, modelled on a combination of Assyrian, North Syrian and Urartian prototypes. It too was high-backed, although it lacked arm rests and the decorative Atlas figures (**Figure 1.26**). The throne tended to rest upon leonine-feet and leaf wreaths, with long, angular, and drooping 'leaves', and a series of alternating *tori* and *scotiae* (see Jamzadeh 1996 and Calmeyer 1996, who have collected these images in separate studies). Sections of heavy bronze fittings of an actual Achaemenid-period throne (**Figure 1.27**, probably from a satrapal palace) were discovered near Samaria in Israel; the two lion paws are 13 cm high and originally encased the wooden legs of the throne. They are certainly similar to depictions of thrones in the Persepolis reliefs, which provide us with the most important evidence of throne decoration (**Figure 1.28**; Tadmor 1974; Kuhrt 2007, 617; Calmeyer 1996). Details of the upholstery of the throne can be made out; these include a textile hanging which is draped over the upright backrest, and a (cushioned?) textile on the seat – it falls over the edge of the seat. It is richly woven with a geometric pattern very similar to that in

Figure 1.26 Achaemenid Great King seated on a throne; detail originally from the east staircase of the Apadana at Persepolis.

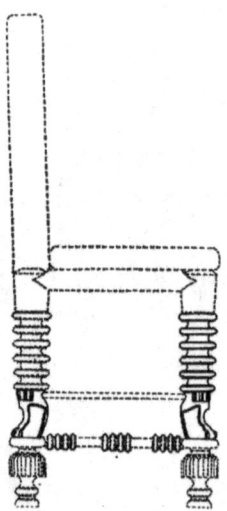

Figure 1.27 Remains of an Achaemenid-style throne discovered at Samaria, north Israel.

Figure 1.28 Patterned textiles on an Achaemenid throne; detail originally from the east staircase of the Apadana at Persepolis.

the large 'Pazyrik Carpet' (**Figure 1.29**; Rudenko 1970), a large woven horse saddlecloth, dating to the Achaemenid period, discovered in 1949, originally in the grave of a Scythian nobleman in the Pazyryk Valley, Siberia. A detail (**Figure 1.30**) shows that the design is composed of a series of ornamental squares and stylized lotus or pomegranate blossoms, very similar to patterns woven into Assyrian and Uratian textiles (**Figure 1.31**).

From Egypt comes a funerary stele belonging to Djedherbes, the son of a Persian-named father, Artam, and an Egyptian-named mother, Tanofrether (**Figure 1.32**). Djedherbes sits on a piece of furniture modelled, in all major respects, on the thrones of Persepolis and Naqš-i Rustam, even to the extent that its high back may be covered by a separate

Figure 1.29 The 'Pazyrik Carpet' – actually an Achaemenid-era felt saddlecloth – perfectly preserved in the ice of the Crimea and housed in the State Hermitage Museum, St Petersburg.

Figure 1.30 Detail of the 'Pazyrik Carpet'.

Figure 1.31 Detail from an Uratrian bronze plaque depicting intricately woven textile designs. From near Lake Van.

piece of fabric. The leonine legs of the throne rest on a *torus* element above a clearly rendered leaf-wreath; above the paw rise a series of *tori* and *scotiae*. There is no doubt as to the Persian origins of this throne type. Moreover, the clothes and beard of the seated figure follow Persian conventions. The image suggests that Persian nobles imitated their royal master and strove to sit on chairs that replicated, in some shape, the royal throne.

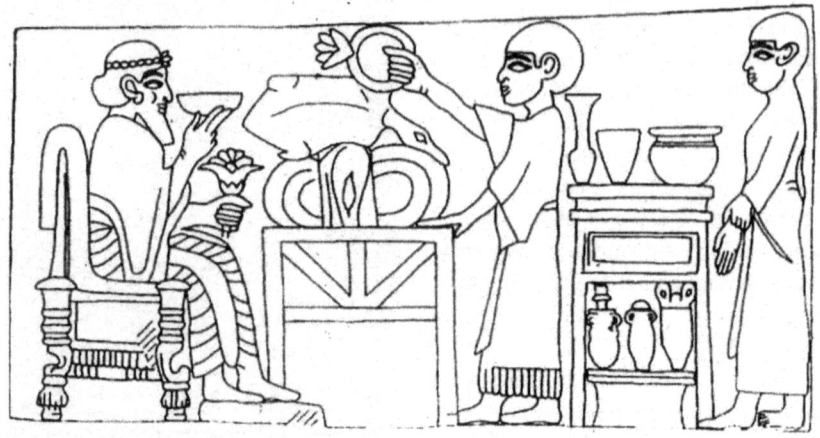

Figure 1.32 Funerary stele of Djedherbes, showing the deceased sitting on a Persian-style throne. From Persian-occupied Egypt.

(ii) Footstool

The Achaemenid Great King had a footstool as well as a throne and this too was an important emblem of his kingship. At the Achaemenid court, there was even an office associated with the footstool, as Deinon (F25a = Ath. 12.514a) notes:

> Whenever the king alighted from his chariot … he neither jumped down (even though the distance to the ground was minimal), nor supported himself upon someone's arm; instead a gold footstool was placed out for him, and he put his feet upon this when he descended. The royal stool-bearer followed him about for this purpose.

The footstool bearer is depicted on the north and east wings of the Apadana at Persepolis (**Figure 1.33**). Quintus Curtius Rufus (5.2.13–15) provides a comical vignette depicting Alexander III misappropriating a low table, which had once belonged to Darius III, as a footstool:

Figure 1.33 Persian nobles perform ignoble tasks at court: a royal groom carrying a saddle cloth and whip and an attendant carrying a footstool with which the Great King will mount his horse. East staircase of the Apadana, Persepolis.

> Alexander now sat on the royal throne, but it was too high for him and so, because his feet could not touch the floor, one of the royal pages placed a small table under them. Noticing the distress on the face of one of Darius' eunuchs, the king asked him why he was upset. The eunuch declared that the table was used by Darius to eat from, and he could not help his tears, seeing it

consigned to such a disrespectful use. The king was struck with shame … and was ordering the table's removal when Philotas said, 'No, Your Majesty, don't do that! Take this as an omen: the table your enemy used for his feasts has become your footstool'.

The story only reconfirms the centrality of this seemingly inconspicuous piece of furniture in royal display and ideology. After all, it was a given that the Great King's feet should never touch the ground and must be protected by soft carpets (Deinon F1 = Ath. 12.514c):

Through the court the king would proceed on foot, walking upon Sardis carpets spread on the floor, which no one else would walk upon. And when he reached the final court, he would mount his chariot or, sometimes, his horse; but outside the palace he was never seen on foot … The throne he sat upon was gold, and round it stood four short golden posts studded with jewels; these supported a woven canopy of purple.

Like the throne, the footstool was loaded with symbolism. In the Near East, it was associated with militarism and with victory over a defeated enemy. Iconographically, defeat is depicted by certain actions that were done by the conqueror to the conquered. There are several methods in which this idea can be achieved, although the most popular way of depicting the vanquishing of an enemy is through reference to the physical body and all that it symbolized. Strong iconographic resemblances exist between the Egyptians, Assyrians, Babylonians and Persians in their desire to craft an image of power in which the foot, and the action of walking over the enemy, takes precedence. Trampling on an enemy body is a sure sign of triumph. Conversely, to be trampled upon is to be dishonoured; to be stood upon is to be shamed. A standard Egyptian motif, dating back to the pre-dynastic period, and running through to the Roman era, depicts the ruler trampling on an enemy as he clutches the prisoner by the hair and delivers a death-blow (**Figure 1.34**). In Assyria the subjugation and humiliation of the enemy was codified in the king's action of placing his foot on the neck of the defeated enemy (**Figure 1.35**), while in Iran, as seen in the Sar-i Pol-i Zahab relief (**Figure 1.36**), Anubanini, king of the Lullubi, holds a bow and a battle axe and stands on the belly of the humiliated foe, as the goddess Ištar pulls two naked

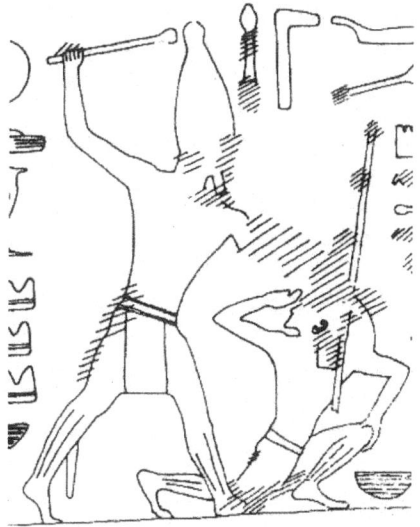

Figure 1.34 Early dynastic representation of a pharaoh defeating a foreign (Libyan) enemy.

Figure 1.35 Tiglath-pileser III of Assyria brandishes his weapons of war and stamps on the neck of an enemy prisoner.

Figure 1.36 Anubanini, king of the Lullubi, humiliates his enemies in the presence of the goddess Ištar; Sar-i Pol-i Zahab relief, western Iran.

captives, tied to each other with ropes, towards the king. Like the naked foe who lies beneath Anubanini's sandal, these captives are being led to their deaths. Some fifteen centuries later, Darius I (**Figure 1.37**) had himself depicted on an enormous relief carved into the side of Mount Bisitun standing upon the belly of the usurper Gaumāta, who lifts his arms in (futile) supplication.

It becomes clear that the footstool becomes a subtle symbolic implement of war, used to give honour to the one placing their feet on the stool or to take honour from the one becoming the footstool, both literally and metaphorically, as seen in Ps. 110:1 –

> The Lord says to my lord:
> 'Sit at my right hand
>   until I make your enemies
>   a footstool for your feet'

Figure 1.37 A victorious King Darius I stands on the belly of the would-be usurper Gaumāta; Bisitun Relief, north-west Iran.

(see also Isa. 66:1 and 1 Chron. 28:2 for Persian-period reflections on God's footstool). Similarly, Shalmaneser III of Assyria is addressed as 'a valiant man, who with the support of Aššur his Lord, has put all lands under his feet as a footstool'. In Egyptian representations one can see that the pharaoh, as a sign of his military victory, actually used captive enemies – the symbolic 'nine bows' – as a footstool or else had images of them carved into the footstool (**Figure 1.38**). It is clear that footstool is mostly used as a metaphor and that in the ancient Near East it was seen as a symbol of the king's military prowess.

(iii) Bench throne

More unique to Persian culture is the employment of a bench throne, divan or couch (OP *gāθu* NP *takht*; **Figure 1.39**). The jambs of the eastern doorway in the Hall of a Hundred Columns at Persepolis show foreign throne-bearers lifting the Great King on high. This might be a purely symbolic image, but it is possible that the iconography may reflect an actual court ceremony in which, at some great festival at Persepolis, twenty-eight courtiers, representing subject nations of the empire, lifted the royal bench-throne supporting the king, and carried him into the main hall of the Tripylon (council hall) where he received ambassadors (Root 1979: 153–61; L'Orange 1953; Shahbazi 2009). Certainly, the transportation of thrones upon palanquins is attested in Egypt and Assyria (**Figures 1.40, 1.41**). A fragmentary Neo-Assyrian text speaks of a king being carried on his throne throughout a city in order to conduct religious rituals:

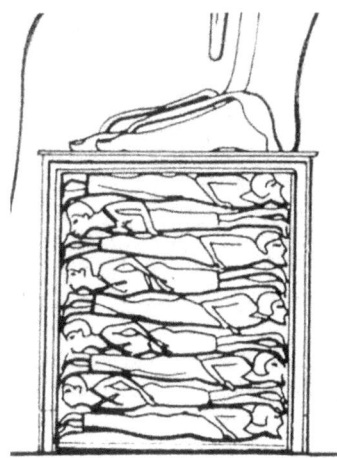

Figure 1.38 Pharaoh Thutmose IV rests his feet on a footstool bearing images of the so-called 'Nine Bows', the traditional foreign enemies of Egypt.

Figure 1.39 Adopting the so-called 'Atlas pose', but in the presence of the Persian military, representatives of the Persian empire lift up the king on a huge bench-throne (*takht*). Detail from the façade of the tomb of Darius I, Naqš-i Rustam.

Figure 1.40 Pharaoh Ramses III is carried on his throne as a kind of palanquin; wall relief, Medinet Habu, Thebes.

Figure 1.41 Assyrian soldiers transport cult images, each sitting on their palanquin-thrones, away from Babylon to Assyria. Relief sculpture, Nineveh.

people who carried the king, he [...] received a robe with fringes [...] When the king has finished the ritual [...] people, who carried [the king to] the temple [...] the king out of the city gate [...] enter the terrace [...] at the entrance of the *Bît-lab ûni* curtain [...] next to the royal throne, they hold the king up on the chair [...]

The couch or divan was an important item of furniture in the homes of the Persian elite and several representations of this important piece of furniture are found in Anatolia (**Figure 1.42**), where it tends to be used as a couch, in the manner of the Greek *kline*. In post-Achaemenid Iran, the *takht* became the dominant style of royal throne. Sasanian kings used it exclusively, rejecting the chair-style throne entirely (**Figure 1.43**).

Figure 1.42 Ivory furniture inlay depicting a Persian satrap or noble reclining on a couch (*takht*) in the presence of a woman (a wife?) and servants; from Persian-occupied Asia Minor.

1:2 citadel of Susa

Susa (OP *Çūšā*; Heb. *Šūšān*; NP *Shush*; Akkad. *šušin*^(ki)) was the principal city of ancient Elam and one of the great royal centres of the Achaemenid monarchs (see Boucharlat 1985, 1997; Dieulafoy 1890–2; Perrot 1981, 2010; Harper, Aruz and Tallon 1992). All biblical references to Susa (Neh. 1:1; Dan. 8:2; Est. *passim*) concern the Persian period or its immediate aftermath and suggest a good familiarity with the topography of the city. An important Jewish community had settled in Susa, probably

Figure 1.43 Silver dish representing a Sasanian Shah, in the company of courtiers, seated on a bench-throne (*takht*). From Iran.

after the Persian conquest of Babylon in 539 BCE. It was still flourishing there in the twelfth century CE.

Susa was not the Achaemenid capital, as it sometimes stated, for there was no such thing. But it was one of several important palace-cities, located at the heart of the Persian empire, which the Great Kings moved into on a regular basis. For the Achaemenids were essentially nomads; they retained the old nomadic lifestyle of their Eurasian ancestors, and the desire to move from one place to another never left them. The regular annual progression of the royal court around the empire was a form of nomadic state-migration. Like all nomads, the court followed the weather patterns. In summer, the court resided in the north of the Iranian plateau in cool mountains of Ecbatana. It journeyed to balmy Babylon and Susa for the winter months, and went to Persepolis and Pasargadae for the freshness of the spring. But come summer, the cycle started again with the court's relocation to Ecbatana. Susa was therefore the principal winter residence of the Achaemenids. It was abandoned well before the heat of summer since the temperatures in Susa were (and remain) scorching. Strabo (*Geog.* 15.13.10–11) noted that snakes or lizards attempting to cross the streets at noon would be frazzled by the sun and burned to death before they could reach the shade. So, in the summer, the Achaemenids decamped to north, to the cool breezes of Media. However, Susa alone is the locale for all the action of Esther. There is no mention of the other imperial palace-cities, nor is the peripatetism of the court acknowledged.

The ruins of Susa evidence more than 5,000 years of human settlement (overviews are provided by Harper, Aruz and Tallon 1992; Allen 2005a: 65–72; Landy 2010). The once great capital of the Elamites, Susa is located in the vast flat plains of south-western Iran, in the foothills of the Zagros Mountains, some 250 miles south-east of Babylon. It was one of the great political and cultural centres of antiquity, and must be placed on a par with the great Mesopotamian centres of Uruk, Nippur, Babylon and Nineveh. Elam was an integral part of the history and culture of Mesopotamia and not a marginal or neglected area of civilization. Elam was an epicentre of Mesopotamian thought and identity although it mustered its own ambitions for self-identity and independence (Potts 1999, 2010, 2011; Álvarez-Mon and Garrison 2012; Henkelman 2003b, 2008). The history of

Susa is inseparable from that of Elam, for a major part of the elements that enable Elamite history to be established derive from the excavations of Susa and its vicinity.

The Achaemenid era was the Golden Age of Susa. The city was incorporated into the Persian empire by Cyrus the Great (cf. Gk. *Sousa* in Hdt. 1.188; 3.30, 65, 70; Strabo 15.3.2), but there is no archaeological evidence of a Persian presence before the reign of Darius I, who was possibly born in the city. Located at the heart of the empire, Susa occupied an important strategic position, far better than Babylon, Ecbatana or Persepolis, to which it was linked by good roads. The royal road directly connected Susa to Sardis in Lydia (Hdt. 5.52–3).

In spite of 70 excavation campaigns, the digs carried out at Susa over several decades have rarely given priority to the Achaemenid period, so our knowledge of the city in the era 559–330 BCE remains surprisingly sketchy. The boundaries of the city were confirmed, however, in the 1969–78 seasons, when the archaeologists also revealed the palace of Darius I, partially reconstructed by Artaxerxes II, and a small pavilion (the 'Shahur palace') outside the walls on the west bank of the Shahur river. The topography and the plan of Achaemenid Susa before Darius I are unknown, but more than three millennia of occupation had shaped three principal mounds: acropolis, city and palace. Darius had surrounded this 100-hectare area in a lozenge-shaped enclosure and reconstructed ruined fortifications to surround it (recorded in DSe; **Figure 1.44**).

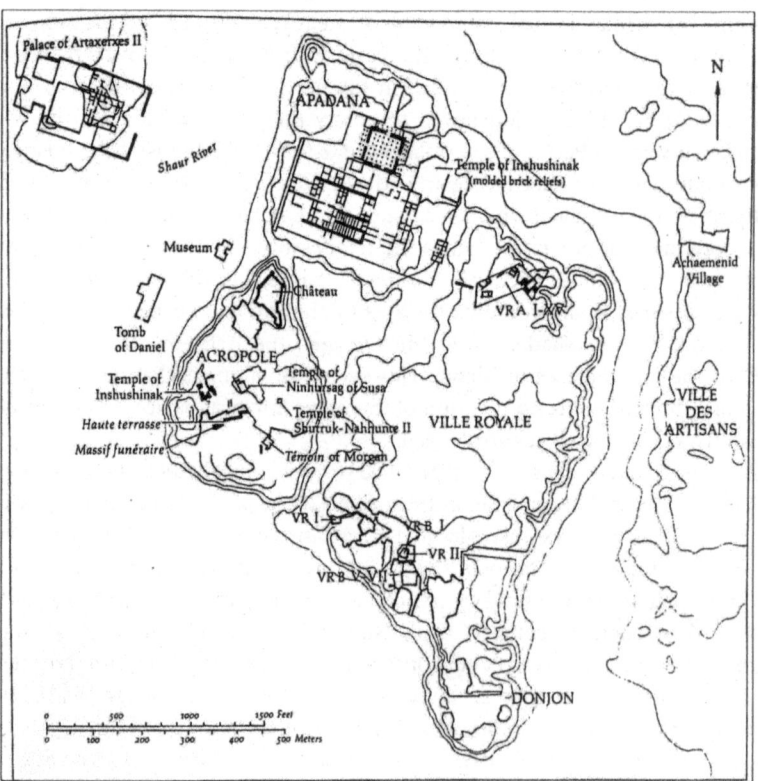

Figure 1.44 Plan of the Elamite city of Susa at the time of the Achaemenids.

He levelled the top of the palace and city mounds to an even height of 15 metres above the plain, and he fixed the boundary of the royal city by a retaining wall which was impressive to the visitor, but without fortification. We know at least four gateways into this area. In essence, Darius created a twelve-acre fortified citadel (OP *didā*, **didām*; Heb. *bîrâ*; Akkad. *birtu*), an upper-city, which accommodated the royal palace, the towering Acropolis (on which Achaemenid burial plots have been discovered), and the so-called *Ville Royale*. This resulted in the creation of a strong city having the appearance of a citadel and dominating the lower-city, which lay in its shadow. Only the enclosure and the royal buildings were built in solid materials of stone and wood. The large area of the *Ville Royale* is completely empty of constructions, suggesting that while the court was in residence at Susa, courtiers, the army and the civil servants lived in tents and other light constructions. A vast tent encampment was also erected at Pasargadae, Persepolis and Ecbatana when the court resided in those areas too, but it is within the walls of the exclusive area of the citadel that the action of Esther takes place.

The lower city encircled the citadel, but nothing is known of the non-royal urban constructions and domestic architecture of Achaemenid Susa. The idea that the lower city was comprised of tents is not easily acceptable in regard to the accommodation of permanent administrative personnel of the province and for the local population. Houses of mudbrick and would probably have served the purpose, although it is surprising that no stone foundations have been excavated. It might be expected that Mordecai and Hadassah resided in the lower city, although Est. 2:5 states that 'there was in the citadel of Susa a Jew of the tribe of Benjamin, named Mordecai'. It implies that Mordecai and his niece lived in the citadel. The distinction between the two parts of the city can be noticed throughout Esther, where 'Susa the citadel' (Heb. *šûšan habbîrâ*) refers strictly to the fortified royal upper-city (thus in Est. 9:6, 11, 12), while Susa (without further qualification) applies to the unfortified lower city (thus in Est. 9:13, 14, 15).

It is worth noting that excavators of the Susa site have often enthused over the correlations to be found between the literary evidence of Esther and what the archaeology unearthed. Jean Perrot (1974: 20) was especially excited: 'On relira aujourd'hui avec un intérêt renouvelé le livre d'Esther dont la description détaillée qui y est faite de la disposition intérieure du palais de Xerxès est en bon accord à présent avec la réalité archéologique', adding (1974: 20, n. 13), 'D'autres indications encore concernant les maisons des femmes, les jardins, tendent à confirmer l'impression que le récit biblique, dont l'historicité reste à établir, a bien sa source à la période achéménide dans le milieu des familiers du grand palais de Suse.'

1:3 third year of his reign

The third regal year of Xerxes fell in 483/2 BCE, just after he had successfully quelled rebellions in Egypt and Babylon which had been provoked by the death of Darius I. The historical reality is completely inconsequential to the plot of the book, however. The reference to the third year of the reign merely suggests that Xerxes was new to rulership, a fledgling on the throne. This fact helps explain his willingness to be guided by advisors and other courtiers; Xerxes has not yet come into his own. The selection of a new consort takes place in the seventh regnal year (2:16), which would be 479 BCE, the year when, in historical terms, Xerxes, having suffered defeat in Greece, returned to Susa via Sardis. Again, the date means nothing; the number seven is much loved by the author of Esther. The reference to Xerxes' seventh year is perhaps there to convince the reader that the bride-search took time to complete. It adds to the perception of the vastness of the empire. It also suggests that, by this time, Xerxes should have matured as a ruler. But had he?

1:3-5 banquet for all his nobles and officials ... princes ... nobles of the provinces ... a full 180 days ... the king gave a banquet

(i) Banquets in Esther

The word 'banquet' (Heb. *mishteh*) occurs 19 times in the MT Esther (Est. 1:3, 1:5, 1:9, 2:18 (twice), 3.15, 5:4, 5:5, 5:8, 5:12, 5:14, 6:14, 7:1, 7:8, 8:17, 9:17, 9:18, 9:19, 9:22). It occurs 26 times in the rest of the Hebrew Bible (Gen. 19:3, 21:8, 26:30, 29:22, 40:20; Jdg. 14:10, 14:12, 14:17; Isa. 25:36 (twice); 2 Sam. 3:20; 1 Kng 3:15; Ezra 3:7; Job 1:4, 1:5; Prov. 15:15; Eccl. 7:2; Isa. 5:12, 25:6 (twice); Jer. 16:8, 51:39; Dan. 1:5, 1:8, 1:10, 1:16). All in all, there are ten banquet scenes in Esther, each of which have significant impact on the action of the book. The story begins with an evocative description of a lavish 180-day-banquet hosted by Xerxes (the reason for the banquet is not given), in which he schmoozes the governors, military elite and princes of the empire (1:1-4). Without drawing breath, the second banquet takes place immediately after the 180-day-feast draws to an end. This time the king throws a seven-day-banquet for all the people who serve the court and reside within the Susa citadel (1:5-8, 10-21). Concomitantly, the third banquet takes place with the second, but this time Vashti is the hostess of the women of the court (1:9). Next, Xerxes celebrates a coronation banquet in Esther's honour (2:18). The king and Haman banquet then together, after Xerxes signs Haman's decree to annihilate the Jews (3:15) and Esther throws banquets six (5:4-8) and seven (7:1-9) in which she invites the king and Haman. The banquet is the place she chooses to reveal her Jewish identity and to name Haman as the mastermind behind the planned pogrom. Together, the Jews party at the eighth banquet, celebrating the new decree that allows them allowing them to defend themselves (8:15-17), and they party even harder with two more celebratory victory banquets (9:17-19). It is clear that the banquets in Esther are places of high drama, where characters – Mordecai, Vashti, Haman and Esther – rise or fall; they are the sites of disgrace, death and of exaltation and jubilation (see further Miles 2015).

The first of the ten banquet scenes, the 180-day party, is undoubtedly the most profligate and eye-catching, although most scholars question its historicity and tend to pass it off as a hyperbolic fantasy. The author of Esther may exaggerate a little, but on the whole, the excesses of Xerxes' five-month banquet would not look out of place in the historical records of Near Eastern kings. Banqueting is not the same as dining. A banquet (Akkad. *naptanu* and *qerētu*) is 'a multilevel, expressive, meaningful communications medium' (Ermidoro 2015: 11). In other words, the banquet is a sort of insignia, pointing to the economic, social and cultural construction of civilization. The importance of dining in this extravagant fashion is explained by Jean Bottéro (2004: 99), who notes that 'A banquet represented something more than the simple provision of daily bread, it gave eating and drinking their full meaning … A banquet broke with the ordinary, occasioned as it most often was by fortunate circumstances in life that were outside the daily routine and thus naturally joyful'.

(ii) Near Eastern banquets

Communal eating was a daily occurrence in Near Eastern societies; eating alone was regarded with suspicion and incredulity. It was unnatural. The only way to enjoy food and drink was in a group – it did not matter the size – but eating was not something to perform in solitude. Monarchs were fully aware of the importance and consequences of sharing food with chosen members of their families and entourage, and also with strangers. Sharing the same food and sitting in the vicinity of the king's table was an important sign, a synonym for being in favour, of being loyal, being a friend, as one Akkad. text is keen to point out: 'Now eat your bread and drink your water under the protection of the king, my lord, and be happy' (cited in Ermidoro 2015: 98). The sovereign shared his meals with his chief officials and courtiers; he conversed with them, discussing affairs of state and foreign policy, putting the world to right. For the generals of the army, the infantry and the cavalrymen, the king's soldiers, who spent many months in foreign lands, conquering and slaughtering, the king had always played the role of quartermaster, a food-provider, but at a banquet, the military elite were rewarded with superior food and drink and basked in the praise of their lord. The monarch showed himself to all, or part, of the population on the occasion of special banquets, where he played the part of leader and patron of his people. As Ermidoro (2015: 91) propounds,

> A banquet represented the moment in which the link between the city and its institutions was forged, and the control of the central administration in both the primary sector and the productive system was made visible to the community, which had the opportunity to verify the ability and the productivity of the élite class, and at the same time to enjoy the proceeds of its own work.

The Nimrud Wine Lists (SAA 7, 7–12), found in Kalhu and which date to the early eighth century BCE (see Fales 1994 for dating), register the wine distributed to various people during a formal occasion – probably a banquet – in the palace (McGovern 2009). The event occurs over several days, during which time the royal privy purse pays for all overheads. The wine rations are therefore listed on a *per diem* basis. The king is listed in the records, of course, as the generous host, and so is the queen and the king's sons. Civilian officials, eunuchs, courtiers, administrators, scholars and diviners, military men, and members of the domestic staff, palace-workers, servants and even musicians are seated with them in a somewhat *ad hoc*, social free-for-all, without much evidence of rank or hierarchy. Kinnier Wilson (1972: 114–20) suggests that at that one banquet, around six thousand people were hosted by the king which, he suggests, took place in the royal residence in Kalhu. The Kalhu palace was also the site of a mega-banquet thrown by Ashurnasirpal II (883–859 BCE) possibly to celebrate the re-establishment of the city as the epicentre of the Assyrian empire. On this occasion, as his so-called Banquet Stele records, the whole city was used for the celebrations. Kalhu became one vast banqueting space as, for ten days, Ashurnasirpal hosted, entertained and fed a staggering 69,574 guests. Extracts from the stele's text are certainly worth citing (Pritchard 1969: 558–60):

> When Ashurnasirpal, king of Assyria, inaugurated the palace in Kalhu, a palace of joy, and erected with great ingenuity, he invited into it Aššur, the great lord and the gods of his entire country. He prepared a banquet […] [The king speaks:] When I inaugurated the palace at Kalhu I treated for ten days with food and drink 47,074 persons, men and women, who were bid to come from across my entire country, also 5,000 important persons, delegates from the country Suhu, from Hindana, Hattina, Hatti, Tyre, Sidon, Gurguma, Malida, Hubushka, Gilzana, Kuma and Mushashir, also 16,000 inhabitants of Kalhu from all ways of life, 1,500 officials of all my palaces, altogether 69,574 invited guests from all the mentioned countries including the people of Kalhu; I furthermore provided them with the means to clean and anoint themselves. I did them due honours and sent them back, healthy and happy, to their countries.

'The overall impression conveyed by the Banquet Stele', Ermidoro (2015: 205) summarizes, 'is of an exceptional exhibit of power and control: there is no other document that expresses so vividly and evidently the magnificence and richness of a state banquet in Assyria, as a tool for celebrating contemporaneously the unrivalled might of the king and the administrative organization under his control'.

(iii) Persian banquets

In Persia, the Great King's table (and by extension that of the royal household), was served with extraordinary abundance, magnificence, efficiency and order. The *Stratagems* of Polyaenus (4.3.32) records an inscribed inventory, purportedly found by the conquering Alexander III, of the foodstuffs brought before the Great King and his household on a daily basis – enough produce to feed no less than 15,000 people, if we accept the words of Ctesias and Deinon (Ctesias F39/Deinon F24 = Ath. 4.146c–d; the origin of Polyaenus' text might in fact lie in the *Persica* of Heraclides or, more likely, Ctesias):

> In the palace of the Persian monarch Alexander read a bill of fare for the king's dinner and supper that was engraved on a column of brass: on which were also other regulations, which Cyrus had directed. It ran thus: Of fine wheat flour four hundred *artabae* (a Median *artaba* is an Attic *bushel*). Of second-rate flour three hundred *artabae*, and of third-rate flour the same: in the whole one thousand *artabae* of wheat flour for supper. Of the finest barley flour two hundred *artabae*,

of the second-rate four hundred, and four hundred of the third-rate: in all one thousand *artabae* of barley flour. Of oatmeal two hundred *artabae*. Of paste mixed for pastry of different kinds ten *artabae*. Of cardamom chopped small, and finely sifted, and formed into a kind of *ptisan* (treated barley?), ten *artabae*. Of mustard-seed the third of an *artabae*. Male sheep four hundred. Oxen a hundred. Horses thirty. Fat geese four hundred. Three hundred turtle-doves. Small birds of different kinds six hundred. Lambs three hundred. Goslings, a hundred. Thirty gazelles. Of fresh milk, ten *marises*. Of sour milk sweetened with whey, ten *marises*. Of garlic, a talent's worth. Of strong onions half a talent's worth. Of knot grass an *artaba*. Of the juice of benzoin (silphium juice?) two *minae*. Of cumin, an *artaba*. Of benzoin a *talent* worth. Of rich cider the fourth of an *artaba*. Of millet seed three *talents* worth. Of anise flowers three *minae*. Of coriander seed the third of an *artaba*. Of melon seed two *capises*. Of parsnips ten *artabae*. Of sweet wine five *marises* ... Of pickled capers five *marises*. Of salt ten *artabae*. Of Ethiopian cumin six *capises* ... Of dried anise thirty *minae*. Of parsley feed four *capises*. Oil of sesame ten *marises*. Cream five *marises*. Oil of cinnamon five *marises*. Oil of acanthus five *marises*. Oil of sweet almonds three *marises*. Of dried sweet almonds three *artabae*. Of wine five hundred *marises*. And if he was at Babylon or Susa, he had one half palm-wine, and the other half grape-wine.

Two hundred load of dry wood, and one hundred load of kindling. Of fluid honey a hundred square cakes, containing the weight of about ten *minae*.

When he was in Media he doled out the following:

Of false-saffron (seed) three *artabae*: of saffron two *minae*. This was for drink and dinner.

He also distributed in largesse five hundred *artabae* of fine wheat flour. Of fine barely flour a thousand *artabae*: and of other kinds of flour a thousand *artabae*. Of rice five hundred *artabae*. Of corn five hundred *marises*. Of corn for the horses twenty thousand *artabae*. Of straw ten thousand load; five thousand wagon loads. Of oil of sesame two hundred *marises*. Of vinegar a hundred *marises*. Of cardamom cresses chopped small thirty *artabae*.

All that is here enumerated was distributed to the soldiers; this is what the king consumes in a day: his lunch, dinner, and in largess.

According to Polyaenus, the menu of the king's dinner varied depending on the residence used by the court: he drank palm and grape wine while he was in Babylon or Susa and added safflower and saffron during his residency in Media, thus adjusting the menu of his repasts according to local traditions and ingredients available from the regional environment. The sheer volume of food and drink recorded by Polyaenus might lead us to suspect that he is merely indulging himself in the familiar Greek *topos* of imagining fantastical Persian excess (Gk. *tryphē*; see Hdt. 1.133; Sancisi-Weerdenburg 1995; Lenfant 2007b), but given that he carefully estimates the size of produce in terms of Greek measurements and that he distinguishes the apportionment of food according to the court's location (Babylon, Susa, Ecbatana and Persepolis), the text can be accorded some esteem ('all of the information *feels* right', says Briant 2002: 288) and can, in fact, be augmented by evidence provided by Heraclides of Cyme (F2 = Ath. 4.145) who similarly lists huge quantities of food served at Persia's court:

> What is referred to as 'The King's Dinner', [Heraclides] says, will seem ostentatious if one hears it described, but if examined carefully, it becomes clear that it has been carefully arranged with economic rigour, like the meals given by other Persian elites too. One thousand sacrificial animals are butchered for the king each day, including horses, camels, oxen, donkeys, and deer; the majority though are sheep and goats. Lots of birds are eaten too: ostriches (a very large creature), geese, and chickens. Each of the king's guests is served with a modest food portion and takes home the leftovers for food the following day. But the majority of the cooked meat and breadstuffs are taken out into the courtyard for the bodyguards and the household troops which the king supports. They break up the half-eaten meat and bread there into portions, divided equally. Just as Greek mercenary soldiers get wages in silver, so these men get food from the monarch to pay for their services. So too in the estates of other eminent Persians, all the food is placed together on a table and when the guests are through with eating, the steward in charge of the table gives some of the leftover food (mainly meat and bread) to individuals in the household, which is how they get their daily provisions. The most esteemed guests therefore visit the king for lunch only, for they asked to be excused for returning again so that they themselves can entertain their own dinner guests.

Here, Heraclides carefully notes how the produce was distributed from the king to his entourage (including men and women of the royal family) and how it was subsequently distributed by the royals and their courtiers to their own respective households. Therefore, the Great King's table was the locus of food distribution to many people of varying social rank (Xen. *Cyr.* 8.3–4 understood the essence of this practice, but he linked it to the monarch's display of beneficence to chosen individuals).

Wouter Henkelman (2010a) has demonstrated how the Greek conception of the King's Dinner is accurately reflected in the Persepolis Fortification Archive (and other Achaemenid-period documents) and he has analysed how the intricate royal food distribution system operated – with livestock and foodstuffs flowing into and out of the royal household (see also Stevenson 1997: 144–52). Known as the J Texts, these Elamite cuneiform tablets list products 'delivered to the king'. They seem to confirm Polyaenus' inventory and show that when the king or a member of the royal family relocated (not necessarily as part of the main court migration) they received food and drink provisions from the central administration (royal individuals included in the J Texts include Darius's wife, Irtašduna in PF 730–2, his son Arsames in PF 733–4, 2035 and his brother-in-law/father-in-law Gobryas in PF 688). Briant (2002: 290) notes though that the J Texts can often merge with the so-called Category Q Texts, relating to travel rations (see also comments by Janković 2008; Potts 2008). Henkelman concludes that 'the crown's internal hierarchy included officials responsible for provisioning the royal table who travelled with the court' and that '[the] redistribution of commodities within the court society was a matter of the court administration … The Elamite and Greek sources both (implicitly) understand the Table of the King as a complex organization with its own rules, hierarchy and bureaucracy' (Henkelman 2010a: 732).

We know something of Persian elite eating-habits, if not much about the recipes they created, and although Kuhrt (2007: 578) notes the fact that 'the ingredients of the meals were not particularly exotic or expensive and were put together in accordance with ideas about maintaining health', the reality is that we have no way of knowing how the raw ingredients were combined or what kind of rich dishes might have been enjoyed (although Batmanglij 2020 strives for an answer). Perhaps Kuhrt says more about current trends in eating habits than anything about authentic Achaemenid eating habits. The fact that Herodotus notes that the Persians had a particular penchant for syrupy or milky deserts (confirmed by the ingredients listed by Polyaenus), suggests that something other than health-food was desired. Moreover, Herodotus says (1.133) that the Persians 'eat only a few main dishes, but they frequently consume an assortment of nibbles – but these are not served together at one time but are distributed randomly throughout the course of the meal'. Xenophon confirms (*Cyropaedia* 1.3.3) this Persian fondness for 'fancy side dishes and all sorts of sauces and meats' (see also Ath. 14. 640f; for the appropriate translation 'nibbles' see Sancisi-Weerdenburg 1997: 341). Taking the Greek reports as her starting point, Sancisi-Weerdenburg (1997: 339) argues for a 'presence at court of specialist cuisiniers, producing not so much food as works of art' and she suggests that 'even if we cannot sketch more than its outlines, there is every reason to qualify cooking at the Persian court as *haute cuisine*'.

The only Classical account to actually specify how the king ate claimed that 'Artaxerxes III stretched out his hands and with his right hand he took up one of the knives laid out on the table and with the other he picked up the largest piece of bread, put some meat on it, cut it up, and ate greedily' (Ael. *VH* 2.17). Thus, flat bread may have been commonly used as a form of edible trencher plate as well as a convenient scoop, but knives used at the table cannot be distinguished typologically from those used for other purposes (nor is it likely that such a distinction was made in antiquity). Silver duck-headed spoons are attested from Pasargadae, although forks only came to be used in Iran during the Sasanian period.

Beyond the daily consumption of food, which even for the court might have been repetitive, better pleasure could be had in eating and drinking in the festive atmosphere of a royal banquet. Elaborate etiquette, conspicuous consumption of food and wine and intense labour in the preparation of food were all hallmarks of Persian banquets, which the Greeks regarded as obscenely decadent. Rich meats, including horse, camel, oxen, wild asses, deer, Arabian ostriches, as well as a variety of geese, were served with various types of bread, sweet grape jelly, candied turnips and radishes, candied capers with salt, terebinth oil, saffron, nuts and huge quantities of fruit – quince, pear, dates, pomegranates, figs, apples, raisins and almonds. Aelian (*VH* 2.17) notes how the Persian king 'ate greedily' a huge portion of meat laid upon a big loaf of bread. It seems that participation in a Persian royal banquet was more of an extreme sport than a chance to relax over a leisurely dinner.

The royal banquet *par excellence* was held on the Great King's birthday (OP *tykta* 'perfect', 'complete'; Hdt. 9.110), a time of great rejoicing amidst the court but also one of ritual importance. The royal birthday might have served as the setting for an annual ceremonial renewal of royal power (as seems to have been the case in the Seleucid period; Bickerman 1938: 246; Sancisi-Weerdenburg 1989: 132–3). This type of royal banquet is depicted by Xenophon (*Cyr.* 8.4.1–5), but it is Herodotus who shows the most interest in the event and several of his stories are set during this important annual court festivity. Thus we learn that the birthday celebration 'is the one time of the year when the king anoints his head and bestows gifts on the Persians' and that 'the law of the Royal Supper stated that on that day no one should be refused a request' (Hdt. 9.109–10), and he notes also that the Persian nobility followed the royal example because 'of all days in the year a Persian most distinguished his birthday and celebrated it with a dinner of special magnificence'; on that day they have 'an ox or a horse or a camel or a donkey baked whole in the oven' (Hdt. 1.133).

(iv) Official guests

The MT Esther uses an OP loanword, *fra-tama*, a derivative of OP *bandaka*, to refer to a loyal servant, a vassal or trusted friend. The OP *bandaka* is from *banda* (cf. the Old Indian masculine noun *bandha* 'bond, fetter') from the Indo-European root *bhendh*, also the source of English 'bind, band, bond'. OP *bandaka* therefore has a meaning similar to that of English 'bondsman'.

Like all other aspects of his official life, the ideology of invisibility governed the Great King's dining habits and according to Heraclides (F2 = Ath. 4.146a), on a daily basis, the sovereign tended to dine alone, hidden from view in a chamber (or some other specified space) and his selected guests sat outside to eat, 'in full sight of anyone who wishes to look on', although the most highly honoured guests were served by the royal butlers in a hall close to the king's dining room:

> Whenever the monarch throws a drinking party (as he often does), he is joined by a dozen people. After they have finished dinner, the king, being alone by himself, and his guests separately, one of the eunuchs summons the men who are going to drink with him. Once they come in, they drink in his presence, although not the same wine; they do so, sitting on the floor, whereas he lies on a gold-footed couch. After they have become very drunk, they leave. The king usually lunches and dines alone, but every now and then his wife and some of his sons eat with him.

Being invited to drink with the king was a mark of exceptional distinction, because it was during these drinking bouts that important matters of state were discussed and personal ambitions might be realized (Hdt. 1.133; Strabo 15.3.20; Ath. 4.144b, 5.102c). Seating placements were also a mark of prestige, as Xenophon (*Cyr.* 8.4.1.3–5) noted:

> When Cyrus [the Great] was celebrating his victory with a banquet, he invited in those of his friends (*philoi*) who showed that they were most desirous of magnifying his rule and of honouring him most loyally ... So when invited guests came to dinner, he did not assign them their seats at random, but he seated on Cyrus's left the one for whom he had the highest regard, for the left side was more readily exposed to treacherous designs than the right; and the one who was

second in esteem he seated on his right, the third again on the left, the fourth on the right, and so on, if there were more ... Accordingly, Cyrus thus made public recognition of those who stood first in his esteem, beginning even with the places they took when sitting or standing in his company. He did not, however, assign the appointed place permanently, but he made it a rule that by noble deeds anyone might advance to a more honoured seat, and that if anyone should conduct himself badly he should go back to one less honoured.

A courtier specifically honoured with a regular fixed place at the king's table was known as a *homotrapezus* ('messmate'), an OP title held by such high-ranking nobles as Megabyzus, Darius I's brother (Ctesias F14 §43), although even foreigners could be awarded this auspicious title too (Hdt. 3.131, 5.24). At a royal banquet, however, the king dined in full sight of this court and guests.

The royal court was the 'household' of the monarch and the attractions of court life for the nobility of the realm were obvious – power, prestige and remuneration could all be obtained through service to the Great King. There was clearly a hierarchy of rank among the many groups who made up the Achaemenid court, although trying to decode the precise function of every royal office within the Persian court is difficult and frustrating. Something of the rich mixture of jobs which composed an ancient Near Eastern royal bureaucracy is reflected in the biblical list of officials who served under King David of Israel (1 Chron. 27:25-34). But for their part, the Greeks found Persian court hierarchy puzzling and consequently their writings on the Persian court fail to provide us with a clear picture of the multitudinous range of court offices. Yet the Greeks were certain of one thing: the Persian Great Kings needed to be surrounded by a variety of courtiers ranging from satraps to stable boys because they were too grand to bother themselves with the mundane tasks of governing the empire themselves (Ps.Arist. 398a–398b):

> The chief and most distinguished men all had their appointed place, some being the king's personal servants, his bodyguard and attendants, others the guardians of each of the enclosing walls, the so-called janitors and 'listeners', that the king himself, who was called their master and god, might therefore see and hear all things. Besides these, others were appointed as stewards of his revenues and leaders in war and hunting, and receivers of gifts, and others charged with all the other necessary jobs. All the Empire of Asia, bounded on the west by the Hellespont and on the east by the Indus, was split up according to race among generals and satraps and subject-princes of the Great King; and there were couriers and watchmen and messengers and superintendents of signal-fires ... It was beneath the dignity of Xerxes to administer his own Empire and to carry out his own desires and superintend the government of his kingdom; such functions were not becoming for a god.

Greek sources suggest that in his youth Cyrus the Great had held several court positions – 'master of the wand-bearers', 'master of the squires' and 'cup-bearer' (Ath. 14.633d; Ctesias F8d* §5; see also Xen. *Cyr.* 1.3.8–9); before grabbing the throne

Darius the Great had been 'quiver-bearer' to Cyrus II and was Cambyses' 'lance-bearer' (Ael. *VH* 12.43; Hdt. 3.139), and before his accession, Darius III had held the title 'letter-bearer' (courier; Plut. *Alex.* 18.7). The Persepolis texts record office-holders such as a 'chair-' and 'footstool-carrier' (PF 0830) as well as a 'bow-and-arrow-case carrier' (PF 1011) who were given sizeable food rations, indicating the high rank of the courtiers who bore these important titles. The entire inner court was under the watch of a powerful official known as the **hazāra-patiš* ('master of a thousand') or *chiliarch* (Keaveney 2010) who (it seems) commanded the royal bodyguard and was responsible for all elements of court security and enjoyed the complete confidence of the ruler, controlling access to his personage through the protocol of the royal audience. Other prominent inner-court dignitaries included the steward of the royal household (perhaps **viθa-patiš*), the royal charioteer and the king's cupbearer. It must be noted, however, that court titles did not necessarily have bearing on the duties expected of the courtier who held them and that nobles with courtly titles perhaps only 'acted' the prescribed roles at state ceremonies. Tobit (1:22), set at the Neo-Assyrian court, notes that a single courtier could, of course, hold multiple offices ranging from king's body-servant to palace pen pusher: 'Now Ahikor was chief cup-bearer, keeper of the signet, and in charge of the administration of the accounts under king Sennacherib'.

Two of the most prominent nobles at Darius I's court, Aspacana (Gk. Aspathines) and Gaub(a)ruva (Gk. Gobryas), were honoured by Darius by being represented on his tomb at Naqš-i Rustam. Between them they were provided with several court titles: 'lance-bearer', 'garment-bearer'(or possibly 'weapon-bearer') and bow-and-arrow-case carrier', but as Henkelman (2003a: 120) has stressed, 'these designations are probably not expressions of actual duties, but, given the status of Gobryas and Aspathines, honorary titles bestowed on privileged court officials, possibly implying some ceremonial obligations. From this perspective "garment-bearer" should not be taken too literally, but be interpreted as "chamberlain"'.

It is clear that the Achaemenids created a complex court structure which, in general, can be regarded as pyramid-like, with the Great King at its apex and the workers (servants and slaves) at large at the base. A comparatively small group of nobles (OP *kara*) occupied a high place in this pyramidal structure, for these were the hereditary Persian nobility, whom the Greeks called the 'People of the Gate' (Plut. *Them.* 26.6), and who were obliged – because of blood and status – to serve at court and wait on the king (Briant 2002: 326–7). A multitude of middle-ranking officials operated in the social-pyramid's space in between the nobles and the workers and communicated between all of the other ranks. Any individual who had rendered important service to the king was a 'benefactor' (Gk. *euergētai*), and his name was recorded in the royal archives (Hdt. 8.85.90; Joseph. *JA* 11.6.4; see further, comments on **6:8 bring a royal robe the king has worn**). Courtiers designated as 'relatives of the king' and 'friends of the king' had the right to eat from the royal table or assist the king as a body servant and these were highly prized and ferociously policed privileges (discussed by Briant 2002: 308).

The title 'friend of the king' had a long pedigree in the Near East, and it is particularly well-attested in the Hebrew Bible (2 Sam. 15:37; 1 Kgs 4:5, 16:11; de Vaux 1961: 122–3, 528). Akkad. texts use the term *rukhi šarri* (van Selms 1957). The title does not seem to have implied any specific function, but being a 'friend of the king' was clearly a closely guarded privilege and a source of pride for those who bore it; thus in Persia, Tiribazus, the powerful satrap of Armenia, was a particularly favoured 'friend of the king' (Artaxerxes II), and, when resident at court away from his satrapy, 'he alone had the privilege of mounting the king upon his horse' (Xen. *An.* 4.4.4; see further Curt. 3.3.14.21 and Briant 2002: 321).

It was important for hereditary nobles to make regular appearances at court, and satraps like Tiribazus were expected to leave their satrapies to pay their respects before the Great King. Masistes was at court at the time he quarrelled with Xerxes (Hdt. 9.108–13), even though he was satrap of far-away Bactria, and starting in 410 BCE, Aršama the long-serving satrap of Egypt took a two-year leave of absence from his official post in Memphis to visit the royal court and to survey his Babylonian estates (Driver 1956: 5–6).

The court was a *locus* of practical political decision-making and imperial power and, as stressed in Esther, the hereditary nobility of Persia made an important contribution to policy making and the governance of the realm (see also Hdt. 3.80–4). The monarch and the royal family formed the nucleus of the court, and the empire was regarded as the Great King's inheritable personal possession; the interests and honour of the dynasty were propelled by the ruling dynasty and its chief adherents who were drawn from Persia's great noble houses (Briant 2002: 334–8). For their part, the nobles organized their own households based on the template of the royal court by employing the same types of staff and celebrating the same rites and rituals as the king (Xen. *An.* 1.6.10). Moreover, the satraps stationed in provinces far away from the heart of the empire fashioned themselves after the royal model. Satraps should not be thought of simply as high-ranking civil servants because, throughout the empire, they represented the king by proxy and, as such, they imitated his behaviour and emulated his taste (Briant 2002: 345–7). But being a satrap was a hazardous business, for the satrap depended personally on the king's good favour and had to watch his behaviour accordingly and there can be no doubt that in their provincial courts satraps were carefully scrutinized by the central authorities for any hint of self-aggrandizement or potential treason (Briant 2002: 338–45).

The letters sent between Aršama in Egypt and the royal court in Iran at the beginning of the fourth-century BCE demonstrate that even when absent from the imperial centre, court nobles in the service of the king kept up a steady dialogue with the central authority (Driver 1956; Lindenberger 2003; Ma and Tuplin 2021). The so-called Passover Edict from Elephantine, for instance, should be viewed as the transmission of a command of Darius II via his Egyptian satrap and therefore a reflection of how political decision-making at court was disseminated to the provinces (Kuhrt 2007: 854, n. 1). Satrapal courts engaged in the same political discourse articulated in the royal court, and a series of Aramaic texts from Bactria offer a rare glimpse of light from a very distant part of the empire to balance the richer Aršama dossier from Egypt and the abundant Persepolis archive, and help demonstrate that an official language of a centralized policy travelled far and wide (Shaked 2004). These sources, coupled with extensive Greek texts, show us the imperial administration at work across the empire and remind us that Achaemenid courtiers were political and bureaucratic animals.

1:3 Medes and the Persians

The most successful of the Eurasian peoples who settled into the Iranian plateau around 1000 BCE were the Medes and the Persians. In the popular imagination, these two Iranian peoples are often moulded into one as though they were, in every way, a single unit. This was not the case. Although they shared a common DNA and many cultural norms and values, the Medes and the Persians had distinctly idiosyncratic identities, and found themselves operating in radically separate geopolitical contexts which resulted in the formation of two very different mindsets (Llewellyn-Jones 2022).

1:4 wealth of his kingdom

Xerxes ruled an empire which stretched out of Persia towards the Mediterranean Sea in the west and to India in the east; it extended south to the Gulf of Oman and north into Russia. It was rich in countless farmlands. Barley, dates, lentils and wheat were grown, and the lands of the empire groaned with precious materials – copper, lead, gold, silver and lapis lazuli. There was no kingdom on earth to rival its wealth.

It was an important obligation of the satraps to send the best produce of their regions to the Great King, for by taking possession of these symbolic gifts the Persian monarch reconfirmed his domination over the empire. Perhaps the most symbolic of all these gifts given to – or demanded by – the king was that of earth and water which appears to have been a prime strategy used by the Persian king to attach himself to areas without resorting to military tactics. The gifting of earth and water (probably presented to the monarch in *physical* form – a silver jar of water, and a golden dish of earth, for instance) therefore represented a country's unconditional surrender to Persia and placed the Achaemenid king in the role of life-giver to his new subjects as he controlled the natural forces that sustained existence. That the king himself always travelled with his own drinking water which had been sourced from a Persian river is a reflection of the same process, and the water of the Choaspes River near Susa linked the king with his homeland no matter where he might be in the Empire and, at the same time, imbued him with the qualities of kingship itself.

The western satrapies were particularly important to the history of numismatics, for it was in Lydia around 650 BCE that the idea of coinage began. The first coinages were made from an alloy of gold and silver called electrum, but king Croesus introduced a coinage in gold and silver, now called 'croeseids' after him. After Cyrus conquered Lydia, the Persian administration continued to mint gold and silver coins like those of Croesus at Sardis but under Darius I the first truly Persian coins were struck, sometime around possibly 515 BCE (**Figure 1.45**). They were minted

Figure 1.45 Silver siglos, minted by the Achaemenid kings in the western satrapies of the empire. Discovered in Athens.

in gold and were named 'darics' (not necessarily after the king) and in silver, named 'sigloi'. Coins in both metals bore the image of a generic Great King, recognizable by his crown, his court robe and his bow. Like the earlier gold and silver croeseids, these coins were struck not at Persepolis or any other Persian centre such as Susa or Ecbatana, but exclusively at Sardis. Later, mints were located in other cities of Asia Minor and some, such as the mint at Tarsus, became important distribution centres. Persian coinage circulated predominantly in the western satrapies and had little impact in the Persian heartlands or the eastern empire, but studies of western coinage reveals a high degree of independence among the communities who issued them.

Every satrapy of the empire (with the exception of Persia) was required to pay tax on an annual basis (Hdt. 3.89, 6.42; Briant 2002: 390–9; Herzfeld 1968: 292–318). Media was assessed at 450 talents of silver and the tribute of 100,000 sheep; Susa paid 300 talents, Armenia 400 and 20,000 prized Nissean horses. Libya and Egypt both provided 700 talents, the products of their fisheries, and 120,000 measures of grain; Arabia gave 1,000 talents-worth of frankincense and Ethiopia provided gold, ebony, and ivory every two years. Babylonia paid the highest silver tax levy – 1,000 talents – and was expected to use the products of its fertile land to feed the court every four months of the year. The annual amount of silver, gold and precious goods amounted to some 14,560 talents, with a purchasing power many times higher than the sum suggests. We know that molten silver and gold was often melted down and poured into amphorae to harden and use as bullion; some was made into coins. Although businesses continued to use credit, many demanded actual silver. By the end of the reign of Xerxes, the payment of taxes in silver became increasingly expected and within a short time, loan sharks and satraps held the bulk of the coinage which led to an increase in inflation as prices for all sorts of goods soared and across the empire, non-Persians suffered.

1:4 the splendour and glory of his majesty

Regardless of time or place, the visual presentation of monarchy is theatrical in its nature. Indeed, the image of a ruler can be seen as an assemblage of theatrical props, costumes and scenery – a *mise-en-scène* of monarchy. In the ancient Near East, kingship was portrayed, in part, through conspicuous displays of ostentation. There was little industry to invest in and so surplus funds were spent on buildings, pageantry and ceremony, clothing, jewels, and the employment of large numbers of retainers. In a world in which literacy was limited, visual display, loaded with symbols of power, was paramount. The splendour and glory of kingship was articulated by and through the paraphernalia of ceremony – thrones, crowns, sceptres, and state rooms – but more than anything, they resided in the body of the king himself. 'Man is a shadow of god', runs one Assyrian proverb; 'the king is the perfect likeness of god', it concludes (Parpola 1970: 112–13). The proverb compares the king to other humans, and contrasts them too, and such a double-layered creed might be corroborated in the *Teachings of Ahiqar* (7:95) too: 'Beautiful to behold is the king ... and noble is his majesty to them that walk the earth'. Similarly, the prophet Isaiah (33:17) was able to promise his listeners that 'Your eyes will see the king in his beauty'. Isaiah's own vision of God (6:1-13) explicitly and implicitly draws on the image of royalty and the physical presentation of earthly monarchy colours his vision. The heavenly king that he witnesses sits on a throne, in a palace, wearing a royal robe; he presides over a court and is surrounded by attendants. It is via the splendid accoutrements of earthly kingship that Isaiah is able to conceive of, and experience, God's glory. Oswalt (1996: 181) defines this divine 'glory' as 'an expression of the stunning importance and reality of God', which succinctly captures what Isaiah sees and experiences in YHWH's throne room. In short, God is glorious. It is easy to understand how, in Esther, Xerxes, sitting in god-like splendour, must have been an impressive, almost overwhelming, sight and how suppliants before his throne were awestruck by his majesty. For god-like Xerxes too is glorious. An indescribable power emanates from his presence – it is his brilliance made manifest.

(i) Physicality of the king

Look at any conventional Persian-made image of an Achaemenid Great King and notice how perfect he is. The monarch's clothed body emanates strength and vitality, his posture encodes military prowess and sportsmanship; his hair and his beard are thick and luxuriant and radiate health and vitality; his face, with its well-defined profile, large eye and thick eyebrow, is as noble as it is handsome. The Great King is, in all ways, a thing of splendour. Much of the visual code of Persian kingship was lifted directly from Neo-Assyrian prototypes. Persian-made images are not portraits of kings in any photographic sense of the word, they are not reproductions of a ruler's true physiognomy. Instead they are cultural representations of the office of kingship. In fact, Assyrian kings had a term for this: they dubbed their royal image as *salam šarrutiya*, 'an image of my (office of) kingship'. These images are imperial pronouncements. We must read them as codes through which the king's body takes on cultural meaning: the manliness, wholeness, beauty. Physical fitness of the monarch's body guarantees his right to rule. The Great King's body was special, sharing in appearance the best physical attributes of Ahuramazda, the anthropomorphic divinity he worshipped (see Bertelli 2001; Hamilton 2005; Sommer 2009; Llewellyn-Jones 2015). The origin and significance of the tradition of the handsome Persian king is unclear although it is probably connected to the connotation that the ruler is superlative in all respects, for as Briant has pointed out, 'a man did not become king because he was handsome ...; it was because of his position as king that he was automatically designated as handsome' (2002: 225–6).

Greek sources do seem to fixate on the body of the Persian monarch, however, and they take an obvious delight in his splendid appearance, making him into a handsome, if nevertheless inherently despotic, opponent. Successive kings are noted for their valour, handsome demeanour and their impressive stature (and coincidentally, a hallmark of Achaemenid art is that kings are made taller than their subjects). They are all 'the most valiant of men' or 'the best-looking of men' and their wives and daughters are equally beautiful – a 'torment' for Greek eyes no less (see Hdt. 7.187; Plut. *Artax.* 1.1) – and together Persian kings and queens are habitually tagged by the Greeks as 'the best looking in all of Asia' (Plut. *Alex.* 21.6, 11). Even Plato could not resist speculating on the striking beauty of the royal Persian physique, which he explained by suggesting that infant princes underwent a strict regimen of massage therapy in which their young oiled limbs were twisted into perfection by their doting eunuch slaves (Pl. *Alc.* 121d; see also Plin. 24.165). Of course, every prince and monarch aspired to match the standard of masculine good looks set by Cyrus the Great – his aquiline nose was allegedly the benchmark of beauty for generations of Persians: 'Because Cyrus was hooked-nosed, the Persians – even to this day – love hooked nosed men and consider them the most handsome' (Plut. *Mor.* 281e; **Figure 1.46**).

There can be little doubt that Achaemenid kings and courtiers wore wigs and false hair pieces and their images at Persepolis and other palace sites certainly suggest that false tresses could be plaited into natural hair and beards. This fashionable caprice must have made hair expensive. Strabo (15.3.21) notes that hair was therefore a taxable item in the Persian empire, while pseudo-Aristotle suggests that the Great King demanded a 'tribute' of hair from provinces specifically

Figure 1.46 Profile of two Persian soldiers. Detail from the east staircase of the Apadana at Persepolis.

for the creation of wigs (2.14d): 'Noticing that the Lycians were fond of wearing their hair long, [Condalus, governor under Mausolus] said that a dispatch had come from the king of Persia ordering him to send hair to make false fringes and that he was therefore commanded by Mausolus to cut off their hair.'

In the ancient world, hair and beards were highly significant and were surrounded by rituals and symbolic undertones; elite men grew their hair long, full, and luxuriant as a supreme mark of high social status and women's beauty was judged by their luxuriant hair (Llewellyn-Jones 2011 and 2015). At the most mundane level, hair signalled a person's state of health or lack of it (poor-quality hair could signal disease or uncleanliness and the tearing out of the hair was a symbol of grief or distress), and

therefore men of the warrior-elite carefully grew and cared for theirs to represent their strength and virility (after all the greatest heroes of Near Eastern antiquity were long-haired: consider Gilgamesh and Samson). They were careful to dress it and arrange it carefully, thereby symbolically 'taming' and 'civilizing' it. Excessive hair-growth had overtones of the barbaric, so that when the Babylonian king Nebuchadnezzar's state of mind finally collapsed and he went into a sharp emotional decline, his courtiers read the external sign when, 'his hair grew as long as eagle's feathers, and his nails were like birds' claws' (Dan. 4:33).

A full, well-set, fragranced beard was a sign of manhood and a source of pride for Persian men (**Figure 1.47**). It was the ornament of their machismo.

Figure 1.47 Detail of the head of Darius I from the Bisitun Relief, north-west Iran.

In Near Eastern cultures the beard was symbolically loaded: it was the object of salutation and the focus of oaths and blessings, although, conversely, the beard could also be a locus of shame, for an attack on the beard was an attack on the individual who sported it, and because the beard was the superlative symbol of manhood, it was a great insult to degrade it: to humiliate them, prisoners of war might have half their beards shaved off. Thus, Israelite prophets threatened the people that the king of Assyria would 'shave your head and the hair of your legs and ... take off your beards also' (Isa. 7:20; see also 2 Sam. 10:4-5). Not surprisingly then, given the close association between the beard and physical power and martial ability, the Great King was depicted with the most impressive beard of all; it far outstripped those of his courtiers in terms of length, fullness and elaboration and it clearly demarcated him as the empire's alpha-male.

One further symbol of monarchy needs to be examined in the context of the king's head – the crowning glory, quite literally, of monarchy – for on top of the Great King's coiffured and oiled locks sat a crown, weighty with symbolic authority. In antiquity, as in later eras, the crown signified some kind of state of honour or dignity for those who wore it because a kind of divine aura emanated from a monarch's crown and raised the wearer up to the most exalted position. The OP word for 'crown' is not known, although various contemporary Gk. terms like *kidaris* or *kitaris*, and *kurbasia*, were possibly derived from OP vocabulary. In keeping with the standard image of a crown, was a rigid metal cylinder with or without crenellated decoration (it is not known whether the king's crown was of a special colour or metal, like gold or electrum). Dalia Levit-Tawil (1983: 72) suggests, however, that the crown which lacks the characteristic crenellations was in fact 'a special turban-like hat' which represented the king as 'lawgiver and chief judge'. While it is possible that Achaemenid kings adopted different forms of crown (crenellated crowns certainly changed shape over the decades; **Figures 1.48, 1.49 and 1.50**), they cannot be considered 'personal crowns' in the way that the crowns of

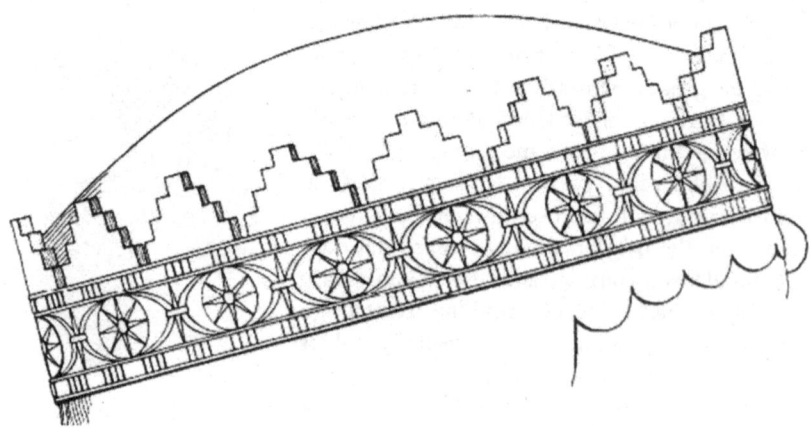

Figure 1.48 Detail of Darius' crenellated crown from the Bisitun Relief.

individual Sasanian kings certainly were (Berghe 1993: 74; see also Henkelman 1995–6 and Root 1979: 92–3). Given the omnipresence of crowns in Achaemenid royal and courtly culture, it is a surprise to find that in Esther, Xerxes is never said to be wearing a crown; perhaps its presence is a given. Vashti (Est. 1:11) and Esther (Est. 2:17) have the honour of wearing crowns, and, like other male courtiers (as represented on the Persepolis reliefs (Tilia 1978: 53–66; Kaptan 2002: 58–60), Mordecai sports 'a large crown of gold' at his triumph (Est. 8:15).

Figure 1.49 Detail of a plain *polos*-style crown; from the east staircase of the Apadana at Persepolis.

Figure 1.50 Stamp seal from Anatolia; a crowned Persian winged sphinx.

Clothing too is an important element of Persian court culture. Its significance could be physical, economic, social or symbolic and the function of clothing, moreover, was multiple. Clothing could protect, conceal, display or represent a person's office or state of being and the fact that garments could wear out or tear is also important. After all, in the ancient world handmade fabrics were costly, scarce and valuable and dyes and decorations added to their worth, so their disintegration or loss was a serious blow to a household economy and personal wealth (see Cleland, Davies and Llewellyn-Jones 2007: 40–1, 205). The Greeks generally regarded Persian dress as beautiful (Hdt. 135; 7.61–2) and expensive (Cook 1983: 138 estimates that by modern standards, King Artaxerxes II stood up in nothing short of three million pounds worth of clothing and jewellery). But what did the royal robe look like? Members of the Achaemenid court wore two distinct types of clothing (Llewellyn-Jones 2010b). The first sort can be called 'riding dress' or 'cavalry costume' (**Figure 1.51**; see Widengren 1956; Vogelsang 2010). Made up of five items of clothing – a felt cap, a sleeved coat (Gk. *kandys*; OP **gaunaka*), sleeved tunic (Gk. *ependytēs*), trousers (Gk. *anaxyrides*) and footgear – this sort

Figure 1.51 Persian riding habit or cavalry dress; from the Apadana at Persepolis.

of dress was ideal for a people so dependent on horses for transportation and warfare, and on the Persepolis Apadana reliefs it is worn by peoples from the Iranian plateau and other related groups (Volgelsang 2010). The Greeks erroneously called this 'Median dress' – yet there is no evidence for it being limited to the Medes, although unfortunately the tag has stuck in much contemporary scholarship (see for instance Sekunda 2010). Interestingly, Achaemenid iconography never depicts the king wearing the riding habit, although it is probable that in reality he did so (for an extended discussion see comments on **Est. 6:8 royal robe the king has worn**; see also Est. 6:9-11, 8:15).

The second form of Persian clothing is known as the 'court robe' (**Figure 1.52**) and may have been of pure Persian invention, although it does bear a resemblance to Egyptian-style royal *mss*-tunics of the New Kingdom period (Root 2011: 426–9 argues that the garment originated in Elam but there is nothing to support this). Constructed from a huge double-square of linen or wool (or perhaps cotton or even silk), and worn over trousers, the tunic was tightly belted at the waist to form a robe with deep folds which created an overhang resembling sleeves (see Beck 1972; Goldman 1964, 1991; Kuhrt 2007: 532). The court robe (Gk. *sarapis, serapeis, kalasireis* or *aktaiai*) was richly woven with intricate designs and ornamented appliqué decorations made from gold and semi-precious stones (**Figures 1.53, 1.54**); it was as costly as it was beautiful (Ath. 12.525d–e). This was the costume of the Great King *par excellence* and he is represented wearing it repeatedly, whether sitting on his throne or actively fighting in battle or killing an animal (mythic or otherwise). In reality the court robe was a highly impractical garment for any form of active combat, so the choice to depict the monarch wearing it with such regularity can only be explained by the fact that it was symbolically important. The court robe represented Achaemenid power and it is probable that it was worn at the

Figure 1.52 Persian court robe; from the palace of Xerxes, Persepolis.

Figure 1.53 Gold disks, used to decorate Persian court garments. Discovered at Susa.

Figure 1.54 Ivory relief of a Persian nobleman in court dress, embellished with appliqué gold disks.

climax of the investiture ceremony, since we know that it was richly dyed and beautifully worked with exquisite designs (Xen. *Cyr.* 8.3.13–14; Curt. 3.3.17–19). Ctesias (F41) recalls that one sort of royal robe was known as a *sarapis*, and here, remarkably, he seems to preserve an authentic ancient Elamite term for a royal garment since the word *sarapi* is found in Middle Elamite texts from the acropolis at Susa, suggesting a long continuity of tradition in ceremonial dress in southern Iran (see Henkelman 2003b: 228–31; for Elamite royal robes in the Achaemenid period see Álvarez-Mon 2009).

(ii) Kingly aura

In the Hebrew bible, the concept of glory (Heb. *kavod*) is used as a stock evaluative term to refer to the greatness and transcendence of YHWH. The glory of God is made visible through an emanation of a kind of radiance, which is closely aligned with notions of beauty, brilliance, magnificence and rapture. To encounter the glory of God is to be overwhelmed by power. But the 'glory' is something that can be seen and experienced too. In Ps. 3:3 the *kavod* of *Elohiym* (God) is paralleled with his 'shield' and in Job 29:20, the *kavod* is paralleled with his 'bow'. In Ps. 24:8 the question is asked, 'who is this king of the *kavod*?', and the answer is given: 'YHWH is strong and mighty, YHWH is mighty in battle.' Therefore, the original meaning of *kavod* is related to battle armaments. Thus, in Exod. 16:7, the Children of Israel will 'see' the 'armament' (i.e., glory) of YHWH, the one who has done battle for them against the Egyptians.

The concept of 'glory', with its martial root, is very old, and is encountered throughout the ancient Near East. In Sumer the brilliance exuded by the gods and heroes is referred to as *melam*, later loaned into Akkad. as *melammu* (Cassin 1968). The term is regularly employed in the Neo-Assyrian period to indicate both divine and royal power, especially the military kind, a development explained by Shawn Zelig Aster (2015, 13) as emerging 'due to the need for the Assyrians to propagate a powerful royal ideology in a manner that was more immediately perceptible to foreigners and which more simply conveyed the force of the royal *melammu*'. In Assyrian royal ideology, *melammu* expressed the insuperable power of the god Aššur (often represented in a sun-burst and wielding a bow; **Figure 1.55**) and his representative, the Assyrian king. By the Neo-Babylonian period, warfare, radiance and *melammu* had formed a single concept, as highlighted in the Ebabbar Cylinder of Nabonidus which evokes the *melammu* of the powerful god Marduk whilst employing other terms that plainly convey the idea of radiance, such as

Figure 1.55 The god Aššur; relief carving from Nineveh.

zīmu and *šalummatu*. In other words, radiance was the visual indicator of *melammu*: 'Your luminous *melammu*, lordly radiance, royal shine, let them walk at my sides, to plunder the land of my enemies' (Akkad. *melammubirbirruka zīme bēlutu šalummat šarrutu anašal ala mat nakrīja šulikuidāja*; Schaudig 2001: text 2.9, 387ii 39–40).

In Persia, divine glory was known in OP as *xᵛarənah* (NP *farr* or *farr-e izadi*). *Xᵛarənah* was derived from an Indo-European root **(s)p(h)el-* meaning 'brilliance' and 'shine', the same that eventually led to 'splendour' in English. When the word evolved and began to be pronounced as *x^varənah*, the idea of a wordplay and punning with *khvar* (sun) became irresistible for the Avestan-speaking priests and hymn-writers, and *x^varənah* was thus intimately linked to the sun. It is clear from a number of passages in the Avesta that *farr* /*x^varənah* was a magic force or power of a luminous and fiery nature. In *Yašt* 10.127 the 'strong' (*uyra-*) *x^varənah* is identified as a 'blazing fire' that precedes the god Mithra in his chariot. In time, the traditional Avestan interpretations, 'glory', 'splendour', 'luminosity' and 'shine' were all connected with the sun and with fire, and gave way to secondary meanings related to prosperity, (good) fortune and (kingly) majesty. Particularly noteworthy is the fact that in Sogdian, the term was often used for 'dignity'. The word *x^varənah* is attested as *farnah-* in Median proper names from the ninth century BCE and in such OP names as Vindafarnah, 'he who finds the *farr*'.

The concept of royal *x^varənah* was a long-lasting theme in Persianate political ideology, and was usually invoked to project legitimacy of rule and divine sanction (see especially Soudavar 2003). In the Early Modern age, for instance, the vizier of the Moghul Emperor Akbar (r. 1556–1605), Abol-Fazl-e Allāmi, justified kingly authority in the following terms:

> Kingship is a light emanating from God, and a ray from the sun, the illuminator of the universe; it is the argument of the book of perfection, the receptacle of all virtues. Modern language calls this light *Farr-e Izadi* and the tongue of antiquity called it *Kayān Kharra* [Kayānid (ie., Achaemenid) Glory]. It is communicated by God to kings without the intermediate assistance of anyone, and men in the presence of it bend the forehead of praise toward the ground of submission.

Figure 1.56 Mughal miniature depicting Jahangir embracing the Safavid king Shah Abbas; late sixteenth century.

The visual symbol of the *x^varənah* that Akbar and his successors chose for kingly representation was a sunburst (*shamseh*). The sunburst radiating from behind the ruler's head became a repeated iconographic feature of Mughal royal portraiture and an important element in projecting legitimacy of Mughal rule (**Figure 1.56**). Indeed, this universal fiery symbol of holiness and/or rulership appears as a halo and nimbus behind the head of Buddha, Jesus Christ, Christian and Islamic prophets, saints and kings and was, in effect, the result of just one more effort to emphasize the power of the *x^varənah*. It is an old Iranian motif, employed for gods and kings (**Figure 1.57**). On a number of Achaemenid-period limestone cylinder seals, a wheel-like nimbus is conspicuously placed below a winged disk. Sometimes a god in a halo-like circle appears beneath a figure of the deity Ahuramazda, rising out of wings

Figure 1.57 Iranian deity, possibly a war god, from Taq-i Bustan, Kermanshah, Iran; Sasanian carved stone capital.

(**Figure 1.58**, or sometimes a winged disk). The figure in the halo below is, I suggest, the *xᵛarənah* itself: it emanates from the god, through the god, and is the glory of the god. The *xᵛarənah* is also found as a wheel-like sunburst on representations of the Heroic Combat scene, emphasizing yet again that divine/royal glory has a martial aspect (**Figure 1.59**).

Thus, the 'glory' which emanates from a charismatic king (note that the Gk. *charis* also denotes 'brilliance') is a way of expressing that divine grace is present with the ruler and rests in and on him. Moreover, the *xᵛarənah* attached itself to Xerxes and his whole dynasty through the sacred power of the blood royal. The *xᵛarənah* was Xerxes' spirit-

Figure 1.58 Persian cylinder seal impression; Ahuramazda, depicted twice. From Persepolis.

counterpart, and it worked with and through the king. However, if the king failed to act in accordance with the Truth (OP *arta*), the *xᵛarənah* could easily disappear, leaving Xerxes an empty shell, devoid of divine light.

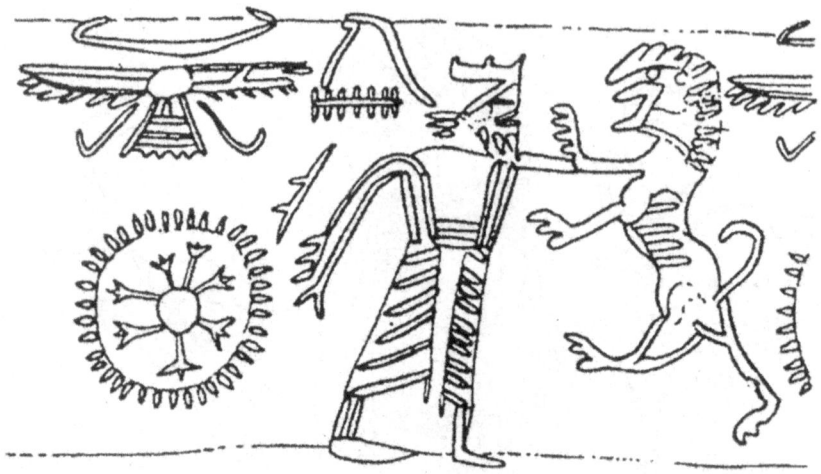

Figure 1.59 Persian cylinder seal impression from Persepolis. The king in combat with a beast is accompanied by the *farr* – radiance of rulership.

1:5 seven days

The number seven, a symbol of wholeness, is noticeable throughout Esther. The party for the people of Susa lasts for seven days (Est. 1:5); on the seventh day, Xerxes sends seven eunuchs to fetch Vashti (Est. 1:10); seven ministers advise the king when Vashti refuses to appear (Est. 1:14). Later, in the harem, Esther is provided with seven maidservants (Est. 2:9) and went on to meet Xerxes for the first time in the seventh year of his reign (Est. 2:16).

From the opening chapter of Genesis 1 (indeed, from the first seven Hebrew words of Gen. 1:1), the Bible makes it is clear that the number seven is significant. It stands for the completed and the perfected. The ancient Iranians held the same concept and this might bolster the presence of 'seven' in Esther. The author of the book riffs on, and toys with, the significance of 'seven' in the Achaemenid period. According to Persian understanding, the world was divided into seven (circular) regions, known as the *haft kešvar*. Seven represented 'totality'. Darius the Great had ascended to the throne thanks to the loyal support of six nobles; together they made a 'Gang of Seven', who overthrew the legitimate king (Bardiya) and established Darius on the throne (Hdt. 7.82–3; see further, comments on **1:14 seven nobles of Persia and Media who had special access to the king**). Subsequently, Darius divided the Persian empire into seven parts (Pl. *Epistel* III). An Aramaic document from Egypt dated to the reign of Darius II designated a district governor as *hpthpt'*, a title derived from the OI **haftaxvapāta* 'protector of one-seventh', suggesting that the division of a region into seven districts was a normal administrative practice, patterned as it was after the Iranian cosmological notion of seven *kešvars*. The position of the Great King among his six magnates is analogous to that of Ahuramazda among the six Aməša Spəntas or sacred spirits. Likewise, Zoroaster and his first disciples made up a heptad.

A single gold cloisonné earring (**Figure 1.60**, *c.* 520–460 BCE) encodes a remarkably sophisticated iconography: it explores the centrality of the number seven in Persian royal ideology. In the centre of the earring a circle encloses the figure of Ahuramazda rising above a winged disk. Seven smaller circles with crescents inside them, separated by gold rhombuses, surround the central one. Six of these circles contain male half-figures similar to the one in the middle of the earring. These figures all face towards the central one. They possibly represent the Persian Great King in his role as 'Lord of the Seven Climes', making a gesture of respect towards his dynastic god. The earring imagery is nothing less than a visualization of the *haft kešvar*.

Figure 1.60 Gold earring with semi-precious stone inlays; Achaemenid. Possibly from Susa.

1:5 king's palace

Xerxes, like all Achaemenid kings, was a builder king. Dynastic and imperial structures were the speciality of Persian monarchs, and between them they erected architectural complexes – fortresses, royal residences and tombs – on a grand scale. Several kings allude to their construction projects in their official inscriptions, often in an attempt to demonstrate dynastic longevity through the exhaustive planning and creation of palaces, tombs and fortresses as symbols of royal power and imperial harmony (DPf; addition by Xerxes: XPf §36–43):

> On this terrace, where this fortified palace (OP *halmarraš*) was built, there no palace had been built before; by the favour of Ahuramazda, I built this palace. And it was Ahuramazda's desire, and the desire of all the gods who are, that this palace should be built; and I built it, and at that time it was built firmly and excellently and exactly as I had ordered it to be. When I became king, much that (is) superior I built. What had been built by my father, that I took into my care and other work I added. But what I have done and what my father has done, all that we have done by the favour of Ahuramazda.

In the inscription, Xerxes dutifully and enthusiastically presents himself as his father's heir in his desire to add to the palace site and to ask for Ahuramazda's blessing.

The Persian palaces were part of the royal *viθ* (Akkad. *bītu*; Elam. *ulhi*), an OP word meaning 'dwelling', 'household', 'economic entity' and 'people of a household'. When Darius I prayed that Ahuramazda would allow 'happiness [to] rest upon this *viθ'* (Dpe §3), he was alluding to both the individuals who made up the royal household and to the physical space which they occupied also. His hope was equally that 'happiness will rest upon this *palace*' (see Kuhrt 2007: 487, n. 4; in the Bisitun inscription likewise, *viθ* is used in the sense of 'house', 'palace' and 'household'; see DB §61–70). The *viθ* was the seat of Persian kingship, for the word certainly refers to the palace or royal residence, which itself was imbued with a deep symbolism reflecting monarchic power. The palace was a centre of active power and given that the court was the administrative hub of the empire, archives, libraries and offices demonstrated that the court was a working machine of royal legislation. Interestingly, in the recent wars and revolutions across the Middle East, the palaces of rulers such as Saddam Hussein in Babylon and Baghdad and the palaces of the Gaddafi family in Libya were attacked in the aftermath of the downfall of their regimes, demonstrating that the intimate symbolic relationship between the ruler, his administration and his palace still exists.

Drawing on the rich resources and the gargantuan labour-force of their vast empire, the Achaemenid kings built lavishly throughout the realm (Briant 2002: 165–70), although the chief palatial sites, crafted from fine stone, mud-brick, glazed-brick and wood, were clustered in the ancestral regions of Fars (the places at Parsagade and Persepolis), Media (at Ecbatana) and Elam (Susa), or in areas of early conquest (Babylonia). With the exception of Persepolis, which was the brainchild of Darius and almost built from scratch (there are *some* indications that the area around Persepolis already had a governmental presence under Cyrus II), Achaemenid royal residences tended to be built on top of earlier areas of habitation and each palace site essentially duplicated the other in form and function, if not in scale. Inge Nielsen reminds us that when trying to understand the layout and meaning of ancient palaces it is important to remember that 'form follows function' (Nielsen 1999: 13), that is to say, royal architecture was intended to conform to, highlight and even augment the needs of monarchy whether in a ceremonial or a domestic sense. To quote Norbert Elias (1983: 9): 'every kind of "being together" of people has a corresponding arrangement of space'. The primary function of the Achaemenid royal palaces was therefore to serve the ceremonial and official needs of Persian kingship and the Persian court and therefore they were places where audiences were granted, business was concluded, embassies were received, judgements pronounced, petitions heard and councils held. Moreover, the palaces were hierarchically charged sites for monarchic display where the king appeared in the full panoply of state, surrounded by his court. The palaces also functioned as residential spaces and each one must have included, to a fuller or lesser extent, living-quarters of the king and some of his family, and maybe even of members of the court. To sustain the royal household, slave dormitories, service quarters and kitchens were needed and to ensure the king's protection, guard rooms must have been present too. Finally, the palaces had an important administrative function, represented by treasuries, offices and archives, all of which needed space. What we see in Achaemenid palace architecture is the idea that space is constructed by the way it is occupied. Our mental maps of the palatial structures of Persia stem from our understanding not only of the physical and material elements of the spaces but of how their occupants functioned within them.

Jean Perrot, whose extensive excavations at Susa have contributed so much to our knowledge of the royal gateway and the palace area, was happy to conflate the evidence he unearthed with the book of Esther, noting that (1996: 254)

> The book of Esther makes Xerxes' palace at Susa the backdrop of its story. The first excavators naturally enough tried to identify the remains they found with the setting of the Biblical account. This identification was always vague. The gate had not been discovered, and the plan and the general scheme of the palace were not understood; even the attribution of the building and its date were uncertain. Today, we have better reasons for thinking that Darius' palace at Susa, begun in 520 BCE, completed by Xerxes ... is indeed the palace in the mind of the author of the book of Esther ... as is evident from his depictions of the gate, the royal apartments, and perhaps the gardens.

Access to the palace from the Royal City was on a pavement of bricks. This pathway passed through a monumental, covered square pavilion, which had two halls and two porticoes with two columns. Begun by Darius, it was finished by Xerxes (XSa). Turning at a right-angle, the road then crossed a brick causeway and ended at the Gate of Darius, another square construction with a hypostyle central hall, which was begun by Darius and, again, finished by Xerxes (XSd). It is reminiscent of the Gate of All the Nations at Persepolis. It was the official entrance to the palace and was flanked by two larger than life-size statues of Darius. Only one of the pair has survived, a very rare example of Achaemenid sculpture in the round (**Figure 1.61**). The king is dressed in the Persian court robe, but the posture, with one foot advanced, the arm folded against the chest, is purely Egyptian. An inscription in Old Persian, Elamite, Akkadian and Egyptian hieroglyphics states, 'Here is the stone statue which Darius ordered to be made in Egypt, so that he who sees it in the future will know that the Persian holds Egypt' (DSab). The statue was made in Egypt, originally intended for the temple of Heliopolis, but was brought to Susa by Xerxes. It is headless, and it has been suggested that, with its companion, it might have sported either pharaonic crowns, Persian headwear, or an amalgamation of both styles (**Figure 1.62**).

Figure 1.61 Egyptian-made over-life-size statue of Darius I, found at Susa.

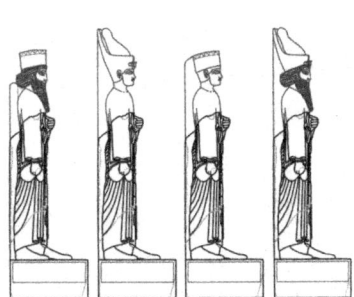

Figure 1.62 Possible reconstructions of the statues of Darius once located at the royal gateway into the Susa palace compound.

The residential palace itself occupies 3.8 hectares. It is organized around three courtyards. The eastern courtyard carried on its northern

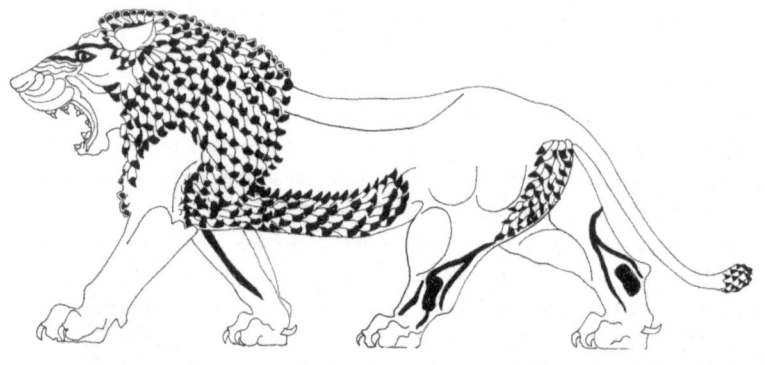

Figure 1.63 Coloured glazed brick relief of a snarling lion; from the main thoroughfare leading to the Ištar Gate, Babylon. Neo-Babylonian period.

face a beautiful lion frieze in enamelled brick (**Figure 1.63**). The royal apartments were difficult to access – and were designed that way intentionally – through doors and zigzag corridors toward the west courtyard. Behind the king's apartment, a series of apartments for the family – the harem – follow a similar plan; they may have included an access stairway to the first floor (**Figure 1.64**). On the north, projecting forward,

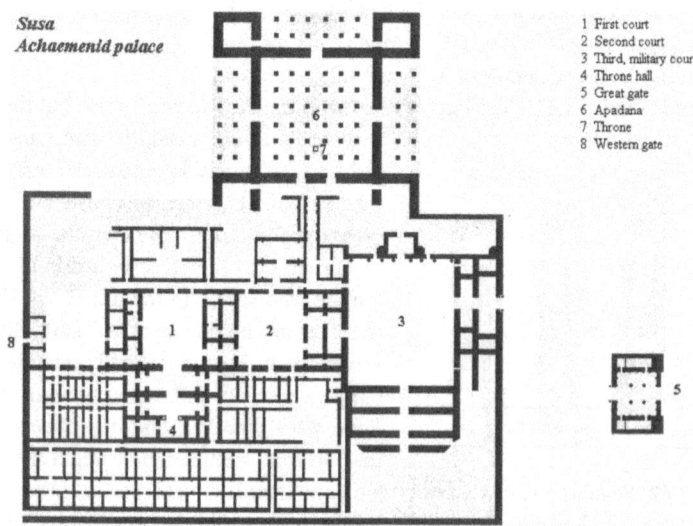

Figure 1.64 Ground plan of the Achaemenid palace at Susa.

Figure 1.65 Reconstruction of the appearance of the Apadana at Susa.

the Apadana, or throne hall, is also the work of Darius, rebuilt by Artaxerxes II following a fire (A²Sa; **Figure 1.65**). The enormous square construction is a little elevated above the open space that surrounds it on three sides. Measuring 109 metres on each side, it has a central hall of 58 metres per side, with 36 columns, topped with massive double-bull-shaped capitals (**Figure 1.66**), supporting a cedarwood roof, and a portico on each of the three open sides with two rows of six columns. The plan of the south side is unclear, but, unquestionably, it had

Figure 1.66 Double bull protome column capital from the Apadana at Susa.

no portico, making the general plan very similar to that of the Apadana at Persepolis. Column bases, shafts and capitals are in stone on imposing stone foundations. Originally 20 metres high, erected on a high platform (OP *takht*, 'throne') and open on three sides, the Apadana would have been impressive, visible from far off, as at Persepolis. The Susa palace, unlike Persepolis, was not burned by Alexander (Perrot 1981), though, and it was still in use when Alexander returned from his eastern campaign in 325 BCE. The palace lost its function after his death in 323 BCE, but remained standing at least for some decades, as did the statue of Darius for several centuries.

Darius was justifiably proud of his newly-built palace at Susa. He commissioned the creation of a fine series of cuneiform texts (DSf, DSaa, DSz) to testify to the multi-ethnic labour-of-love which went into its construction. Found buried under the doorways into the Apadana, the so-called Susa Foundation Charters are a series of multilingual inscriptions which provide valuable information about Darius' titles and the construction of his palace. Since the time of the archaic dynasties of Babylonia, it had been the tradition in Mesopotamia to bury a foundation tablet under the thresholds of palaces to invoke the protection of the gods. The Achaemenid kings enthusiastically upheld this custom, since similar texts were discovered at the Apadana at Persepolis too. Darius' inscriptions speak of the fine timbers, stone and precious materials which went into constructing the palace and they emphasize the geographical span of Darius' empire which allow such diverse and rare materials to be used. Most importantly, the Charters tell of the ethnic mix of workers who had come to Susa from lands far-off to work on the completion of the palace. In the texts, Darius tells of how his palace had its foundations built on solid ground and how his workers had dug 40 cubits down into the earth in order to reach base rock and how they filled the foundations with rubble, packed tightly together to form a secure base for a palace that would last for eternity. He continues (DSf):

> This palace which I built at Susa, from afar its ornamentation was brought … The sun-dried brick was moulded, the Babylonian people performed these tasks. The cedar timber, this was brought from a place named Lebanon. The Assyrian people brought it to Babylon; from Babylon the Carians and the Greeks brought it to Susa. The *yakâ*-timber was brought from Gandara and from Carmania. The gold was brought from Lydia and from Bactria, which here was wrought. The precious stone lapis lazuli and carnelian which was wrought here, this was brought from Sogdia. The precious stone turquoise, this was brought from Chorasmia, which was wrought here. The silver and the ebony were brought from Egypt. The ornamentation with which the wall was adorned, that from Greece was brought. The ivory which was wrought here, was brought from Nubia and from India and from Arachosia. The stone columns which were here wrought, a village named Abirâdu, in Elam – from there were brought. The stone-cutters who wrought the stone, those were Greeks and Lydians. The goldsmiths who wrought the gold, those were Medes and Egyptians. The men who wrought the wood, those were Lydians and Egyptians. The men who wrought the baked brick, those were Babylonians. The men who adorned the wall, those were Medes and Egyptians. Darius the King says: At Susa a very excellent work was ordered, a very excellent work was brought to completion.

The Susa Charters list no less than sixteen regions of the empire that furnish raw materials or labour to Darius' building project; eight more countries provide the talented craftsmen. Sardians worked stone and wood; Egyptians worked wood and created the palace reliefs; Medes worked gold and crafted palace reliefs. Some of the workmen were common hard-laborers: Babylonians who did the foundation work; Syrians, Ionians and Carians who transported lumber from Lebanon to Babylon and on to Susa. The Susa Charters also show how foreign workers were often kept together, corralled into units, as they constructed certain parts of the palace. It is important to note that the presence of so many foreign workers at Susa was a direct response to the Persian empire's desire to mark its presence in stone. For the first time in their history, the Persians needed to build palaces, governmental centres and all the necessary infrastructures of a ruling state. Building was undertaken on a massive scale in order to manage the unparalleled reaches of their vast empire. The Susa Charters demonstrate how manpower and specialist workers were urgently needed in Persia to build on an extraordinary super-scale, and the huge territory that Darius and his predecessors had conquered allowed the Persians to prioritize foreign techniques of building and decorating. All in all, Darius' palace at Susa is a masterpiece of multinational design and manufacture.

1:6 is a catalogue of luxury (although linguistically, verse 6 is difficult. It contains nouns found nowhere else in the Bible: *karpas, baḥaṭ, dar* and *sōḥāret*; see below for fuller discussion). The verse elaborates on the realia of the Persian court and focuses on its visual splendour. It is one of the most visually evocative verses of Esther, if not the whole Hebrew Bible (as noted by Day 2005: 26–7). Its fascination with the visual appeal of Persian luxury is consistent with contemporary Greek accounts too. Theopompus (F263a/b), for example, notes that at the king's court, 'There were many splendid textiles and cloths, purple and multi-coloured weavings, others white; many tents fitted out in gold and equipped with everything necessary. There were garments and expensive couches, and then drinking cups and bowls of chased silver and gold, some covered with precious gemstones, other beautifully and elegantly wrought.'

1: 6 garden (see also 1:5 enclosed garden)

The Heb. *bitan* is derived from the Akkad. *bitānu*, meaning a colonnaded pavilion set within a garden. In other words, in Esther, the huge crowd assembled at Susa was treated to an *al fresco* banquet in the royal garden. Xerxes was no doubt delighted to see how the fine garden, planted by his father, had matured with tall cypress trees running in straight avenues alongside bubbling streams which passed through endless stone water-channels and little pools. It was paradise.

It was under the Achaemenids that the notion of an earthly paradise took hold. Gardens were a key part of Persian cultural expression and throughout the empire these carefully cultivated parklands were living symbols of Persian dominance. The OP for 'garden', **paridaida*, is related to the Av. *pairidaēza-* and Med. **paridaiza-* (from **pari*, 'around' and **daiza*, 'wall', i.e., a walled garden). It was transliterated into Gk. as *paradeisos*, then rendered into the Lat. *paradisus*; from there the word entered into European languages as, for example, French *paradis*, and English *paradise*. The word entered Semitic languages too: in Akkad. it is found as *pardesu*, and in Heb. as *pardes* (Neh. 2:8; Eccl. 2:5; Song 4:13). In Arab. it turns up as *ferdaws* (Koran 18.107, 23.11). The concept of a 'paradise' may be located in the Sumerian epic of *Gilgamesh*, but the conception of a heavenly garden on earth existed independently in the Indo-Iranian tradition. Strictly speaking, a Persian 'paradise' was a walled-in green space with clear demarcations between the cultivated and tamed 'within' and the untamed and uncivilized 'without'. The concept that can be found in the Bible's book of Genesis where the Garden of Eden, the locale of the 'garden of God' is modelled on a Persian paradise.

Ecclesiastes (2:4-6), probably an Achaemenid-period creation, has a Persian-style Jewish prince proclaim his royal prowess through his botanical accomplishments:

> I made great works:
> I built houses and planted vineyards for myself;
> I made myself gardens and parks,

and planted in them all kinds of trees.
I made myself pools
from which to water the forest of growing trees.

The text demonstrates that an effective ruler was not just a warrior and sportsman but a gardener-king too. A successful king was cultivator who personally tended to agricultural matters to ensure the prosperity of his realm (and in this light the Great King ordered his satraps to create and maintain *paradeisoi* in their provinces; Xen. *Cyr.* 8.6.12). Xenophon was both flabbergasted by, and full of admiration for, prince Cyrus the Younger's vigorous and sophisticated gardening skills (*Oec.* 4.8–13; 4.21–5) and the Latin Vulgate version of Esther (1:5) stresses that the royal garden at Susa 'was planted by the care and the hand of the king'. Achaemenid kings were keenly interested in horticulture and encouraged the efforts of the satrapies toward innovative practices in agronomy, arboriculture and irrigation. Xenophon (*Hel.* 4.1.15–16; 33–6) regularly encountered them as he trekked the western half of the realm and the astonishing beauty of various *paradeisoi* clearly left a mark on him:

> The place where the palace of Pharnabazus was located was surrounded by many large villages, all stored in abundance, and there were many wild animals found around about – some in enclosed *paradeisoi*, others in open areas. There was also a river teaming with fish flowing near by the palace. And besides all this there was winged game in plenty for those who knew how to get it.

Gardening was a Persian obsession. The pedestrian Greeks never understood its appeal. For a Greek, a garden was merely a place to grow radishes.

A Persian royal *paridaida* can be understood in two ways: i) a formal walled garden attached to a palace or pavilion, ii) a large area of uncultivated land enclosed in a perimeter wall, a kind of safari park, well-stocked with game. The text of Esther refers only to the former, palace-style garden, although this too could be enormous. It was of a type already located in the Neo-Assyrian world, where rulers such as Tiglath-pileser I spent lavishly on creating green spaces in and around their palaces. His inscriptions tell how he brought plants from all known regions of the world to Assyria and cultivated them within the royal gardens to be a place *ana multa'it belūtīja*, 'for the leisure of my majesty'. He bragged, 'I took cedar … [and] oak from the lands which I had dominion … and planted [them] in the orchards of my land' (Brown 1996: 67; Novak 2002), thereby emphasizing that an exotic garden symbolized the monarch's control of a huge territory. Later, Ashurnasirpal took up the idea of a universal garden when in his palace, close to his new founded residential city of Kalhu, he laid out a huge *kiri rišate*, 'garden of pleasure'. Sargon II erected his own new residential city Dur-Šarrukin in the middle of a spacious garden which was called *kirimāḫu*, 'mighty garden', and erected a panorama platform from which to observe it. A cylinder text commemorating the founding of Dur-Šarrukin (cited in Tomes 2005: 76–7) enthusiastically praises Sargon for the care he showed in the planning and cultivation of the garden:

> The sagacious king, full of kindness, who gave his thought to … bringing fields under cultivation, to the planting of orchards … to make these regions ring with

the sound of jubilation, to cause the springs of the plain to gush forth, to open ditches, to cause waters of abundance to rise high ... like the waves of the sea.

A series of reliefs found in the palaces of Nineveh reflect the layout of the royal gardens. One of them, dating to the reign of Ashurbanipal, shows a hill planted with different trees and irrigated by a system of channels and an aqueduct (**Figure 1.67**). A pavilion with a columned hall (Akk. *bītanu*) is situated on top of the hill. Another, very well-known, relief (**Figure 1.68**) shows King Ashurbanipal and his wife dining within the botanical garden of the Nineveh place. The decapitated head of the Elamite king Teumman that hangs down from a palm tree reminds us that a royal garden was also a political, ideological and ceremonial site. The assemblage of city, palace and gardens was a symbol of the charismatic king as the creator of civilization. Its universal characteristics, with flora and fauna of all

Figure 1.67 Stone relief depicting an Assyrian royal garden at Nineveh, including a pavilion with a standing sculpture of a king.

Figure 1.68 Garden banqueting scene from the palace of Ashurbanipal at Nineveh.

conquered regions within its walls, emphasized the claim of the Assyrian monarch to rule the entire universe as the *šar kibrāt erbettim*, 'King of the Four Quarters'.

The earliest reference to a Persian-style garden comes in the form of a Babylonian text dating to regnal year 5 of Cyrus II which speaks of a *pardēsu* near Uruk: 'Šapik-zeri has received 1 shekel of silver from Marduk-rimanni for the shift-workers of the *pardēsu* in the presence of Apla, son of Tabnea and Nadin, his third man (on the chariot). Month of Tebetu, 22nd day, 5th year of Cyrus, King of Babylon, King of all

Lands' (Bremmer 2008: 37; Dandamanev 1984). The earliest gardens on the Iranian plateau associated with the Achaemenids are located at Pasargadae, the royal park residence of Cyrus the Great (c. 559–530 BCE), the founder of the Persian empire. The formal garden was Pasargadae's chief jewel. An expansive area of rich cultivation linked a gateway and two pavilion-like palaces together into a single, unified whole. The layout of lush green spaces interspersed with palaces, pavilions and audience halls became a defining feature of Persian garden-design (Gharipour 2013). Dressed-stone water channels unified the garden through a carefully planned geometric layout by creating an elegant fourfold design, or NP *chahar bagh*. This distinctive feature was destined to become a major characteristic of garden design throughout the Islamic world from Samarkand to Seville (Mahmoudi Farahani, Motamed and Jamei 2016). Through the intricacy of its *chahar bagh* design, the garden of Pasargadae became a living reflection of the royal title Cyrus inherited from his Assyrian predecessors and had emphasized in his Babylonian propaganda cylinder: 'I am Cyrus ... King of the Four Quarters of the World.'

It is during the reign of Darius I that more regular references to *paradeisoi* are found in the Persepolis Texts. These enable us to speculate more fully on their maintenance and use (PT 59; for a full exploration of Persian *paradeisoi* see Tuplin 1996: 80–181). In addition to textual sources, archaeological evidence of Achaemenid gardens exists at Persepolis, Susa and other royal and satrapal sites throughout the empire. Beyond the obvious sensual hedonism offered by royal gardens, like their Assyrian antecedents, the Persian *paradeisoi* were encoded with a rich political and ideological symbolism. The royal gardens were an empire in miniature, and plants, birds and animals from every area of the king's dominion were resettled and replanted within their confines (Bremmer 2008: 38; Uchitel 1997). We hear of Achaemenid monarchs enriching their *paradeisoi* with foreign shrubs and fruit trees (PPA31). The idea of the king creating a fertile garden – displaying both symmetry and order – constituted a powerful statement symbolizing monarchic authority, fertility, legitimacy and divine favour (even gods were portrayed as gardeners, see *Psalm* 80:11, 104:16; Homer, *Iliad* 5.693). As a potent symbol of resistance to Persian rule, the rebellious citizens of the city of Sardis completely destroyed the royal garden 'in which Persian kings took their relaxation' (Diod. Sic. 16.41).

Of all the plants cultivated in royal gardens, trees were the most important. Not only did they provide practical cooling shade, but they were symbolically rich too. Near Eastern kings were traditionally identified with (or even *as*) fine trees. The Sumerian monarch Šulgi for instance was at one and the same time 'a date palm planted by a water ditch' and 'a cedar planted by water' (Widengren 1951: 42) and famously the kings of Israel were depicted as both a 'shoot' and a 'branch' of the Davidic house (Isa. 11:1). Assyrian kings were frequently represented standing next to the so-called 'Tree of Life' – an important cult symbol across the Near East generally (**Figure 1.69**). This special relationship between kings and trees lies behind the

Figure 1.69 Tree of Life guarded by *apkallu*; stone relief from Nimrud.

infamous Herodotean story of Xerxes' infatuation with a plane tree (Hdt. 7.31), which Briant (2002: 235) suggests shows evidence for the existence of a Persian tree cult (see further Ael. *VH* 2.14). Several seal images support this idea. One inscribed with Xerxes' name (SXe; Kuhrt 2007, **Figure 1.70**) shows the monarch about to decorate a tree with jewellery, an exact visual parallel to the Greek account. Other seals show the monarch in close proximity to date palms. The Great King was equally associated with the grape vine as a symbol of fecundity and strength and, according to Herodotus (1.108), the king of Media dreamed that a vine emerged from the genitalia of his daughter, thereby predicting that Media would be overthrown by his daughter's unborn son (the future Cyrus II). This may well have its origins in a Persian story about Cyrus' birth and might help explain the symbolism of the golden jewel-encrusted vine which supposedly decorated either the royal bed chamber or audience chamber (Athen. 12. 514f–515a; 539d).

Figure 1.70 Persian cylinder seal impression; Xerxes offers gold decorations to a sacred tree.

1:6 hangings of white and blue linen, fastened with cords of white linen and purple material to silver rings on marble pillars

Given the temperature at Susa, even during winter, can be high, *al fresco* dining was a practical solution to overheating (Baldwin 1984: 58). A textile awning was extended from the pavilion out into the garden where it was attached to poles planted into the soil. Very strong cords would have been needed to support the awning if it was carried across the garden, perhaps a space just over 18 metres. The canopy kept the diners in the shade and filtered welcoming cool air into its enclosure. A similar structure can be found on the Hellenistic-era Palestrina Mosaic (**Figure 1.71**). It is secured with guide ropes and excess fabric is gathered in tie-backs. The Persians were descended from Eurasian nomads and the nomadic way of life never left them. Tents and canopies were part of their daily life and when the Great King progressed around his domains he slept in a tent of great size and beauty (Llewellyn-Jones 2013a). Made from colourfully woven textiles and leather panels and supported by a framework of pillars, in all respects, the king's tent was a collapsible version of a palace pillared-hall and it is reasonable to think of the *bitānu* at Susa as a stone version of the royal tent (Xerxes' lavish campaign tent – ideal for 'glamping' – is described in Hdt. 9.82). No doubt Xerxes sat in the shaded porticus of his elegant little pavilion of stone and wood beneath the wide awning which effectively extended the palace into the garden and drew the garden back into the palace. When Alexander III of Macedon celebrated a series of interracial marriages at Susa in 324 BCE, he erected a colossal

Figure 1.71 Detail from the Hellenistic-era Palestrina Mosaic depicting Nilotic scenes, including a palace façade with textile awnings.

awning in the palace garden for the occasion. It was supported by 50 golden pillars and had enough space to hold a hundred couches (Polyaenus 4.3.24; Arr. *Anab.* 7.4.4–5.6; Miller 1997: 51; Spawforth 2007a: 94–7, 112–20).

Est. 1:6a should be read as, 'bleached white fabric, finely woven material, purple wool, held fast with cords of fine linen and purple wool'. The 'bleached white' fabric is perhaps best rendered 'bleached white cotton' (on the colour see Noonan 2021: 134–5). This unique biblical reference to cotton uses the word *karpas*, which is a cognate of the Sanskrit word for cotton *kârpâsa*, implying a direct link between the native Indian origin of the plant and the Persian court. This is unsurprising since by the end of the 6th century BCE, India was under Persian political control. The attestation in the Persepolis archive of travellers on their way to India around 500 BCE receiving provisions from the Persian central administration underlines the type of long-distance commercial networks supported by the Persian empire (PFT 2057). Indian cotton may have become more common in the Mediterranean world after the conquests of Alexander: it later became a common cultigen in the Eastern Mediterranean. Moreover, Neo-Elamite texts from Susa reveals that hundreds of *kuktum* (cotton) garments, sometimes classified as blue, white, streaked or partly coloured, were stored in the royal treasury. References to these luxury textiles pre-date Xerxes' reign by almost a millennium, proving that the use of cotton in the Near East was very old (Álvarez-Mon 2015). Cotton had several primary advantages over flax in textile manufacture: it did not require retting, and is naturally whiter and more amenable to dyes. Cotton was also combined with other materials (linen and wool) to produce cloth of mixed fibres, as seen here in Esther.

The whiteness of the cotton canopy is striking however. Since most textile fibres are naturally a dull off-white, in the ancient world pure whiteness was achieved only by bleaching and fulling, and was probably at least as difficult to obtain and maintain as any dyed colour. It was very expensive process and the cost of a huge crisp white cotton awning would have been affordable only to a monarch like Xerxes.

However, it was purple that was the undisputed royal colour of antiquity (Reinhold 1970). Yet its centrality to the conception of power and wealth did not really focus on the *colour* purple *per se*, since not all purples were equal, and not all purples were truly purple. The symbolism of purple was very much bound up with its origins though, since the rare shellfish dyes used to make purple dyes were prized not only for their distinctive colour qualities, but also because they were difficult to obtain and to apply to textiles. Shellfish dyes produced a range of colours, from what we would call deep crimson red, through purple, to violet or even 'Prussian' blue, all of which appeared to have shared the cultural associations of 'purple' throughout antiquity.

The process of murex dyeing was lost in Late Antiquity (probably due to the shift from outdoor to indoor ritual and status activities in the Byzantine period) and was only rediscovered in the nineteenth century. Since then, scholars have debated exactly how the dye was made and used. Each purple dyeing requires removing the tiny dye sacs of hundreds or thousands of individual shellfish. These must be chemically 'reduced' to form a water-soluble compound which can be applied as a dye – essentially a form of fermentation, probably using a variety of processes in antiquity. Along with the species and origin of the shellfish, these produced variations in the finished colour. Experiments have also suggested that purple dye application is light-sensitive so that the colour becomes blue if exposed to light during the formation of the dye bond (Ziderman 2004). This reduction process makes mordanting unnecessary, and promotes a very fast dye-bond, not subsequently degraded by exposure to light or washing. Meanwhile, the colours produced are visually bright, rich and complex, contrasting favourably with the generally relatively dull and frequently fading colours of plant dyes. So, the value of purple dyes was not only aesthetic or economic, but also practical. Purple remained both a status symbol and, because of its origin, an important item of trade, throughout antiquity.

The finely woven textiles with their rich purple hues and gleaming white sheen, were the product of a successful Persian imperial trade network. But a Jewish audience might have more naturally found resonances between the elegant splendour of Xerxes' garden 'tent' and the priestly description of the tabernacle (Exod. 25:4; 26:1, 31, 36; 27:16 etc.) and the Chronicler's details of the furnishings of Solomon's temple in Jerusalem (2 Chron. 3:14). Indeed, it is possible that the Chronicler's description of the Solomonic temple and palace were inspired by Achaemenid palace prototypes.

The cotton and linen awnings of Xerxes' pavilion were attached to the cords with silver rings which were fixed into the pillars of the portico. These are said to be marble (or alabaster). But the pillars at Susa are not of marble, but of a dark-blue crystalline limestone; marble was never used as major building material by the Achaemenids. The region around Susa was devoid of good stone but Darius' Susa Charters make it clear that stone for the pillars was brought from the village of Abiradu in Elam (see further, Boucharlat 1997).

The Heb. *šeš*, may probably be taken to mean almost any fine quality stone and perhaps a better rendering would be 'well-dressed stone'. It is derived from Egy. *šs*, 'alabaster' (Noonan 2021: 209–10). The so-called 'marble' of Solomon's architectural works was probably alabaster 'marble', the go-to building material for the rulers of the ancient Near East. There can be no doubt that Herod the Great, following later Greco-Roman tastes in architecture, employed Parian or other gypsum-based alabaster 'marble', both in the construction of the Jerusalem Temple and his palaces.

1:6 couches of gold and silver

In Persia, as in other parts of the Near East and Greece, male party-goers reclined on their left elbows on couches (**Figures 1.42, 1.68**; see Dentzer 1971). The reclining position implied a need to be served but also the leisure of the occasion. The couch was an object of luxury and, for some critics of elite, it had connotations of a life spent in indolence. The Hebrew prophet Amos (6:4a) describes the wealthy nobility of Samaria as those 'that lie upon couches of ivory' and was ready to chastise them for stretching themselves 'upon their couches, and eat lambs from the flock … [and] who sing idle songs to the sound of the harp' (6:4b-5). Exquisitely carved ivory inlays for couches have been discovered at Nimrud and other Assyrian sites (Curtis 1996) as well as at Samaria (Tappy 2001). The solid gold and silver couches at Susa are a step above even the ivory beds of the Assyrians. Furniture of this sought was looted by the Greek soldiers following the Battle of Marathon, and again after the Greek's ultimate victory over the remaining Persian invasion at the Battle of Plataea. The tent which Xerxes had used during his Greek campaign of 480–479 BCE had been given to Mardonius to use as the general continued the war with the Greeks. Abandoned post-battle, the Spartan leader Pausanias saw the royal quarters for himself and was overawed by the golden and silver couches with sumptuous coverings which had been left behind (Hdt. 9.82).

There are no known images of an Achaemenid Great King reclining on a couch and the motif is oddly absent from the artistic repertoire at the centre of the Persian empire. However, in Achaemenid-occupied Asia Minor, mortuary reliefs very frequently show male banqueters reclining on their left elbows against a pile of cushions, overtly raising a cup of specifically Achaemenid shape (**Figure 1.72**). Often a female sits upright at the foot of the couch, her feet upon a footstool. She frequently holds a symbol of fertility in her hand, such as an egg or a budding flower. The visual representation closely resembles the most famous banquet scene carved on the walls of the seventh-century Assyrian king Ashurbanipal's palace at Nineveh (**Figure 1.68**).

Figure 1.72 Banqueting scene. A nobleman reclines on a couch while his wife, seated beside him, proffers a fruit. Funerary stele from Achaemenid-occupied Anatolia.

1:6 a mosaic pavement of porphyry, marble, mother-of-pearl and other costly stones

This problematic vocabulary of stones is difficult to apply to the material culture of ancient Persia. Heb. *bahat* is identified with 'alabaster', but as we observed earlier, it probably refers, at least in this context, to crystalline limestone. Mosaics have not been found in Persia. Omanson and Noss (1997: 23) suggest that the term 'mosaic' is out of place and should be replaced with 'pavement' or simply 'floor'. What is important, they note, is that the 'floor' is coloured in red, white, black and gold. This certainly fits with what we know about the interior décor of Near Eastern palaces which often installed painted stone reliefs on the floor. Several stone doorsills have survived from Neo-Assyrian palaces (**Figure 1.73**) and had no doubt been used in Achaemenid structures too. They were designed to mimic carpets and were, in a sense, a solution to the everyday practical problem of carpet wear in a heavily used space (such as a doorway). They would also have been painted, and where real carpets would eventually need replacing, these panels would presumably have needed to be repainted regularly. Of course, Achaemenid palaces were filled with fine carpets and hangings, but none survive. Most would have been stolen by Alexander of Macedon. Those at Persepolis no doubt perished in his arson attack on the palace in 330 BCE. Representations of textiles in other media help to compensate for this loss, particularly when, as with **Figure 1.73**, the designs and patterns that would have been used in real carpets are depicted in detail.

Figure 1.73 Neo-Assyrian stone relief which once decorated Ashurbanipal's palace at Nineveh. It represents a woven carpet.

'Mother-of-pearl' is the translation of Heb. *dar*, which occurs only here in the Hebrew Bible. In NP 'pearl' is *dorr*, but it is a late loan word from Arabic. The indigenous Iranian MP term for 'pearl' is *moravārīd*, a borrowing from the Gk. *margaritē*. Since there is no evidence for the use of mother-of-pearl in ancient Persia, Gindin (2016: 55) rightly supposes that the *dar* of Est. 1:6 is 'gold', taken from OP *daraniya*.

1:7 Wine was served in goblets of gold, each one different from the other, and the royal wine was abundant

Wine was a cultural phenomenon in Achaemenid Persia, 'evidenced in its widespread prestige, appeal, and consumption' (Dahlén 2020: 99). The Persians were 'very fond of wine', Herodotus insisted (2.33), and it does appear that the Persian elite were genuine wine connoisseurs. The empire's excellent road system made it possible for Persia's nobility to obtain speciality wines from far-off places – Armenia, Sogdia, Macedonia, Carman, and Cilicia. Xenophon noted that Artaxerxes II had 'vintners scouring every land to find some drink that will tickle his palate' and refers to the abundant choice of wine at the court. For the Achaemenids the presence of fine wines at the king's table was a symbol of the king's power and his capacity to attract tribute. The royal cupbearers, among the king's most trusted courtiers, were excellent wine connoisseurs, *au fait* in the knowledge of different vintages. The Greek Heraclides, resident in Persia for some years, observed that the king 'does not drink the same wine' (Ath. 4.145–6) as his companions but had his own choice wine. This was the 'royal wine' referred to in Esther. Posidonius of Apamea (Ath. 4.145c) noted that Darius III exclusively drank Syrian wine from Chalybon (Helbon), a district on the slopes above Damascus, while Polyaenus (4.3.32) adds that the king's wine menu in Ecbatana differed from that in Susa and Babylon, where half the wine was from grapes and half from palm dates. There is even mention of royal vine-cutters (or grafters) who were charged with carefully pruning precious grape vines from Lebanon and transporting and replanting them in Persian soil (PF-NN1564; see further Batmanglij 2008 for Iran's longstanding love affair with wine).

The Persepolis Fortification Tablets attest that there was a special wine department in Persepolis with stations and warehouses in various places in the Pārs region. The texts show that wine was a common ration for different categories of functionaries and courtiers who received it as payment. The payments made to everyone from the chief administrator down to the lowliest worker were all in terms of commodities:

> Parnaka [the head of administration at Persepolis] received as rations 90 quarts of wine [1 quart = 0.97 litres] entrusted to Karkis. For a period of one day, at a village named Hadarakkas. Hisbes wrote the text. Mannunda communicated its message. Regnal Year 23 [of Darius I], month 2, day 25. The sealed document was delivered.
> (PF 665)

> Zišsawiš received as rations 90 quarts of wine supplied by Muska. For a period of 3 days. at Parmadan and Pirradase (?). Month 9. Regnal Year 18 [of Darius I].
> (PF 673)

The presence of Greeks in the Persian heartland is even attested by one of the Treasury Tablets dealing with wine transactions, for it was written in Greek. Some people were given wine in huge quantities: Irdabama, the mother of Darius I (and grandmother of Xerxes), who possessed estates and a large workforce of slaves and administrators, received by far the largest amount of wine of any other member of the court. On one occasion 2,360 quarts of wine were sent to her at Susa (PF 737). Wine was also used in religious rituals as libations and offerings (see, for instance, PF 759).

Xenophon's experiences as he marched through the Persian empire altogether capture another side of wining and dining in Persia. In Babylonia, he observed, they drank 'date wine' and 'a sour drink made the same by boiling dates'. In eastern Turkey they quaffed 'old wines with a fine bouquet' and either used 'a reed [to] suck the [barley] wine into one's mouth' or drank straight from 'the bowl ... sucking it like an ox' (*Anab.* 1.5; 2.3; 4.4–5).

Gold and silver tableware was commonly used by the Achaemenid court and Persia's aristocracy (Moorey 1980). The rich variations in design are notable. At a court banquet all guests drank from cups or bowls of silver or gold. Wine was only served in clay vessels when the Great King wished to insult or humiliate an individual (Athen. 11.464a). 'Every year the king sends rich gifts to the man who can show the largest number of sons', Herodotus wrote (1.136), and according to Xenophon (*Cyr.* 8.2.3–4, 6, 8; 3.3, 33; 4.24, 27; 5.29), gold drinking vessels were one category of such royal largesse. This form of payment in kind offers one explanation for the circulation of Achaemenid metal plate and other luxury items to the extremities of the Persian empire and beyond.

The royal court always travelled with 'water, ready boiled for use, and stored in flagons of silver' together with 'many gold and silver drinking cups' (Hdt. 1.188; 6.1.190). The Persian monarch was said to have presented one favoured courtier with 'one hundred large *phialai* of silver and silver mixing bowls' and 'twenty gold *phialai* set with jewels', which may be a reference to the cloisonné work typical of Achaemenid goldsmiths (Athen. 2.48f). Vessels are carried by as many as twelve of the twenty-three delegations shown on the Apadana reliefs at Persepolis. Among these are amphorae with plain or fluted bodies and opposing plain or zoomorphic handles. These are shown being carried by members of delegations I (Medes; **Figure 1.74**), III (Armenians; **Figure 1.75**) and VI (Lydians; **Figure 1.76**). Silver and gilt-silver versions of these vessels survive, either complete or as isolated handles or spouts. Pairs of horizontally fluted or plain beakers are shown being carried by members of delegations XII (Ionians; **Figure 1.77**) and XV

Figure 1.74 Delegation I (Medes) from the east staircase of the Apadana at Persepolis.

Figure 1.75 Delegation III (Armenians) from the east staircase of the Apadana at Persepolis.

Figure 1.76 Delegation VI (Lydians) from the east staircase of the Apadana at Persepolis.

Figure 1.77 Delegation XII (Ionians? Greeks?) from the east staircase of the Apadana at Persepolis.

(Parthians (?); **Figure 1.78**); less ostentatious versions are also carried by delegations I (Medes), IV (Arians (?); **Figure 1.79**), VI (Lydians), and VII (Drangians; **Figure 1.80**). Pairs of plain bowls with rolled-over rims and plain hemispherical bowls (*mastoi*) are carried by delegation XIII (Bactrians (?); **Figure 1.81**); small alabastrons are carried nested in baskets by delegation XVIII (Indians (?); **Figure 1.82**), and another type of lidded vessel is shown being carried by a member of delegation XXIII (Nubians; **Figure 1.83**). Finally, pairs of plain or horizontally fluted shouldered bowls (*phialai*) are depicted on the Apadana being carried by delegations V (Babylonians; **Figure 1.84**), VI (Lydians), VIII (Assyrians; **Figure 1.85**), XII (Ionians) and XV (Parthians (?)). The ubiquitous presence at the Persian court of tableware in precious metals was noted frequently by the Greeks and the presence of gold and silver cups became a shorthand for the bigger picture for Persian extravagance. When the Athenian comic Aristophanes lampooned the luxury-loving Athenian ambassadors who travelled to Susa on diplomatic missions, he noted especially the 'hardships' they encountered in the royal dining hall: 'And those pitiless Persian hosts', the dignitaries, well-fed and fat with Persian generosity, complain, 'they compelled us to drink sweet wine. Wine without water! From gold cups!' (*Arch.* 72–3).

Shallow lobed bowls are a particularly distinctive type of Achaemenid tableware, although, strangely, they are not represented at Persepolis. Four complete silver examples

Figure 1.78 Delegation XV (Parthians?) from the east staircase of the Apadana at Persepolis.

Figure 1.79 Delegation IV (Arians?) from the east staircase of the Apadana at Persepolis.

Figure 1.80 Delegation VII (Drangians) from the east staircase of the Apadana at Persepolis.

Figure 1.81 Delegation XIII (Bactrians?) from the east staircase of the Apadana at Persepolis.

Figure 1.82 Delegation XVIII (Indians?) from the east staircase of the Apadana at Persepolis.

Figure 1.83 Delegation XXIII (Nubians) from the east staircase of the Apadana at Persepolis.

are inscribed: 'Artaxerxes the Great King, King of Kings, King of Countries, son of Xerxes the king [who was] son of Darius the king; in whose royal house this saucer [or wine-drinking vessel] was made' (Simpson 1998; **Figure 1.86**). The rhyton, or 'pourer', is another quintessential Persian form of vessel which is nevertheless also absent from depictions at Persepolis. It typically consists of a conical or trumpet-like horn, usually hammered from relatively thin sheet metal and inserted. sometimes at right-angles,

Figure 1.84 Delegation V (Babylonians) from the east staircase of the Apadana at Persepolis.

Figure 1.85 Delegation VIII (Assyrians) from the east staircase of the Apadana at Persepolis.

into a proportionately much smaller cast or hammered animal-headed *protome*, with a pouring hole or spout typically in the muzzle or chest (**Figures 1.87, 1.88, 1.89**). Most surviving rhytons are silver, although gold and bronze versions are also known. Other sorts of tableware included hemispherical cups, either plain gold or silver decorated with gold cut-outs (**Figure 1.90**), cylindrical plain bronze beakers, shallow silver or gold bowls decorated with petals radiating from a central rosette or animal figures (**Figure 1.91**), twin-spouted amphorae and gold jugs with zoomorphic handles.

Figure 1.86 Silver dish inscribed with the name and titles of King Artaxerxes I.

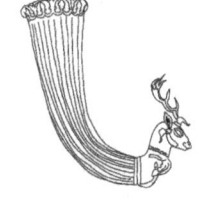

Figure 1.87 Silver Achaemenid animal rhyton in the form of a stag.

Figure 1.88 Gold Achaemenid rhyton in the form of a mythical beast.

Figure 1.89 Silver Achaemenid animal rhyton in the form of a ram or ibex.

Figure 1.90 Silver and gold figurative Achaemenid bowl.

Figure 1.91 Gold Achaemenid dish decorated with rampant lions.

Excavated examples of drinking vessels demonstrate they could comfortably hold a litre of wine or even a litre and a half. At a royal banquet, an 'abundance' of drink (as the author of Esther put it) was guaranteed.

1:8 wine stewards

Xenophon refers to encountering villagers in eastern Turkey who drank barley-wine from large bowls: 'Floating on the top of this drink were the barley-grains and in it were straws, some larger than others. When one was thirsty, one had to take these straws into the mouth and suck. It was an extremely strong drink unless one diluted it with water, and extremely good when one was used to it' (Xen. *Anab.* 4.5). The purpose of the straws was to avoid drinking the coarse sediment in the drink, especially the dregs of the bowl. This had been a popular form of drinking throughout the Levant, Mesopotamia and the Persian Gulf from as early as the third millennium BCE. But the Persian court rejected the custom as a vulgarity. Instead, the Persian elite sieved the wine as it was poured. For this purpose, a perforated ladle was used. The employment of royal servants whose task this was is suggested by Athenaeus' reference to 'wine filterers' in Darius III's household (13.608a). A depiction of a satrap's cup-bearer on a fifth-century Lycian tomb-painting at Karaburun, Turkey, indicates that the ladle was suspended from the little finger of one hand, with the other three fingertips supporting the sides and bottom of a bowl (**Figure 1.92**). Xenophon (*Cyr.* 1.3.8–9) describes the etiquette of wine service:

Figure 1.92 Satrap or nobleman reclines on a couch in the presence of slaves, including a fan-bearer and a cup-bearer. Painted tomb fresco from Achaemenid-occupied western Asia Minor.

For these cup-bearers to kings perform their business very cleverly; they pour in the wine without spilling it and give the cup, holding it on three fingers, and presenting it in such a manner as to put it most conveniently into the hand of the person who is to drink ... For these cup-bearers to kings, when they give the cup take a little [wine] out with a small ladle which they pour into their left hand and swallow; so that, in case they mix poison in the cup. It may be of no profit to them.

The royal cupbearer was one of the most prestigious offices at court and was held only by the monarch's most trusted courtiers, like the Jewish eunuch Nehemiah who performed that duty for Artaxerxes I (Neh. 1:1; it was Nehemiah's routine proximity to the king as his cupbearer which later saw him rise to power in Judah). The king's cupbearer was charged with managing of all of the court's wine-pourers and tasters although he alone poured the king's wine into the royal cup and tasted the monarch's drink, drawn off in a silver ladle to check that it was poison-free. The threat of poison might be a reason why the Great King drank a wine unique to him.

1:9 Queen Vashti

There is no evidence for a queen or any other woman named Vashti in the Persian sources. Linguistic efforts to link Vashti to Xerxes' only named queen, Amestris (Hdt. 7.61, 9.108–13; Ctesias F13), have been unsuccessful. The name does have two possible OP roots though: *vaštī*, 'that which is desired' (the feminine form of the verb *vaš*, 'to wish'), and *vahištī*, 'the best'. Its etymology could approach that of *Vištā* – which is present in the OP name Vištāspa – rather than the OP terms suggested above.

Connecting Vashti to the Elamite goddess Mašti is etymologically unlikely, since there is little evidence to confirm the deity's presence in the Elamite pantheon at all (Gindin 2016: 64). Like the version of 'Xerxes' presented in Esther, 'Vashti' too is an invention. She represents queenship and personifies correct womanly behaviour. 'The identity of Vashti is crucial', Moore states (1971: 8), 'only to those modern scholars ... who have a strong apologetic interest in the *strictly* historical accurateness of Esther' (see further Arnold 2000: 63–7; Gehman 1924: 322–3; Gerleman 1966: 60; Gertoux 2015 – all of whom argue for an identification of the historical Amestris with Vashti or Esther).

Achaemenid kings were polygynous – that is to say, they had sexual access to many women: consorts, concubines and even slaves. The consorts of the Great Kings were responsible for promulgation of the Achaemenid dynasty. Royal power was transmitted directly through the wombs of the royal wives. Darius the Great was married to at least six women (and there may have been more) and his marriage alliances were undertaken to endorse his legitimacy as Persia's monarch. His marriage to a daughter of Gobryas, a significant nobleman, before becoming king tied together two important Persian houses; he had three sons with her. After his accession, he married Atossa, the daughter of Cyrus II, who had previously been wife to both Cambyses II and King Bardiya; Darius had four sons with her. He was also wed to Artystone, another daughter of Cyrus II, who gave him at least one son. Next to be married was Parmys, daughter of Bardiya, and then Phaidymie, daughter of the nobleman Otanes; earlier, she too had been King Bardiya's wife. Another spouse, Phratagoune, daughter of the nobleman Artanes, gave Darius two more sons. Darius therefore had six wives at the same time. In addition, the king had numerous concubines and fathered children by many of them too (Llewellyn-Jones 2022).

A sense of royal polygyny is gained in Esther. Yet, in spite of its focus on women and power (or lack of power), the Book of Esther gives a very skewed picture of the norms of Persian royal matrimony. It suggests that, to all intents and purposes, at worst, Xerxes was a serial monogamist, moving on from one queen (Vashti) to another (Esther). Greek texts have a tendency to repeat the same misconception. Indeed, our knowledge of the names of Achaemenid royal consorts is chiefly derived from Greek sources. They usually provide the name for just one wife for each Great King. Reliance on the Greek and Hebrew sources (see also Neh. 2:6) would suggest that Persian monarchs were monogamists.

Dominique Lenfant suggests that belief in the presence of numerous royal consorts at the heart of the imperial Persian world is 'an over-reading, the result of a projection of modern stereotypes onto antiquity' (Lenfant 2019: 33). But Greek sources – Lenfant's core study – cannot be used as evidence for a lack of institutional polygyny or polygamy; the truth is that often the Greek writers did not know about the workings of the marriage practices of Persian royalty, although they were prepared to make bold guesses. Dismissing the existence of polygamy and polygyny on the grounds that Greek literary sources do not support the notion seriously damages our understanding of the nature and functioning of royal marriage within absolutist forms of Near Eastern dynastic government. Multiple marriages to a series of consorts, and the accumulation of women as concubines too, was a hallmark of dynastic rule throughout the ancient Near East and therefore to write polygamy and polygyny out of the history of the Achaemenid world makes no sense in any *longue durée* approach to the history of marriage. Lenfant notes 'we do not have any non-Greek source giving some indication about the plurality of wives', but this notion is too closely tied to a modern conception of what defines marriage and how we go about looking for evidence of wedlock in the linguistic minefields of the past. Lenfant is in danger of another form of Orientalism, whereby the realities of eastern practices are nullified in the danger that, ironically, they read as Orientalist. Let us not be under any illusion here: in Persia, as in all other Near Eastern societies, the taking of multiple wives was a political act and a male ruler's sex-drive is never the explanation of polygamy or polygyny. Women were gathered together in ancient court societies to fulfil social, cultural and ritual roles and to undertake (it was hoped) important functions in dynastic continuity as wives, concubines and mothers. Rather than deal with the problems (and potentials) of royal polygamy, Lenfant opts to write it out of history.

This idiosyncratic appearance of Persian 'monogamy' in the Greek sources is the result of two factors: first, for the Greeks, there was a preoccupation with the 'norm' of monogamy. They preferred to think of the Persian king as a one-woman-man (at least when it came to a wife; they were happy to imagine him with countless concubines). Second, the Greeks knew very little about the workings of the Great King's harem. They simply did not have access to details such as the names of the king's wives. The Greek representation of Persian royal monogamy is certainly wrong. Great Kings took multiple wives so that they could father many heirs.

The explanation of the fixation on royal monogamy in Esther, however, is different. Here monogamy serves the story best. Xerxes' remarriage is a straight swap; Esther replaces Vashti in a simple but effective 'reversal of fortunes' scenario. In the story, the presence of multiple consorts and concubines was not wanted, even though in reality they filled the court, as the author of Esther must surely have known. Vashti therefore becomes the sole wife of Xerxes. But the imposition of monogamy on the story reconfirms the opinion that Esther is a-historical and, at the most, a work of 'historical fiction'. As Jean-Daniel Macchi (2018: 97) notes, 'it is useless to identify Amestris with Vashti or Esther. The authors of the book of Esther certainly did not want to push the historical fiction to the point of staging the famous Amestris'.

1:9 banquet for the women

Greek reports that high-ranking consorts sometimes dined with the Great King are probably correct. Plutarch (*Mor.* 140B 16, probably using Ctesias as his source) notes, for instance, that:

> The lawful wives of the Persian kings sit beside them at dinner, and eat with them. But when the kings wish to party and get drunk, they send their wives out and call for the dancing girls and the concubines. They are right in what they do because they could not condone their laddish behaviour in front of their consorts.

However, Greek references to the presence of royal women at the king's table make it clear that the dining occurs within the inner court of the palace, that is to say, inside the domestic heart of the structure. This was a place of relative privacy, of social separation. A sharp spatial and representational divide between the public and domestic sits at the heart of Iranian tradition, as it did in much of the ancient Near East and still does in parts of the modern Middle Eastern world. The NP word *andarūnī* literally means 'the inside'. It is a term used by Iranians for the private family quarters of a home and for the people who inhabit it. It is used in opposition to *birun* – which refers to the public space and the sphere of a household used for welcoming and entertaining guests. In contemporary Iran, the *andarūnī* consists of all the males of a family and their respective wives, mothers, grandmothers and a whole array of male and female offspring ranging from babies to adolescents. When a large mixed sex company gathers, the men will congregate in the *birun* while the women will occupy the *andarūnī*. This ancient practice is what defines the separation of the sexes during the great banquet in Esther. Vashti entertains the female guests inside the palace in accordance with rules of proper decorum and courtly etiquette.

Figure 1.93 Women preparing a banquet; detail from an incised bronze belt from Urartu.

Figure 1.94 New Kingdom Egyptian all-female banquet scene; wall painting from Thebes.

Figure 1.95 New Kingdom Egyptian all-female banquet scene; wall painting from Thebes.

Figure 1.96 North Syrian ivory relief furniture inlay depicting a woman drinking and accompanied by servants and a pet rabbit.

Representations of all-women banquets (or their preparation) are not uncommon in the art of the Near East (**Figure 1.93**). There were many opportunities for women to mix exclusively, especially at times of domestic celebrations such as weddings, births and even funerals where women tended to play the major ceremonial roles. The XVIII Dynasty tombs of the Egyptian nobles Nakht and Nebamun depict registers of women party-goers wearing elaborate linen clothes and large festal-wigs. They are entertained by female musicians and dancing girls (**Figures 1.94** and **1.95**). Representations of enthroned or otherwise seated women enjoying a beverage and dishes of food are known in Mesopotamia, Anatolia and Iran (**Figures 1.96, 1.97, 1.98, 1.99**). They are attended exclusively by female servants. One Middle-Elamite seal, later used in the Achaemenid period, shows a seated female drinking from a cup whilst in the presence of female

Figure 1.97 Enthroned woman (queen? goddess?) receives food and drink from slaves. Incised bronze plaque, Urartu.

Figure 1.98 Noblewoman holding a flower and wreath and wearing a linen gown sits on a high-backed throne or chair. Ring impression; Achaemenid-occupied Anatolia.

Figure 1.99 Semi-nude women recline under a grape vine to enjoy a feast. Sasanian silver dish.

servants (**Figure 1.100**). It belonged to a significant royal commissioner named Rašda whose many jobs included taking care of the vast workforce of Irdabama, the Queen Mother. Scenes of all-girl orchestras, dance troops and other entertainers exist outside of Egypt too and strongly suggest the importance of all-women social gatherings (**Figures 1.101, 1.102**). Vashti's exclusive banquet for female guests is perfectly at home in a Near Eastern context.

Figure 1.100 Elamite seal impression from a seal belonging to Rašda, Steward of Lady Irdabama, mother of Darius I.

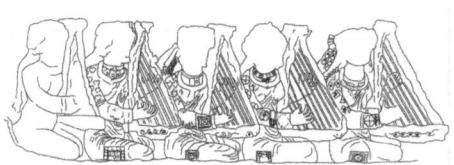

Figure 1.101 Group of female harpists. Late Sasanian period, from Taq-i Bustan, Kermanshah, Iran.

Figure 1.102 Group of all female singers, musicians, and entertainers. Detail from an incised bronze belt, Urartu.

1:10 eunuchs

The Heb. *sāris* appears forty-five times in the Hebrew Bible; twelve of its appearances are in Esther. Debate and doubt also surrounds the historical validity of royal eunuchs, the (supposedly) castrated males who served at the Persian court as high-ranking officials, bureaucrats and attendants (in ancient Assyria they also seem to have been military personnel). If these individuals were indeed castrati, then as a kind of 'third-sex' they were able to negotiate the permeable barriers of the inner court and outer court in their crucial capacities as messengers and trusted body-servants (Llewellyn-Jones 2002). Pierre Briant, however, has vehemently rejected the notion that all individuals identified as 'eunuchs' in the context of the Achaemenid empire were castrated males and suggests instead that 'eunuch' was how 'Greek authors transmitted a term that the court of the Great King considered a court title' (Briant 2002: 276–7). His debate centres on the problem of whether the Akkad. term *ša rēši* (lit. 'of the head') should be translated 'eunuch' (see further Oppenheim 1973). The translation 'eunuch' for *ša rēši* has been open to considerable scholarly debate among Assyriologists and given that the same term in found in Achaemenid-period Babylonian sources, its interpretation continues to be an issue for the study of the Persians too.

Were 'eunuchs' really 'castrati' at all? Perhaps, it has been suggested, there were two 'types' of 'eunuch' at the Persian court. The first, the castrati who served the needs of the court at large and (for a minority) tended to the Great King himself as body-servants, administrators or even as advisors. The other 'types' of 'eunuch' were those courtiers who performed the services expected of eunuchs but without the need for castration. 'The term "eunuch" is sometimes a taboo word', write Omanson and Noss (1997: 32). 'It may have a very negative connotation', they continue, 'or the practice may be entirely unknown ... The significance of the term [in Esther] is not, however, that these were emasculated men, but that they were important officials in the royal court'. For Omanson and Noss, 'eunuch' was a court title but not a physical state of being. But this idea remains mere speculation (for overviews of the debates see Jursa 2011 and Pirngruber 2011).

Shaun Tougher in his major studies of eunuchism in antiquity has wisely warned that 'being too sceptical [about the sources and hence the presence of eunuchs in the Persian court] can be as dangerous as being gullible' (Tougher 2008: 20). Briant and others find it difficult to accept that castrated males could be powerful courtiers and elite officials, or even military men, but this is to do a grave disservice to a wider knowledge of eunuch history. After all, eunuchs are attested in many Near Eastern courts (Guyot 1980; Grayson 1995; Deller 1999; Pirngruber 2011), and they became hallmarks of the royal courts (and noble houses) of later times too. In Ottoman Turkey, Mughal India, Ming and Qing China, and Safavid and Qajar Iran, eunuchs dominated the court, working as body servants, administrators high-ranking officials, and members of the military (Lal 1988; Peirce 1993; Tsai 1996, 2002). Certainly, eunuchs were still to be found in the Middle East in the nineteenth century, and well into the opening decades of the twentieth century too. However, although it was calculated that no less than 8,000 eunuchs a year were imported into Arabia, Turkey and Egypt from other countries of the Middle East in 1890, by the 1930s N.M. Penzer (1936: 43), who made a pioneering study of eunuchs and the Ottoman harem, was only able to trace one or two of these 'strange beings' (as he termed them) in the whole of Turkey. Castration did not bar eunuchs from access to court positions; it facilitated employment. It would seem odd to write Achaemenid eunuchs out of a world history of castrati or to consider them 'outsiders' in courtly culture. Puzzlingly, this is Maria Brosius' approach in her study *Women in Ancient Persia* (1996) and Lenfant's more recent exploration of eunuchs in Ctesias' work too (2012).

According to Greek reports (where we clearly see the Greeks trying to come to terms with an alien practice), the Persians valued eunuchs for their honesty and loyalty, since the process of castration made men, like gelded horses and dogs, docile and more malleable (Hdt. 8.105) and Xenophon unambiguously affirms that Cyrus the Great had first introduced eunuchs into his guard for just this reason – although in reality this cannot be qualified (*Cyr.* 7.5.60–4). Herodotus recounts an interesting tale of how a Greek-speaking youth, Hermotimus of Pedasa, was captured and sold to the slave-dealer Panionius who specialized in trading beautiful boys to elite customers in Asia Minor, having first castrated them. Hermotimus subsequently found himself at the Persian court where he quickly caught the eye and gained the favour of Xerxes who charged him with the privileged and trusted task of tutoring the children of the royal harem (Hdt. 8.103–5; see Hornblower 2003). Herodotus further ascertains (3.92) that Babylon was required to send the Great King an annual tribute of 500 boys who were to be castrated and turned into eunuchs and by implication it is possible that the five boys he mentions being sent every three years from Ethiopia and the 100 boys sent by the Colchians to court as tribute were castrati also (Hdt. 3.97). There may be truth in Herodotus' report (certainly human tribute was demanded in Ottoman, Safavid and Qing times). Herodotus also points out that at the suppression of the Ionian revolt, the Persians emasculated the prettiest boys they captured and shipped them off to Iran (Hdt. 6.9, 32). It is possible that the beardless youthful-looking servants depicted on some of the doorjambs at Persepolis are eunuchs, perhaps the young castrati sent to Persia as tribute (**Figure 1.103**) but this is by no means certain (Olmstead 1948: 314; Cook 1983: 136; on the physical repercussions of castration see Bullough 2002). He is elegantly dressed in a long court robe; his hair is twisted into tight curls and caught into a small *chignon* at the nape of his neck; a fillet or metal headband crowns his head. The eunuch's face is smooth, clean-shaven and youthful; his eyes are wide and alert and his mouth extends into a serene smile. His presence on the doorjamb confirms the idea that the rooms beyond this doorway were given over for the private uses of the king and his immediate family. All in all, some six eunuchs are depicted in the Persepolis reliefs, often (but not always) accompanied by a bearded official who is no doubt meant to contrast with the eunuchs' smooth effeminacy. The eunuchs frequently carry towels, ointment jars, parasols and flywhisks, all of which allude to their roles within the close entourage of the king and, perhaps, the women of the harem.

Figure 1.103 Stone relief sculpture of a eunuch; palace of Darius, Persepolis.

Perhaps it is more logical to accept the presence of genuine castrati at the Persian court and we need not look for excuses to exonerate the Achaemenids of the practice of castrating boys and men. It is also hard to tell how many eunuchs were employed at the Persian court or within the royal harem at any one time, but even in the fragments of Ctesias there are at least sixty. If we accept the logical presence of bona fide eunuchs within Persian society then we can note that some of them clearly rose to positions of high influence, prestige and outright power at court. The roles eunuchs played at court were as diverse as they were complex. Ctesias (probably using authentic Iranian sources for his history) begins his examination of each successive Great King's reign with a kind of litany which lists the key eunuchs at court and implies that their names and deeds were remembered for generations after their deaths alongside the monarchs they served:

> Artasyras, the Hyrcanian, held the greatest sway with him (Cambyses II), and of the eunuchs Izabates, Aspadates and Bagapates were influential: the latter was also influential with Cambyses' father …
>
> (Ctesias F13 §9)

> So Ochus, who was also called Darius (II), ruled alone. There were three eunuchs who held sway with him: the foremost was Artoxares, second Artibarzanes and third Athöus.
>
> (Ctesias F15 §51)

If we follow the fourth-century Greek sources then we are alerted to the preconception that from the end of the reign of Xerxes, eunuchs began to acquire increasing power at court and that they routinely entered into plots and even became involved in regicide (see comments on **2:21 Bigthana and Teresh**). But how much of this can be taken at face value is difficult to know, given the Greek penchant for using eunuchism to disparage Persian values and traditions.

Neither male not female, the eunuch was considered to be genderless or, at least, gender-fluid. The eunuch therefore gained the privilege of being able to occupy simultaneously the public world of male politics and the private world of female society. The eunuch became the vital connection between the outer court and the inner court. In Esther, eunuchs negotiate their way between the public worlds of men and the private worlds of women. As has been stressed by Keith Hopkins (1963, in a Late Roman context that works for Persia too), the constructed fluidity of movement from outer court to inner court resulted in an increase in power wielded by ambitious eunuchs, even within the harem, and the eventual rise of the phenomenon of eunuch 'king-makers'. In the hectic world of the court, eunuchs provided the ruler with a way to cope with the demands of his office, and to keep him in touch with the two worlds of the public and the domestic, whose spheres of interest often overlapped and sometimes clashed. In the Achaemenid court institution, eunuchs were both necessary and insignificant. The eunuchs of Persia depended for their survival upon the favour of the king. If they managed to serve him well, then the rewards could be great – wealth, high rank and access to the person of the king himself. But with power came the risk of vice, of abrupt demotion, and of execution, a theme which permeates the book of Esther.

1:10 Mehuman, Biztha, Harbona, Bigtha, Abagtha, Zethar and Karkas

The Hebrew versions of the names of Xerxes' seven eunuchs have attracted considerable debate, much of it revolving around the issue of the dating of Esther. D.N. Freeman (cited in Moore 1971: 9) argues that 'If these names were mere creations without historic verisimilitude, then the case for a Hellenistic date [for Esther] would be advanced thereby. In other words, if they were a second-century composition, one might naturally expect there to be anachronisms and plain errors of this kind'. His observation that there is a total lack of Greek influence in the names establishes for him a secure Persian-period date for the book. Berlin too finds the Persian-sounding names convincing, 'although whether they are authentic is not clear' (2001: 13). She makes the pertinent observation that on the Greek stage, playwrights sometimes gave their Persian characters fake Persian-sounding names and that this might be happening in Esther too. Yamauchi, however, comments on 'the care that the Hebrew scribes exercised in transmitting such foreign names' (1990: 238). Gindin (2016: 67–72) argues that the names of the eunuchs have solid Iranian etymologies:

(a) Mehuman = Vahumanah (Av. *vohumanah*), 'good thought', the name of one of the seven celestial beings in the Iranian pantheon. In Middle Persian, the name is found as Bahman. Yamauchi (1990: 238) argues for the presence of the name in PF 455 as 'Mihimana'.
(b) Biztha = Bagazāta, 'born of the god' or, perhaps better, from OP *besteh*, 'bound'. For Yamauchi (1990: 238), the name is found in PF 1793 as 'Bakatanna'.
(c) Harbona = Harvona (Av. *Xwarnah*), 'glory', 'splendour'. It might have a less grandiose meaning, linked to NP *kherbân*, 'donkey-driver'.
(d) Bigtha = Bagadāta, 'god-given', 'whose law is divine', or 'gift of god'.
(e) Abagtha = the same name as 'Bigtha'/Bagadāta, but with a prefix. The estimated meaning is 'law received from god'. Alternatively, it derives from Av. *gabata*, 'fortunate one'.
(f) Zethar = Zaθura (Av.), the name given to a libation poured into water. In Middle Persian the name morphs to *zōhr*, and in New Persian it is *zūr*, 'power'. However, the name might be reflected in the MP *zaitar*, 'conqueror'.
(g) Karkas = Kahrkāsa (Av.), 'vulture' (New Persian *karkas*). Yamauchi (1990: 238) argues that the name is to be located in PF 10 as 'Karkiš'.

It can be safely argued that the author of Esther had knowledge of some Persian names (see further Duchesne-Guillemin 1953; Gehman 1924; Mayrhofer 1973).

1:11 royal crown

Very few images of queens are preserved from the Achaemenid period, yet when they do appear they all wear crowns or other types of diadems. In Near Eastern antiquity, as in later times and places, the crown signified some kind of state of honour or dignity for those who wore it. The Heb. *ăṭārâ* is generally used in the bible to refer to a piece of jewellery symbolizing leadership. Envisaged as golden (2 Sam. 12:30; 1 Chron. 20:2), it is sometimes parallel to flower garland (Prov. 4:9). Indeed, Egyptian crowns were often embellished with a garland motif, some are in gold with flower medallions. The Nimrud ivories too show possible metal crowns with a series of rosettes. From excavations, such as at Megiddo, a type of frontlet tied in back and having rosettes and pomegranates has been found. It could be a rendition in gold foil of a garland with flowers and fruit. Vashti's royal crown (Heb. *keter malkhut*) is not described. The term is unique to Esther (see also 2:17 and 6:8), but is probably reflected in the post-biblical semitic root **ktr*, 'to encircle', as well as the Gk. *kitaris*.

Figure 1.104 Fragmentary Neo-Assyrian relief depicting a queen wearing a mural crown. From Nineveh.

The most common Achaemenid female crown, however, did not contain floral motifs. It was the so-called 'mural crown' which apparently represented a city wall, with square towers. It is a design well attested outside of Iran in the Neo-Assyrian period, where it was worn by Assyrian queens (**Figures 1.104, 1.105**), and was known too in Elam. The Assyrian type crown is well-fitting on the head, so that the upper part of the head protrudes from the upper edge of the crown, which is decorated, at regular intervals, by towers, probably square, standing on a triple base line, and with crenellated tops protruding from the upper edge of the crown (Gansell 2014a: 411; Stol 2016: 43; Svärd 2016: 131; Pinnock 2018).

Figure 1.105 Detail of the head of the wife of Ashurbanipal, showing her wearing a mural crown. From Nineveh.

The Achaemenid variation is taller, unembellished, and sits higher up on the head (**Figures 1.106, 1.107**). It is less diadem-like than its Assyrian counterpart and sits on top of a curled short 'bob' hairstyle or in combination with a veil. A tiny scrap of woven tapestry found at the periphery of the Achaemenid empire in a frozen tomb at Pazyryk, which can be dated to the late fifth century or early fourth century BCE (**Figure 1.108**; Brosius 1996: 85; Rudenko 1970: 296–7, pl. 177; Scarce 1987: 34, pl. 9; Henkelman 1995–6: 289), confirms

Figure 1.106 Egyptian-blue miniature head of a Persian woman, boy or eunuch wearing a crenellated crown. From Persepolis.

the importance of the veil in Achaemenid elite society. The repeated design, shown also in reverse, depicts women standing near an incense burner, perhaps in an act of worship. The small figure at the rear wears a mural-crown on top of her bobbed hair, but the figure at the front, the hierarchically more important position, who is rendered on a larger scale, wears a turret-crown over which is draped a long veil, reaching to the back of her knees. It is

Figure 1.107 Flat gold metal sheet in the form of a crowned woman; Achaemenid period, discovered close to the Oxus River.

Figure 1.108 Detail of a textile fragment representing Achaemenid women; from the Crimea.

woven with a decorated edge, the pattern of which – a series of coloured triangles and dots – is echoed on her large robe. The long veil gives a visual authority to the leading woman, adding a sense of superiority to her position. It suggests that at the Persian court female hierarchy was codified through the visuality of dress and that rank was encoded through appearance.

It is hard to know whether all crowned women in the rare depictions of women we have from Achaemenid Persia should be regarded as royal. A woman represented on a grave stele from Daskylion in Anatolia, for instance, is seated on a couch next to her husband; she wears a tall mural crown (in this instance partly covered by a veil). She is probably not to be regarded an Achaemenid princess although she borrows from Achaemenid fashion in her bid for a high-status representation (**Figure 1.72**). The image on the stele suggests that the Persian style of veiling had taken hold among the nobility of Cilicia. Unlike the Persian style, however, this Cilician noblewoman has tucked the veil behind her ears to show off her large hoop earrings to better advantage. While some wealthy rulers or nobles living on the peripheries of the Achaemenid empire may have aspired to be seen as cultured Persians and would have dressed accordingly, others retained a distinctive native or ethnic style. In fact, dress as an indicator of rank and nationality was obviously an important aspect of life for some settlers in foreign lands who were keen to hang onto their ethnic identities. Similarly, an Anatolian gold ring depicts a 'Persian' wearing a Greek-style linen *chitōn* (**Figure 1.109**). Her hair is dressed in a long plait, typical of the fashion in Achaemenid Anatolia, but her head is ornamented with a Persian-style mural crown. It is impossible to know if the woman is of royal status. Even if she was, is she of the Achaemenid royal house, or from the family of a local dynast?

1:11 her beauty ... for she was lovely to look at

Figure 1.109 Ring seal depicting a seated, crowned, lady with a bird. Achaemenid-occupied Asia Minor.

There are as many conceptions of beauty as there are cultures. Every society defines beauty, predominately female beauty, according to a set of commonly held criteria operating around the construction of gender, class and aesthetics which are specific to a time and a locale. In antiquity, we find societies accepting common shared ideals of beauty over a wide geographical and chronological framework, although we can also pinpoint more unique forms of beauty in almost all individual ancient cultures too. Most ancient societies accredited their gods with holding and extolling the ideals of beauty. Divinities by definition are beautiful: Innana's beauty radiates like the dawn, and Ishtar too, in a piece of divine self-promotion declares, 'at my appearance my glow is like the sun's'. The beauty of the gods is augmented by having shining skin, sometimes of gold, and hair of lapis lazuli. The goddesses of the Near Eastern pantheons are particularly prized for their beauty and a common mythological *topos* revolves around the male (mortal and immortal) desire to sexually possess and dominate the beautiful female. The male gaze falling on the beauty of goddesses is not without its consequences, however: goddesses may well revel in their looks, but the unsolicited ogling of a man invokes their anger and retribution. Beauty is desirable yet destructive.

Ancient texts often speak of beauty in abstract terms, employing rich metaphors and similes (usually drawn from nature) to evoke the qualities of beauty. Egyptian love songs of the New Kingdom offer a vivid set of examples: mouths are lotus buds, breasts are mandragoras, arms are branches and teeth are pomegranate seeds (Gardiner 1931). The biblical Song of Songs is clearly composed in the same tradition: eyes are doves, hair is a flock of goats, teeth are newly-shorn sheep, the neck is an ivory tower and the breasts are twin gazelle fawns (Fox 1985; Keel 1994). Sumerian, Assyrian and Babylonian descriptions of beauty tend to be less coy in eroticism (Leick 1994).

A cultural typology of beauty – that is, a classification based on 'types' specific to any given culture – needs to be applied to any attempt to analyse the aesthetic constructs of a social group. A modern, western, typology which describes beauty as dark, fair, black or white, or bodies as stocky, fat, obese, thin, skinny or underweight is value laden and therefore has limitations as a cross-cultural classification system (Gansell 2014a). Whilst any or all of these terms may carry negative associations in one society, in another culture they might be regarded as positives. As Amy Gansell (2014b: 28) has pointed out, 'In the Hebrew bible, female (and male) beauty is frequently referenced using ... modern translations ... including "beautiful", "fair", and "lovely". [These] only imperfectly capture the connotations and ambiguities of their ancient usage'. She notes too that in the bible, a woman's beauty is usually regarded as an asset, although it can expose her to dangerous situations, as is the case with Vashti (see also 2 Sam. 13:1-4).

Cultural typographies of beauty and the body clearly operated in antiquity. In India during the fourth and third centuries BCE, for instance, it has been noted that four traditional 'types' of female can be found in the iconography: 1) *padmini* or Lotus Woman, 2) *chitrini* or Art Woman, 3) *shankhini* or Conch Woman and 4) *hastini* or Elephant Woman (Degeorge 2013). Each female 'type' was characterized by certain physical attributes which placed them on a 'ranking scale' according to ancient Indian concepts of desirability, with the Lotus Woman being the most desirable and the elephant woman being the least. Remarkably these classic types of categorization still echo in current evaluations of women's appearance in modern India (Eicher and Evensen 2015: 286). Creating a typology that spans all physical types and cultural groups is difficult given that some typologies have limited usefulness within even a single society because of implicit gender or racial bias. Moreover, even in one period, such as the floruit of the Achaemenid empire, regional variations in cultural typologies become clear. In Persian-occupied Anatolia, for instance, glyphic art shows a very localized form of female beauty: the women are depicted with conspicuously large buttocks, which are given particular emphasis by the drapery of their robes (**Figure 1.110**; Llewellyn-Jones 2009a and 2010a). This steatopygic fatness is the most notable feature of the representation of women on Anatolian gems but is not attested in any of the representations of women elsewhere in the Persian empire.

Figure 1.110 Bulla depicting a woman in a linen court robe. Achaemenid-occupied Anatolia.

Can we get any other impression of a distinct Persian typology of female beauty? There are no contemporary Achaemenid texts that extol the virtues of the beauty of Persia's women, but Greek authors fixated on the subject. Persian queens are habitually tagged as 'the best-looking women in all of Asia'. When Plutarch (*Alex.* 21.6, 11) recounted Alexander's capture of the harem of Darius III after the Battle of Issus, he noted that

> The wife of Darius was said to be the most beautiful princess of the age, just as Darius was the tallest and most handsome man in Asia; their daughters inherited

their parents' looks ... When Alexander saw their beauty and stateliness, he took no more notice of them than to say, jokingly, 'These Persian women are a torment for our eyes!' He was determined to demonstrate his chastity and self-control by disregarding the beauty of their appearance – so he walked past them as if they were made of stone.

This same erotic charge emerges in Iranian Avestan religious texts – especially in a series of ancient hymns which praise the goddess Anahita's divine beauty as being 'fair of body, most strong' and as 'tall'. The lyrical catalogue of the goddess' charms focuses on her dress and body: 'her belt is tightened and her well-shaped breasts are defined ... wearing shoes up to the ankle, wearing a golden veil, and radiant.' In later Zoroastrian Pahlavi texts, beautiful women known as *dēn* (Av. *daēnā-* or female personifications of 'conscience') take on Anahita's appearance and lead souls of the righteous dead into paradise. Individual *dēn* are praised for being 'beautiful in appearance, well grown and full of virtue, with prominent breasts, with breasts jutting out, and with long fingers and a body as brilliant as her appearance' and as 'having white arms, strong, plump, of great stature, that is young and tall, with prominent breasts, delicate skin ... her body so beautiful as the most beloved of all creation' (see Agostini 2010). The image of the ideal Persian beauty was promulgated throughout antiquity and was still to be found in the writings of al-Tabari on the histories of the Persian kings. Once, al-Tabiri claimed, when King Khosrow Parvez was asked to describe 'the best and most desirable women' (cited in Vahman 1985: 670), he answered without hesitation,

> The best is the girl in the age between childhood and adulthood, not too big, not too small, not too thin, not too fat, well-built, with a beautiful face, beautiful in all aspects, with an even forehead, with arched brows, almond-shaped eyes, well-proportioned nose. Her lips thin and red like rubies, her mouth small and her teeth like pearls, with a gracious smile, a rounded chin, an elegant neck, rosy cheeks, silken skin, jet black hair, wasp-waisted, breasts round like apples.

To judge from the artistic repertoire, the facial features of ancient Persian women shared the same stock features configured by artists throughout Mesopotamia. The female face is characterized as round ('moon-faced' was a term used in the Parthian period) with full, plump, cheeks. Eyes are large, noses are prominent and mouths are tiny and bud-like (**Figure 1.111**). Fleshiness was certainly thought beautiful, and artists carefully rendered double chins and dimples, as well as the Venus-rings of flesh-folds that circled the neck (**Figure 1.112**). A limestone half-round relief of an elite (royal?) woman adopting the 'hand-over-wrist' prayer-gesture, now in Brooklyn (**Figures 1.113, 1.114**;

Figure 1.111 Neo-Assyrian ivory furniture inlay depicting a female face. From Nimrud.

Figure 1.112 Neo-Assyrian ivory furniture inlay depicting a seated female. From Nimrud.

Goldman 1991: 88), renders her facial features fashionably round and full. Facial plumpness often signalled the presence of a curvaceous body. Given the multiple pregnancies and somewhat inactive or secluded lives of many aristocratic women in ancient Near Eastern societies, a tendency to run to fat was commonplace. But curvaceousness was not undesirable: Near Eastern art celebrates the beauty of the fleshy female figure. Fatness was thought to be the best feature of female beauty, the most desirable and beautiful stuff of all. When the Israelite women of Samaria are criticized by the prophet Amos for their luxurious lifestyles (4:1) he labels them 'cows of Bashan'. In other words, Amos conjures up an image of well-fed and beautiful aristocrats, albeit lazy wives.

In Achaemenid Persia the most common female body 'type' found in art might be called, by our standards, 'voluptuous'. In the artworks much of the viewer's attention is drawn to the breasts. The Brooklyn noblewoman has very full, rounded, breasts which are only accentuated by the positioning of her hands. The females depicted in the Pazyryk textile follow the same conceit. It can be noticed that the weaver has placed a disk on each woman's breast – this is not an attempt to show bare breasts, but can be interpreted as either a desire to show the shape of the nipple underneath the dress or indicate that the disk is part of the ornamented appliqué designs which regularly decorated court robes. A caryatid figure on an incense burner found at Amman similarly has

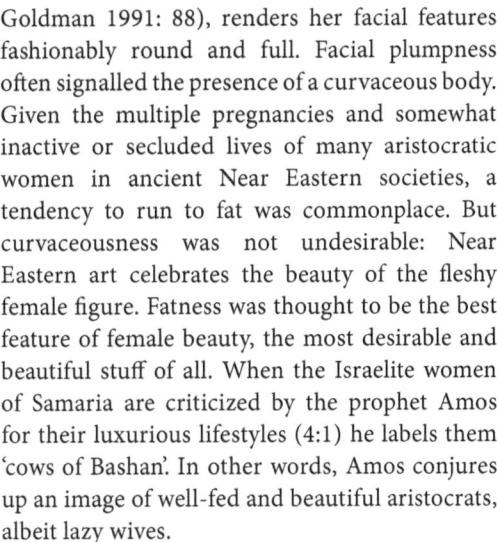

Figure 1.113 Limestone plaque depicting an Achaemenid woman in a court gown.

Figure 1.114 Limestone plaque depicting an Achaemenid woman in a court gown.

breasts which project, full and uplifted, from beneath her robe (**Figure 1.115**; Goldman 1991: 89; Khalil 1986). Two headless ivory figurines discovered in Achaemenid-era Phoenician Levant depict women with splayed hands who cup their breasts and raise them up (**Figures 1.116, 1.117**). One of the figures has indents on the breasts suggesting a nipple beneath the fabric, as might be portrayed on the Pazyryk tapestry. A more complete figuring, also from the Levant, but this time carved from bone, shows a woman in an Achaemenid-style court robe and an Egyptian-looking wig, supporting her breasts with her two hands (**Figure 1.118**). This motif of full and uplifted breasts has a central place in the art of the ancient Near East. Countless female idols are known adopting this position, as they lift up their breasts, as though offering them forward. Often called 'Astarte Figures' or 'Astarte Plaques' (although there is nothing to link them exclusively to this or any other goddess) the figurines confirm that breasts were

Figure 1.115 Detail of a bronze caryatid figure of an Achaemenid woman in a court gown and jewellery. From Jordan.

Figure 1.116 Ivory figurine of a woman in Achaemenid dress lifting her breasts; from Phoenicia.

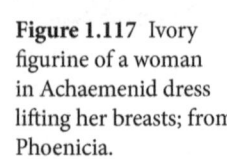

Figure 1.117 Ivory figurine of a woman in Achaemenid dress lifting her breasts; from Phoenicia.

Figure 1.118 Bone figurine of a woman in Achaemenid dress lifting her breasts; from the Levant.

Figure 1.119 North Syrian ivory figurine of a fertility goddess.

Figure 1.120 Egyptian First Intermediate Period wall relief depicting an emaciated woman.

powerful symbols of women's fertility, nourishing powers, and overabundance (**Figure 1.119**; Green 2019: 181–4, 193–6). The image of the shrivelled breast was, conversely, at once both disquieting and repulsive, signifying, in some instances, divine punishment (**Figure 1.120**; Hos. 9:14). The Achaemenid Phoenician ivory figurines are part of a long Levantine tradition, but in southern Mesopotamia the theme can also be located in the many hundreds of terracotta figurines and plaques that have been unearthed. Elam in particular has yielded significant numbers of naked females, often with extenuated pubic triangles and thighs, in which the cupped breasts are further emphasized with the addition of a *baudrier* – a

Figure 1.121 Clay mould figurine of an Elamite fertility goddess; from Susa.

Figure 1.122 Stone relief of a woman in Achaemenid dress with a flower; from Phoenicia.

Figure 1.123 Clay plaque of a woman in Achaemenid dress lifting a breast; from Phoenicia.

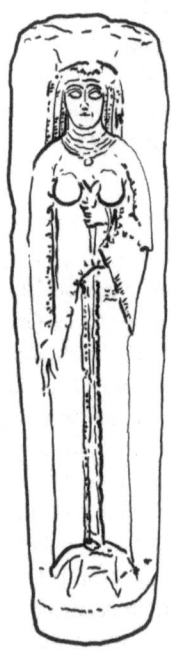

Figure 1.124 Clay plaque of a woman in Achaemenid dress holding a flower; from Phoenicia.

textile or leather harness decorated with shells or jewellery which criss-crosses between the breasts (**Figure 1.121**; Daems 2018). However, during the Achaemenid era, female fertility figurines eschew nakedness all together and stay strictly clothed (**Figures 1.122, 1.123** and **1.124**). Thus, the Persian form of the 'Astarte Plaques' articulate the concept of abundance from within the all-concealing garment worn by high-ranking Persian court ladies. This particularly Achaemenid take on the old Semitic-style fertility motif can be located too on a series of perfume flasks in the shape of women where either both breasts are offered or a single breast is lifted as if to offer succour (**Figures 1.125, 1.126**). However, the image of the naked female breast, indeed, the naked body, is completely unknown in Achaemenid era iconography. In Achaemenid Iran, feminine beauty was expressed through clothes as much as through physical attributes.

Figure 1.125 Bronze cosmetic container in the shape of a woman in Achaemenid dress.

Figure 1.126 Terracotta cosmetic container in the shape of a woman in Achaemenid dress.

1:12 Vashti refused to come

As Jo Carruthers (2008: 61) has rightly noted, 'Vashti fascinates her readers'. Queen Vashti has been criticized for her loose morals and championed for her feminist opposition to the patriarchy. Her disobedience is not explained in the bible, but it has been interpreted as pride, foolishness, modesty and immodesty, virtuousness, bravery, brazenness and even madness (Carruthers 2008: 67–83). The only way to understand the story is to place it into its historical context, as Macchi (2018: 99) understands: 'Her summons requires her to choose between two contradictory obligations – the rules of etiquette prevent her from appearing, but the king's order compels her to go'.

Vashti's rebuff of the king's orders brings about her swift downfall in a story reminiscent, in many ways, of the themes in the Herodotean tale of Gyges and Candaules' wife (Hdt. 1.8) and the story of Amyntas, a Macedonian nobleman who entertained his Persian guests by instructing his (usually sequestered) wives to sit with his guests and entertain them as they got drunk. The Vashti episode finds further reflection in the Greek account of Aspasia, the much-loved concubine of Prince

Cyrus the Younger. Aspasia of Phocis was renowned for her breathtaking, god-given, beauty: 'of hair yellow, locks a little curling', her admirers lyricized, 'she had glorious eyes, delicate skin, and a complexion like roses … Her lips were red, teeth whiter than snow … Her voice was sweet and smooth, that whosoever heard her might justly say he heard the voice of a Siren' (Plut. *Per.* 24.11; *Art.* 26.5–9; see also Ael. *HV.* 12. For an exploration of the story see Brulé 2003: 198–203; for further details see Llewellyn-Jones 2002: 36). She was also known to be pure-minded, modest and determinedly, resolutely, categorically, chaste. She had been delivered to Cyrus as a war-captive, one of many virgins who were gifted to him from the campaigns in Ionia. He desired ornaments for his harem, and accepted the young women as concubines. Aspasia was presented to Cyrus one evening, after he had enjoyed a good supper. He went off to drink with his companions, as was usual in Persian high society (drink was enjoyed only after a meal had been consumed), and during the drinking bout, four of the Greek girls were brought to him. Aspasia was among them. When they came into Cyrus' presence, three of the girls smiled and blushed appropriately but Aspasia kept her gaze on the ground, her eyes full of tears. When Cyrus commanded them to sit down by him, the rest instantly obeyed, but Aspasia refused, until a eunuch pushed her down by force. When Cyrus touched their cheeks and fingers and breasts, the three girls responded willingly. But when he approached Aspasia, she wept, saying that her gods would punish him for his forwardness. As Cyrus reached across to grasp her breast, Aspasia rose up, and would have fled the scene had not the eunuch stopped her and forced her back into her seat. Cyrus was hooked. On the spot he declared her to be his chief favourite and made her a concubine of the highest rank. She was escorted into the harem and provided with a private chamber of superlative quality, such as might be given to a royal consort.

The Greek sources are united in confirming that the women of Persia did not drink with their husbands. While it was all very well for concubines and slave girls to appear at male drinking parties, the appearance of high-ranking women in such company would be thought very improper (Plut. *Artax.* 5.3; *Mor.* 140b). In the ancient Near East, as in parts of Greece, a high-ranking woman felt no honour in being put before the public view (Llewellyn-Jones 2003: 155–214). Authority and prestige lay in a woman's removal from the overt public view and in her separation from the gaze of strangers. This was certainly the case among high-status women where numerous social conventions (including veiling and the demarcation of space) ensured their public invisibility and thereby boosted their sense of honour and, simultaneously, the honour and status of their male kin. In Persia it was important for the status and honour of Achaemenid royal women that their public invisibility was publicly demonstrated.

The play on visibility and honour and shame would help explain the complete absence of the human female form in the official palace art of the Persian empire (it has already been noted that women are rarely depicted in Achaemenid art and then are only represented in small-scale art works, although sometimes of precious and semi-precious materials; see Brosius 2010a and Llewellyn-Jones 2010a and 2010b). Women were not readily looked upon in real life so as to augment and ensure their social honour and they were not viewed in large-scale artworks for the same reason. The high social rank of royal females, like that of the Great King himself, was stressed by their conspicuous invisibility (which is not to be confused with seclusion or lack of authority). While we should not necessarily believe Plutarch's exaggeration that Persian women were locked away behind doors (*Them.* 26.5), his reports (and those of other Greeks) of women travelling in curtained carriages (Gk. *harmamaxae*) is certainly believable and gives us a sense of how the Persians conceived of elite women's public life.

The *harmamaxa* was a deluxe four-wheeled 'chariot-wagon' composed of an enclosed box, long enough to recline in, which was richly upholstered and decorated with hangings. It was a vehicle supremely suited to transporting women and it was used by Persians for 'shuttling their harem about' (Oost 1977/8: 228) and perhaps it was this type of vehicle that was provided for a group of women called (Elam.) *dukšišbe ... puhu Mišdašba pakbe*, 'royal ladies ... girls, daughters of Hystaspes' who are recorded travelling from Media to Persepolis in PFa 31 (Brosius 1996: 93). When the king travelled with his court and set up camp, the *harmamaxae* could be placed together to produce a harem wing on wheels (as suggested by Hdt. 9.76; see Miller 1997: 51). That Artaxerxes II's main consort, Stateira, had a *harmamaxa* which often appeared with its curtains open, in order that the young queen might greet the women of the empire, is highly unusual: 'What gratified the Persians the most was the sight of ... Stateira's carriage, which always appeared with its curtains up, and thus permitted the women to approach and greet the queen' (Plut. *Artax.* 5.6). Plutarch (*Mor.* 173f) also says that Artaxerxes encouraged his wife to do this. Certainly, her imperious mother-in-law, Queen Parysatis, regarded Stateira's eccentricity as a breach of court protocol and an affront to decorum. In this respect, the king's mother is probably more in accord with orthodox royal conceptions of female visibility. Interestingly, Persia's royal concubines operated in this sphere of high-status invisibility as well. Plutarch (*Artax.* 27.1) records that the Persians 'are very jealous, especially about anything that pertains to love-lives, so that it is death for anyone merely approaching and touching a royal concubine, but even when somebody, during a journey, overtakes or crosses the path of the *harmamaxae* in which they are transported, he is punished with death.' Xenophon (*Hell.* 3.1.10) recalls that Mania, the extraordinary female governor of Dardanus in Achaemenid-occupied Asia Minor, a dependant of the satrap Pharnabazus, watched and even commanded battles from the protection of her curtained wagon. This demonstrates best of all the way in which women participated very actively in society while retaining a sense of harem.

The high rank of Persia's royal females, like that of the Great King himself, was stressed by their conspicuous invisibility. This is the key needed to unlock Vashti's story. If there is a judgement to be made on 'correct behaviour', then Xerxes needs to be the focus of the investigation, for it is he, not his consort, who breaks the social conventions. Drunk with wine and power, Xerxes makes a tremendous mistake in instructing Vashti to leave the women's quarters to display herself to the public male gaze. His command is dishonourable. It shames him, his consort and his household. It is shocking in its inappropriateness. Xerxes should never have voiced such an egregiously tasteless directive. Vashti maintains her dignity as she preserves her invisibility within the court of women, but Xerxes loses his honour in the endless overflowing golden goblets of wine.

1:12 the king became furious and burned with anger

Xerxes' anger was a popular literary trope. Herodotus' description of Xerxes' anger in the face of a storm which prevented his soldiers from crossing the Hellespont and entering Europe is infamous (Hdt. 7.21):

> Xerxes flew into a rage and he commanded that the Hellespont be struck with three hundred strokes of the whip and that a pair of foot-chains be thrown into the sea ... He also commanded the scourgers to speak outlandish and arrogant words: 'You hateful waters, our master lays his judgement on you thus, for you have unjustly punished him even though he's done you no wrong! Xerxes the king will pass over you, whether you wish it or not! It is fitting that no man offer you sacrifices, for you're a muddy and salty river!'

In Esther, the king's wrath is of a similar magnitude (and is described in doublets). The Heb. *yiqṣōp* and *bā'ara bō* give onomatopoeic resonance to the spluttering anger brewing up inside him. Xerxes anger wells up later in the book too, and it is royal rage which brings about Haman's death (Est. 7:7). The anger motif crafts Xerxes as an impulsive individual, driven too much by his emotions. It is the antithesis of the mindset lauded by Achaemenid monarchs in their inscriptions, the touchstone of which is carved into the façade of the tomb of Darius I at Naqš-i Rustam. In his personal credo, Darius asks its readers to 'make known what kind of man you are', and goes to some length to articulate his own conception of self: 'I am not hot-tempered. When I feel anger rising, I keep that under control by my thinking power. I control firmly my impulses' (DNb §2b). Darius liked to portray himself as a rational and considered monarch who never acted in haste or in panic. It was his sheer force of personality that guaranteed his subjects received the benefits of his considered and learned judgements. Darius would have been disappointed with the biblical Xerxes' recourse to anger. It was un-kingly and decidedly un-Achaemenid. In Esther, Xerxes' inability to assuage his own anger leads him to dark places.

1:13 it was customary for the king to consult experts in matters of law and justice

(i) Advisors

As noted above (see comments on **1:3 nobles and officials**), Achaemenid kings frequently consulted their most highly favoured courtiers in matters of law and justice (Heb. *dāṯ* and *dīn*). They 'were closest to the king' (Est. 1:14), which might be better rendered as 'they were privileged to see the king's face', that is to say, they got to enjoy private discourse with him. While some high-ranking courtiers no doubt often saw and spoke with the monarch, for most members of court the king was inaccessible, and seeing and speaking to the sovereign was tightly controlled. Courtiers had to follow certain formulations of etiquette and most would not have dared to speak directly to their sovereign (the king however could permit a courtier to speak and express an opinion, see Neh. 2:1-6, 8).

Texts from across the ancient Near Eastern world speak of the ardent desire of courtiers to behold the faces of their monarchs. The Assyrian Bel-ibini, far away from court in one of the western provinces, for instance, writes to King Ashurbanipal earnestly professing how 'I long for the sight of the king my lord, that I might see the face of the king my lord' (cited in Tomes 2005: 82). The governor of Calah addresses the same ruler, imploring, 'Let an order be given to the Palace Overseers ... Let them allow me to see the face of the king, my lord, and may the king look at me' (cited in Tomes 2005: 82). Some individuals, regularly admitted into the royal presence, come across as smug, as demonstrated in a tomb-inscription of Ineni, a favoured courtier of the New Kingdom pharaoh Thutmose II: 'I was a favourite of the king in his every place; greater was that which he did for me than for those who preceded (me). I attained the old age of the revered, I possessed the favour of seeing His Majesty every day' (Breasted 1906: II §117; see further Tomes 2005: 81). Courtiers who regularly served in the royal presence were therefore to be congratulated: 'Happy is the man whom you have chosen to approach you/And to live in your court!' (Ps. 65:5); 'Happy are they who live in your house/Who are always praising you!' (Ps. 84:5).

It is difficult to know if Achaemenid monarchs appointed nobles to specific roles on an official 'Privy Council' or 'Cabinet'; it was perhaps more of an *ad hoc* arrangement, much depending on the king's will and on the oscillating fortunes of the great noble houses of Persia. In Esther, Haman's story might well be a typical scenario. When Artaxerxes I ascended the throne after the assassination of Xerxes (in which he had played a major role), he undertook a series of pogroms aimed at his father's ministers and advisors. Artaxerxes reorganized the affairs of the empire in his own interests. He dismissed the satraps who were hostile to him and chose replacements from among his friends and supporters – those that seemed, to him, most able and most loyal. The removal of existing ministers and the appointment of new ones is only attested in relation to Artaxerxes I. No other Achaemenid monarch attempted to do so radical an act.

The so-called 'Constitutional Debate' found in Herodotus' *Histories* (3.80–2) has long been the subject of intense interest among Herodotean scholars. In it, Darius I, newly ascended to the Persian throne, sits in council with two of his closest nobles, Otanes and Megabyzus. Together they debate the various systems of rulership which Persia might adopt under its new ruler. They settle on unchecked sovereignty. Some hold that the debate is authentic, grounded in Persian sources traceable to the occasion while others aver that the passage is fictitious, whether Herodotus or another invented it (a summary of opinions is provided by Asheri, Lloyd and Corcella, 2007: 471–2). Although Herodotus asserts its authenticity (Hdt. 3.80.1; 6.43.3), he is actually engaging in an anachronistic fiction. Nevertheless, even if this particular debate never took place, the image of a Persian king in consultation with his advisors is certainly drawn from real-life practice. Likewise, the presence of the king's councillors in Esther makes much sense.

(ii) Law and justice

Achaemenid kings conceived of themselves as defenders and champions of law and justice. They had been invested with authority by the god Ahuramazda himself and as Great Kings by the grace of the god, they were put on the throne to ensure that justice prevailed throughout the empire. The OP term for the divine commandment, as well as the royal one, is *dāta*. It is one of the keywords of the Achaemenid royal inscriptions; it means, to all intents and purposes, 'law'. This word became the hallmark of the Achaemenid civic order, because *dāta* was nothing more than the expectation of loyalty (OP *arta*, 'truth') to the monarch. The OP *dāta* is sometimes more ambiguous though. For example, in a Persepolis tablet, it designates 'regulations' that the heads of government warehouses had to follow (PF 1980 and PF 1272: Elam. *dātam*). Nonetheless, the term *dāta* was borrowed by countless non-Iranian languages across the empire as local laws were adopted on an imperial level. In Babylon, for instance, the king's law was known as *dātu ša šarri*. In Esther, *dāta* appears nineteen times to refer to a court regulation (e.g., Est. 1:8: wine reserved for the king) or to refer to an established custom (Est. 1:15: judgment of Esther) or to Xerxes' edict (Est. 1:19). Here the translation of *dāta* as 'law' (in LXX translated via the Gk. *nomos*) is perfectly appropriate.

It was Darius the Great who was instrumental in establishing Persia's law codes; he was particularly interested in legislation that had been formed in various parts of his empire in what he called 'the olden days'. Mesopotamia had a long and noble legacy of law-giving, stemming from the great Hammurabi of Babylon who around 1745 BCE codified a collection of 282 rules, established standards for commercial interactions, and set fines and punishments to meet the requirements of justice. Egypt too had established laws which had been in operation for millennia and, indeed, the verso side of a papyrus document known as the Egyptian Demotic Chronicle contains the copy of a decree from King Darius written in 519 BCE (cited in Johnson 1974):

> Darius made the chiefs of the whole earth obey him because of his greatness of heart. He wrote (to) his satrap in Egypt in Year 3, saying: Have them bring to me the scholars [...] They are to write the law of Egypt from olden days [...] The law ... [...] of the temples and the people, have them brought here ... He wrote matters [...] in the manner (?) of the law of Egypt. They wrote a copy on papyrus in Assyrian [Aramaic] writing and in documentary [demotic] writing. It was completed before him. They wrote in his presence; nothing was left out.

The laws of the Achaemenid empire reflect both continuity with the ancient legal traditions of Mesopotamia and Egypt, while being both creative and flexible enough to attend to changing circumstances and new apprehensions.

Achaemenid kings were not above the law. Rather, they were an integral part of it. They decided legal cases mostly in accordance with local circumstances on a case-by-case basis. The shrewd and diplomatic nature of their decisions, which often featured rewards more than punishments, resulted in a reputation for virtuousness. Darius emphasized his role as a fair judge in an inscription found on his tomb (DNb §2). Having the reputation for impartiality obviously mattered to him:

> What is right, that is my desire. To the man following the Lie I am not friendly … The man who co-operates, for him, according to the co-operation, thus I care for him; who does harm, according to the harm done, thus I punish him. It is not my desire that a man should do harm; moreover that (is) not my desire: if he should do harm, he should not be punished. What a man says about another man, that does not convince me, until I have heard the statement of both. What a man achieves or brings according to his powers, by that I become satisfied, and it is very much my desire; and I am pleased and give generously to loyal men.

Among the peoples of the empire, the Persian kings were generally characterized as fair and wise (Xerxes, together with Cambyses II, tend to be the exception to the rule). Judicial administration was ultimately under the authority of the king, and texts document his supervisory role. Although the king rarely adjudicated individual cases, they did rely on judges and officials to do so in his name. Ordinary judges were appointed from among the Persian nobility (often for life) and it was their task to arbitrate on any cases that came before them and to legislate as required.

1:14 Karshena, Shethar, Admatha, Tarshish, Meres, Marsena and Memukan

The list of names is perhaps a comic device which, as Berlin (2001: 16) proposes, 'increases the odds that the lists are playful devices, like the names of the seven dwarfs in *Snow White*'.

1:14 seven nobles of Persia and Media who had special access to the king

As noted above (**1:5**), seven was a highly symbolic number. The 'seven' mentioned here are attested too in Ezra (7:14) and Josephus (*Ant.* 11.31) who mentions 'the so-called seven houses of the Persians'. Plato held that Darius I had divided his empire into seven parts and governed it alongside seven Persian nobles. Darius had been one of seven conspirators who overthrew King Bardiya in a revolution that was to have a dramatic impact on the dynastic history of Persia: it paved the way for Darius' accession to the throne. According to Herodotus (3.70–3, 76–9) it had been agreed between the seven that those who had engineered the *coup d'état* had free access to the king without being formally presented unless, it was stipulated, the monarch happened to be having sex with one of his wives or concubines at the time. Any initial privileges which the co-conspirators had enjoyed were quickly revoked by Darius; and there is no evidence to suggest that they, or their descendants, were thereafter exempt from the rules of court protocol. Nevertheless, the presence of the 'seven' in Esther shows how the tradition of the seven great Persian houses lingered.

1:15 what must be done to Queen Vashti? ... if it pleases the king

A similar scenario is set up by Herodotus (3.31) when he narrates how Cambyses II (whom he crafts as an out and out madman) went against Persian tradition and enforced the legitimation of a breach of the law through the royal judges. The king, Herodotus claims, is intent on marrying one of his sisters and solicits his Privy Councillors for advice on how that might be brought to pass. Meekly, they tell him that the king's word is law and that if he wishes to marry his blood-kin then this would automatically become a legality. This reveals a specific feature of boundless despotism, which is constantly pointed out by Herodotus in the course of his exposition on Cambyses. In Esther, Memucan's advice to the drunk Xerxes has a similar ring to it. In both stories the kings are remarkably passive; it is the advisors who are the 'policy-makers'. This motif runs throughout Esther (see 2:2-4, 3:7-9, 5:14, 6:7-9). The vigour with which Memucan advocates the dismissal of Vashti from her role as queen suggests that he has perhaps plotted her fall for some time.

1:18 There will be no end of disrespect and discord

Memucan's scenario of an empire-wide women's revolt is the stuff of Greek comedy. Aristophanes' *Lysistrata* of 411 BCE, for instance, is set in an Athens in which male leadership has been replaced by that of women. The comic creates a world of terrifying topsy-turvydom in which women are responsible for the running and maintenance of the *polis*, like lunatics taking over the asylum. Heleen Sancisi-Weerdenburg has argued that the pernicious roles attributed by the Greeks to Persian queens were widespread literary cliché which endorsed the idea that women and power should not mix (Sancisi-Weerdenburg 1987a: 43, 38). Certainly, Plato's representation of the imperial women as the harbingers of royal degeneracy and the root cause of the inevitable decline of Persia's empire is representative of the wider Greek paranoia about, and misunderstanding of, the part played by Persian women in Achaemenid court society (*Laws* 694b–696a). Cruel, capricious and uncontrolled, the Greek image of Persian queens contributed to the emasculation of the Great King and, by extension, his empire.

1:19 if it pleases the king

A customary salutation when making a suggestion to the king. The result of good advice is the king's pleasure, a common *topos* in Near Eastern texts: 'And then it pleased the heart of His Majesty more than anything in this whole land' (Hallo 1997: I, 104); 'The woman pleased the heart of his majesty greatly and beyond anything. So her titulary was established as Great Royal Wife Nefrure' (Hallo 1997: I, 135).

1:19 which cannot be repealed

The idea that Persian laws cannot be revoked appears again at 8:8 and in Dan. 6:8, 9, 12. Fox (1991: 22) rightly speculates that 'it seems an impossible rule for running an empire'. Indeed it is. Such an inflexible law would be crippling to good governance, and there is no extrabiblical evidence for it. In fact, Great Kings are shown reverting decrees and orders. Darius I, for example, ameliorated his decree to execute the entire family of the nobleman Intaphernes and allowed his brother-in-law and eldest son to live (Hdt. 3.119; see also Plut. *Artax*. 27). Yet much in the fictitious plot of Esther revolves around the historically implausible farce that a royal decree once issued cannot be revoked.

1:19 Also let the king give her royal position to someone else

As noted at **1:9**, Esther encourages the reader to think of Xerxes as a one-woman-man. He is married first to Vashti and upon her repudiation, he takes Esther as his new wife. This picture of modest serial monogamy does not fit the norms of Persian or other Near Eastern royal marriage practices. Kings could have (and often had) numerous wives at one time, in addition to even more concubines. The monogamy of Xerxes suits the story of Esther, but it does not reflect the realities of the Achaemenid court.

It is difficult to know if a Persian king picked out a 'chief' wife – on par with the pharaonic Egyptian tradition of appointing a Great Royal Wife (*hmt nsw wrt*), who ranked higher than the other royal wives (*hmt nsw*; Robins 1993) or whether precedence in the Achaemenid harem pecking-order was negotiated on a more *ad hoc* basis. There does not seem to have been an official Persian title for a 'chief' wife, which suggests that it was not a recognized court position. Some historians have suggested that the reports of intrigues, factions and insurgences at the ancient courts are more literary motifs than authentic records of actual events (Briant 2002: 322), but it is more likely that the conservative nature of the courts themselves truly engendered repetitive actions on the part of frustrated courtiers. As Arthur Keaveny (2003: 123) astutely notes,

> Monarch after monarch was surrounded by thrusting officials and relatives. Given that this circumstance did not change we need not wonder if, in reign after reign, they led to the same ... consequences. It is the unchanging nature of court life over a long period rather than a *reprise de motifs littéraires* which led to the repetitious nature of the tales.

Within the female household of the royal palaces of the Near East, status was dependent upon gaining and maintaining the king's favour. One text, quite unparalleled in Neo-Assyrian history, shows a king, Sennacherib, clearly smitten by one of his wives: 'As for Tašmetum-šarrat ... my beloved wife, whose features [are] perfect above all women, I had a palace of loveliness, delight and joy built ... May she be granted days of health and happiness ... May she have her fill of well-being' (cited in Macgregor

2017: 85). Women who had an emotional or sexual hold on the king to this degree would have had (even if only temporarily) greater status than those who had no access to his heart or his bed, and therefore we can speculate how competition to attract and keep the king's sexual attention could be intense. The title 'favourite of the king', found with intermittent regularity in the Near Eastern sources, suggests that some women – but not *all* women – were recognized as having a particular significance in the king's affections. This, it seems, is true of both Esther and Vashti.

Love and sexual attraction aside, in the cut and thrust world of the court, it is increasingly clear that the position of a primary or favoured wife was not necessarily a stable one given that the king's affections might change, or rival candidates for his affection (perhaps championed by noble families) might arise and supplant his previous love. A king might show his preference for a particular woman by appointing her son as his heir. The new heir might be the son of a high-ranking consort, a lesser wife or of a concubine. As Zafrira Ben-Barak (1986: 93) is keen to emphasize, 'Women … had therefore covertly to plan and establish a sophisticated power-base … in their bid for power. To this end they gathered supporters to their … side from various political strata in the realm.' To all intents and purposes, it suggests that Vashti has no one to support her. As she slips from Xerxes' favour, so too the courtiers abandon her. They possibly even actively manoeuvred her downfall. When her turn comes to have her authority and position challenged by Haman, Esther is luckier. She had her uncle to look out for her and to advise her, so that she manages to maintain her position as a consort.

Rivalry was endemic at court. Palaces were dangerous places to be. A Neo-Assyrian text labels the royal court with its antagonistic (sometimes vicious) inhabitants as 'the lion pit'. A set of Sumerian proverbs (Alster 1997: I, 147) also explore this theme: 'A palace is a huge river; its interior is a goring ox … A palace is a slippery place where one slithers; If you say, "Let me go home!", just watch your step … A palace … is a wasteland. [As] a freeborn man cannot avoid corvée work, a princess cannot avoid th[is] whorehouse.'

The hub of dynastic and political life, the Achaemenid court was a hazardous locale, a stage on which the games intrigue, faction and revenge were played out with astonishing regularity (see Wiesehöfer 2010: 521–3). The tension of court politicking permeated every aspect of the royal household and few individuals were untouched by some form of intrigue. Court nobility was highly susceptible to political machinations and personal rivalries and the book of Esther demonstrates this clearly, based as it is on a story of destructive intrigue(s). Esther reveals that while courtiers were allied to holding office, the fact that 'every court job was temporary and could be transferred from one day to the next' (Briant 2002: 258) meant that courtiers feared for cherished posts which could be revoked at any moment, leaving them marooned within the competitive structure of the court. Of course, none of this was unique to Persia, for court societies of all periods have suffered from the strain of imposing and then maintaining power. Allowing for some differences of institutions, the Persian court was subject to the same kind of pressures which have afflicted the courts of absolute rulers down to the time of Stalin, or Kim Jong-un, or Donald Trump.

Vashti's final fate is not revealed. Over the centuries, divorce, exile and execution have all been proposed for her (Carruthers 2008: 88–9). In a genuine historical situation, it is possible that a rejected royal consort merely faded away into the background of the court. Maybe she was sent away from the main court to one of the king's many estates, or to her own landholdings. In the royal game of snakes and ladders, the king's women were the playing-pieces in the politics of the harem. As one woman fell from grace, another rose to the heights of favour, only – perhaps – to lose the king's favour herself. This scenario is played out many times in the ancient evidence. The many Persian women who were married at the mass-weddings of Susa in 324 BCE were soon repudiated by their Macedonian husbands in favour of Macedonian women. In the Hellenistic courts, Arsinoe I was passed over in favour of Arsinoe II, Laodice in favour of Berenice Phernophoros, and Amastris in favour of Arsinoe II (Ogden 1999). Divorce was unknown in royal contexts, but 're-grading' or 'demotion' was common.

1:19 enter the presence of King Xerxes

The honour of being in the presence of the king, to be seen and recognized by the king, is the ultimate mark of prestige at court. To be denied access to the king was social death. This is what Xerxes' rejection of Vashti means for the dishonoured queen.

We have seen how courtiers articulate the pleasure felt by many who bask in the presence of their sovereign's gaze (see comments on **1:13**). Most desperate of all is the plea of the Assyrian courtier Barhalza, located some distance away from his lord and master Esarhaddon in a province far west of Nineveh: 'Like sunshine, all countries are illuminated by your light. But I have been left in darkness; no one brings me to see the king' (after Tomes 2005: 81).

1:22 dispatches to all parts of the kingdom ... own script ... their own language ... native tongue (see also 3:12 and 8: 10 mounted couriers, who rode fast horses especially bred for the king)

(i) Dispatches

The smooth-running of the Persian empire was facilitated by an excellent infrastructure, the most sophisticated of any ancient civilization (Hdt. 5.52–4; Ctesias F 33; Xen. *Cyr.* 8.6.17–18). First-rate roads connected the main satrapal centres of the empire with the imperial core, thereby allowing kings a way to maintain control over conquered provinces. The most important of these highways was the Royal Road (Almagor 2020) which ran for a staggering 1,500 miles (2,400 kilometres). A major branch connected Susa to the cities of Kirkuk, Nineveh, Edessa, Hattusa, and Sardis in Lydia, which was a journey of ninety days on foot; it took ninety-three days to reach the Mediterranean coast at Ephesus. Another road from Susa, the eastern branch, was connected to Persepolis and Ecbatana and thence went onwards to Bactra and Pashwar. Yet another branch of this road steered west and crossed the foothills of the Zagros mountains, went east of the Tigris and Euphrates rivers, through Cilicia and Cappadocia and ended at Sardis, while an alternative route led into Phrygia. One more highway connected Persepolis to Egypt via Damascus and Jerusalem. The roads were all designed to interconnect with rivers, canals and trails, as well as ports and anchorages for sea travel. Together they made the Persian transportation system the wonder of the age. The roads were measured in 6-km (3.7-mile) intervals known as *parasangs*, and road-stations were set up around every 28 km (17.4 miles) of the route to accommodate weary travellers.

Similar to the great medieval caravanserais of the Silk Road, the Persian way-stations were composed of rectangular mudbrick and stone buildings with multiple rooms around a large courtyard affording accommodation for humans and pack-animals alike. It is estimated that around 112 way-stations existed on the main branch between Susa and Sardis alone, but there were many hundreds more set up on alternatives roads.

A fast and efficient postal relay system (OP *pirradaziš*, 'express runner', see PF 1285, perhaps from OI **frataĉiš*) connected the major cities of the empire (Hyland 2019: 151, n. 2, with further references). Fast communication of dispatches was the order of the day as the Persian bureaucracy demanded an efficacious and reliable communications channel. The result was that the Persians created the earliest form of the pony-express. Herodotus (8.98) enthusiastically reports its efficacy:

> There is nothing mortal that is faster than the system that the Persians have devised for sending messages. Apparently, they have horses and men posted at intervals along the route, the same number in total as the overall length in days of the journey, with a fresh horse and rider for every day of travel. Whatever the conditions – it may be snowing, raining, blazing hot or dark – they never fail to complete their assigned journey in the fastest possible time. The first man passes his instructions on to the second, the second to the third and so on.

Useful information about the Royal Road system comes from the Persepolis Fortification Tablets which record the disbursement of traveller's rations or provisions along the way, describing both their destinations and points of origin (Henkelman and Jacobs 2021). The 'travel ration' texts attest to the systematic criss-crossing of vast swathes of the empire by men and women on state business (delivering messages, money or goods) or conducting private affairs (honouring work contacts or attending religious ceremonies). The texts record the food rations which individuals received on their journeys. Three tablets (PF 1318, PF 1404 and PF 1550) confirm that individuals undertook journeys of enormous breadth – from India to Susa, Sardis to Persepolis and, strikingly, from Susa to Kandahar in Afghanistan:

> 11 BAR of flour Abbatema received. For his own rations daily he receives 7 BAR. 20 men received each 2 QA. He carried a sealed document of the king. They went forth from India. They went to Susa. 2nd month, 23rd year. Išbaramištima (is) his elite guide. The seal of Išbaramištima was applied (to this tablet).
>
> 4.65 BAR of flour Dauma received. 23 men (received) each 1½ QA. They went forth from Sardis. They went to Persepolis. 9th month. 27th year. (At) Hidali.

1 QA of wine (was) supplied by Karkašša. 1 woman went from Susa (to) Kandahar. She carried a sealed document of the king, and she received it. Zišanduš (is) her elite guide. 22nd year. 2nd month.

All roads were guarded and policed. They were kept safe for private individual travel by highway patrols stationed at regular points on all thoroughfares. Traffic police had the right to stop and search any lone traveller or caravan. Brigands, highwaymen and beggars met with heavy punishments, and their missing eyes or limbs were warnings to all potential thieves and petty criminals who thought to defy the good order of the king's law.

(ii) Script and language

The legal materials of the Achaemenid period were written primarily in either the Neo-Bab. dialect of Akkad. on clay tablets or in Aramaic on perishable materials, although a few extant clay tablets also hold some Aramaic dockets along with the cuneiform (Magdalene 2007). Additional materials may be written in the vernacular of a particular colonized region, such as the Demotic legal corpus in Egypt. Because a large quantity of the texts in Aramaic script from the centre of the empire has decomposed, we are left chiefly with cuneiform tablets. Thousands of such tablets exist from the reign of Cyrus through to the revolts of Xerxes' reign, when the major archives break off. A small amount of later cuneiform materials from Judahite communities in rural Babylonia survives (Alstola 2020) and so does the archive of the wealthy and influential Murašû family-bankers that are crucial to understanding later Persian law, edicts, decrees and other communications (Stolper 1985). It is very difficult to know if the cuneiform material is truly representative of Persian legislation in all geographic regions of the empire across the entire Persian period.

The Persians never forced their language on subject peoples. They preferred to utilize local languages for their decrees and they employed Aramaic as a form of *lingua franca* throughout the imperial territories to help facilitate effective – unbiased – communication. This ancient Semitic language had been widely in use throughout the Near East in the eighth century BCE and had been employed by the Assyrians as an effective method of international communication. The Persians used it as a language of diplomacy and administration so that it served the same purpose as Latin would later do in the Middle Ages. Diplomats and scribes were well-versed in Aramaic (it is not known if kings were even literate) and its efficacy as a bureaucratic tool can be seen in the fact that the language was still functioning in the Near East well into the Hellenistic period and beyond. Aramaic was easy to read and write (it was a fluid cursive script) and it could be scribbled in ink onto papyrus, wood, pot sherds, bone or other easily portable surfaces. For this reason, Achaemenid-period Aramaic documents have been discovered as far afield as southern Egypt and eastern Bactria (modern Tajikistan and Uzbekistan). At a local level it was often translated into the native language of the area. Scribes needed to be, at the very least, bilingual, a fact which is attested in the Persepolis tablets which record the presence of boys writing on parchment – which means they were writing in Aramaic – rather than in Elamite or Babylonian on clay. A document from Uruk dating to the fourth regnal year of Cyrus II confirms that a group of local craftsmen undertaking works on behalf of the king were addressed in Aramaic: *ina lišānišunu iqbū* ('spoken in their own language as follows'; see Weisberg 1967: 15). A decree sent by Darius I to the satrap Gadatas of Magnesia, concerning the affairs of the local temple of Apollo, was discovered carved into a marble stele. It is written in Greek, but was probably originally composed in Aramaic and translated, read out and inscribed in Greek for the benefit of the local population (Meiggs and Lewis 1988: 20–2, no. 12). Ezra (4:7) reports that the opponents of the plan to rebuild the Jerusalem Temple wrote a letter to Artaxerxes I in Aramaic to express their objection to the reconstruction of the city walls. The Great King replied, writing back,

> The letter you sent us has been read and translated in my presence. I issued an order and a search was made, and it was found that this city has a long history of revolt against kings and has been a place of rebellion and sedition. Jerusalem has had powerful kings ruling over the whole of Trans-Euphrates, and taxes, tribute and duty were paid to them. Now issue an order to these men to stop work, so that this city will not be rebuilt until I so order.
>
> (Ezra 4:18-21)

The king's reply suggests that copies of royal correspondence and decrees were kept in palace archives (Aram. *separ dokrānayyā'*, lit. 'book of records'; see further Ezra 6:1-2; Est. 2:23, 6:1). Our overall impression is that throughout the Persian empire peoples and communities operated (or had at least some capacity to operate) in more than one language. It is also certain that kings, satraps, army commanders and provincial governors all had official translators working in their service (Briant 2002: 507–10, 956).

Chapter 2

1 Later when King Xerxes' rage had abated, **he remembered Vashti and what she had done and what he had decreed about her.** 2 Then the king's **personal attendants** proposed, '**Let a search be made for beautiful young virgins for the king. 3 Let the king appoint commissioners in every province of his realm to bring all these beautiful young women** into the **harem** at the citadel of Susa. Let them be placed under the care of **Hegai**, the king's eunuch, who is in charge of the women; and let beauty treatments be given to them. 4 Then let the young woman who delights the king be queen instead of Vashti.' This guidance grabbed the attention of the king, and he followed it.

5 Now there was in the citadel of Susa a Jew of the tribe of Benjamin, named **Mordecai** son of Jair, the son of Shimei, the son of Kish, 6 who had been carried into exile from Jerusalem by Nebuchadnezzar king of Babylon, among those taken captive with Jehoiachin king of Judah. 7 Mordecai had a cousin named **Hadassah**, whom he had brought up because she was an orphan. This young woman, **who was also known as Esther, had a lovely figure and was beautiful.** Mordecai had taken her as his own daughter after her father and mother died.

8 When the king's order and edict had been proclaimed, many young women were brought to the citadel of Susa and put under the care of Hegai. Esther also was taken to the king's palace and entrusted to Hegai, who had charge of the harem. 9 She pleased him and won his partiality. Immediately he provided her with her **beauty treatments** and the choicest food. He assigned to her **seven female attendants** selected from the king's palace and moved her and her attendants into the best part of the harem.

10 Esther had not revealed her race and family background, because Mordecai had prohibited her to do so. 11 Every day **he walked back and forth near the courtyard of the harem** to find out how Esther was and what was happening to her.

12 Before a young woman's turn came to go in to King Xerxes, she had to finish **twelve months of beauty treatments** arranged for the women, six months with oil of **myrrh** and six with **perfumes and cosmetics**. 13 And this is how she would go to the king: Anything she wanted was given her to take with her from the harem to the king's palace. 14 **In the evening she would go there and in the morning return to another part of the harem to the care of Shaashgaz**, the king's eunuch who was in charge of the **concubines**. She would see the king again unless he was pleased with her and beckoned her by name.

15 When the turn came for Esther (the young woman Mordecai had adopted, the daughter of his uncle Abihail) to go to the king, she asked for nothing other than what Hegai, the king's eunuch who was in charge of the harem, proposed. And Esther won

the goodwill of everyone who saw her. 16 **She was taken to King Xerxes in the royal residence** in the tenth month, the month of Tebeth, in the seventh year of his reign.

17 Now **the king was attracted to Esther more than to any of the other women**, and she won his favour and liking more than any of the other virgins. So he set a royal crown on her head **and made her queen instead of Vashti**. 18 And the king gave a great banquet, **Esther's banquet**, for all his nobles and officials. He proclaimed a celebration throughout the provinces and distributed gifts with kingly munificence.

19 **When the virgins were assembled a second time**, Mordecai was **sitting at the king's gate**. 20 But Esther had kept undisclosed her family background and race just as Mordecai had told her to do, for she continued to follow Mordecai's directives as she had done when he was bringing her up.

21 During the time Mordecai was sitting at the king's gate, Bigthana and Teresh, two of the king's officers who guarded the doorway, became irate and **conspired to assassinate King Xerxes**. 22 But Mordecai found out about the plot and told Queen Esther, who in turn informed the king, giving full credit to Mordecai. 23 And when the report was investigated and found to be factual, the two officials were **impaled on poles**. All this was logged in the **book of the annals** in the presence of the king.

Commentary

2:1-2 he remembered Vashti and what she had done and what he had decreed about her ... personal attendants

The morning after the night before (the timing of 'later' is unspecified), Xerxes wakes, with a hangover, no doubt, and the events of the previous evening slowly come back to him. He realizes the gravitas of the situation. He has repudiated his principal consort (note that in this verse Vashti does not have the honourific 'Queen' attached to her name). The deed has been done and he sits in wonderment at his action.

An interesting anecdote recounted by Herodotus (1.133) says that the Persians were used to negotiating while in a drunken condition, but that the decision was later confirmed when they were sober, and vice versa:

> If an important decision is to be made, they [the Persians] discuss the question when they are drunk, and the following day the master of the house where the discussion was held submits their decision for reconsideration when they are sober. If they still approve it, it is adopted; if not, it is abandoned. Conversely, any decision they make when they are sober, is reconsidered afterwards when they are drunk.

The report is part of a repertoire of stereotypes about Persian wine drinking in the *Histories*. It cannot be taken as truth, of course, but it has certain literary resonances with the Esther story: decisions made in haste in the heady atmosphere of an all-male booze-up can have devastating repercussions. The court acted quickly and overnight Vashti has been quietly moved out of the palace. In Esther, however, there is no reassembly of the councillors who so fervently pushed the king towards dismissing Vashti from her queenship. Memucan, the mastermind behind Vashti's fall, is nowhere to be seen. To all intents and purposes, the Persian form of decision-making *in vino veritas* fails because no one is around to pick up the pieces and reopen the debate about Vashti's suitability to remain as queen. Xerxes may have 'morning after regrets' (Moore 1971: 25), but the imperial debating system has broken down and he is in no position to renege on his drunken pronouncement. As Proverbs warns, 'Better to be slow to anger than be mighty, to have self-control than to conquer a city' (Prov. 16:32).

Xerxes' personal attendants then step in. These are not the men of the banquet or the officials of Est. 1:13, but youthful pages or body-attendants, perhaps even young eunuchs. The Heb. *na'ra* and *šāratīm* evoke the types of personnel connected to the domestic quarters of the king's palace, especially to the royal bedchamber (the feminine forms are found in Est. 2:9; 4:4, 16 for the queen's personal attendants). 'The change of advisors', Macchi (2018: 120–1) correctly explains, 'underscores the organizational complexity of the Persian court and the rigidity of the positions everyone occupies'. It is this group of youngsters who save Xerxes further embarrassment and offer a solution, elaborately spelled-out, to his marital crisis.

Certain individuals with regular (and on the face of it) menial labour-tasks, like the boys of the king's chamber in Est. 1:3, were servants with a uniquely close access to the king (and even to the king's actual body in the cases of wardrobe officials, grooms, barbers and beauticians). Though they might be ignobly born, or even foreign castrati, these individuals had the potential to wield great power and influence, albeit informally and without official channels. Close access to the monarch not only meant the opportunity to importune a favour, but also implied to all onlookers that the privileged gainer of access had some kind of eminence. Tom Bishop (1998: 89) has perceptively noted that 'the court often functioned like a series of locked rooms, with those on the outside always trying keys, and those on the inside constantly changing the locks'. Throughout Esther the concept of an 'inner court' and an 'outer court' is of singular importance (see Est. 4:11; 5:1; 6:4). The Persian court can best be understood as operating around these two axes. The people who naturally orbited within the Great King's inner court were members of the royal harem – in other words those people who were under his immediate protection, including his mother, wives, concubines, sons and daughters, siblings and personal body-servants (including eunuchs). Nobles from the highest-ranking families of the realm, even those granted the honorific title 'Friend' of the king, bureaucrats and administrators, ambassadors and foreign visitors, physicians, and sundry other officials such as grooms and dog-handlers, all made up the outer court. The people of the inner-court had greater potential to influence the king because of their routine close physical proximity to the monarch and due to the amount of time they spent with the monarch in his 'down time' when he was more open to casual conversation and unsolicited advice.

2:2-3 Let a search be made for beautiful young virgins for the king. Let the king appoint commissioners in every province of his realm to bring all these beautiful young women

(i) 'Beauty Contests', storytelling and the Persian tradition

Scholars have been sensitive to the folk tale quality of Esther's structure and content (as they have been with the Joseph story of Gen. 37–50; Niditch 1987). The characters of Esther are drawn from a rich motif-index of stock-types: wicked villains, fair maids of humble origin who become princesses, wise councillors, ineffectual kings and banished, innocent, queens. As Niditch (1987: 127–8) comments, Esther's 'magic-like setting is plush with the trappings of court; servants, purple furnishings, fetes, food, and magnificent clothing. Its literary patterns follow well-worn models at generic, morphological, and typological levels, patterns found in the tales of Abraham, Jacob, and Joseph and sharing much with the tales of other cultures'. The Cinderellaesque structure of Esther, with its inherent rags-to-riches story, includes some very familiar fairy-tale motifs, such as a bride-finding quest and the concealed identity of the heroine (Anderson 2004; see further Thompson 1955–8: Motifs T91.6.2; T121.8). With very good reason, some scholars have suggested that these plot turns are based on ancient stories, perhaps specific Persian (or older) tales, which were borrowed and adapted by the Jewish author(s) of Esther (Bardtke 1963: 248–52; Bickerman 1967: 171–234, Dalley 2007; Grossman 2011 argues compellingly for a deeper Jewish meaning hidden behind the outward simplistic folkloric story of Esther, perhaps expressing a concealed contempt for the Persian authorities).

Alter (2015: 94) comments that 'the fairy-tale character of the story [of Esther] becomes especially clear' in the second chapter of the book. Many modern commentators have found it impossible to resist the urge to liken Xerxes' search for a virgin bride to *A Thousand and One Nights* (Arab. *'Alf layla wa-layla*; see Moore 1971: 26 and, especially, Silverstein 2018). They have good reason to do so. The well-known frame-story of the collection (best known in its final Arabic form) is that of King Šahriār's sexual exploitation of a different bride every night, who is thereafter dismissed and executed the following morning. It is the beautiful and clever Scheherazade who brings an end to the atrocities by capturing his imagination and his heart and winning for herself both her life and the queenship, while her father is rewarded with the post of vizier of the realm. The fable-like qualities which the *'Alf layla wa-layla* shares with Esther are notable (see esp. Est. 8:2, 15) and should not be dismissed lightly. There is clearly an element of folk tale at work here. It is possible that the *'Alf layla wa-layla* preserves a more original form of the Esther story, presented outside the frame of a religious text (de Goeje 1888). The oldest testimony to the existence of a collection of tales bearing the title *A Thousand and One Nights* is given by Mas'ūdī (d. 956 CE) who refers to work full of tales translated from Persian, Sanskrit and Greek, including the 'book entitled *Hazār afsāna*, or *The Thousand Tales*, because a tale is called in Persian *afsāna*'. Ebn al-Nadīm writes that the *Hazār afsān* is said to have been written for Princess Homāy, daughter and consort of the Sasanian shah, Bahman. In Iranian tradition she had a second name, Čehrāzād. Moreover, Homāy's paternal grandmother was called Esther (Estār), a fact that linked Bahman with the Children of Israel. Thus, a Čehrāzād/Scheherazade figures in the list of sovereigns attributed by a thousand years of tradition in pre-Islamic Iran. In another connection Masʿūdī refers to a certain Dīnāzād (in the Arab tales she is Scheherazade's sister), who also echoes Esther's story, since she is a captive Jewess, a spouse of Nebuchadnezzer, who promoted the return of the Jews to their homeland. The names of the three characters who play a key part in the frame-story of the *Alf layla wa-layla* are Iranian.

Šahrīār is a MP name (*šahr* + *dār*) which literally means 'holder of a kingdom, possessor of ruling power'. Čehrāzād, another MP name, is composed of *čehr*, 'lineage' and *āzād* (going back to Av. *āzāta*) and it came to mean 'noble' and 'exalted'. In Sasanian Persia, *āzād* referred to the nobility as a whole. Čehrāzād, therefore, means 'of noble lineage'. Dīnāzād is the MP *Dēnāzād, composed of *dēn* (Av. *daēnā-*), 'religious sensibilities' (and regarded as a goddess), and *āzād*. The name therefore means '[the goddess] Dēn [is] exalted.' Names with *dēn* appear elsewhere in MP, notably the Sasanian queen Dēnag mentioned in Šāpūr I's great inscription on the Kaʿba-ye Zardošt at Naqš-i Rustam. That the prologue and frame-story of the *Alf layla wa-layla* have a Persian origin cannot be doubted. Its relationship to the storytelling tradition out of which Esther was derived, though difficult to pin down with precision, is more than simply feasible.

The idea that the formative events described in Esther chapter 2 leads to a 'beauty contest' (De Troyer 1995: 50; Klein 1995: 157) – a quest to find the next Miss Persia – is compelling. But it is important to separate the beauty contest folk-motif from a genuine historical practice in which young (presumably fertile) women were conscripted into the imperial harem (see below (iii)). Ringgren (1981: 60) is surely correct to note that the beauty contest in a royal context is a 'standing motif' in myths, folk tales, fairy-stories (on which see Anderson 2000: 24–40) and romantic fiction. For instance, in Book 5 of Chariton's late Hellenistic novel, *Callirhoe*, the Greek heroine arrives in Persian-occupied Babylon, transported there in a curtained carriage. As she steps out, the Babylonians gawp at her beauty (*Cal.* 5.2). A group of aristocratic Persian women go to the royal harem and tell queen Stateira about the lovely Greek girl who has arrived in the city; they fear that the queen's reputation as the most beautiful women in Asia is under threat and so they decide to hold a beauty contest within the city (*Cal.* 5.3). However, since Stateira cannot show herself in public, a substitute, the Persian noblewoman Rhodogyne, is chosen to represent the queen by proxy. All Babylon witnesses the beauty competition. Callirhoe is declared the winner and at the end of the contest she retires to the seclusion of her covered wagon (*Cal.* 5.3) until King Artaxerxes commands his eunuchs to bring Callirhoe to his palace (for a discussion see Llewellyn-Jones 2013b). The Persian scenes in *Callirhoe* invite the gaze. The reader views the pageantry and splendour of Persia in its heyday, although it is an exotically fictionalized Persia of the imagination, a world in which all eyes are seduced into feasting upon the sights of the harem. In both *Callirhoe* and Esther, the image of the harem and of its beautiful 'chosen' women offer an 'open sesame' to a largely unknown, alluring world.

(ii) Virgins

The Heb. *bĕtûlâ* (which occurs fifty times in the Hebrew Bible) is translated 'virgin' in most standard translations of Est. 2:2, although the term actually has a more open meaning: 'girl of marriable age', 'girl past puberty', 'teenager' (Wenham 1972 and Wadsworth 1980). Of course, this does not suggest that the idea of virginity must be rejected; indeed, given the nature of Near Eastern society, the virginity of unmarried girls is almost a given. Cooper (2002) has concluded that Sumerian and Akkadian had no specific word to indicate a virgin since it was supposed that every girl was a virgin before her marriage. The Akkad. *batultu*, a close cognate of the Heb., has a general meaning of 'young, unmarried girl', and is not necessarily related to a physical state of being, although, tellingly, there is no masculine form of the noun. To show when a young woman was 'ready for a man', observations of her physical development became key. A Sumerian love song uses explicit language to state that her breasts have enlarged and that her pubic hair has sprouted (Wilcke 1985: 242). In Ug. the term *btlt* occurs as an epithet of the goddess Anat, sometimes wife or sister of El. The OP word is unknown, but the MP *dōšīzagīh* also implies the inherent virginity of an unmarried young woman; it is likely that any OP term had the same connotation. There is no word for 'virgin' in ancient Egyptian, but we should not suppose that Near Eastern peoples attached no value to the idea. However, the concept of *virgo intacta* had little hold in Near Eastern cultures.

Every use of *bĕtûlâ* in the Hebrew Bible is ascribed a specific role (eg. Gen. 24:16; Num. 31:18; Joel 1:8). In Esther, young women, virgins, are selected for the harem because of their promise of fertility. Chastity (but not necessarily virginity) immediately before marriage was expected in Near Eastern societies. A Babylonian woman testified before a temple official, for instance, 'My husband NN has taken me for his wife as a virgin (Babyl. *batūltu*)' – which in this context means that she was 'pure' (Babyl. *ellu*) and that she had entered marriage respectably, as a *batūltu* (Jursa 2008: 29). Pre-marital chastity was an essential prerequisite for entry into a royal harem, as the legitimacy of any offspring born to a king could be thought suspect (see Lev. 21:13 for chastity before marriage). The young women we meet in Esther, who had been corralled together and brought into Xerxes' harem at Susa, must have been closely watched by the eunuchs and female servants for any signs of pregnancy. It is for this reason, as much as for lessons in court etiquette and personal grooming, that the girls spent a full year within the harem of 'novices' before meeting the king for sexual congress.

The ugly story of the fate of the ten concubines of King David, who had been captured by his rebellious son Absalom when the prince stormed Jerusalem during his attempted *coup d'état*, is instructive of the way in which the chastity of royal concubines was of supreme importance (2 Sam. 15–20). Andrew Hill (2006: 135) suggests that the ten concubines were 'Jebusite … tokens of an alliance or treaty between David and the residue of the local regime in Jerusalem after its capture by David's mercenaries'. If so, then they were tribute gifts and consequently of political value to the crown. Following the Bathsheba scandal, God had threatened David with the promise that 'I will take your women before your eyes', and this was indeed brought to pass when Absalom decided to go 'in to his father's concubines in the sight of all Israel' (2 Sam. 16:22). The concubines themselves are violated by Absalom as part of a public spectacle, for it is on the rooftop of David's palace that the prince has congress with the girls. The concubines are soiled and contaminated by his penetration of their bodies, even though those bodies are not really their own, but the legal property of King David. Absalom's rape of the king's concubines is intended to strengthen his political standing as a would-be king and he is assured by Ahitophel's suggestion that if he goes 'in to [his] father's concubines … the hands of all who are with you will be strengthened' (2 Sam. 16:21). In the conventions of ancient Near Eastern royal protocol, the politics of David's marriages and alliances, and contemporary civil order, Absalom's sexual violation of David's concubines decimates every treaty, family tie, economic connection, political authority and relationship which is connected to these ten women. More appallingly, when Absalom's rebellion fails and David arrives back at 'his house at Jerusalem', the victorious king takes the ten concubines and puts them in a guarded space within the palace. David, we learn, 'provided for them, but did not go in to them'. In other words, he ceased having any social or sexual contact with them (2 Sam. 20:3a) and leaves the ten concubines 'shut up until the day of their death, living as if in widowhood' (2 Sam. 20:3b). In effect, the women become the living dead (see further, studies by Linafelt 1992; Kuhrt 2001b; Gaca 2011).

(iii) The sex-trafficking of women: war captives and tribute

Behind the folk tale beauty-contest veneer of Est. 2:2-4 there is a historical reality. In Persia, as in many other ancient (and later) societies, women were often presented to the monarch as a gift, as tribute or as chattel. Women were regularly acquired as war booty or were captured from rebellious subjects. Herodotus confirms that after quelling the Ionian uprising, 'the most beautiful girls were dragged from their homes and sent to Darius' court' (6.32; see also 4.19; 9.76; Plut. *Mor.* 339e) and the Persian practice of taking concubines as war booty is corroborated by a report in a Babylonian chronicle that following the Persian sack of Sidon in 345 BCE, Artaxerxes III transferred to his Babylonian palace large numbers of women (Glassner 2004: 240 no. 28):

> [Year] 14, Umasu, who is called Artaxerxes: In the month of Tashritu [11 October–9 November 345 BCE), [were brought] the prisoners of war which the king took from Sidon to Babylon and Susa. That month, day 13, some o[f them] entered Babylon. Day 16, the remaining women prisoners which the king sent to Babylon, that day they entered the palace of the king.

The Persian evidence finds a neat comparison in an inventory of female captives from Nineveh, dated to the latter part of the reign of Esarhaddon (Fales and Postgate 1992: 24). Women from different locales across the empire are all bound for the imperial centre:

> 36 Aramean women; 15 Kushite women; 7 Assyrian women, maids [of theirs]; 4 replacements …; [x] 3 Tyrian women; [n] Kassite women (break of some 4 lines) … [n] female Corybantes; 3 Arpadite women; 1 replacement; 1 Ashdodite

woman; 2 Hittite women and [n] [-ean] women: in all, 94 women and 36 maids of theirs. Grand total, of the father of the Crown Prince: in all, 140 (women) … [Furthermore] 8 female chief musicians; 3 Aramean women; 11 Hittite women; 13 Tyrian women; 13 female Corybantes (?); 4 women from Sah[…]; 9 Kassite women: in all, 61 female musicians.

Brosius (1996: 32) suggests that many of the captive foreign women who entered the Persian palaces came from families of high social status, although it is very difficult to verify that idea. The Egyptian pharaoh refused to send his daughter to Cambyses' harem for fear that she would be destined for servitude and not marriage (Ctesias F 13a).

The tale of Esther is therefore premised on the notion that imperial power could be translated into reproductive opportunities. The empire-wide hunt for suitably fertile, and preferably pretty, girls is a historical reality. Satraps, regional governors and specially commissioned scouts – as noted in Esther – were required to conscript and send to Persia human 'gifts': handsome castrated boys and pretty fertile girls. It was the equivalent practice of the Chinese Tang emperors to levy tribute in the form of young women and have attractive candidates gathered by their agents throughout the empire. We know that during the Ming period, when our records are more fulsome, that human tribute, including female servants, eunuchs and virgin girls, came from China's various ethnic tribes and from Mongolia, Vietnam, Cambodia, Central Asia and Siam. In a total of seven missions between 1408 and 1433, Korea sent a total of 114 women to the Ming court, consisting of 16 virgin girls (accompanied by 48 female servants), 42 cooks and eight musical performers. Central Asian women were provided to the Zhengde Emperor, especially Uighur and Mongol girls. The same practice of conscription and selection was routine in the Qing dynasty – in a triennial draft of 'beautiful women' – and in the Ottoman and Mughal empires, as well as in Safavid and Qajar Iran (Duindam 2016: 108–20).

Ericka Shawndrinka Dunbar (2022) has named the practice of accumulating young women and boys for the purpose of sex-servitude as it surely is: sex trafficking. She observes (2022: 118) that in Esther, 'there is a gendering of the geopolitical space. In the text, Persia is masculinized in its representation as the dominant geopolitical body that controls feminized and subordinate locales between India and Ethiopia. The colonized territories, meanwhile, are represented by feminized entities (namely, the virgin girls) who are taken and penetrated … by the Persian King'. After all, 'these girls do not appear to be acting of their own volition; rather they are repeatedly acted upon, being "sought", "gathered", and "taken"' (2022: 24).

A Darwinian perspective on the themes of reproduction and imperialism reveals that the amassing of females for procreative purposes has been an important feature of many absolute monarchies. In fact, the capture, guardianship, and sexual monopoly of numerous women often lay behind male competitive aggression as demonstrated by wars, succession fights and coups. Military success translated into territorial and economic success. By extension, the more military success a ruler enjoyed, the bigger harems he acquired. The physical manifestation of a monarch's power was attested in the social grouping of women and their offspring.

The aggressive guardianship of women and especially the herding together of groups of females is known in Darwinian terms as 'female defence polygyny'. In the animal kingdom, when females are clumped together, they can be monopolized sexually. The same can be said of human sexual relations. According to the sociologist Laura Betzig,

> Darwinian theory predicts that to the extent that conflicts of interest among individuals are not overridden by common interest, or by an overpowering force, they will be manifested, and they will, ultimately, be reproductively motivated ... *Hierarchical power should predict a biased outcome in conflict resolution, which should in turn predict size of the winner's harem,* for men, a measure of success in reproduction.
>
> (Betzig 1986: 9; italics in original)

In her cross-cultural study of leadership and (what she terms) 'differential reproduction', Betzig attempts to determine just how often power has been used to the end of reproduction throughout the course of history. The results are illuminating. Yet, she notes, owing to a variety of physiological and social checks (such as concealed abortion, miscarriage and infidelity), even successfully polygynous men are severely constrained in their reproductive success by the fertility of their mates. Thus, regardless of socio-economic status, only men with extensive and well-guarded harems are able to raise their average lifetime fertility beyond a dozen children or so. For this reason, progressive accumulation of sex partners is bound to pay off in reproductive terms, and cultural and legal institutions that put no numerical limit on the number of women under the control of individual men are therefore most adaptive, thus historically enabling rulers and nobles to monopolize women on a grand scale.

Betzig notes that Dahomey, a powerful west African empire of the nineteenth century, provides, in many ways, a typical case. There the royal harem allegedly consisted of thousands of women, constantly replenished by war captives selected by or for the king. In the African kingdom of the Asante, at the end of the nineteenth century, the number of women available to the king ranged from two to a thousand. The king himself was credited with 3,333 consorts, a symbolic figure that is nevertheless suggestive of the order of magnitude and of the unquestioned association of cultural success with reproductive success. The pattern was already well-established in the pre-Islamic Near East. While in the twelfth century BCE, long before the apogee of the Neo-Assyrian empire, the Assyrian king Ninurta-tukul-Ashur controlled about 40 wives, at the height of the Sasanian empire, Khusraw II can be credited with up to 12,000 consorts and concubines. In a much earlier period, the successful territorial expansion policy of King Zimri-Lim of Akad increased the number of palace women in Mari from 44 to 232, whereas the rulers of the less powerful kingdom of Arrapha had to make do with a few dozen women per palace. The kings of Israel could be portrayed as moving from seven-plus wives under David to 700 under Solomon and back down to 18 after the division of the Kingdom in the reign of Rehroboam. The most fertile Egyptian Pharaoh, Ramses II, ruled at a time of almost unprecedented imperial expansion. He is said to have fathered around 99 sons and 120 daughters, taking in turn at least four daughters as Great Royal wives and fathering children with them too.

In her ground-breaking study of the Ottoman imperial harem, Leslie Peirce makes a vital observation on the nature of absolute monarchy and the intimate relationship with its royal women (1993: 3):

> Sex for ... any monarch in a hereditary dynasty, could never be purely pleasure, for it had significant political meaning. Its consequences – the production of offspring – affected the succession to the throne, indeed the very survival of the dynasty. It was not a random activity ... Sexual relations between the [ruler] and chosen women of the harem were embedded in a complex politics of dynastic reproduction.

Taking this logical idea very seriously, it is clear that any trivialization in which the harem is viewed as a fantastical Orientalist brothel-like pleasure-palace fails to do justice to its central role in the political milieu of a royal court or, indeed, of empires at large.

2:3: harem

Heb. *beyt hanashiym*, 'house of the women', see also Est. 2:9, 11, 13, 14.

In ancient Persia, polygamy was the preserve of the ruler, the noblemen of his family and his elite affines. According to Herodotus, 'every [Persian] has a number of wives, a much greater number of concubines' (1.135), an image also later presented by Strabo (15.3.17): 'They marry many wives and also maintain a number of concubines for the sake of having many children'. While this scenario of empire-wide polygyny should not be taken at face value, it may well be representative of the elite of Persian society in the Achaemenid period since Persian nobles, and certainly satraps, imitated royal polygyny and as a mirror-image of the royal court, they housed numerous women within the satrapal palaces. Pharnabazus, the satrap of Phrygia, for instance, kept a court full of concubines, female servants and entertainers (Xen. *Hel.* 3.1.10).

The term 'harem' is generally employed to describe a cultural phenomenon primarily known today from Islamic cultural spheres (although the practice was actually global). 'Harem' denotes a physical sphere in which the female family members and younger children of a ruler/potentate as well as their servants lived, segregated from the public (Turk. *harem* from Arab. *harām*, 'forbidden', 'taboo', 'inviolable'; Peirce 1993: 3–5). However, 'harem' can also refer simply to women and their blood-kin when grouped together; 'harem' does not necessarily need a defining space. Walls are not that important. 'Harem' is also a term of respect, evoking personal honour. In Near Eastern royal practice, 'harem' can be employed to refer to the people who came under a monarch's immediate protection – wives, concubines, children, siblings and other blood-kin, as well as slaves (gender was not an issue). The people who made up the king's inner court, the royal domestic sphere, were the 'harem'. In his discussion of the Middle Assyrian Palace ('Harem') Edicts, van de Mieroop has pointed out that because stereotypical 'harem' images have not been sufficiently interrogated in scholarship, we assume that indigenous ancient evidence will automatically reflect the oppressed status expected of women in ancient societies (van der Mieroop 1999: 149–51). We conveniently apply the preconceived vision of the 'sequestered' woman to the notion of 'harem'. So let us be clear about this: to think of 'harem' in terms of secluded female-only space or as a form of oppressive purdah is a fundamental misconception of the nature of the term and of the institution (Yeazell 2000; Llewellyn-Jones 2009b).

However, it is not easy to find Near Eastern linguistic parallels for the words scholars often throw together to suggest 'harem'. Terms like Akkad. *bitanu* ('domestic quarter') or Heb. *penîma* ('inside [of a building]') express some of the attributes of the concept of harem, but not all of them. Marsman suggests that the use of *bit sinnišati* ('women's house') or *sikru* ('enclosure') from the Assyrian title used of court ladies *sekretu* ('enclosed woman'), which is certainly suggestive of restrictive access, might be ancient parallels of 'harem', but, like the Heb. *beyt hanashiym*, 'these do not quite satisfy the gender diversity of the living institution' (see also Weidner 1954).

It is difficult to know how the ancient Persians actually referred to a harem – either in its physical or ideological form – although it has been suggested that the OP **xšapā.stāna*, meaning 'place where one spends the night' might have been employed (Shahbazi 2004) but it is hard to qualify this. The OP *viθ*, as used by Darius I in his inscriptions, seems to carry with it the triple sense of 'dynasty', 'house' ('palace') and 'household', so *viθ* might have been used to describe the harem in its double meaning of a (flexible) space and a people, but it is impossible to say so with any certainty. Another candidate for 'harem' is the OP *taçara*, 'suite of rooms', but this, while attractive, is far from certain. Besides, the word does not have a double meaning to incorporate the people who might inhabit those rooms.

Whatever it was called, an *ideology* of 'harem' is a hallmark of all ancient Near Eastern monarchies. It makes little sense that in the long history of Near Eastern monarchy this important institution should be absent from the Achaemenid period (Llewellyn-Jones 2022: 173–92). Despite the illuminating work of Marsman (2003) on the institution of the royal harem in antiquity, studies of the ancient Persian court tend to underplay the place and role of the harem or else deny its presence totally (contra Llewellyn-Jones 2013a, 2013b, 2019, 2022; Stoneman 2015). Kuhrt, for instance, generally questions the practice of royal polygamy in Near Eastern civilizations and is reluctant to acknowledge the institution of the harem in any Near Eastern society, arguing that historians rely too heavily on its existence to explain or concoct a ranking-system for royal women (Kuhrt 1995: 149, 526). More puzzling is Maria Brosius' methodical ostracism of the concept of 'harem' from her studies on royal women in Achaemenid Persia (1996; 2021: 102–4). While she notes the wide array of royal females found at the Achaemenid palaces, she makes no effort to integrate these women into the matrix of court society. This makes no sense. In any developed royal court system, the presence of women of defined and designated social status would have called for a codified hierarchical structure. Such a structure must have been reflected in issues such as court protocol and even the use of designated (if not permanent) social and living spaces.

Heleen Sancisi-Weerdenburg (1987a) has argued that the pernicious roles attributed by the Greeks to Persian harems, concubines and queens were nothing more than a widespread literary cliché. But as Christopher Tuplin (1998a: 105) points out, 'Scholarly failings must reflect modern misunderstanding of Greek texts, not Greek misunderstanding of Persian realities'. Following Sancisi-Weerdenburg's lead, however, Briant (2002: 283) confidently speaks of 'the myth of the [Persian] harem'. Indeed, the word 'harem' so effectively conjures up the misguided stereotypes promulgated by Orientalist art, literature and cinema that Briant seems unable to move beyond the fantasy and see the harem for the court institution it really was. He reluctantly, and obliquely, concedes, however, that 'the term *harem* must be retained for convenience'. That is at least a pragmatic, if unnecessarily dismissive, concession. Balcer (1993: 273–317) and Spawforth (2007a: 93, 97, 100) both employ 'harem' as the simplest and most effective way to talk about the women and personnel of the Persian inner court without any pejorative associations. There is no reason to abandon using the term 'harem'. We can use it safely, without an Orientalist gloss and free of misconceptions or preconceptions, if scholarship rises above and beyond the harem cliché. Having no OP term at our disposal, 'harem' is best used to describe the composition and ideology of the Persian inner court.

(ii) Functioning

The harem of the Great King does not fulfil the two main criteria of the Ottoman paradigm which has proved so influential in our conceptualization of the institution: there is no evidence that all women and children were gathered at one location, nor that they were cut off from public life. Properly speaking, the harem of the Great King comprised a conglomerate of phenomena, which can be distinguished in different ways:

a) the women and children who belonged to the royal household, particularly the queens, concubines, princes and princesses;
b) related institutions, including administrative organizations and personnel; and
c) associated localities and places, like palaces and royal apartments, regional estates, as well as agricultural land and manufacturing workshops.

There is nothing that indicates that the female members of the royal family were cut off from wider court life (see above, comments on **1:9 banquet for the women**; **1:12 Vashti refused to come**). On the contrary, sources reveal that they regularly accompanied the ruler at feasts and banquets and even at audiences. They accompanied the king as he journeyed around the empire. When the king was progressing through the empire with his entourage, a 'travelling harem' went with him.

Royal women could also travel independently of the king, accompanied by their own retainers and courts. Darius the Great's mother, Irdabama, is attested at the ceremonial cities of Persepolis and Susa, and even as far away from the Persian heartland as Borsippa in Babylonia (Brosius 1996: 130–41; Henkelman 2010a: 693–7). She clearly travelled widely around central Iran and Mesopotamia with her own courtly entourage and she and her court are often represented travelling independently of the Great King's court (Briant 2002: 191). As part of her personal progress through the empire's heartland, Irdabama could deputize for the king in his absence. Like Irdabama, Darius' favourite consort, queen Irtaštuna, held at least three estates and travelled around the empire's core, sometimes with Irdabama (PFa 14a) and sometimes in the company of her son,

Prince Aršama (PF 733, PF 734). Interestingly, European monarchies of the Middle Ages and Early Modern periods employed much the same tradition and European queens and queen mothers frequently travelled with their own households, setting up courts in places often far from the king, but always re-joining the monarch's court for religious festivals, state ceremonies or family events. Of more surprise perhaps, is the fact that some of the highest-ranking women of the Mughal imperial harem operated the same system and traversed northern India in curtained palanquins surrounded by armies of courtiers – and all without breaching the very strictest form of Muslim purdah demanded by Mughal royal society (Lal 2005).

The Persepolis Fortification Texts suggest that royal women of the highest ranks enjoyed exceptional autonomy (Brosius 1996: 123–46). The same can be made of Greek tales of royal women hunting in the open (Ctesias F15 §55; Athen. 12. 514b). The hunt could be enjoyed without breaching rules of segregation by controlled access to game parks or even the erection of screens behind which the royal women could sport freely; in later times, both these measures were adopted for Mughal harem women (Lal 1988: 60, 129, 185–6, 201).

In spite of their ability to travel independently of the king, to reside at their own estates, and enjoy the thrill of the hunt, in no way do these freedoms negate the idea that high-ranking royal females were still components of the royal harem. It shows the structure of the institution was maintained with or without their physical presence, and that 'harem' operated in multiple spaces simultaneously.

Nevertheless, access to the royal women was without doubt restricted and was controlled by officials and guards. It is also unlikely that all royal wives, daughters and younger princes lived together in one location. It is more probable that only the principal consorts and their (infant?) children, as well as the king's mother, resided close to the ruler, but even then, not at all times. The majority of the secondary wives and their entourage, as well as concubines and their servants, probably resided in separate areas in the main residence, in the tented accommodations which clung to the court – for around the stone palaces, tented cities accommodated the bulk of the royal entourage. In Esther there is evidence for at least two harem-spaces in operation at Xerxes' court: one (Est. 2:8) was for 'novices', a training-ground for newly acquired girls (a somewhat dormitory-like space, perhaps). This was under the governance of Hegai. The second harem (Est 2:14), perhaps a more comfortable space with demarcated private personal areas, was inhabited by new girls who had recently pleased the ruler and by women already established as concubines. This was headed by the eunuch Shaashgaz. When Esther becomes Xerxes' consort (Est. 2:17), she moves to another space, close to the king, within the domestic heart of the palace-proper. Levenson (1997: 62) proposes that to mark a distinction between the 'ordinary' harem of the court women and those of Xerxes' successive queens – Vashti, then Esther – the Heb. *beyt hanashiym* 'should be re-vocalized as *beyt mēlākôt*, "house of queens"'. There can be little doubt that royal women had their own apartments (Briant 2002: 283–4) either in tents, wagons or palaces; Herodotus (3.68–9; 7.2–3) certainly thought as much when he described the physical layout of the inner court of Susa. When the Greek doctor Democedes arrived at the court of Darius I, he was escorted by a eunuch to meet the king's wives in their apartments (Hdt. 3.130).

(iii) Archaeology and iconography

The original excavators of Susa maintained that a harem quarter had been located in the north-west corner of the palace of Darius. It comprised a long corridor-like block of some eight small rooms with en suite storage areas (Dieulafoy 1888; **Figure 2.1**). This identification has been doubted (Moore 1971: 18). *If*, however, these rooms were part of the domestic structure of the palace, then they offered very little accommodation and only very few individuals could be lodged there. The archaeological remains of Persepolis offer more lucrative evidence though. In his *History of the Persian Empire*, Olmstead paints an atmospheric picture of an L-shaped building at the southern edge of Persepolis which both Herzfeld (1941) and Schmidt (1953) identified as the harem: 'Surrounded by the guardrooms of the watchful eunuchs was a tier of six apartments to house the royal ladies. Each tier consisted of a tiny hall whose roof was upheld by only four columns and a bedroom so minute that even with a single occupant the atmosphere must have been stifling' (Olmstead 1948: 285; **Figure 2.2**). Brosius (2007: 33) dismisses Herzfeld's and Schmidt's designation of the area out of hand: 'no structure has been identified at Persepolis which could have served as the women's quarters'. Indeed, the building has often been classified as an overflow storeroom of the nearby Treasury (Wilber 1969: 73). Yet the position of the L-shaped building towards the back of the terrace provides strong support for it being a (temporary) residential area of the palatial complex. A series of uniform apartments within the complex, each consisting of a main room connected with one smaller room or two such subsidiary chambers, echoes those at Susa. The argument for a living space is therefore enhanced.

Figure 2.1 Series of rooms making up the 'harem wing' of Xerxes' palace at Persepolis.

Figure 2.2 A room and antichamber; part of the 'harem wing' of Xerxes' palace at Persepolis.

The L-shaped building lies well inside the area of the palace platform defined by excavators as a private area, out of bounds to visitors. In fact, Herzfeld argued for the strict separation of this area from those accessible to the public on the model of similar layouts of the majority of other ancient Near Eastern palaces (Herzfeld 1941: 226; Allen 2007: 328). At Persepolis the protection of these structures by the thick southern fortification wall immediately behind the L-shaped structure contributes to the function proposed here for the building. One would expect to find accommodation used by the king and the royal family to be best protected. Indeed, the presence of guard-reliefs at major entrances to the compound suggests that security was paramount (Root 1979: 10 – but figures of soldiers carved into the connecting wall between the upper terrace and the harem are usually overlooked by scholars). Crucially then, this space at the terrace rear was allocated as living quarters for at least some of the royal family. It was hidden by high fortifications and well-guarded by the military. It was both secure and private.

The harem is grouped with other palatial residential structures both on and off the platform and it is actually integral to the building immediately above it – identified as Xerxes' palace and private residence. Xerxes' palace is connected to the harem by two grand well-worked flights of stairs, which must have been utilized by the king or his courtiers when they required direct access to the rooms below (**Figure 2.3**; Schmidt 1953: 244). They could move between the two parts of the palace without having to traverse any public space. Schmidt's excavations found that the lower flights of steps were formerly enclosed whilst the upper section was open and that the more monumental, well-dressed and polished western stairway also contained one of the few physically evidenced (well-worked) doors in the area. Schmidt also identified a direct access route, via the stairways, connecting the harem with the Council Hall and the Hall of a Hundred Columns, allowing the king and the royal family to move

Figure 2.3 Staircases connecting Xerxes' palace with the 'harem wing' at Persepolis.

conveniently and directly from their private apartments to the public areas without breaching security (Schmidt 1953: 255).

As to the harem apartments themselves, they are laid out in two rows, all interconnected by long narrow corridors. There were 22 apartments, each consisting of a large hypostyle room with one or more adjoined chambers (Schmidt 1953: 137, 260; Herzfeld 1941: 229). The main rooms are well decorated with niches and plastered walls and elegant stone door lintels and column bases which are so well crafted that the general execution of the stonework are just as fine as the palaces of the kings (Wilber 1969: 94). The average apartment measures approximately 10 × 10 metres – and while in no way a negligible living space, it would be hard to imagine royal personages passing their days perpetually in a room this size. This alone helps negate the image of royal women living in strictly guarded confinement – the claustrophobia would have been cruel. Briant rightly voices his concern that it is not at all clear 'that the royal princesses lived cloistered in their apartments' (Briant 2002: 285). It is better to think of each chamber as perhaps a separate (and temporary) domestic quarter (for sleeping?) and anti-chamber or storage area but not as a room used by a single occupant all of the time. It was not a living space *per se*.

A big courtyard in the main wing of the building and the large room attached to it is therefore best interpreted as a communal space for the harem rather than for a grand individual's private use (as Schmidt proposed), since it lacks the domestic quarter/ante-chamber units which accompany the main halls of Darius' and Xerxes' palaces. In view of the regulated control of movement to this area, both from within and outside the space, it could have functioned as an audience chamber for royal women or princes or perhaps even the king when he chose to remain there. It is very likely that in this large hall a space was set aside for other activities, including communal eating and entertainment as well as the collective rearing of younger children. We must certainly be rid of any notion of women shut up all day in cramped isolated cells. The cluster of defined 'apartments' certainly accords with Diodorus Siculus' description of residences on the terrace (7.70–1): 'Scattered about the royal terrace were apartments of the kings and members of the royal family as well as quarters for the great nobles'. Variations within the standard model of the chambers may provide a convenient indicator of some hierarchy among the inhabitants, although this assumes that greater living space is an indicator of status. More sub-chambers could also reflect the presence of a larger number of attendants.

The whole court could not have resided in the limited terrace area, and within the harem itself space was at a premium. It is tempting to conclude that the mass ranks of the court women generally resided in tents and covered-wagons strewn about on the plain below and (those of highest rank perhaps) within the mud-brick and stone buildings, whilst the permanent stone buildings of the terrace were reserved for a privileged few, members of the inner royal family. Favoured consorts and royal mothers were the most likely to have their own apartments and, consequently, commanded the most intimate access to the king.

No Persian iconographic evidence exists for the harem. It is Egypt that offers the best artistic representations, although we should not imagine that a direct replication of the Egyptian harem system operated in Persia too. But the Egyptian materials do provide an interesting template of possibilities (Spence 2007 and 2009; Yoyotte 2008). The harem quarters depicted in the tombs of the officials at the royal city of Amarna apparently lay inside the residential palace of the pharaoh Akhenaten (Davies 1908). In the tomb of Ay (**Figure 2.4**), the artist adopts a bird's-eye view of the harem building, combining it with a more standard two-dimensional side-on representation. A surrounding enclosure wall demarks the buildings of the harem complex; it leads to a garden of

Figure 2.4 Schematic view of a New Kingdom Egyptian 'harem wing' from the tomb of Aye, Amarna.

trees. Inside there are numerous rooms: columned halls for communal use, anterooms for the storage of musical instruments and other paraphernalia, and large pantries and kitchens, full of jars, dishes and food stuffs. These latter facilities are separated from the 'residential' rooms by a wide (open air?) corridor which is staffed by cleaners and, notably, a security guard (chatting to a colleague as he leans against a wall). Inside the 'residential' rooms, women are engaged in music and dance (rehearsals, perhaps for a performance in front of pharaoh?), grooming and hairdressing, and eating. Access to the complex is controlled through one door at the far lower right of the scene, an area populated by more male overseers and guards. A similar layout of space is depicted in the representation of the Amarna royal harem in the tomb of Tutu

Figure 2.5 Schematic view of a New Kingdom Egyptian 'harem wing' from the tomb of Tutu, Amarna.

(**Figure 2.5**). Again, the division of space is accented by the presence of women within the columned halls and of men in the outdoor spaces, stationed at the entranceways. The iconographic evidence corroborates Charlotte Booth's (2015: 106) description that 'the harem was a noisy bustling place, with all the royal wives and their children, king's sisters and aunts, women inherited from his father's harem as well as all the attendants and servants'.

2:3 Hegai

Possibly from the OP *haga or *hagahya, which would correspond to the two versions of the name found in the MT of 2:3, 8, 15 – Hege and Hegai – it is difficult to construct a feasible etymology for the name, although Gindin (2016: 88) suggests a Sanskrit root meaning 'to adhere to, to look after', which would fit the bill nicely. In the Septuagint he is simply Gai. Hegai appears to be the eunuch overseer of the 'first harem'; he is in charge of the novices who are brought, undisciplined in the etiquette of the court, into the palace. Later, after their instruction is complete, having found favour with Xerxes, some of the young women 'graduate' to a higher-ranking harem under the supervision of a eunuch named Shaashgaz (2:14).

2:5 Mordecai

Berlin (2001: 24) is correct to state that, 'in a book that is as nonhistorical as Esther, there is little point in looking for historical or biographical information on Mordecai's genealogy ... the introduction of Mordecai is syntactically similar to the introduction of Job (Job 1:1-2), giving us the sense that we are in folktale mode'. Certainly, the name Mordecai, derived from the Babylonian Marduka, is realistic and the Babylonian version of the name is found in Achaemenid sources. A Persian text dating from the last years of Darius I or the early years of Xerxes mentions a government official in the employ of Ushtannu, the satrap of Babylon named Marduka, who served as a civil servant. PF 81 also refers to an official named Marduka authorizing a grain shipment in the twenty-second regnal year of Darius I, but there is no compulsion to link either of the men to the character in Esther (Clines 1991; contra Yamauchi 1992; Gertoux 2015: 28). The obvious connection of the name Mordecai to that of the Babylonian god Marduk, just as the name Esther corresponds to Ishtar (see below), is well known and adds credibility to the idea that sitting behind the court novella of Esther is a Mesopotamian folk tale about some kind power-struggle among the gods (Dalley 2007). Gindin (2016: 91) notes an interesting folk etymology used among Iranian Jews in which the NP *morde* (dead) has been combined with the Heb. *hai* (alive).

2:7 Hadassah ... who was also known as Esther

That the Book's heroine is known by two names is not surprising because it was common in antiquity for Jews to utilize different names, one typically Hebraic and the other more linked to the non-Jewish world (Dan. 1:7; 1 Macc. 2:2-5). Hadassah is the Heb. for 'myrtle', a small scented evergreen shrub which has very positive associations in the Hebrew Bible (Isa. 41:19, 55:13; Testen 1998). Ancient Persians seem to have appreciated its fragrance too, at least if we follow Herodotus' account (8.99) of the celebrations they held on hearing of Xerxes' capture of far-off Athens in 480 BCE: 'they strewed all the roads with myrtle boughs and burnt incense and gave themselves up to feasts and to celebrating'. In Mesopotamia, myrtle was a plant frequently offered to the supremely sexualized goddess Ishtar, possibly because its white star-like flowers so closely resembled the deity's astral symbol of the morning star. It is probable that the name 'Esther' derives from this starlike connection to both the fragrant plant and the sex-goddess. Moreover, a cultic title sometimes associated with Ishtar, Akkad. *hadaššatu*, meaning 'young woman' or 'bride' (Dalley 2007: 169) might help explain the folk-tale-like use of Hadassah. Deriving 'Esther' from the Semitic name 'Ishtar' is clearly credible, but so too is its derivation from the OP *stāra*, 'star', a word-sound common to almost all Indo-European languages, including the Hittite *haster* (Gindin 2016: 97). *Stāra* would also link 'Esther' to the goddess, of course. Outside of the Hebrew Bible, however, the name Esther is entirely unattested. Bold attempts have been made to read 'Esther' as 'Amestris' (OP Amāstrīs, 'Strength') the name of Xerxes' formidable principal wife given by Herodotus, but they are entirely unconvincing (Gertoux 2015: 20–5). Esther is either a fabricated name or a reference to the star-goddess Ishtar.

2:7 had a lovely figure and was beautiful

See comments on **1:11**. Esther's beauty is the only attribute needed to secure her a place in the harem; beauty was the only requirement of a concubine.

2:9, 2:12 beauty treatments ... twelve months of beauty treatments prescribed for the women, six months with oil of myrrh and six with perfumes and cosmetics

The Persians understood the appeal of what might today be termed a 'makeover' and elite men and women readily utilized make-up and other artificial beauty enhancers (**Figures 2.6, 2.7, 2.8, 2.9**). According to Xenophon, Cyrus the Great appreciated the effectiveness of cosmetics in enhancing the appearance. The story goes that Cyrus especially admired his grandfather Astyages' use of eye liner, rouge and wigs (Xen. *Cyr.* 1.3.2–3) and so, '[Cyrus] encouraged the fashion of painting beneath the eyes so that they might seem more lustrous than they are, and of using cosmetics to make the complexion look better than nature had made it. He also took care that his associates did not spit or blow their noses in public' (Xen. *Cyr.* 8.1.40). The Persian use of kohl is attested in iconography, where make-up lines drawn around the eyes are delineated (**Figure 1.46, Figure 2.10**), but also in Achaemenid-period

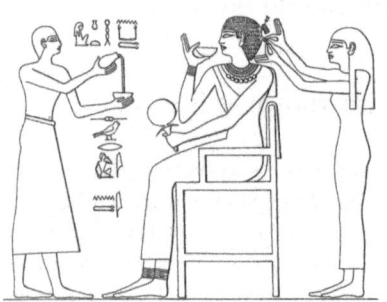

Figure 2.6 Scene of Queen Kawit with her hairdresser and page; sarcophagus from Deir el-Bahri.

Figure 2.7 Egyptian prostitute applies make-up; New Kingdom erotic papyrus from Deir el-Medinah.

Figure 2.8 Ramesside wall painting of a young Egyptian woman with an elaborate hairstyle and heavy eye make-up.

Figure 2.9 Female party-goers in elaborate wigs have perfume cones applied to their heads by a naked slave girl. New Kingdom, from Thebes.

archaeological finds from north-west Iran which have yielded delicate coloured glass and bone kohl tubes (Dayagi-Mendels 1989: 46; the rich Egyptian evidence is discussed by Manniche 1999). Two exquisite high-quality kohl containers now in the al-Sabeh collection are crafted from very fine silver, beautifully rendered into images of elite ladies wearing fine court robes, crowns and jewellery (**Figures 2.11** and **2.12**). In common

Figure 2.10 Neo-Assyrian limestone relief depicting the head of a male courtier wearing kohl around his eyes. From Nineveh.

Figure 2.11 Silver perfume flask representing a woman in Achaemenid court dress and a crown. Provenance unknown.

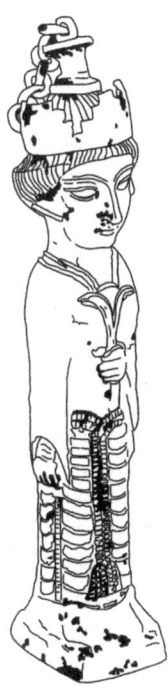

Figure 2.12 Silver perfume flask representing a woman in Achaemenid court dress and a crown. Provenance unknown.

with many courts of the Near East, the Achaemenids also created a stratum of specialist slaves who were trained as beauticians, some of whom could become influential at court – no doubt because of their close proximity to the ruler or his family (Xen. *Cyr.* 8.8.20). Professional perfumers had access to the most desirable and costly fragrances and were certainly to be found at the Persian court – when Alexander of Macedon captured the harem of Darius III in the aftermath of the Battle of Issus, he acquired many of the body-servants of the king and his women, including 70 wine-bearers, 46 florists (for making chaplets) and 40 perfumiers (Ath. 13.608a). Small unguent-bottles or perfume flasks are carried by eunuch servants on the walls of Persepolis (**Figure 1.103**).

Traditionally, Persian women wore seven forms of cosmetic enhancement (NP, *haft qalām arayīsh*), and although it is difficult to pinpoint each of them in the ancient sources, it is highly likely that all seven elements were known to the Achaemenids. The items are: henna (for staining fingers, toes, hands and feet), white face-powder, powdered rouge, kohl for eyeliner, thick woad or indigo used for thickening the eyebrows, perfume or scented oils, and gold dust to be sprinkled on the skin and hair. The year-long beauty regime described in Esther is regimented according to courtly prescriptions, although B.W. Jones (1977: 175) noted that it was 'conspicuous consumption in the extreme' (De Troyer 1995 has little to offer in the way of analysis of the beauty treatment sequence, despite a promising title: 'An Oriental Beauty Parlour', although Groves 2003 makes some very perceptive points). The cost of running a royal beauty salon must have been considerable as many of the perfumes and oils used in there were imported luxury items: one Indian perfume known as *labyzos*, much beloved of the Achaemenid aristocracy, was even more expensive than the costly myrrh which was brought in from Arabia (Deinon F25a = Ath. 12.514a). Nard, saffron, cane, cinnamon, frankincense and sandalwood were also known to the Persians. Of course, all perfumes and fragrant waters, even locally sourced varieties, required much skill and effort to produce the final product, while qualities and grades of oils affected perfume production too.

Especially important in the ancient beauty regime was the application of perfumed oil or paste onto the skin. Sandalwood or turmeric as well as saffron were staple, if expensive, products employed for the purpose. The paste, with a base of flour and mustard seed, might be applied to the body and left on for several days in order to help moisturize the skin and keep it supple and it is possible that many women hoped that it would help lighten the skin tone too, since all aristocratic women aimed for a pale complexion (Baldwin 1984: 68). Queen Hatshepsut adorned herself with a high-end product: a paste made from myrrh oil or stacte (Manniche 1999: 67). One Egyptian New Kingdom love poem (Manniche 1999: 91) describes how a frustrated lover yearns to perform the menial task of washing away the remains of perfumed oil found on the garments of his beloved:

> I wish I were her laundryman,
>   Just for a single month.
> Then I would flourish by donning her garment
>   And be close to her body.

> I would wash away the unguent from her clothes
> And wipe my body in her dress.

All over the Near East, aromata of various kinds were used to beautify men and women, their clothes, textiles and living spaces. Some people even used balls of incense as a kind of chewing gum to combat halitosis. Incense was burnt at parties and banquets to help create a heady atmosphere. The use of incense as a cosmetic was intended to impress, to please and to seduce. In Ruth 3:3, the heroine is instructed to anoint herself for the meeting with Boaz – her limited budget meant that she probably used olive oil mixed with some aromatics. In Prov. 7:17, an adulteress sprinkles her bed with myrrh, aloe and cinnamon to make it attractive. Similarly, an Aramaic papyrus from Egypt gives an account of a sexual union between a king and a goddess Nanaya: 'The bed of rushes they have laid down, perfumed fragrances for your nostrils … Horus-Bethel will lay you on a bedspread … on fragrant embroidered covers'. The king perfumes his clothes with myrrh, aloe and cassia at the royal wedding (Ps. 45:9). This theme continues in Song of Songs, where references to incense are both metaphors for the beauty of the beloved (4:6) and the result of a lavish use of incense materials as perfume (5:5). Here, the use of incense as a cosmetic may be a desire to elevate the relationship between man and woman into a sphere as close to the divine as possible. Incense and sex belong together, just like incense and the worship of the divine belong together in the relationship between humans and gods.

William Albright (1982) has drawn attention to the ancient practice of using cosmetic burners in the beautification of women, especially during the Achaemenid period, and in doing so, he drew attention to the work of Sir S.W. Baker and his 1868 book *The Nile Tributaries of Abyssinia* (London, 1868) in which was chronicled the same practice among Sudanese and Arab women:

> The women have a peculiar method of scenting their bodies and clothes, by an operation that is considered to be one of the necessaries of life and which is repeated at regular intervals. In the floor of the tent or hut … a small hole is excavated sufficiently large as to hold … a fire of charcoal … into which the woman about-to-be-scented throws a handful of various drugs. She then takes off the cloth or tope which forms her dress, and from her neck to the ground like a tent. … None of the precious fumes escape, all being kept under the robe, exactly as if she wore a crinoline with an incense burner … She now begins to perspire freely in the hut or tent, and … the volatile oil from the burning perfumes is immediately absorbed [by her skin]. By the time that the fire has expired the scenting process is completed and both her person and the robe are redolent of incense with which they are so thoroughly impregnated that I have frequently smelled a party of women a full one hundred yards distant.
>
> (Cited in Albright 1982: 263)

Albright notes how in Esther, 'it now seems obvious that the periods of conditioning [for the young women] were accompanied by the extensive use of fumigation, which would have both hygienic and therapeutic value'. Indeed, incense-burners are familiarly

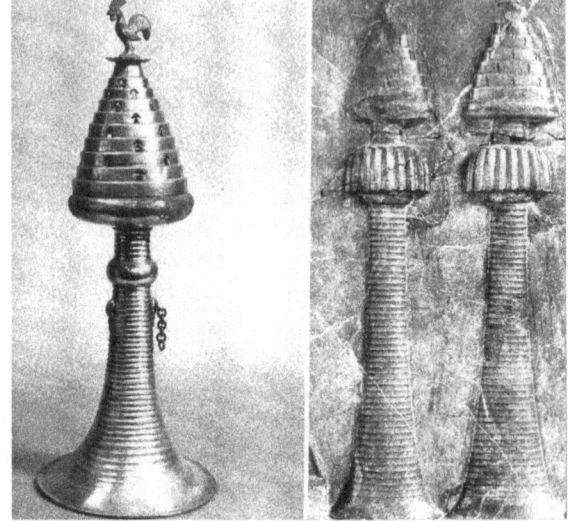

Figure 2.13 Achaemenid-period bronze incense burner; possibly from the Levant.

Figure 2.14 Achaemenid-period silver incense burner from Asia Minor with a stone relief showing incense burners from Persepolis.

encountered in Persian iconography, often (but not exclusively) in the context of women (**Figures 1.93, 1.100, 1.108**). The Menil Collection contains a large floor-standing bronze burner dating to the Achaemenid period (**Figure 2.13**) in which perfume resin was burned and finds from Persian-occupied Anatolia include fine silver examples, neatly paralleling the burners depicted in the court art found in central Iran (**Figure 2.14**). Of special interest is a well-cast bronze burner discovered in Amman (**Figure 2.15**): the censing bowl is supported by a female caryatid figure wearing Persian court robes and jewellery (**Figure 1.115**; see Khalil 1986). It supports the notion of a link between women, cosmetic burners, and perfumed fumigation.

2:9 female attendants

Countless women could be found at the Persian court. There were women from just about every rank and position, but the majority of them were nameless female administrative personnel, women attendants (such as those chosen to serve Esther),

Figure 2.15 Achaemenid-period bronze incense burner with caryatid figure; from Jordan.

and, at the lowest rung of the social ladder, the female slaves. The story of Esther stresses the fact that before her entry into the royal harem as a concubine, the heroine was raised in comparatively humble circumstances and it is certainly the case that the majority of women located in the Persian palaces came from poor families (Peirce 1993). Briant (2002: 279) makes the important point that not all captive women were bound for the privileges of the royal harem either, and that most of them would have disappeared into the huge regiment of domestic staff who worked throughout the places as Akkad. *arad šari* ('royal slaves') and *arad ekalli* ('palace slaves').

2:11 he walked back and forth near courtyard of the harem

It appears from the text that the harem had a courtyard which men were permitted to enter (Hancock 2013: 73). It is very difficult to verify this. The Greek historian Plutarch was keen to maintain that Persian men rigorously policed their wives and concubines, 'and no outside eye is allowed to see them, and even at home they live shut up in their own quarters' (*Them.* 26.5). It must be recognized though that Plutarch was writing during the first century CE when the romantic stereotype of the secluded Persian woman had become a stock image in Greek fictional literature. It was the Greek-speaking authors of the new genre of the novel who first gave rise to a vogue for romantic adventure stories set within the palaces of Achaemenid kings and their romantic tales deliberately played with the tensions associated with viewing women in the harems of eastern monarchs. The Greek novelists, working from the fourth-century BCE *Persica* of Ctesias, Deinon and Heraclides of Cumae, concocted their stories long after the fall of the Persian Empire and while they recognized the historical truth that royal Achaemenid women had been part of a regulated court society in which the harem played a key role, the stories which they composed were intended to arouse the passions of (male) readers who saw in them an open licence for erotic voyeurism. Chariton's novel *Callirhoe*, written at some time in the period 25 BCE to CE 50, is generally regarded as the earliest extant piece of Greek prose fiction and tells the story of a beautiful Greek girl, Callirhoe, who is forced into concubinage in the harem of Artaxerxes II. By locating his story in old romantic Persia, and within the harem of his imagination, Chariton allows a distinct form of Orientalism to permeate his narrative. In fact, *Callirhoe* can be seen as a formative contributor to a long line of beautiful, if deeply misunderstood and precarious, Orientalist clichés that permeate later Greek works of literature (Llewellyn-Jones 2009b and 2013b).

By the first century CE the romantic 'harem-motif' had embedded itself so firmly within the popular imagination of Greek and Roman readers that historians like Plutarch were using the stereotypical image of the secluded Oriental harem as factual content in the construction of their Eastern biographies and histories. It is also vital to recall that in writing his Greek *Lives* Plutarch had a particularly virulent anti-Persian prejudice (see Llewellyn-Jones and Robson 2010: 40–3). Plutarch's *Life of Themistocles* has a definite agenda and his *Boys' Own*-style adventure-story of the Greek statesman's flight from Persia in a curtained carriage, travelling disguised as a woman, necessitates Plutarch's exaggeration and solicits his opinion about the extreme control which the despotic Persians have over their women. However, in his *Life of Artaxerxes*, which revolves around the workings of the inner court in some detail, and is derived in large part from Ctesias' and Deinon's observations of court life, nothing of this strict barbaric 'Oriental seclusion' is suggested (for the unreliability of Plutarch on the Themistocles matter see Nashat 2003: 21, 23).

Maria Brosius is correct in championing the idea 'that there is no truth in suggestions that women lived in seclusion and were confined to the palace' (Brosius 1996: 188). To think of 'harem' in terms of secluded female-only space or as a form of oppressive purdah (or 'Oriental seclusion') is a crucial misconception of the nature of the term and of the institution (Llewellyn-Jones 2022: 174–5). As has been noted, royal women operated in a wide array of public spheres: travelling the country, having economic autonomy and political agency, and even hunting in the open countryside. Herodotus notes that eunuchs regularly admitted men into the harem to engage in business (3.130). He tells how one nobleman, Otanes, had access to the harem and often spoke with his daughter, Phaidyme, who was one of the wives of Darius the Great (3.68).

1:14 In the evening she would go there and in the morning return to another part of the harem to the care of Shaashgaz, the king's eunuch who was in charge of the concubines. She would not return to the king unless he was pleased with her and summoned her by name

Any young woman who found favour with the king during the night did not return to the harem of novices, under Hegai's administration, but advanced into the main harem. In other words, successful, pleasing, sexual congress persuaded the Great King that the girl was worth keeping. Presumably, if the girl remained untouched by the monarch, she was sent back to Hegai. What happened then? Did she stay under the supervision of Hegai? In all probability she became one of the many palace slaves who kept the harem functioning. The only girls to escape servitude are those the monarch 'summoned by name'. As Macchi (2018: 129) stresses, 'This motif sets the stage for the passage in which Esther, having become queen, declares that she has not been summoned and may therefore not approach the king (4:11). Her status as queen does not free her from the same constraints as the concubines'.

For 'another part of the harem', the literal translation is, 'to a second house of women'. This is under the watch of another eunuch, Shaashgaz. His name holds no special significance, but his appearance at this juncture in the story serves to demonstrate yet again the extreme level of hierarchical structure in operation at the Persian court (see Llewellyn-Jones 2013a). From this point, Esther is identified as a concubine (Heb. *pîlegeš*; see, importantly, Davidovich 2007 on concubinage in the Hebrew bible).

For the sake of having many children, Persian rulers had a number of wives and much greater number of concubines. In spite of the Orientalist lure of erotic exoticism that has been built up around them, concubines were not living sex-toys. Like the king's consorts, royal concubines too were expected to act for the benefit of the ruling dynasty and provide healthy, and numerous, children. In their desire for multiple heirs, the kings of ancient Persia were not content to rely on the child-bearing capabilities of their consorts, but actively sought to procreate with concubines whom they sought to monopolize sexually.

Concubinage was a difficult existence. Concubines tended to oscillate between being 'royal ornaments' (as the Egyptians often classified these palace women) and figures of state. A remarkable set of reliefs from the so-called 'High Gate' of the palace of Pharaoh Ramses III at Medinet Habu gives us a rare glimpse inside the inner-quarters of the royal residence and depicts concubines as ornamental beauties. The pharaoh is shown relaxing with his concubines, all of whom are depicted naked or semi-nude (except for jewels, wigs, headdresses and the occasional sensational pair of sandals).

Figure 2.16 Stone relief from the 'Syrian' gatehouse at Medinet Habu, Thebes. Pharaoh Ramses III and concubines. New Kingdom.

In one scene, girls are laden with feather fans, baskets of fruit and other titbits; they approach the seated pharaoh who stretches out his fingers and tickles the chin of the girl who stands before him (**Figure 2.16**); in another scene, Ramses plays a game of *senet* (a form of chess) with one girl, as he drapes himself around the shoulder of another who extends her arm around the king's torso and tweaks his nipple (**Figure 2.17**).

Figure 2.17 Stone relief from the 'Syrian' gatehouse at Medinet Habu, Thebes. Pharaoh Ramses III and concubines. New Kingdom.

A third scene shows Ramses gifting a necklace to a delicate girl depicted on minuscule scale (**Figure 2.18**). In texts which accompany the scenes, the concubines refer to Ramses by his pet-name, Sisi (see further Yoyotte 2008 and Roth 2012).

Some concubines were trained to be skilled musicians, cultured dancers and brilliant story-tellers and were highly prized for their services in the arts of entertainment (**Figures 2.19, 2.20, 2.21**). In Persia, royal concubines were expressly noted for their musical

Figure 2.18 Stone relief from the 'Syrian' gatehouse at Medinet Habu, Thebes. Pharaoh Ramses III and concubines. New Kingdom.

Figure 2.19 Female musician; painted ostraca from Deir el-Medinah, Thebes; New Kingdom.

skills: 'During dinner (the king's) concubines sing and play the harp, one of them taking the lead as the others sing in chorus' and we learn that 'at night they sing and play on harps continually while the lamps burn' (Heraclides F1, F2; also E1). Ctesias (F8d*) notes that some concubines specialized in playing the cithara, which, when placed alongside the harpists and singers, feasibly suggests a 'complex and developed form of musical entertainment' could be found at court (Kuhrt 2010: 907). We know of a court tradition for stories told though music from passing references to singers at the court, and songs about the heroic deeds of Cyrus the Great seem to have been especially popular (Xen. *Cyr.* 1.2.1; Deinon F9 = Ath. 14, 633c–e). But perhaps the concubines' musical repertoire went beyond heroic tales about Cyrus to include love songs and tragic romances like the doomed love-affair of Stryangaeus and Zarinaea recorded by Ctesias (F7, F8a–c; Llewellyn-Jones and Robson 2010: 36–9) which was almost certainly based on an Iranian poetic tradition and the story of Zariadres and Odatis, preserved in precis by Chares of Mytilene (= Ath. 13.575) who ascertains that it was 'very well-known among the barbarians … and … [was] exceedingly popular'.

Figure 2.20 Group of Egyptian female musicians, possibly concubines. From Thebes, New Kingdom.

Figure 2.21 Female musician at a Canaanite court. Detail from the 'Megiddo Ivory'; late Bronze Age.

Concubines were not courtesans or prostitutes and must not be classed even as reputable disreputable women. In no way should these women be confused with courtesans or mistresses. Nonetheless, in legal terms it is doubtful that concubines were ever thought of as being 'married' to a king. There were, as far as we know, no vows or financial transfers of bride-price or dowry and no ceremony or banquet of celebration. When a grey-haired monarch, as Darius the Great was at the close of his reign, selected his fiftieth girl from amongst the novices of the harem (perhaps a woman of a conquered province, or one of his dancers) as his latest love-interest, was this ever a marriage? No, it was not. Yet concubinage could lead to a stable relationship with the king. An established concubine would find prestige and honour within the harem-system when children she had borne the king were officially acknowledged as his. Nevertheless, unlike a wife, a concubine did not have the same status socially or legally as her mate. Dinon (= Ath. 13.556b), a Greek who lived in Persia for several years, gives an interesting glimpse of how court etiquette was employed within the female household to carefully demarcate concubines from more superior royal ladies: 'Among the Persians', he noted, 'the queen tolerates an enormous number of concubines because … the queen is treated with deference by the concubines. In fact, they do obeisance in front of her.' Some sort of hierarchical structure seems to be reflected in an all-female audience scene on a cylinder seal, possibly from Susa (similar models are found in Neo-Elamite and Archaic Greek contexts too; see Brosius 1996: 86 and 2010a; Lerner 2010). According to the Persepolis tablets, high-ranking women of the royal house were honoured with the OP title *duxθrī (lit. 'daughter'), which has been preserved in Elamite transcription as dukšiš (pl. dukšišbe), which can be generically translated as 'princess' or 'royal lady' (e.g. PF 1795; PF 823). The OP word for 'concubine' is not known, but philologists reconstruct an OI term harči- (derived from the Armenian harč) as 'secondary wife' or 'concubine'. It is unlikely that concubines were given the title dukšiš because in the highly formalized hierarchical structure of the court, these foreign women were always on a lower rung of the social ladder from that of royal consorts.

Nevertheless, concubines had an important part to play in the fortunes of the Achaemenid dynasty. They were expected to be fertile sexual partners and as such, they were as much responsible for a dynasty's promulgation as any royal wife. The lives of these women were not for themselves, but for creating other lives. They were required to keep intact the dynasty, and secure future generations to come. As we have seen, they were supposed to be physically appealing since the arousal of desire in the ruler was essential. King Artaxerxes I fathered at least eighteen sons from his concubines and Artaxerxes II had no less than 150 sons by his. The birth of a son possibly terminated the concubine's sexual relationship with the ruler, even if their relationship was one of passion. Court tradition dictated that she could give him no more male children (there were no concubine-born Persian kings who had full-blood brothers). If the concubine gave the monarch a series of daughters, then the sexual relationship could continue, but once the couple were blessed with a son, sexual congress seems to have ceased and the ruler moved on to a new concubine. From there on, the singular purpose of the concubine-mother was to work towards her son's political advancement. While the official take was that sons born to concubines were regarded as inferior to any child born to a royal wife, the history of the succession of the Achaemenids tells another story. Not infrequently the son of a concubine ascended his way to the throne. Darius II, the son of a Babylonian concubine, for instance, was crowned Great King on the death of his father, Artaxerxes I. Greek writings about the sons and daughters of Persian concubines consistently – but inaccurately – refer to them as 'bastards' (*nothoi*; see Hdt. 3.2.2). But in Persia, there was no stigma attached to being the offspring of a concubine and in the harem status-system, the child of a concubine always outranked its mother, since the child took its eminence (and the blood-royal) from its father.

Concubinage was not necessarily a dormant institution and some concubines – like Esther – gained access to high status. Some became the mothers of kings (although this is never stipulated for Esther). But the great majority of concubines must have passed their lives as nameless nonentities in a court full of competitive women. The reality of the harem was that circumstance or personal ambition could change the hierarchy, and with it the course of dynastic politics. Antagonism between concubines and between wives and concubines was common. Women who had sexual relations with the king would have had (even if only temporarily) greater status than those who had no access to his bed, and therefore we can speculate how competition to attract and keep the king's sexual attention could be intense. Concubinage was not a satisfying state of existence.

What of the number of concubines found at the Persian court? How many were there? Greek authors, captivated by their own erotic seraglio fantasies, claimed that there were around 360 royal concubines in the royal harem – one (almost) for each day of the year. Very few Greeks ever saw into the domestic quarters of the palace of Persian Great King and so the subject of his harem was ripe for titillating speculation. Diodorus Siculus (17.7.77) was just one of many Greeks who fantasized about the Persian king's sex-life, conjuring up the image of 'concubines, outstanding in beauty, selected from all the women of Asia'. He daydreamed how 'each night these women paraded about the couch of the king so that he might select the one with whom he would lie that night' (see also Ath. 12.514b and 13.557b; Plut. *Art.* 27). The Greeks envisaged the royal concubines as abandoned, licentious girls, and as beautiful off-limits eastern erotica. The heated fantasy of a carousel of nubile concubines, there to be ogled and stripped, gladdened the heart of many a Hellene. But in their wonderment the Greeks did perceive something else besides: the fact that the Great King had the ability and resources to amass, house, support and sexually exploit so many women. In truth, the ranks of the royal concubines were never fixed at 360.

There was a continual traffic in concubines and female slaves entering into the harem, and although it is impossible to state with any authority the exact number of women who found themselves in concubinage throughout the Achaemenid era, we must suppose that the numbers ran from a few dozen to many hundreds, depending on the fortunes of conquest, the payment of tribute and the sexual inclination of any Great King.

The accumulation of females on an imperial scale spoke for the monarch's virility as well as his wealth. Consorts and concubines were there to provide for his bodily comforts and for the needs of the dynasty. Their bodies were symbols of his dominance – not simply of man over women or of master over slaves, but of monarch over empire. Like the diverse food served at the royal table, the precious stones and timbers brought to the workshops at Susa, or the rare flora planted in the royal gardens, the women who lay in the king's bed were physical manifestations of the Persian empire itself. Through their fertility the monarch populated his court and prolonged his dynasty.

2:16 She was taken to King Xerxes in the royal residence

Given that the focus of the passage is Esther's recognition as queen, it is probable that the 'royal residence' (Heb. *bet ha-malkhut*) referred to here is a ceremonial hall or throne room, like the Apadana. It should be distinguished from the *bet ha-melekh*, the Heb. term used to refer to the royal living quarters and to the palace compound as a whole (Berlin 2001: 13, contra Macchi 2018: 130). This is Esther's first appearance in the ceremonial hall of the palace, a place which will take on great significance for her in the future.

2:17 Now the king was attracted to Esther more than to any of the other women

The author emphasizes yet again Esther's sublime appearance and the hold which her beauty has over the king – this will serve her well. Of course, according to the story, Esther's ultimate value is the inner-beauty – the loyalty and courage – which compels her to act to save her people (Davidson 2007: 278–80; see further perceptive comments from Berlin 2001: 29).

Perhaps the most vivid biblical portrayal of beauty and the sexual joy of married love can be found in Prov 5:15-23 where the author councils with frank eroticism, the joys of sexual attraction:

> May your fountain be blessed,
>   and may you rejoice in the wife of your youth.
> A loving doe, a graceful deer—
>   may her breasts satisfy you always,
> may you ever be intoxicated with her love.

Figure 2.22 Queen Ankhesenamun shares an intimate moment with her husband, Tutankhamun. New Kingdom, from Thebes.

Figure 2.23 Ivory plaque depicting a kissing couple; north Syria.

Figure 2.22 depicts an intimate moment between a young king, in this instance Tutankhamun, and his wife, Ankhesenamun, who languidly reclines in his lap as he pours perfume into her cupped hand. The image is ripe with sensuality as it toys with the double meaning of the Egyptian verb *sti*, 'to pour' and 'to ejaculate'. Yet, as Keel (1978: 284) observes, 'Despite the intimate character of the scene, the king and queen wear the full trappings of office; for despite its intimate scope, it is not a private scene. What happens here serves the preservation of the dynasty.' An ivory plaque from Ugarit (**Figure 2.23**) shows another young royal couple in an intimate embrace; their mutual desire is apparent in their intense gaze, the interlocking of their limbs and the gentle caress which the king gives to his wife's breast.

2:17 he set a royal crown on her head and made her queen instead of Vashti

There is no hint of a marriage ceremony between Xerxes and Esther. In fact, we know nothing about ancient Persian wedding rites, nor do we hear about any formal ceremonial in which a woman was recognized as queen; it is very unlikely that royal consorts went through a coronation ritual (after all, as has been noted, even kings precluded the idea of a coronation in place of the more culturally significant investiture ceremony). The crown mentioned here in v. 17 simply cements the idea that Esther has replaced Vashti who was last seen in the same crown in 1:11.

However, Esther's entrance into the 'royal residence' does herald her entry into the world of court politics.

Perhaps the most fantastical aspect of the Esther story is the idea that a Persian king would take a Jewish girl – or any foreign woman – as a consort. The earlier Persian kings, including Cyrus II, had certainly taken non-Persian brides as important consorts, but given the tribal structure of Persian society the powerful nobles were coerced into good behaviour through marriage alliances with the royal house. Over many generations the Persian elite had intermarried and all shared common blood through grandchildren, nieces, nephews and cousins. Even interfamilial marriages were seen as advantageous, especially the well-established uncle–niece unions which were common to all tribes. Marriages were political affairs and bonded the tribes in a rich nexus of intermingled DNA. Having ascended to the supreme position of monarch, both Cyrus the Great and Cambyses II depended upon the support of tribes in south-western Persia, and in exchange for their loyalty, the kings had rewarded them appropriately with marriage alliances for their offspring. These were lucrative matches which brought economic privileges, including estates and fiefdoms, to tribal chiefs. King Bardiya himself had been a willing participant in this process when he took as his wife Phaidymē, the daughter of the nobleman Otanes. This was the girl's second marriage into the royal house. She had already been married to Cambyses II in a union that had been arranged by Cyrus and Otanes, two old saddle-buddies who saw nothing but good coming from the wedding of their offspring. Otanes was the most respected of all the nobles and took precedence over his peers. He wielded the most clout and had more influence on the ruling family than any other courtier. He had served the house of Cyrus very well and very profitably. With Cambyses dead, Otanes saw to it that the widowed Phaidymē became consort to the new king, her former brother-in-law, so that the bond of allegiance that had been established between Otanes and Cyrus would remain active. In spite of this, as Bardiya began to place limits on the powers of the tribal leaders, so the nobles turned together in order to oust him.

From the reign of Darius the Great, Achaemenid kings only made marriage alliances with the daughters or sisters of great Persian nobles. Before he ascended the throne, Darius had married the daughter of the nobleman Gobryas. It was not a love-match, but the result of careful, economic, negotiations between Gobryas and his peer, Hystapses, Darius' father. Hystaspes took the union between the two tribes even closer when he gave one his daughters, Radushdukya, to Gobryas as a wife, making him Darius' father-in-law and brother-in-law simultaneously. The Achaemenid kings also married within the dynastic family itself by taking cousins, nieces, sisters and half-sisters as consorts. Yet there is no evidence that a Great King had a foreign woman, a non-Persian, as a consort; such women could only be allocated a concubine or slave status.

2:18 Esther's banquet

Although there is no evidence for a wedding ceremony per se, royal nuptials were one of the grandest occasions for royal display throughout the ancient Near East, celebrated with feasts and parties. This feast celebrates Esther's elevation to queenship. As such,

Esther herself is present, although that does not mean that she was on full display to the assembled gathering. The presence of high-status women at royal banquets is attested in the sources (Heracleides F2 = Ath. 4.145), but this did not mean that the etiquette of segregation was contravened or compromised. Royal women could be simultaneously present and invisible.

2:19 When the virgins were assembled a second time

The acquisition of women for the royal harem continues into another year. Girls used as items of diplomatic exchange and the acquisition of women as war booty was a regular event at the courts of the Near East and in the case of the Esther-story, even though Xerxes has taken a new consort, the mechanics of the court continue as normal and a new contingent of young women is brought into the palace (Groves 2003 suggests that the girls are brought to court to satisfy the passions of the insatiable Persian monarch, but there is nothing to support the reading).

2:19 sitting at the king's gate

(i) Gate structures

Gates existed in the Near East from the earliest days of palace and city construction and evolved as part of the general development of fortification architecture and the architecture of display. Gateways (or gatehouses) of palaces and fortresses were usually flanked by rectangular towers. Natalie May (2014; see also Frese 2020) proposes that gates functioned in a series of intertwined ways across the ancient Near East and she suggests nine key elements to their socio-cultural importance:

1. a sacred and/or ceremonial space.
2. a place for the installation of royal monuments (stele or sculptures).
3. a place for performance (processions, military parades and ceremonials).
4. a place for the public appearance of the king.
5. a location for public assembly.
6. a location for public jurisdiction (a place to appeal for justice, to petition the king or his ministers, a place for judgement).
7. a place for public executions.
8. a place for economic exchange (markets).
9. a place where security was tantamount.

From Achaemenid Iran, only one city gate, the eastern gate of the Ville Royale in Susa, is known. Labelled the 'Artisans' Gate' by archaeologists, it was a solid construction with a rectangular plan, measuring 35 m long by 18.8 m wide. It was made up of two long rooms flanked at their extremities by smaller rooms. The base of the walls was made of square baked bricks. Internal passageways interlace the structure. Access to the gateway was via a mud-brick ramp and a door facilitated access to the royal quarter for the population of the suburbs. Its form, a cubical structure projecting from the line of the walls, with a central entrance passage flanked by pairs of deep recesses, can be traced to Hittite models, as at Carchemish and to city gates from Palestine, Israel and other parts of the Levant. A much-ruined gate at Iṣṭakhr, near Persepolis, which perhaps belongs to the late Achaemenid period, was once surrounded by a fortified wall.

A spectacular archaeological discovery was made in 2015 at a site in Fārs province known as Tol-e Ajori ('Hill of Bricks'), located near Firuzi Village in very close proximity to Persepolis. There a joint Iranian-Italian archaeological mission unearthed the remains of a huge gatehouse, once integrated into high walls which probably encircled much of the Persepolis area. To all intents and purposes a city gate, it was square in shape, 30 m long on each side, with walls 10 m thick, and decorated with colourful glazed brick panels with figurative designs. Around the gate excavators unearthed small pavilions and found, as at Pasargadae, clear traces of perfectly planned formal gardens. Intriguingly, studies of the bricks have revealed striking iconographical similarities with panels from Nebuchadnezzar's buildings in Babylon, particularly the figural imagery of fantastic beasts found on the famous Ishtar Gate. The massive gateway, with its blue-glazed brick coating, was once a near copy of that famous structure. When compared with other architectural structures in Achaemenid Pārs, in plan, in building and in decoration, the gate-structure was absolutely unique. The monumental Babylonian-style gateway was surely the work of Cyrus II. In fact, the attribution of the building to him seems to be confirmed through the finding of a brick fragment containing the beginning of a cuneiform inscription painted in the glaze on which is part of the Akkad. *šarru*, 'king'. The discovery of King Cyrus' gateway so close to Persepolis means that the history of that key Achaemenid palatial site has undergone radical revision in recent years. What was thought to have been virgin territory, untouched before Darius I started to build there in *c*. 518 BCE, can now be viewed as having been a flourishing royal centre well before that time. The gateway might have started taking shape, if Cyrus had sent Babylonian craftsmen to Pārs, as early as 538 BCE, shortly after the conquest of Babylon itself, thereby pre-dating Darius' palatial structures by at least two decades.

Palace gatehouses are better attested in the archaeology of Iran. At Susa, the 'Darius Gate' was an independent building, separate to the main palace complex. This is the space where, in the mind of the author of Esther, Mordecai sat. Certainly, the first French excavators were convinced that Esther displays a remarkable degree of accuracy when the archaeology is brought into play (Perrot 1974: 20; Yamauchi 1990: 300). Measuring 40 m × 28 m, Susa's royal gatehouse height must have reached to at least 16 m. The foundations of the gate were complex. The entrance was 5 m wide and was flanked by two (lost) sculptures. Only the displaced sockets of the doorway remain because the building has suffered from much erosion over the centuries. Enough remains however to show that the gatehouse had a central square room (21.1 m

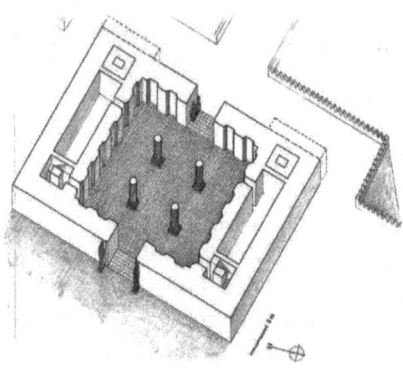

Figure 2.24 Plan of the royal gateway into the palace compound at Susa; Achaemenid period.

sides) with four columns (**Figure 2.24**) carrying a trilingual inscription by Xerxes: 'King Xerxes says: By the grace of Ahuramazda, King Darius, my father, built this palace' (XSa). The rear exit, facing towards the royal residence, was flanked on the outside by two colossal statues of Darius I. That on the southern side was of Egyptian origin and had been brought to Susa by Xerxes (**Figure 1.61**). It was still *in situ* when found in 1972. The other statue survives in only a few fragments.

Dating also to the reign of Darius (most probably) is a gatehouse found at Pasargadae. A once glorious monumental gateway stands close by the ruins of a pavilion-palace built earlier by Cyrus the Great. It was the only entrance portal in the entire palatial complex but its former grandeur is now indicated by a single standing doorjamb decorated with a high-relief sculpture of a four-winged male figure wearing an Elamite garment and an elaborate Egyptian-style crown (**Figure 2.25**). For centuries this curious hybrid figure has been identified as a portrait of Cyrus the Great himself, but that is simply not the case. Its angel-like wings show it to be a Babylonian-style guardian-spirit known as an *apkallu*, a divine superintendent who functioned as part of Pasargadae's defence system. The *apkallu* protected the palace from any malevolent force. The gateway stood in splendid isolation; it had no associated wall because, unlike other palace-sites throughout the Near East, Pasargadae had no fortifications to encircle it, located as it was deep in

Figure 2.25 Relief sculpture of a guardian figure from a surviving doorjamb at the entrance gate to Pasargadae, Iran. Late Teispid–early Achaemenid period.

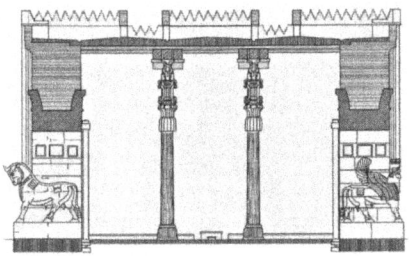

Figure 2.26 Cross-section of Xerxes' Gate of All Lands at Persepolis.

the Persian homeland. The absence of defences only strengthened the symbolic power of the gate as both a magical and a ceremonial portal through which foreign diplomats, suppliants and tribute-bearers processed to greet their king. Pasargadae was not totally without defences, however, for overlooking the complex from a high mound was a great fortified platform known as the *Tal-e Takht* – 'Hill of the Throne'. Under the later Achaemenids, the hillside developed into a sprawling citadel with substantial mud-brick defences which was used as a military garrison.

Persepolis was adorned with two impressive gateways, the Gate of All Lands (**Figure 2.26**), named as such by Xerxes, who commissioned its construction, and the Unfinished Gate, still a work-in-progress when Persepolis was burned by Alexander III of Macedon in 330 BCE. Xerxes' gate, the most complete gatehouse to have survived, is built on an epic scale, consisting of one large square room, lined with stone benches (interrupted at the doorway); here diplomats and visitors would sit before being escorted towards the Apadana. A cedarwood roof was supported by four huge stone columns resting on bell-shaped bases. Outside, the austere mud-brick walls were relieved by frequent niches. The east, west and south walls were each the locations for huge stone doorways; cedar doors with bronze hinges were once *in situ* (pivoting devices found on the inner corners of all the doors indicate that they must have had two-leaved doors). A pair of massive bulls flanked the western entrance and two Assyrian-style *lamassu* (human-headed winged-bulls; **Figure 2.27**) stood at the eastern doorway. Trilingual inscriptions were carved high above the colossal sculptures:

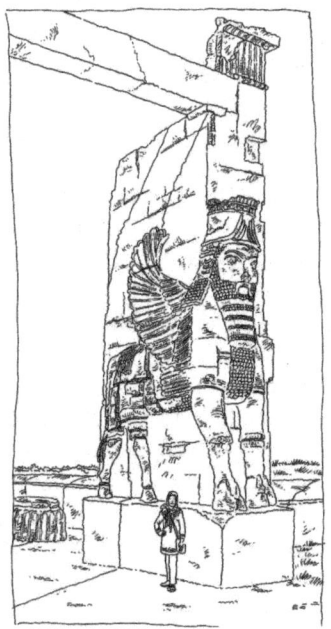

Figure 2.27 Human-headed winged bull guardian figure, part of Xerxes' Gate of All Lands at Persepolis.

A great god is Ahuramazda, who created this earth, who created heaven, who created man, who created happiness for man, who made Xerxes king, one king of many kings, commander of many commanders. I am Xerxes, the Great King ... the son of Darius, an Achaemenid. King Xerxes says: by the favour of Ahuramazda this Gate of All Lands I built. Much else that is beautiful was built in this [place], which I built and my father built. Whatever has been built and seems beautiful – all that we built by the favour of Ahuramazda.

(XPa)

(ii) The gate as a place of justice

The gate was a site for royal administration, but there was commonly held Near Eastern association between the gate and justice (2 Sam. 15:2; Dan. 2:49). Xenophon (*Cyrop.* 8.1.6) reported that Persian royal officials frequented the king's gate, where they would receive petitions and report official communications. According to Herodotus (3.70), following the arrest, imprisonment and condemnation to death of the nobleman Intaphernes (OP Vindafarna), his wife sat at the gateway into the Susa palace in order to petition Darius I for clemency. Messages, relayed by eunuchs, travelled back and forth between the gate and the private quarters of the king as Intaphernes' wife made use of the gate's association as a place where justice should be upheld. The royal gatehouse was a conspicuous place to sit and Intaphernes' loyal wife took advantage of the conspicuous visibility the gate afforded to highlight her plight. Mordecai employs the same tactic in 4:1-2.

(iii) Mordecai at the palace gatehouse

The gate plays a significant part in Mordecai's story and his presence there is mentioned ten times, each reference charting his dramatic rise to prominence at Xerxes' court (2:19, 2:21; 3:2-3; 4:2, 4:6; 5:9, 5:13; 6:10, 6:12). As Berlin (2001: 31) has correctly observed, the gate says more about Mordecai than his physical location, since the verse 'states his official position in the royal court'. He is an employee of the royal civil service and his specific role, Berlin speculates, was as a functionary in the office of the secret police. The Great King policed his realm carefully and throughout the empire he maintained a tight network of spies. Known as the 'King's Ears' (OP *gaušaka*), they reported back to the central authority any hint of rebellion in the satrapies or any flicker of insurrection in the provinces. Seditious speech was carefully monitored too. A court official bearing the curious title 'the King's Eye' (OP *spasaka*) was in charge of the intelligence-gathering and reported directly (and perhaps on a daily basis) to the Great King himself. One Greek author, Aristotle of Stagira, was most impressed by the efficiency of the Persian spy-system, writing that: 'The king himself, they say, lived in Susa or Ecbatana, invisible to all, in a marvellous palace. Outside these the leaders and most eminent men were drawn up in order, some called "guards" and the "king's eyes and ears", so that the king himself might see everything and hear everything.'

If Mordecai was indeed a member of the royal intelligence service (not a particularly high-ranking one, it should be conceded), then the ease of access which he had to the courtyard in front of the harem can be explained by virtue of his office. His position meant that he was well placed to hear about the plot devised by Bigthana and Teresh, two of the king's officers who guarded the gate.

2:21 conspired to assassinate King Xerxes

No reason is given for why Teresh and Bigthana wanted to assassinate Xerxes. Was it part of a bigger plan? Were they agents of a higher power at court (after all, they were guardians at the gate)? Or were they acting alone in a somewhat haphazard plan to overthrow the status quo? Esther is silent on these questions. Moreover, why, if he was indeed an official in the secret service, did Mordecai feel the need to reveal the plot to Esther? Why did he not report his findings to the correct authorities? As Grossman (2011: 78) notes, the narrator leaves the questions completely unanswered.

The basic idea of an assassination attempt is feasible enough though. The Persian court was the locale of intrigue, subterfuge, cruelty and danger as Achaemenid kings, queens, courtiers and servants plotted against their opponents and murdered their rivals, or else were outmanoeuvred and assassinated first. The fictional plot of Esther revolves around this historical fact. Rivalry, treachery and vendetta were ever-present even within the inner circle of the royal family itself as succession issues plagued the political heart of the dynasty. Throughout its history the Achaemenid family's inability or inertia in establishing any rules of primogeniture led to chaotic family discord, tumultuous political upheaval and bitter personal power-plays so that succession issues became a perennial crisis for the Achaemenids who exacerbated the matter with poisons, plots and murder.

The first audience of Esther would have known that Xerxes did indeed meet an ignominious end at the hand of assassins. Regicide plagued the Achaemenids, as the table below reveals. No less than seven of the twelve Achaemenid Great Kings met their deaths at the hands of an assassin of some sort (and only three monarchs had the luxury of a peaceful death); to this we can add the murder (or execution) of at least two Crown Princes:

Name of Great King	Nature and Date of Death
Cyrus II	Battlefield; November 530
Cambyses	Natural causes (?); after 18 April 522
Bardiya	Assassination; 29 September 522
Darius I	Natural causes; after 17 November 486
Xerxes I	Assassination; between 4 and 8 August 465
Artaxerxes I	Natural causes; after 24 December 424
Xerxes II	Assassination; early 423
Darius II	Natural causes; April 404
Artaxerxes II	Assassination; after January 358
Artaxerxes III	Assassination; after 26 August 338
Artaxerxes IV [Arses]	Assassination; Summer 336
Darius III	Assassination; July 330
Name of Crown Prince	**Nature and Date of Death**
Darius, son of Xerxes I	Assassinated; soon after 8 August 465
Darius, son of Artaxerxes II	Executed; Summer (?) 370

The evidence confirms that Xerxes' death came about early in August 465 BCE. A Babylonian astrological text refers to the assassination of the king by his son (BM 32234; Stolper 1985: 196–7):

> ... in 18 [...]; 40 (duration) of onset, to[tality and clearing up], the 'garment of the sky' was present; (the moon) was eclipsed in the area of the rear group of four stars of Sagittarius. (There was an) intercalary month Ulul. On the fourteenth (?) day of the month Ab [i.e. 5 June 465 BC], Xerxes – his son murdered him.

What do we make of the Babylonian evidence that Xerxes was murdered by his son? Which of his three sons did the deed? The Greek stories about Xerxes' murder (Ctesias F 13 §33–4; F13b*) smack of an elaborate cover-up by Prince Artaxerxes and it is highly likely that he, perhaps with several eunuchs, banded together to rebel against Xerxes. In the coup, the prince availed himself of the opportunity to dispose of both his father and his elder brother in an audacious, ambitious (and successful) bid for the throne. However, the Babylonian evidence states that the perpetrator of Xerxes' murder was clearly his son – and no other. Perhaps Artaxerxes was the sole operator of the deadly deed. Certainly, his scheming ambition paid off nicely. By January 464 BCE Artaxerxes I was recognized as the new Great King. As far away as Elephantine in southern Egypt, a papyrus document reads: 'On the 18th day of Kislev, that is the seventh day of Thoth, in the year 21 of Xerxes, the beginning of the reign when king Artaxerxes I sat on his throne' (Llewellyn-Jones 2022: 274).

2:23 impaled on poles

Impalement (OP *uzmayāpati kar*; Akkad. *zaqīpu*; Gk. *anastaurizein* and *anaskolopizein* (which can also translate as 'crucify'), see Hdt. 3.159; 4.43; 6.30; 7.194; 9.78; Ctesias F 9[6], F 14[39 and 45], F 16[66], F 26[12.7]; Arr. *Anab.* 4.7.4) was a form of capital punishment frequently employed by Achaemenid rulers. In his Bisitun Inscription, which narrates his suppression of rebellions which broke out at the time of his accession, Darius the Great records the torture and execution of rebel ringleaders:

> Fravartish was seized; he was brought before me. I cut off his nose, ears and tongue, and tore out one eye. He was held in fetters at my palace gateway; all the people saw him. After that, I impaled him at Ecbatana; and the men who were his foremost followers, those I hanged at Ecbatana in the fortress ...
>
> [I] took Cicantakhma prisoner, brought him to me. After that I cut off his nose, ears and tore out one eye. He was held in fetters at my palace gate; all the people saw him. After that, I impaled him at Arbela ...
>
> Vahyazdata and the men who were his foremost followers – at a place called Huvadaicaya in Persia – there I impaled them.
>
> For Arakha, who had lied and called himself Nebuchadnezzar, and the men who were his foremost followers, I gave the order: that Arakha and the men who were his foremost followers were impaled at Babylon.
>
> (DB §§32, 33, 43, 50)

Figure 2.28 Neo-Assyrian stone relief depicting the sack of a city; prisoners are impaled before the city walls. From Nineveh.

Transgressors against the earthly and cosmic order designated by *dāta* ('law') were penalized by the Great King in person, or at least this was claimed. Impalement is the only death penalty for rebels against royal authority known from Persian inscriptions (Jacobs 2009: 134), and as such it also entered the Greek tradition, as shown for example by Ctesias' account of the execution of the Egyptian rebel Inaros (Llewellyn-Jones 2022: 283).

As a method of execution, impalement was inherited from the Neo-Assyrians, whose relief sculptures depict scenes of impalement with some regularity (**Figure 2.28**). It is important to distinguish between the two types of impalement encountered in the Assyrian corpus: i) the impalement of living victims (**Figure 2.29**) and ii) the impalement of corpses or parts of a corpse (in particular the decapitated head – as happened to Saul's dead body (1 Sam. 31:10); **Figures 2.30 and 2.31**). This latter method of impalement is distinguished in the royal texts by the Akkad. term *ina gašīši rattû*, 'to fix to a pole'. For the still-living victim, impalement was a horrific end to life. Stripped naked, the condemned was positioned on top of a long, sharpened, wooden stake that entered his body through his anus. The process of dying was a long, drawn-out, and agonizing affair that lasted for many hours, sometimes for days. The cause of death was via shock, body-trauma, loss of blood and blood poisoning (Jacobs 2009: 137–8).

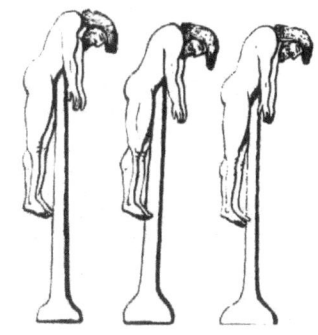

Figure 2.29 Neo-Assyrian stone relief depicting impaled prisoners. From Nineveh.

Figure 2.30 Neo-Assyrian bronze relief depicting impaled and mutilated prisoners. From Balawat.

Figure 2.31 Assyrian impalement scene from the Balawat Gates.

Both types of impalement were useful methods of terrorizing an audience in a targeted, measured and memorable way. Thus, following the siege of Suru in 882 BCE, Aššurnasirpal II had a tower erected opposite of the city gate to serve as a stage for the spectacle of flaying and impaling prisoners of war:

> I built a tower opposite [the] gate. I flayed the nobles, as many as had rebelled against me. I clothed the tower with their skins. Some I spread out within the tower. Some I impaled on stakes above the tower. Some I arranged on stakes in a circle (*ana zaqīpī ušalbî*) around the tower. I flayed many across my land. I clothed the city walls with their skins. I cut up the flesh (even) of criminal eunuchs and royal eunuchs
>
> (see Radner 2015: 207–8)

Closely linked to the concept of impalement are the notions of disgrace and defilement (Gen. 40:19; Deut. 21:22; Josh. 8:29, 10:26). The public visibility of a hanging corpse or a head on a spike caused revulsion and brought shame on the victim, even after death. When Xerxes had the head of Leonidas, king of Sparta, impaled on a spike, the action was meant to accentuate the ignominy of the Greek's defeat – which is certainly how Herodotus (7.238) interpreted it: 'This, to my mind, is the most convincing piece of evidence … that during his lifetime Leonidas had been more of an irritation to Xerxes than anyone in the world.' In Esther, the impalement of Bigthana and Teresh clearly foreshadows both Haman's attempt to have Mordecai brought to the stake and Haman's own impalement following his swift fall from grace.

2:23 book of the annals

The Persians were fanatical about administrative records, and a testimony to their bureaucratic efficiency is seen in the so-called Persepolis Fortification Tablets, a huge series of (mainly) Elamite cuneiform texts dating chiefly to the reign of Darius I. Of course, these cuneiform administrative documents are a long way off any official royal record, although we do hear of kings issuing official letters and edicts and copies of these must have been stored in a central archive (Hallock 1985 and Briant 2002: 422–4). Stronk (2004–5: 107–9) argues that the claims made by the Greek historian Ctesias to have used royal documents must be taken seriously and cites the biblical evidence to support his case: both the books of Ezra (4:15) and Esther (2:23; 6:1; 10:2) refer to official documents, or books of annals. Ezra (5:2–6:2) even speaks of a 'house of books (or archives)' in Babylon where official documents were stored. This should come as no surprise because the archival library system in Neo-Babylonia was strong and had taken its inspiration from the Assyrians. Assurbanipal, Assyria's last important ruler, had founded a library 'for royal contemplation' but also to archive official royal documents (Casson 2001: 9–16 and Beaulieu 2007; see also Brosius 2003).

Arthur Christensen, however, thought that the 'book of annals' was far more than dry annals records of daily events or military conquests. He regarded them as an account of royal events woven into an epic storyline, 'une littérature d'amusements' (Christensen 1936: 117) and cites Esther 6:1-2 as support. Here, argues Christensen, the insomniac Xerxes looks for distraction and to keep the monarch entertained throughout the long sleepless night, the royal records which were read out to him must been more than a dry list of daily events. Christensen goes further, however, and suggests that Persian epics of later centuries – the highly fragmentary MP Book of Rulers (*Xwaday Namag*), and the eleventh-century NP *Book of Kings* (*Shahnahmeh*) by Ferdowsi – as their names suggest, were a continuation of a tradition of Achaemenid royal records and stories (Christensen 1936: 119).

It is difficult to imagine that entertainment was the primary function of royal chronicles, however. Dorothea Weltecke (2000) has suggested that ancient annals were never intended to be thought of as stories nor as 'historiae'; for her, annals were simply records of past events, disconnected from any kind of narrative. Certainly, the well-known Babylonian Chronicles appear to be extracts taken from running annals wherein the compilers entered anything noteworthy. The purpose of such a compilation is something of a mystery, but Alan Millard (1980) argues that Esther 6:1-2 provides a solution:

> There is no reason to doubt the story [that sleepless Xerxes has the chronicles of his reign read to him]. It reflects a court custom. The running record was kept so that the king himself might see how he and his country were faring. In that would be an indication of the gods' favour or disapproval, since everything that occurred was under their control. In addition, chronicles of earlier kings would show what they had done, maybe in similar circumstances, thus offering precedents and warnings.

It is unlikely that any Persian 'book of annals' was a narrative in the way that Christensen wanted to see it, but, as in the Mesopotamian tradition, it was more likely to have been a continuous historical account of events arranged in chronological order without analysis or interpretation. That does not mean, however, that the material had been randomly collected or compiled, or had been arbitrarily collected. Nor did it lack drama (as any reader of the Assyrian royal annals knows). Grayson's (1972: ix) definition of the genre of Near Eastern royal annals is the clearest and best in its simplicity: 'it is a prose narration of events in chronological order normally written in the third person'.

Chapter 3

1 After these events, King Xerxes honoured **Haman** son of Hammedatha, the Agagite, elevating him and giving him a seat of honour higher than that of all the other aristocrats. 2 All the royal administrators at the king's gate **knelt down and paid honour** to Haman, for the king had commanded this for him. **But Mordecai would not kneel down or pay him honour.** 3 Then the royal officials at the king's gate asked Mordecai, 'Why do you flout the king's edict?' 4 Day after day they spoke to him but he refused to conform. Therefore they told Haman about it to see whether Mordecai's behaviour would be endured, for he had told them he was a Jew.

5 When Haman saw that Mordecai would not kowtow or pay him honour, he was infuriated. 6 Yet having learned who Mordecai's people were, he scorned the idea of killing only Mordecai. Instead Haman looked for a way to annihilate all Mordecai's people, the Jews, throughout the whole of Xerxes' empire.

7 In the twelfth year of King Xerxes, in the first month, the month of Nisan, **the pur (that is, the lot) was cast** in the presence of Haman to select a day and month. And the lot fell on the twelfth month, the month of Adar.

8 Then Haman said to King Xerxes, 'There is a certain people spread among the peoples in all the provinces of your empire who keep themselves detached from others. Their norms are different from those of all other people, and they do not obey the king's laws; it is not in the king's best interest to put up with them. 9 If it pleases the king, let a decree be issued to destroy them, and I will donate **ten thousand talents of silver** to the king's **administrators for the royal treasury.**' 10 So the king took his **signet ring** from his finger and gave it to Haman son of Hammedatha, the Agagite, the adversary of the Jews. 11 'Keep the money,' the king told Haman, 'and do with those people what you will.'

12 Then on the thirteenth day of the first month the royal scribes were summoned. They wrote out in the script of each province and in the language of each people all Haman's orders to the king's satraps, the governors of the various provinces and the nobles of the various peoples. These were written in the name of King Xerxes himself and sealed with his own ring. 13 Dispatches were sent by couriers to all the king's provinces with the order to destroy, kill and annihilate all the Jews – young and old, women and children – on a single day, the thirteenth day of the twelfth month, the month of Adar, and to steal their goods. 14 A copy of the text of the edict was to be issued as law in every province and made known to the people of every race so they would be ready for that day. 15 The couriers went out, spurred on by the king's mandate, and the edict was issued in the citadel of Susa. The king and Haman sat down to drink, but the city of Susa was bemused.

Commentary

3:1 Haman

The name 'Haman' is attested only in Esther and no Achaemenid-period text records its use anywhere in the empire. However, it is possible – likely even – that the name is related to the Elamite deity Hamban (or Humman) who figures prominently in the Persepolis archives. If this is the case, then the Esther story might have its roots in an ancient tale of conflict between the Babylonian gods Ishtar and Marduk and the Elamite deity Hamban.

Haman's rise to power is not explained. He is awarded 'a seat of honour higher than that of all the other nobles', that is to say, he occupied the top seat at the council table (it is unnecessary to think of a physical seat or throne, cf. Macchi 2018: 146). Xenophon (*Cyr.* 8.4.5) was aware of the Achaemenid preoccupation with the nuances of power and place, noting that Cyrus the Great,

> gave public recognition to those who stood highest in his esteem, beginning even with the places they took when sitting or standing in his company, although he did not assign them the appointed honour permanently. He made it clear that through good deeds one might advance to a seat of honour, but that bad conduct would lead to a demotion of status.

As Esther demonstrates, the Achaemenid monarchs constructed their royal court as an effective political tool in order to consolidate and augment an absolutist rule through which the Persian nobility and civil service could be tamed and domesticated; stripped of effective power and occupied instead with the minutiae of etiquette and courtly ceremonial, the elite of Achaemenid society became obsessed with their positions in the orbit of the Great King.

3:2 knelt down and paid honour to Haman ... But Mordecai would not kneel down or pay him honour

Notions of hierarchy and status were so deeply entrenched in the cultural systems of Persia that power manifested itself in multiple displays of non-verbal communication, and particularly in the act of showing reverence to the monarch or his representative (in this case, Haman). Much has been written on the nature of non-verbal communication in ancient Near Eastern civilizations (see especially Gruber 1980 with a full bibliography), although the nuances of body language and greetings of respect amongst the Persians are complicated by a lack of specific Achaemenid sources and an overdependence on the Greek understanding of Persian non-verbal customs. Unspontaneous, semi-ritualized gestures were a hallmark of Persian social communication, at least according to Herodotus (1.134) who describes in some detail a series of greeting-gestures used in daily life:

When one man meets another on the road, it is easy to see if the two are equals; for, if they are, they kiss each other on the lips without speaking; if the difference in rank is small, the cheek is kissed; if it is great, the humbler bows and does obeisance to the other.

These same gestures were, it would seem, inflated and further ritualized at the Persian court. Common rules of respectful deference are often multiplied and formalized where a strict etiquette of formal codified gesture is required, and the Persians seem to have transformed the gestures of *la vie quotidienne* into a rarefied form of etiquette. Known to the Greeks as *proskynesis*, the exact nature of the ceremonial obeisance to a Persian monarch is debated (Frye 1972; Fredricksmeyer 2000). Etymologically, *proskynesis* incorporates the idea of a kiss (Gk. *pros* 'towards'; *kyneo* 'to kiss'), but when Herodotus says that one should perform *proskynesis* to a superior while prostrating oneself or bowing down, the term must describe an act performed once one is bowed or prostrate, which is, as on the Persepolis Treasury Relief, kissing from the hands (**Figure 3.1**). At the centre of the Treasury Relief, a courtier dressed in a riding habit – possibly the *chiliarch* – performs a ritual gesture of obeisance to the monarch. He stoops forward and raises his hand to his mouth and makes a gesture that is

Figure 3.1 Detail of a limestone relief depicting a royal audience scene. Originally from the east staircase of the Apadana, Persepolis.

Figure 3.2 Egyptian tomb wall painting from Memphis showing foreign petitioners or prisoners in front of Egyptian officials; New Kingdom.

closely associated with the *salaʿam*, or formal greeting, used in other ancient Near Eastern courts (**Figures 3.2, 3.3**) and at later Muslim courts such as those of the Safavids, Ottomans and Mughals.

Importantly, for the Greeks, the gestures which spoke of respect in a Persian context were regarded as suitable only for a religious act. Bowing and kowtowing were performed before a god, so that for a Greek to do

Figure 3.3 Elamite captives kowtow to Assyrian soldiers. Stone relief from Nineveh.

obeisance before a man, even a Great King of Persia), undermined the very concept of *eleutheria*, or 'freedom' (Xen. *Hel.* 4.1.35). Classical authors note that performing *proskynesis* before the Great King was a non-negotiable rule for an audience (Frye 1972; Fredricksmeyer 2000) and this is clearly what the Persian *chiliarch* Artabanus intended to convey to Themistocles when he briefed the Greek about the courtly ceremonial:

> 'Amongst our many excellent customs, this we account the best, to honour the king and to worship him (*proskynein*), as the image of the god of all things (*eikōn theou*). If then you approve of our practices, fall down before the king and revere him, you may both see him and speak to him; but if you think otherwise, you will need to use messengers to intercede for you, for it is not our national custom for the king to grant audience to any man who does not pay him obeisance' ... When Themistocles was led into the king's presence, he kissed the ground in front of [the Great King] and waited silently.
>
> (Plut. *Them.* 27.4–5; 28.1)

Likewise, the *chiliarch* Tithraustes advised the Greek Conon that any man who appeared before the Great King must render to him 'a rite of adoration (Lat. *venerai*)', a term specifically defined by Nepos as *proskynesis* (*Conon* 3.3; see also Ael. *HV* 1.21). The misunderstanding of the Persian act of *proskynesis* as a veneration of divine monarchy (a claim never made by the Achaemenid kings themselves, nor understood that way by the Persians) accounts for several Greek tales which take the distaste for this act of social submission as their theme. Herodotus (7.136) tells how the Spartans Bulis and Sperchis refused to prostrate themselves before Xerxes in a royal audience at Susa, even though the royal guards thrust their heads to the ground:

> they came to Susa, into the king's presence, and when the guards commanded and would have compelled them to fall down and bow to the king, they said they would never do that. This they would refuse even if they were thrust down headlong, for it was not their custom, said they, to bow to mortal men, nor was that the purpose of their coming.

Aelian (*HV* 1.29) describes the Theban Ismenias as 'ingenious and typically Hellenic' in his ruse to dodge paying the required homage to the Great King (compare Plut. *Arta.* 22.8). Notoriously, it was with this background of misunderstanding that, in the summer of 327 BCE, Alexander of Macedon provoked unrest among his Macedonian followers when he introduced *proskynesis* to his court and army (Taylor 1927).

In a Near Eastern context, the Persian practice of bowing and kissing as a sign of submission and respect looks very much at home. Kowtowing, prostration, kissing the ground or even kissing the hem of a garment or the feet of the monarch or his representative were familiar gestures in Assyrian court protocol, and some Near Eastern texts record an elaborate and flowery language of bodily self-debasement utilized to render homage to the monarch. One of the Amarna Letters (EA 320; Moran 1992: 350 and Pritchard 1969: 490) makes much of the obsequiousness of the gesture:

> To the king, my lord, my god, my sun, the sun from the sky: message of Yidya, the ruler of Ashkelon, your servant, the dirt at your feet, the groom of your horses. I indeed prostrate myself, on the stomach and on the back, at the feet of my king, my lord, seven times and seven times. I am indeed guarding the place of the king where I am. Whatever the king, my lord, has written me, I have listened to very carefully. Who is the dog that would not obey the orders of the king, his lord, the sun of the sun?

A Babylonian emissary, ushered into the presence of Esarhaddon of Assyria and squatting before the throne, offers a similar response: 'I am a dead body. Let me behold the face of the king my lord, and die' (Portuese 2020: 119).

Some sources suggest that status-levels between monarch and subjects were carefully negotiated through different gestures of respect (2 Sam. 14:33; 1 Kgs 1:19; **Figures 3.4, 3.5**). It appears that in Persia royal women were constrained

Figure 3.4 Jehu, king of Israel, kisses the ground before Sennacherib, king of Assyria; 'Black Obelisk' from Nimrud.

Figure 3.5 Foreign tribute bearers present themselves to an Egyptian vizier; tomb painting from Thebes; New Kingdom.

to follow the same rules of etiquette and show due deference to their social superiors: 'the queen is treated with deference by the concubines; in fact, they do obeisance in front of her (Gk. *proskynousi goun autēn*)' (Athen. 13.556b; **Figure 3.6**). Rich Neo-Assyrian sources demonstrate how dominance and submission were encoded in ritualized greetings too. Four significant moves were used to greet a superior (and the monarch in particular): standing erect with head held high (a rare mark of distinction given to only the most highly-favoured individuals), kissing the ground or the feet (Akkad. *kaqquru našāqu*) and grasping the feet (Akkad. *šēpu sabatu*; see Portuese 2020: 110–22). Stooping, bending and lowering the head (Akkad. *kanašu kišādu*, 'to bend the neck') were all marks of social humility.

Figure 3.6 Woman performs a full prostration before the image of a god. Egyptian papyrus painting; New Kingdom.

In Esther, Mordecai's refusal to kowtow to Haman, or show him any degree of respect cannot, unlike the Greek claim, be associated with any 'democratic' stance, since the Hebrew Bible proves that prostration before superiors was a standard cultural code amongst the Jews and that religious sensibilities did not enter into the picture (Gen. 23:7, 43:28; Exod. 18:7; 1 Kgs 1:23). The reason for Mordecai's rejection of all norms of etiquette must lie in the ancient ethnic tensions which existed between the Jews and the Amalekites (Exod. 17:18-19; Num. 24:7; 1 Sam. 15) and, as Berlin (2001: 35) observes, a 'Greek cultural value, which disdained bowing to the Persians, is transmuted into a historic Jewish enmity, which prevented a Jew from bowing to an Amalekite.'

3:7 the pur (that is, the lot) was cast

There can be little doubt that the word 'pur' was a later, Maccabean-period, insertion in the MT text; it anticipates the insertion of the entirety of chapter 9 (esp. 9:24-6). Note how the author of Esther provides a gloss of the word to aid his Hellenistic audience (Kitz 2000; see further, Introduction). The reason for casting lots is not given, although it can be assumed that it was to fix a date for the extermination of the Jews. In and of itself, there is nothing unusual about casting lots (**Figure 3.7**). In antiquity this was a common strategy by which to determine an event, since it was thought that the gods (or other supernatural forces) spoke through dice or any other tokens of prophecy. Indeed, the word 'pur' is derived from Akad. *puru* ('to fall', 'to throw'; compare Hittite *pul*) and Mesopotamian evidence for divination through lots is plentiful. It was customary, for instance, upon a person's death, to divide the

Figure 3.7 Assyrian dice recovered at Tepe Gawra.

inheritance among the eligible heirs by lot, a convention expressed through the phrase, 'they made the division (of the property) and cast lots (to distribute it)'. (The practice was still in operation in Roman Judaea, as recorded in the Gospels in connection with the crucifixion – Matt. 27:35; Mark 15:24; Luke 23:34; John 19:24). Even state-decisions were determined by the casting of lots, as an inscription dating to the reign of Shalmaneser III attests: 'In my thirty-first year (i.e. 828 BCE), I cast the lot … in front of the gods Ashur and Adad' (Hallo 1983: 20). The king's purpose was to decide on the appointment of royal councillors. A small archaeological find of an inscribed clay cube (**Figure 3.8**), used as a lot, which once belonged to an Assyrian courtier named Iahali, contains an inscription which states,

Figure 3.8 Clay cube lot belonging to Iahali; Neo-Babylonian.

> Oh Assur the great lord, oh Adad the great lord, the lot of Iahali the grand vizier of Salmaneser king of Assyria, governor-of-the-land (for) the city of Kibshuni (in) the land of Qumeni, the land of Mehrani, Uqu and the Cedar Mountain, and minister of trade – in his year assigned to him by lot may the harvest of the land of Assyria prosper and thrive, in front of the gods Assur and Adad may his lot fall.
>
> (Hallo 1983: 20)

The practice is well-attested in the Hebrew bible too (Lev. 16:8; 1 Sam. 10:20-1) and the Persians certainly employed the casting of lots as part of the decision-making process (Hdt. 3.128; Xen. *Cyr.* 1.6.46, 4.5.55) We can imagine that the inscribed lots or other token (including knucklebones) were thrown, either by their owners or by a third party (for impartiality), and that decisions were reached by the location in which they fell (**Figure 3.9**).

Figure 3.9 Hellenistic wall painting depicting a girl playing with gaming lots.

3:9 ten thousand talents of silver

Haman offers Xerxes a bribe of silver talents (there is little to support Vogelstein 1943 who argues that Haman was simply participating in the socially acceptable game of *bakshish*). Bribery was a perennial problem in the Achaemenid administration (as it has been everywhere in history) and Xenophon (*Cyr.* 8.8.13) was quick to note that the payment of the largest bribe had results: appointments to high position, contracts and lucrative trade deals (**Figure 3.10**). When put into context, the size of Haman's bribe is quite incredible. The annual tribute the Persians demanded from Media, for instance (Hdt. 3.95), was assessed at 450 talents of silver and the tribute of 100,000 sheep. Susa paid 300 talents, Armenia 400 silver talents and 20,000 prized Nissean horses. Libya and Egypt both provided 700 talents, the products of their fisheries and 120,000 measures of grain; Arabia gave 1,000 talents-worth of frankincense, and Ethiopia provided gold, ebony and ivory every two years. Babylonia paid the highest silver tax levy – 1,000 talents – and

Figure 3.10 Detail from a south Italian red-figure vase (The Darius Vase) showing a 'Persian' tax collector recording payments.

was expected to use the products of its fertile land to feed the court three times a year. The annual amount of silver, gold and precious goods amounted to some 14,560 talents, with a purchasing power many times higher than the sum suggests (Hackl and Ruffing 2021). Therefore, according to the standard weight measure established under Darius I, Haman's bribe amounted to some 333 tons of silver – almost the equivalent to the taxation which was accrued from the entire empire.

3:9 administrators for the royal treasury

The Persian royal court was both the household of the extended royal family, and the central organ of the entire state administration. The Achaemenids revelled in administrative red-tape (a love-affair they shared with their Assyrian and Elamite forebears) and their palaces included substantial spaces given over to imperial bureaucrats. Labelled by archaeologists 'Treasuries', these large buildings were both imperial storerooms and the offices of many thousands of civil servants. From sites as wide apart as Aswan in Egypt to Bactra in Afghanistan, surviving administrative documents (in these cases written on clay, papyrus, wood and strips of bone) testify to the tight administrative grip the Achaemenid kings had over their empire. Nothing was too trivial to be logged. The number of nails needed to repair a wooden boat in Upper Egypt or the fact that a plague of locusts meant that a mud-brick wall could not be built in Bactria – each and every case was individually recorded, signed-off, reported to the central administration in Persia and methodically filed away.

The administrative heart of the Great Kings' realm was located at Susa. A man-made canal connected this great city to the Persian Gulf and the River Tigris, and roads to Ecbatana, Babylon and Persepolis radiated out from the city's bureaucratic offices. Orders emanated from Susa to all provinces of the empire and reports from far and wide came back to the civil servants who manned the offices there. Susa was a hotbed of officialdom. It was there that high-ranking satraps rubbed shoulders with courtiers, and low-paid civil servants got glimpses of foreign diplomats on ambassadorial embassies. All life converged at Susa for the purpose of imperial business. The major chancelleries of state were bursting with civil servants, and scribes engaged in writing, sealing, posting and archiving thousands upon thousands of administrative clay tablets and other documents. Susa was the hub of the empire's bureaucracy, but similar, smaller offices were to be found at Persepolis, Ecbatana, Babylon, Memphis, Bactra, Sardis and all the other important urban centres of the realm. Red tape encircled the Persian world.

3: 10 signet ring

Gold, silver and bronze signet rings with stamp seals embedded into them have been found throughout Achaemenid Asia Minor, Babylonia and the Levant (**Figure 3.11**). Interestingly, in terms of artistic style and flavour, many of the seal images found in Asia Minor show a heavy Greek influence, with foreshortened human and animal figures, some three-quarter faces, some frontal faces, and realistic renditions of poses and anatomy (Llewellyn-Jones 2009a). Consequently, it is obvious that the seals belong to a heavily Hellenized environment and that they were, more than likely, created for and utilized by the Persian and Persianizing courts of Asia Minor or even by the dignitaries of the semi-independent kingdoms of Anatolia, and perhaps even the luminaries of the Syro-Phoenician coastal city-states. Yet the language they speak is undeniably 'Persian': in battle scenes between Persians and Greeks, for example, the Greeks are always shown as the vanquished foe. In one case (**Figure 1.9**), the Great King himself kills a naked hoplite representing, perhaps, the king's rule over the entire Greek people (or at least his anticipated hold over the western Greeks). In another seal image (**Figure 3.12**), Persians clash with nomadic, trouser-wearing, nomads. One especially striking ring-seal (**Figure 3.13**) bears the name of the owner (probably), Athenades, and shows a Persian archer sitting on a folding chair inspecting an arrow (the motif is better known from

Figure 3.11 Ring with seal impression; from Achaemenid-occupied Anatolia.

Figure 3.12 Battle scene of Persians fighting nomadic peoples; cylinder seal impression.

Figure 3.13 Gold ring with incised image of a Persian archer; inscribed with the owner's name – Athenades.

a series of coins from the fourth century BCE minted in the Levant). It is a fine example of goldsmith's work from Achaemenid Anatolia.

It should be noted, however, that the Persians much preferred to use cylinder seals crafted from semi-precious stones (although they were outlasted in popularity by ring-seals, which became the most common ring type in the Hellenistic and Roman worlds). Cylinder seals were worn around the neck on a chain or string and were sometimes placed on a spindle to enable them to be rolled into wet clay easily (**Figure 3.14**). To make the processing of documentation more straightforward, everyone involved in the Achaemenid bureaucracy, from the Great King to the lowliest scribe, possessed his own cylinder seal. Royal women too were in charge of their own seals. The seal was a visible emblem of office that could be carried and shown to everyone. It acted like a warrant, or a sheriff's badge, giving officers of the empire the stamp of power (Garrison 2021). The seal would be applied to all official documents, pressed into a wet clay tablet to leave its imprint as a kind of 'signature'. A seal, or rather its impression, conveyed the authority of its owners and the seal-imprints could sanction action and expenditure. While a seal remained with the owner, clay tablets imprinted with the seals of civil servants and officers of state could travel far and wide. It is possible to locate tablets created in Persepolis in far off Kandahar, Sardis, Bactra, Damascus and many other distant clerical centres. Every seal was inscribed with a bespoke image and each image was unique to one owner, which makes it possible to trace an individual's 'signature' throughout the whole archive of documents, and to pin-point his role in the administration.

Figure 3.14 Example of a cylinder seal in its setting.

The Director of the Persepolis Civil Service, a man named Parnaka, owned a very fine seal indeed. It was an antique Assyrian-made piece depicting a warrior grasping a somewhat confused ostrich by the neck and brandishing a sword (**Figure 3.15**). His deputy, named Zišsawiš also had a smart seal-design: it showed a winged cow suckling her calf, enjoying the protection of a four-winged daemon (**Figure 3.16**). Whenever civil

Figure 3.15 Seal impression of Parnaka (PFS 9) from Persepolis.

Figure 3.16 Seal impression of Zišsawiš (PFS 83*) from Persepolis.

servants saw the ostrich- or the cow-figures imprinted into a clay tablet, they recognized the owners of the seals immediately and acted on their orders. Cylinder seals and signet rings were apt to get lost and needed replacing. When Parnaka mislaid his ostrich-design seal he had it replaced with another, this time showing a warrior throttling two lions (**Figure 3.17**), and quickly issued a memo to his team stating that, 'The seal that used to be mine, is now lost. As a substitute, I now use the seal that can be seen in this letter.' As a matter of security,

Figure 3.17 Second seal impression of Parnaka (PFS 16*) from Persepolis.

Ziššawiš was therefore forced to abandon his regular seal and to use a new design too. Fortuitously his loyalty to the crown was rewarded when Darius the Great gifted Ziššawiš a brand-new seal representing the king himself standing in a date grove in front of a fire altar in the presence of Ahuramazda (**Figure 3.18**).

Figure 3.18 Second seal impression of Ziššawiš (PFS 11) from Persepolis.

Chapter 4

1 When Mordecai learned of all that had happened, **he tore his clothes, put on sackcloth and ashes, and went out into the city, wailing loudly and bitterly.** 2 But **he went only as far as the king's gate, because no one clothed in sackcloth was allowed to enter it**. 3 In every province to which the edict and order of the king came, there was great mourning among the Jews, with fasting, weeping and Lamentation. Many sprawled on the ground in sackcloth and ashes.

4 When Esther's eunuchs and ladies-in-waiting came and told her about Mordecai, she was in great anguish. She sent garments for him to put on instead of his sackcloth, but he would not take them. 5 Then Esther beckoned **Hathak**, one of the king's eunuchs assigned to attend her, and ordered him to find out what was upsetting Mordecai and why.

6 So Hathak went out to Mordecai in the open square of the city in front of the king's gate. 7 Mordecai told him everything that had happened to him, including the precise amount of money Haman had promised to pay into the royal treasury for the obliteration of the Jews. 8 He also gave him a copy of the text of the edict for their annihilation, which had been published in Susa, to show to Esther and explain it to her, and he told him to tell her to go into the king's presence to beg for clememcy and plead with him for her people.

9 **Hathak went back and reported to Esther what Mordecai had said**. 10 Then she told him to say to Mordecai, 11 'All the king's officials and the people of the royal provinces know that **for any man or woman who approaches the king in the inner court without being summoned the king has but one law: that they be put to death unless the king extends the gold sceptre** to them and spares their lives. But **thirty days have passed since I was called to go to the king**.'

12 When Esther's words were told to Mordecai, 13 he sent back this response: 'Do not think that because you are in the king's palace you alone of all the Jews will escape. 14 For if you stay voiceless at this time, relief and deliverance for the Jews will arise from some other place, but you and your father's family will perish. And who knows but that you have come to your royal position for such a time as this?' 15 Then Esther sent this message to Mordecai: 16 'Go, call together all the Jews of Susa, and fast for me. Do not eat or drink for three days, night or day. I and my entourage will fast as you do. When this is done, I will go to the king, even though it is prohibited by law. And if I perish, I perish.' 17 So Mordecai went away and carried out all of Esther's instructions.

Commentary

4:1 he tore his clothes, put on sackcloth and ashes, and went out into the city, wailing loudly and bitterly

Figure 4.1 Professional mourners accompany the deceased on a barge; wall painting from a tomb at Thebes; New Kingdom.

Mordecai expresses his anguish over the injustice of Haman's edict with visual and audible force. Termed 'petitionary mourning', Mordecai's display of public grief is best understood as relating to a calamity yet to come (see also Jon. 3:5; analysed by Seidler 2019). His purpose is to solicit attention and to draw attention his – and his people's – plight. Loud wailing was used ritualistically and symbolically throughout the ancient world to acknowledge and emphasize distress and apprehension (**Figures 4.1, 4.2, 4.3**). Public lamentation (mostly the preserve of women) also involved specific actions such as tearing clothes, throwing dust on the head and squatting close to the ground (Pham 2000; **Figures 4.4, 4.5, 4.6**). Each element of lamentation encoded a message of loss as the mourners lowered themselves into the dust as witness to a traumatic change in circumstances. In the Babylonian version of the Descent of Ishtar into the Underworld, Papsukkal, the vizier of the

Figure 4.2 Mourning women, stripped to the waist, on the sarcophagus of King Ahiram of Byblos.

Figure 4.3 Fragmentary relief sculpture of Egyptian mourning women. Late Period, from Thebes.

Figure 4.4 Mourning women squat close to the ground. Egyptian tomb painting, Thebes.

Figure 4.5 Mourning women squat close to the ground. Egyptian tomb painting, Thebes.

great gods, undertakes formal mourning: 'He wore mourning clothes, his hair was unkempt. Dejected, he went and wept before Sin his father, his tears flowed freely before king Ea' (Hallo 1997: 382).

Displays of anxiety and of grief were ritualistically codified and were *de rigueur* for both sexes, almost demanded by etiquette, in fact, and the Hebrew Bible is rich with such examples (the Persians were in no way out of step in this regard). Formal mourning at the death of a loved-one or a person of consequence was always accompanied by conspicuous displays of grief and wealthier families employed the services of professional mourners too. Tearing one's garments was a fitting response to personal calamity (Judg. 11:35; 1 Sam. 13:19) and even in courts of law judges who were witnesses to blasphemy were required to tear their garments as a formal response (Ezra 9), and in royal courts monarchs ripped their clothing as a sign of outrage (2 Kgs 5:7; 2 Kgs 6:30; see further Köhlmoos 2019). It is possible that tearing one's garments resulted in nudity (or partial nudity): the chest or breasts, stomach and even the genitals might be displayed as a consequence. Certainly, an exposure or partial exposure of the body would make sense of Job's (1:21) famous lament, 'Naked I came from my mother's womb, naked I shall return.' The female figures on the so-called Memphis stela (**Figure 4.7**), an intriguing pictorial record from Achaemenid-period Egypt, are naked from the waist up and tear their hair in another gesture of ritual lamentation.

Figure 4.6 Large group of professional mourners; Egyptian tomb painting; New Kingdom.

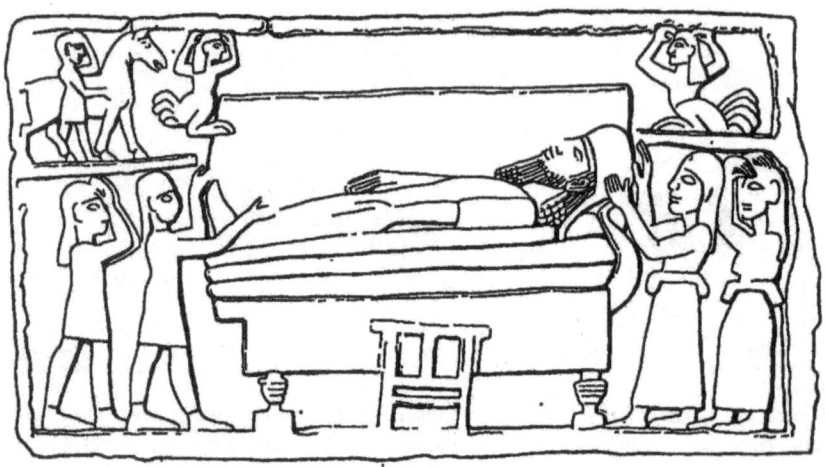

Figure 4.7 Funerary stela of a Persian nobleman from Persian-occupied Egypt (The Memphis Stela).

Wearing sackcloth – a coarse, loosely woven material made of goat-hair (it was also called haircloth) or plant fibres which, as its name suggests, was commonly used for sacking – was an extension to the conspicuousness of lamentation (1 Kgs 20:31-2) and self-humiliation (2 Kgs 19:1; Isa. 37:1-2). Uncomfortable to wear and with an obvious association of uncleanliness, the wearing of sackcloth garments (sometimes simply a belt or loincloth, Isa. 32:11) demonstrated the wearers' relationship with pain and preoccupation with suffering; it stressed that they had turned their backs on society and no longer participated in its norms. The employment of ashes, dirt or dust – smeared over the face and scattered over the head – is a visual extension of the motif of social distancing evoked by public lamentation. The ashes were a symbol of insignificance or nothingness (Gen. 18:27; Isa. 44:20; Mal. 3:21; 13:12; 30:19). In Babylonian mythology, ashes were thought of as the food of the inhabitants of the underworld. For men, an unshaven, unkempt appearance was part of the codified signs of lamentation: a remarkable ostraca sketch of a young Ramesside pharaoh shows him mourning his dead father and royal predecessor (**Figure 4.8**): stubble grows on his unshaved chin and tear stains (highlighted by the kohl eye make-up he wears) run down his face.

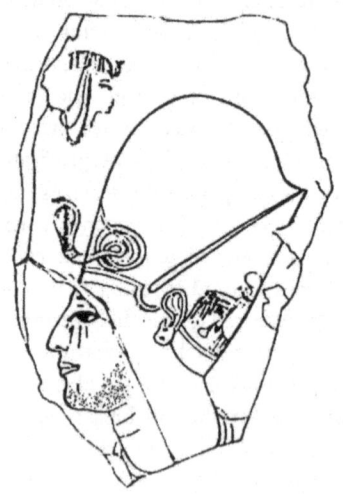

Figure 4.8 Ostracon showing a grieving Ramesside pharaoh. From Deir el-Medinah; late New Kingdom.

4:2 he went only as far as the king's gate, because no one clothed in sackcloth was allowed to enter it

The royal enclosure was a place of formality where the rules of etiquette were strictly enforced; the disorder of mourning, with all its connotations of social topsy-turvydom, in such a heightened environment was not welcomed. Throughout the Near East orderly behaviour within palaces was looked for and some monarchs went as far as to establish strict codes of behaviour for all their courtiers. Cleanliness and propriety were expected, even (especially) amongst the royal cooks and food-bearers as one Hittite text (Hallo 1997: 217–18) makes clear:

> Let those who make the daily bread be clean. Let them be washed and trimmed. Let (their) hair and finger[nails] be trimmed. Let them be clothed in clean garments ... When a servant stands before his master, [make sure] he (is) washed and has clothed (himself) in clean (clothes).

Part of the Persian prohibition of mourning dress within the confines of the Great King's living space might be explained through a desire to keep the monarch away from the contamination of grief (see for instance Hdt. 3.117, 119). Certainly, Nehemiah, the much-favoured cupbearer of Artaxerxes I, feared the king's anger when he appeared before the throne looking gloomy: 'I had never been sad in his presence', Nehemiah (2:2) was keen to stress.

4:5 Hathak

The etymology of the name is uncertain, but it might be connected to the OP *$hantaka$, 'the runner'. It would make sense of his office, as the one who runs between Mordecai and Esther delivering missives (see **4:9 Hathak went back and reported to Esther what Mordecai had said**) – a standard occupation for court eunuchs it seems.

4:11 for any man or woman who approaches the king in the inner court without being summoned the king has but one law: that they be put to death unless the king extends the gold sceptre

(i) Audience ceremony

In any monarchic system, ceremony naturally revolves around the figure of the ruler; ceremonies have always been the favourite way for a regime to exhibit its political clout, and when properly employed, ceremony nearly always produces the desired results by appealing to people of diverse backgrounds and beliefs. Alongside promoting a regime's power and stability, ceremony serves to reveal its ideological basis and worldview to its targeted population.

Messages lie encoded in various components of the rituals of Achaemenid court ceremonial: the architectural venue for ceremonies or the route of imperial processions can offer significant clues about the meaning of ceremonies to the life and ideology of the dynasty. Similarly, as has been noted, thrones, footstools, parasols, flywhisks, sceptres, crowns and robes are loaded with symbolic implications, although many of the subtleties of these objects of symbolic importance still require serious scholarly exploration. Moreover, the identity of courtiers participating in ceremony, their attire as well as their stance, imparts a mass of information about the self-perception of the ruling elite.

Achaemenid court ceremonies maintained and reinforced hierarchy within the elite and delineated power relations between courtiers, the royal family and the monarch himself. Persian monarchs relied upon formalized etiquette and court ceremony to create a special aura around the throne. A deliberate separation and distancing of the king from the gaze of his subjects, even from much of his court, meant that elaborate rituals were enacted through which courtiers and visitors might get limited access to the royal personage during a tightly controlled and stage-managed audience ceremony. The Book of Esther highlights the notion of having access to the royal presence and what that meant for state policy.

We might think of the Great King, costumed in his finery as an actor in a great royal drama (and his courtiers as part-players and spectators) because events at court, like coronations and investitures, royal audiences and imperial parade-reviews, were clearly focused on a kind of 'performance', since they were set far apart from everyday life by being 'scripted' or turned into ceremony (see Elias 1983: 94, 97; Burke 1994; Strootman 2007: 10). As actors in the royal drama, courtiers (even queens) had their cues for entrances and exits. A Neo-Assyrian text highlights the choreographed nature of the royal audience:

> As soon as the king is seated on his seat, the overseer of the palace enters [kisses] the ground before [the king], and gives (his) report before the king. The overseer of the palace [goes out] and brings in the palace herald. The palace herald e[nters], kisses the ground before the king, and stands with the standard opposite [the king]. The palace herald gives (his) report before the king. [The overseer of the palace goes out and] brings in the grand vizier. [The grand vizier en]ters, [kisses the ground] opposite the king before the threshold, and stands opposite the king. The palace herald and the] grand vizier go out. [After they have l]eft, the crown prince enters. He keeps his right foot stiff [ ], places [a]ll his [...] on the ground [ ], leans [...] [and] occupies (his) place. [The (other) sons of the king enter] and stand [opposite the king]. [The ...] gives (his) [repo]rt. [The ... ente]r [and giv]e [(their) reports before the king].
>
> (cited in Portuese 2020: 115)

The Esther story operates on the understanding that the choreography of courtly etiquette was inflexible in structure and that an unscheduled, spontaneous, appearance before the Great King, without the rigmarole of the correct audience-protocol, was unwanted and even dangerous for the rogue actor.

Narrative accounts of audiences with the Great King form a significant corpus in Greek and biblical writings on the Persian court (Philost. *Imag.* 2.31; the same is true of satrapal audience scenes – see Xen. *Hel.* 1.5.1–3; Plut. *Lys.* 6; see especially Allen 2005b), but nothing remotely comparable exists in the Achaemenid literary tradition. Instead, we must turn to a rich stratum of iconography for information on the intricacies of the ceremony. Representations of the royal audience come in the form of numerous seal- and gemstone-images (**Figure 4.9**), a small painted image on a sarcophagus (**Figures 4.10** and **4.11**), and from the sculptured monumental doorjambs

Figure 4.9 Achaemenid royal audience scene; seal impression from Persian-occupied Anatolia.

 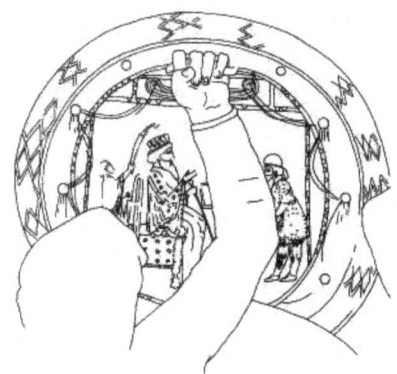

Figure 4.10 Persian soldier with shield raised; from the Alexander Sarcophagus; early Hellenistic period from Sidon.

Figure 4.11 Achaemenid royal audience scene painted inside the shield depicted in Figure 4.10.

at Persepolis (see Allen 2005b; Kaptan 2002: 31–41), although the finest surviving examples come in the form of two big stone reliefs once located at the staircases to the Apadana (later moved to the Treasury; see Abdi 2010; **Figure 4.12**). The Great King is shown in audience in a 'frozen moment'; he wears a court robe and crown and holds a pomegranate blossom and holds a sceptre (see below). In order to 'accentuate the immutable character of kingship' (Briant 2002: 221), the Great King is accompanied by the Crown Prince who is depicted wearing the same garb as the king, and who is given the prerogative of holding a flower too. Also in attendance are high-ranking members of the court and the military (Abdi 2010: 277–8; Kuhrt 2007: 536). Two incense-burners help to demarcate the royal space (and accentuate its sacredness), as does the dais upon which the throne is placed (Brettler 1989: 85–6) and the baldachin, decorated with an image of Ahuramazda, which covers the scene (the relief image closely echoes a Greek description: Dinon F1). The theatrical paraphernalia of the throne room, and the awesome setting of the Apadana was intended to instil fear and wonder in suppliants; the figure of the king, the protagonist of the drama, must have been an impressive, almost overwhelming, sight (the Greek version of Esther 15:5-7 brilliantly captures the scene of the terrified queen approaching the enthroned king, who is described as looking 'like a bull in the height of anger').

Figure 4.12 Achaemenid royal audience scene; originally attached to the north staircase of the Apadana at Persepolis.

Evidence for the protocol policy cited in Esther – execution for anyone who appears before the king without his summoning – is scarce, although Herodotus (3.118) makes the point that when Darius I ascended the throne, he passed legislation stressing that only representatives of the six great Persian families who had helped him seize the throne might have unprecedented access to his person (although even this privileged few could not approach the king if he was in the company of his women). The case of Intaphernes subsequently acted as a litmus test for the legislation. One of Persia's great *khāns*, Intaphernes was a man of spectacularly high standing. He had supported Darius' accession to the throne when, in 521 BCE, he went as a general at the head of an army to eliminate one of the men who had usurped the throne of Babylon in the first year of Darius' reign. Intaphernes was the second man in the empire and Darius listed him first among those he called his 'followers'. In spite of this, shortly after his accession, Darius had Intaphernes executed. The charge was treason.

According to Herodotus (3.70), who was probably reiterating a well-known Persian account (possibly originating with the family of Intaphernes itself), Intaphernes had entered the royal palace at Susa wishing to enjoy a private audience with Darius, but the palace chamberlain and the eunuch messenger thought otherwise and refused him leave to pass into the domestic interior of the palace. They told him that the king was, at the time, in bed with one of his women. Intaphernes suspected them of lying, and in anger he drew his dagger and sliced off their noses and cut off their ears. He then attached the grisly trophies to his horse's bridle, which he tied around the necks of the mutilated retainers. In this hideous state, the shellshocked servants presented themselves to Darius and rattled off the events that had occurred. Fearing that the other six nobles had conspired in this act and that another coup was at hand, Darius sent for each of them. He carefully questioned them, individually, about their thoughts on Intaphernes. When he had ascertained, and was satisfied, that Intaphernes had acted without their knowledge and that a power-struggle was not imminent, he had Intaphernes arrested. His children and all his male relatives were taken into custody too. Darius was convinced that Intaphernes had conspired with his family and that they intended to remove him from the throne and found a new dynasty. Shortly afterwards, they were all condemned to death. The story suggests that Intaphernes was flaunting his insubordination by violating rules of protocol. It is probable that Darius took this as an excuse to rid himself of a powerful *khān* who had come uncomfortably close to his throne.

There is no doubt that access to the Persian Great King was not immediate, but mandated. Greek accounts stress the fact that no one was allowed free passage into his presence without the express permission of the *chiliarch*, Gk. 'commander of a thousand' (Nepos, Conon 3.2–3; Plut. Them. 27.2–7, Barjamovic 2011: 40–1; Llewellyn-Jones 2013a: 31, 43, 71–2; in the Neo-Assyrian court the role of introducer to the king and chief of palace protocol was the *ša-pān-ekalli*, 'the one in front of the palace'; see further Groß 2020: 73–98 and Portuese 2020: 105–10). The question arises, therefore, as to why Esther did not simply petition the *chiliarch* for an audience with the king. It is possible that it was Haman himself who held the position of *chiliarch* and that Esther did not want to arouse any suspicion by communicating with him (Moore 1971: 49).

(ii) sceptre

Outside of Esther there is no attestation of the protocol of the king extending his sceptre to suppliants. There is plenty of iconographic evidence for the king's employment of a sceptre as part of his official paraphernalia, however, and the object – which appears more like a staff or walking stick – is frequently depicted in Achaemenid art (**Figures 1.15, 1.26, 1.28, 1.52; Figures 4.12, 4.13**). The sceptre is certainly to be found in depictions of the royal audience

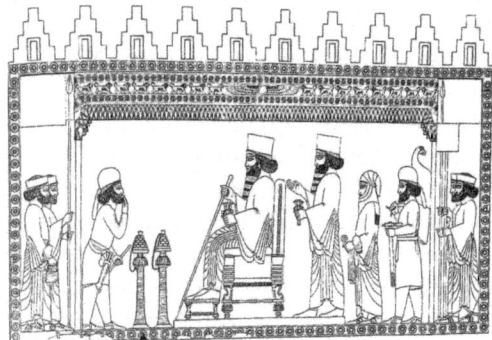

Figure 4.13 Achaemenid royal audience scene; originally attached to the east staircase of the Apadana at Persepolis.

Figure 4.14 The Greek god Zeus; red-figure vase painting; early Classical period; from Athens.

Figure 4.15 Great King in procession; doorjamb at the palace of Xerxes, Persepolis.

(**Figures 3.1**, **4.12**) and the Greeks used it to demarcate figures of Zeus, the king of the gods, in their artworks (**Figure 4.14**) and subsequently employed a sceptre as a shorthand to depict the image of the Persian Great King too (**Figures 4.15**, **4.16** and **4.17**). Like much else at the Persian court, the royal staff-like sceptre was inherited from a Neo-Assyrian prototype where it was known by the Akkad. *ḫattu* or *šibirru* (see Portuese 2020: 138–9; **Figure 1.21** and **Figure 4.18**). Portuese (2020: 139) suggests that the staff-sceptre carried 'profound meanings to show the shepherding role of the Assyrian king and his paternalistic attitude towards his flock, since it is never [shown] during warlike scenes'. The shepherd image was effectively used of Sargon II of Assyria: 'May the king, my lord, the good shepherd … truly tend and shepherd them (his people). May Ašur, Bel, and Nabu add flocks to your

Figure 4.16 Detail from a south Italian red-figure vase (The Darius Vase) showing a 'Persian' monarch in audience.

Figure 4.17 A Persian 'king' shown with his bow and sceptre; from a red-figure drinking cup; early Classical period from Athens.

Figure 4.18 Neo-Assyrian king with sceptre stands with his designated heir; stone relief sculpture from Nineveh.

flocks, give them to you, and enlarge your spacious fold; may the people of all countries come into your presence!' (cited in Tomes 2005: 79). Near Eastern royal imagery frequently cast the king in the role of the shepherd of his people: the Israelite king David was a shepherd-ruler par excellence, a man whom Yahweh 'took … from the sheepfolds … to be shepherd of … his people' (Ps. 78:70) and the Hebrew conception of Cyrus the Great likewise depicted the Achaemenid monarch in the same light (Isa. 44:28). Rooted deep in the sheep–shepherd relationship, the image of the shepherd-king stresses his care and compassion for his people and, simultaneously, the dependence of the people on the ruler to meet their needs. In addition, the metaphor of people as sheep emphasizes their passivity – an ideal state-of-being in ancient royal ideology, because it was wilfulness and disobedience of the people that kings most feared. However, a scene from the Assyrian palace at Kalhu depicts Tiglath-pileser III, seated on a high throne, using his sceptre to pin down a foreign suppliant who grovels before him (**Figure 4.19**). Less of a shepherd's staff and more of a warrior's spear, Tiglath-pileser's sceptre shows that royal dominance could be encoded in the more overt use of this significant ceremonial prop. It is feasible that the Achaemenid monarch enjoyed a similarly flexible use of his sceptre.

Figure 4.19 Tiglath-pileser III uses his sceptre to humiliate a foreign suppliant. Stone relief sculpture from Kalhu.

4:11 thirty days have passed since I was called to go to the king

Esther's month-long absence from the king should not be taken as her loss of Xerxes' favour. It is, instead, typical of the polygynous nature of the royal household. The highest-ranking women of the royal family did not always reside with the king. Sometimes they resided at their estates and at other times they were in his orbit, but did not share his bed. Given the number of concubines and other sex-partners the king could potentially enjoy, the royal consorts enjoyed his intimate companionship infrequently. Many concubines spent their entire lives in the palaces without any contact with the Great King.

In many polygynous court cultures, the observation of a strict hierarchy amongst women resulted in the regimentation of their sexual congress with the ruler. In China, to give but one example, it was believed that organizing the emperor's sex life was essential to maintaining the well-being of the entire Chinese state (Rawski 1998). The Chinese calendars of the tenth century CE were not used to keep track of time but rather to keep the emperor's sex schedule in check and the rotation of concubines sleeping with the emperor was kept to a strictly regimented order. Secretaries were employed to record the emperor's sex life in annals so that the conception of children could be calculated to the day of intercourse. In imperial China, age was determined from the moment of conception, not the time of birth and it was believed that women were most likely to conceive during the full moon, when the Yin, or female influence, was strong enough to match the Yang, or male force, of the emperor. The empress and other wives slept with the emperor around the time of the full moon because it was believed children of strong virtue would be conceived on those nights. The lower-ranking concubines were tasked with nourishing the emperor's Yang with their Yin, sleeping with him around the time of the new moon.

It is interesting to note that Esther specifically notes that it had been thirty days since she was last called to Xerxes' bed. Might this suggest that she simply had to wait her turn and that the Achaemenids, like many other royal dynasties, scheduled sexual congress with the monarchs in a formal way? The possibility is real.

Of course, another reason for Esther's absence from the Great King's bed might be explained through biology: menstruation. A menstruating woman could be referred to as someone who was 'unclean' and menstrual blood was regarded as dangerously polluting. Menstruating women in the royal archives of Mari had to leave the palace and live elsewhere for five or six days. After that time, she would be clean again: 'Today the slave-girl of the king (a concubine) has become clean and has entered the palace' (cited in Stol 2016: 439). A regulation in an Assyrian harem (edict 7) also stipulates temporary exclusion: 'When the time for making sacrifices draws near, a palace woman who is menstruating (lit. unapproachable) shall not enter into the presence of the king' (Roth 1995: 200 §7). In Zoroastrian tradition of the Sasanian era, menstruation was thought to be so polluting that women were kept well apart from men (see Secunda 2020).

Chapter 5

1 On the third day Esther put on **her royal robes** and stood in **the inner court of the palace, in front of the king's hall**. The king was sitting on his royal throne in the hall, looking towards the entrance. 2 When he saw Queen Esther standing in the court, he was delighted with her and held out to her the golden sceptre that was in his hand. So, Esther advanced and touched the tip of the sceptre.

3 Then the king asked, 'What is it, Queen Esther? What is your request? **Even up to half the kingdom**, it will be given you.' 4 'If it pleases the king,' replied Esther, 'let the king, together with Haman, come today to a meal I have prepared for him.' 5 'Bring Haman at once,' the king said, 'so that we may do what Esther asks.'

So the king and Haman went to the meal Esther had prepared. 6 As they were drinking wine, the king again asked Esther, 'Now what is your petition? It will be given you. And what is your request? Even up to half the kingdom, it will be granted.'

7 Esther replied, 'My petition and my request is this: 8 If the king regards me with favour and if it pleases the king to grant my petition and fulfil my request, let the king and Haman come tomorrow to the banquet I will prepare for them. Then I will answer the king's question.'

9 Haman went out that day happy and in high spirits. But when he saw Mordecai at the king's gate and observed that he neither rose nor showed fear in his presence, he was filled with rage against Mordecai. 10 Nevertheless, Haman restrained himself and went home. Calling together his friends and **Zeresh**, his wife, 11 Haman bragged to them about his affluence, **his many sons**, and all the ways the king had honoured him and how he had elevated him above the other aristocrats and bureaucrats. 12 'And that's not all,' Haman added. 'I'm the only person Queen Esther invited to accompany the king to the banquet she gave. And she has invited me along with the king tomorrow. 13 But all this gives me no pleasure as long as I see that Jew Mordecai sitting at the king's gate.'

14 His wife Zeresh and all his friends said to him, '**Have a pole set up, reaching to a height of fifty cubits**, and ask the king in the morning to have Mordecai impaled on it. Then go with the king to the banquet and have fun.' This suggestion pleased Haman, and he had the pole set up.

Commentary

5:1 her royal robes

A better translation of the Heb. might be, 'she clothed herself royally' (Macchi 2018: 185), i.e., she dressed in her best (but not specifically royal) garments. It is, according to Berlin (2001: 52), part of the 'dress for success motif' encountered elsewhere in the bible (Ruth 3:3; Ezek. 16:9-15; Jdt. 10:3-7).

It is fair to say that there is a paucity of evidence for female dress in Iran in the Achaemenid period. There are no indigenous Persian texts which tell of women's dress and material sources are limited in this respect too (as recognized by Brosius 1996: 84). However, enough visual evidence survives for us to make some cogent points about female dress (**Figures 1.98, 1.107–1.110, 1.113–1.116, 2.11** and **2.12**) and, more importantly, to begin to expand our engagement with ancient Persian gender ideologies – an important subject which is woefully lagging behind in scholarly studies when compared to the significant advances made over the last two decades in the fields of Near Eastern and Biblical Studies and the bold strides made since the 1980s in the study of gender in the Classical world (of particular importance is the work of Bahrani 2001; see further Green 2019 for a summary of important issues arising in Near Eastern gender studies).

To all intents and purposes, elite women of the Achaemenid court wore the same voluminous, richly ornamented garments as men. In anthropological terms this is very unusual. There are few places or times (perhaps none) in the world and its history in which no sex-differentiation in dress exists. Those who participate inside any given culture learn how to distinguish males from females at an early age, although there are no universal patterns in dress which are considered appropriate for each sex. In societies where dress does not distinguish the secondary sexual characteristics, the sexes are clearly distinct but distinguishing between the sexes is possible even in societies where bodies are covered or concealed by garments – such as in ancient Iran. The Persian elite, like all cultural insiders, must have used other clues to facilitate sex differences through hairstyles, cosmetics and even perfumes. Some gender markers, like male beards or female head veils, were obvious sex-distinguishers, but others were perhaps more subtle: make-up was used by both sexes, but were there variations in style or application? Jewellery seems to offer no distinct clues to gender-appropriateness, but might there have been sex demarcations? Certainly, the discovery of a rich horde of jewellery (including lion-headed torcs and bracelets, cloisonné earrings and roundels, and many necklaces) in an Achaemenid-era grave at Susa in 1901 gave no clues as to the sex of the deceased (the loss of the human remains means that sex-identification is impossible, although Jacques De Morgan (1905) thought them to have been of a middle-aged woman). Nor can we pronounce (as yet) on colour ideologies in ancient Persia or say that fashionable gender identity was demarcated along lines of hue, colour, colour-saturation or even the patterning of garments, although it is highly likely that there were distinct nuances in dress which are not apparent to us. There is enough iconographic evidence to show that bracteates were used to decorate both male and female court robes. All in all, it is not too much of a semantic stretch to classify the garment worn at court as 'unisex'.

Was Persian courtly hierarchy apparent through dress? In what ways were Esther's 'royal robes' a mark of distinction of office? It is very hard to be precise about this point, but there is some evidence for status-distinction in Achaemenid women's dress. The De Clerq seal, now in the Louvre (**Figure 5.1**), clearly represents a female audience

Figure 5.1 Achaemenid seal impression of a female audience scene (De Clerq Seal); possibly from Susa.

scene, on a par with representations we have of male royalty (Brosius 1996: 86 and 2010b; Lerner 2010). The parallel with the king's audience is explicit and is proof of the high regard in which royal women were held. A woman sits on a high-backed throne, her feet raised up on a footstool, and wearing the same type of crown and veil as the large female encountered in the Pazyryk textile fragment (**Figure 1.108**). She sniffs a pomegranate flower while young girl, her hair in a long plait, offers a bird as a gift. Behind the incense burner, which stands centrally demarcating the space, there approaches another crowned and veiled woman, but in contrast to the seated female's veil, this woman wears a shorter, narrower veil which emerges, it appears, from underneath her crown so that it does not envelop her body; it reaches to her buttocks and seems to terminate in a decorated border – perhaps a cross-fringe (Lerner 2010: 159 identifies the veil as 'diadem ribbons', but this is erroneous). It could be argued that rank among royal women – and here I suggest we have either the enthroned mother of the king, a royal daughter and a royal consort, or, just as feasibly, a series of consorts and concubines of differing ages and rank – was expressed through dress as much as through posture and body-language. The size and volume of the seated woman's veil seems particularly significant. Status in terms of age and status appears to be codified through the varying levels of physical concealment it offered. The bird-bearer's lack of head-covering amplifies her youth and her junior status, it seems, among the other

Figure 5.2 Achaemenid cylinder seal impression of seated woman spinning and flywhisk-bearing attendant. Unknown provenance.

assembled women (although Lerner 2010: 160 suggests the figure is that of a boy and that the 'plait' is a kind of side-lock-of-youth worn by Levantine princes). It is highly likely that within this court system, dress was used as an important, if subtle, status-indicator. After all, in other court societies throughout world history, rank has always been carefully codified through elements of dress. Among the royal ladies of Achaemenid Persia, it might have been played out through the use of dress accessories such as headdresses and veils as well as through other wealth-indicators such as jewellery and fine textiles.

A seal in Buffalo (**Figure 5.2**) gives, perhaps, further evidence of this. It depicts an enthroned woman with an attendant behind her, who holds a flywhisk over the seated female's head in the manner of representations we have of the Great King (Lerner 2010: 154). While the iconography incorporates elements of standard 'audience scene' motifs (throne and incense burner), there are noticeable differences, most obviously the fact that the seated woman, the higher ranking of the two females, is spinning. The royal trappings which surround her (including the flywhisk-bearer herself) suggest the seated figure's high rank, whilst her spinning must be related to the gendering of her person. Both wear the Achaemenid court robe (the gown of the flywhisk-bearer trails on the floor behind her) but they are distinguished by their headwear. The flywhisk-bearer wears the distinctive Persian bob-hairstyle and what Lerner (2010: 154) has identified as 'a tight-fitting cap with a long pig-tail or tassel at the back'. This is not the case: the artist is attempting to show that the woman is wearing a short head veil (similar to that found on the De Clerq seal, **Figure 5.1**) over her carefully arranged bouffant-style hair and there is no need to over-read the image by looking for any form of 'cap' here. The seated spinning woman does wear something quite unique, though, because it appears that her head is draped in a cloth which has been wrapped around to form a kind of turban. This headdress is not attested elsewhere on any other representation of a woman in Achaemenid art, although turbans and headwraps of various forms can be found worn by many male delegations on the north and east staircases of the Persepolis Apadana, on the so-called Atlas-pose scenes on Persepolitan doorjambs and tomb façades, and on the base of the statue of Darius I from Susa (**Figures 1.13, 1.76**). It is possible that the seated spinning woman, of clear high rank, is distinguished by her head-covering as perhaps foreign-born or non-Persian, but we cannot go any further with this idea.

5:1 the inner court of the palace, in front of the king's hall

This must be the area of the Susa palace which it was forbidden to enter until summoned (4:11). It probably refers to the Apadana – the site of official receptions (**Figure 5.3**).

Figure 5.3 Reconstruction of the façade of the Apadana at Susa.

5:3 Even up to half the kingdom

As well as being a common biblical idiom to express a large gift (1 Kgs 13:7), this is a popular, and very ancient, folktale motif. Herodotus employs it in the story of Xerxes' adulterous love for his daughter-in-law-cum-niece towards the end of the *Histories* (9.109). He promised the girl, Artaÿnte, cities, gold, a personal army and half his kingdom (Llewellyn-Jones 2022: 265–70; the motif is found in other Herodotean stories, at 5.24 and 7.135). In the New Testament Gospels, the same promise is made to the unnamed daughter of Herodias who danced for the pleasure of Herod Antipas (Mk 6:17-29; Mt. 14:3-12).

5:10 Zeresh

Haman's wife plays a small but important role in the story. She encourages his crimes and spurs him to action. Her name might derive from Av. *zairiçi*, 'blonde' or be associated with the Elamite deity Kiriša (Macchi 2018: 194). Gindin (2016: 163) argues that the name Zeresh (Av. Zaurviš) is the name of an Avestan demoness, patroness of old age and poisonous plants. Given that she is 'determined, brutal, and devoid of scruples' (Macchi 2018: 195), adopting the name of a demoness works well for Zeresh.

5:11 his many sons

According to the addition to the original text, Haman has ten sons (Est. 9:10). All ancient societies thought that a father with many sons was a blessed and fortunate individual (Gen. 29:31–30:24; 35:16-29; 1 Chron. 3:109; 2 Chron. 11:21; Job 1, 42:13; Eccl. 2:7). The pressure felt by men, especially nobles and kings, to father many sons was tantamount to their success and reputation (**Figures 5.4** and **5.5**). Appeals to the gods are telling of the pressure they were under. Kirta, the childless princeling of Ugarit pours forth an anguished cry to his gods to grant him male heirs: 'What to me is silver,

Figure 5.4 Representation of the sons of Ramses II; Ramesseum, Thebes; New Kingdom.

Figure 5.5 Representation of the sons of Ramses III; Medinet Habu, Thebes; New Kingdom.

or even yellow gold, together with its land, and slaves forever mine? A triad of chariot horses from the stable of a slave woman's son? Let me procreate sons! Let me produce a brood!' (Parker 1997: 13–14).

Herodotus noted that the Persians regarded it 'the greatest proof of manly excellence' to father a healthy line of sons, affirming that,

> after valour in battle it is accounted fortunate to father a great number of sons. The king sends gifts yearly to the man who begets the most. Strength, (the Persians) believe, is in numbers. They educate their boys from five to twenty years old, and teach them only three things: riding and archery and to speak the truth. A boy is not seen by his father before he is five years old, but lives with the women: the point of this is that, if the boy should die in the interval of his rearing, the father would suffer no grief.
>
> (1.136)

5:14 Have a pole set up, reaching to a height of fifty cubits

A cubit is around 45 to 50 centimetres (Scott 1958). At a height of 50 cubits – 25 metres or 82 feet – Haman's impalement-pole would reach the height of a modern seven-storey building. It would be the highest structure in all of Susa. The measurement is, of course, satirical.

Chapter 6

1 That night the king could not sleep; so, he ordered the book of the chronicles, the annals of his reign, to be brought in and recited to him. 2 It was found recorded there that Mordecai had exposed Bigthana and Teresh, two of the king's officers who safeguarded the doorway, who had contrived to assassinate King Xerxes.

3 'What honour and recognition has Mordecai received for this?' the king asked. 'Nothing has been done for him,' his attendants answered. 4 The king said, 'Who is in the court?' Now Haman had just entered the outer court of the palace to speak to the king about impaling Mordecai on the pole he had set up for him. 5 His attendants answered, 'Haman is standing in the court.' 'Call him in,' the king ordered. 6 When Haman entered, the king asked him, 'What should be done for the man the king delights to honour?' Now Haman thought to himself, 'Who is there that the king would rather honour than me?' 7 So he answered the king, 'For the man the king delights to honour, 8 **have them bring a royal robe the king has worn and a horse the king has ridden, one with a royal crest placed on its head. 9 Then let the robe and horse be entrusted to one of the king's most noble princes. Let them robe the man the king delights to honour, and lead him on the horse through the city streets**, proclaiming before him, "This is what is done for the man the king delights to honour!"'

10 'Go at once,' the king instructed Haman. 'Get the robe and the horse and do just as you have recommended for Mordecai the Jew, who sits at the king's gate. Do not overlook anything you have recommended.'

11 **So Haman got the robe and the horse. He robed Mordecai, and led him on horseback through the city streets, proclaiming before him, 'This is what is done for the man the king delights to honour!'**

12 Afterward Mordecai returned to the king's gate. But Haman hurried home, with his head covered in shame, 13 and told Zeresh his wife and all his friends everything that had happened to him. His advice-givers and his wife Zeresh said to him, 'Since Mordecai, before whom your downfall has started, is of Jewish blood, you cannot stand against him – you will surely be ruined!' 14 While they were still talking with him, the king's eunuchs arrived and harried Haman away to the banquet Esther had organized.

Commentary

6:8–6:9, 11 have them bring a royal robe the king has worn and a horse the king has ridden, one with a royal crest placed on its head. Then let the robe and horse be entrusted to one of the king's most noble princes. Let them robe the man the king delights to honour, and lead him on the horse through the city streets ... So Haman got the robe and the horse. He robed Mordecai, and led him on horseback through the city streets, proclaiming before him, 'This is what is done for the man the king delights to honour!'

The author of Esther skilfully toys with the narrative here. Haman, the conniving, cunning courtier, every inch the polished politician, supposes that the king means to honour him – 'Who is there that the king would rather honour than me?', he asks himself – and, puffed up with pride, he rolls off the list of honours a man found worthy of such tribute might expect. He is then told by the king that the dignity should be given to Mordecai for services rendered and, crestfallen, Haman begins to plot the hateful destruction of the uppity Jew and of his despised race. The honouring of Mordecai acts as the author's catalyst and he uses it to put the final strand of the plot of the story into motion.

Commentators have traditionally used this passage to cast light on Haman's hateful character. His self-pride is evident in the scene, although his self-awareness is clearly severely limited. When the king asks him to cite what honours should be given to a man worthy of the dignity, scholars assume that, on the spot, Haman immediately invents a list of rewards he would like to have bestowed upon himself, and he rattles them off, one after the other, with dazzling élan. This spur of the moment response to Ahasuerus' question is, scholars maintain, tellingly loaded and it speaks of both Haman's mounting self-confidence and of his dangerous, almost palpable, ambition. Haman longs to wear the king's robe and his golden crown and to ride upon the king's horse not simply because he wants to 'masquerade as the king'; no, 'Haman wants to *be* the king' (Berlin 2001: 11. Similar judgements are provided by Levenson 1997: 97; Fox 1991: 77; Laniak 1998: 101. See further, Wahl 2009: 135–43).

Haman is penned as a villain of grotesque passions and unstrained ambitions and contemporary exegetes are merely repeating what ancient interpreters of Esther have long claimed. In Edition E of the Septuagint, for example, the Great King accuses Haman of aiming to 'deprive us of our kingdom' (16:12-16) and the MT's own inclusion (7:8) of Xerxes' claim that Haman attempted to ravish the queen (which, in fairness, he never attempted to do), plays on the common motif of a usurper taking a king's wife or concubine (2 Sam. 3:7, 16; 21-2; 1 Kgs 2:15-17, 22. Plut. *Art.* 26.6; Xen. *Cyr.* 5.2.28. See further, Llewellyn-Jones 2013a, 116–22). As Adele Berlin (2001: 14) sees it, Xerxes, 'perhaps naively, or perhaps not, is accusing Haman of wanting to replace the king – an act of treason ... the villain gets the punishment he deserves for something he did not do'.

Issue can be taken with modern exegetes on one key issue, however: the reading of Haman drawing up of a wish-list of honours at 6:7-9 as an act of vainglorious spontaneity needs refining. What happens if we regard Haman, the consummate courtier, as merely citing a well-established court practice? In this alternative scenario, Haman answers the king not with a register of his private fantasies of aggrandizement but with a rota of what royal tradition has long deemed necessary for a formal court recognition of rewards – a *bone fide* Persian Honours List, as it were. Haman knows the correct court protocol and he anticipates that he will be the recipient of it and, while the joke is on him when Xerxes reveals that it is Mordecai who is to be the chosen dignitary, nothing is lost in the narrative pleasure of the moment if we grant that Haman recites the standard formula for honouring an individual in the king's favour.

(i) Gift-giving at the Persian Court

In Achaemenid royal ideology the interplay between loyal service and the receiving of a royal gift was profoundly important. The monarch was perceived as receiving the gifts of his people in the form of loyalty, service and produce, and in turn he was honour-bound to demonstrate his thanks though the bestowal of largesse. The concept of a reward for loyalty is a theme clearly propounded in Darius I's Bisitun Inscription: 'The man who cooperated with my house (*viθ*), him I rewarded well; he who did injury, I punished thoroughly' (DB §63), and again on his tomb at Naqš-i Rustam he states: 'What a man does or performs … with that I am satisfied' (DNb §8e). This strategy finds parallel with Xerxes' statement that 'I generously repay men of good will' (XPl §26). Pierre Briant (2002: 302–20) has carefully explored how royal benefactors were rewarded by the king with gifts of clothing, jewellery, livestock and land, and has noted that even foreigners who worked at court could benefit from this gift-giving system. Xenophon (*Anab.* 1.2.27), for instance, records clearly the way in which a Great King expressed his favour to a courtier through the use of gifts: 'Cyrus presented him with the customary royal gifts – that is to say, a horse with a gold bit, a necklace of gold, a gold bracelet, and a gold scimitar, (and) a Persian robe'. This formalized gift-giving of 'unequal exchange' as Briant (2002: 316) terms it, bears a striking resemblance to the Honours List articulated by Haman in Esther. The act of gift-giving on this scale was an important tool for the Achaemenid monarchy, as it established as system of debt and dependency on the part of the Persian nobles and other courtiers.

The royal benefaction found in Esther finds, in fact, many parallels in the Greek corpus. Xenophon believed that it was Cyrus II who had begun this practice of lavish gift-giving (Gk. *polydoria*), but ever since Cyrus' time, generosity had become one of the hallmarks of the qualities of Achaemenid kingship. Although this Cyrus-centred aetiology might be doubted, nevertheless stories of Cyrus' largesse create a picture of imperial gift-giving on an imperial scale:

> Cyrus began the practice of lavish gift-giving … Who is known to adorn his friends with more beautiful robes than the king? Whose gifts are so clearly recognized such as the bracelets, necklaces, and horses with gold-studded bridles as those which the king bestows? (Xen. *Cyr.* 8.2.7–8)

The sheer number of gifts doled out by the king suggests that the imperial textile workshops and stables were kept occupied year-round. Before a major parade, for instance, Cyrus is supposed to have 'distributed amongst the nobles the most beautiful robes ... for he had a great many made, with no lack of purple dye, red, and scarlet, or sable' (Xen. *Cyr.* 8.3.3) and Herodotus (3.84) notes that 'Every year ... clothes and other gifts held to be of great value' were distributed by the king to his loyal courtiers. Briant (2002: 307) notes that 'these robes and jewels were not baubles; they were resplendent marks of the king's favour ... [T]he royal gift was symbolically charged ... With all of the Persian nobles wearing sumptuous robes and prize jewellery, we should not be surprised that the ceremony of awarding gifts was held in public.' Indeed, the honour bestowed upon Mordecai is amplified through the centrality of the public aspect of the ceremony – in particular the horseback ride through the streets and squares of Susa.

(ii) *Khal'at*

The gift-giving and public demonstration of a monarch's esteem accords closely with an ancient ritualized honour ceremony studied by Stewart Gordon (2003). Known as *khal'at*, the origins of the ceremony can be traced back to Eurasian customs that entered into Persia via the nomadic peoples of the Steppes around 1000 BCE. It was also known in Mesopotamia, as demonstrated in an inscription of Ashurbanipal, who honoured the vassal king of Egypt, Necho, with gifts: 'I clad him in a garment with multicoloured trimmings, placed a golden chain on him ... put golden rings on his hands ... and ... a golden dagger. I presented him with chariots, horses, and mules as a means of transportation befitting his position' (cited in Queen-Sutherland 2016: 353).

Khal'at can be defined as both the ceremony of gift-giving and as the gift itself. In more specific terms, *khal'at* was a gifted robe of honour. In the pre-Islamic and later Islamic courts of the Near East and Central Asia, *khal'at* were bestowed by rulers on their courtiers, visiting dignitaries or other deserving people as marks of high honour, as a way of securing loyalty, and of securing legitimacy. As Stewart Gordon explains (2010: 462), 'At its simplest, a king or his representative bestowed on another person ... an outer [garment] ... In a robing room adjacent to the court, the recipient donned the ... outfit, re-emerged to the acclaim of the assembled nobles and – if not so before – was deemed "suitable" to take his place in court.' While robing ceremonies themselves no doubt evolved and changed over the centuries, the fundamental importance of *khal'at* never changed – the gifted robe served as a bond between superiors and subordinates (see further Komaroff 2011).

There are no Achaemenid visual representations of the *khal'at* ceremony (iconographic evidence does, perhaps, survive from the Sasanian period, see Rose 2001). Pictorial evidence is more abundant from early Islamic age: a miniature from the *Jami'al-Tawrikh* of Rashid al-Din, *c.* 1307 CE, for instance, depicts Mahmud of Ghazna receiving a robe of honour from the Caliph al-Qadir Bi'llah in 1000 CE; having decided that the courier who brought him the robe was unsuitable to touch him, he puts the robe on himself, without assistance, in the presence of his nobles (**Figure 6.1**;

Figure 6.1 Miniature painting from the *Jami'al-Tawrikh* of Rashid al-Din, *c.* 1307 CE; from Baghdad.

see Blair 1995 for a discussion). According to Gordon (2001), the *khal'at* traditions of the pre-Islamic and Islamic royal courts followed six distinct norms:

1. Presentation of *khal'at* was highly personalized. The gift of luxurious robes reinforced the direct relationships between a leader and his honoured subject.
2. The robe was granted from the hand of the leader before the whole band of nobles, representing solidarity with that band, cross-cutting family and dynastic ties; in other words, those distinguished through the wearing of gifted robes formed an elite club.
3. A central and enduring connection existed between robing and horses, as well as highly decorated horse-trappings.
4. As an indicator of wealth and status in itself, the robe was nevertheless always accompanied by something gold (headdress, weaponry, jewellery, horse trappings; **Figure 6.2**).
5. The *khal'at* robe was always a shaped and sewn garment rather than a wrapped or draped one, and it was always compatible with horse riding; in fact, in many of its later manifestations the robe of honour often had side- or back-slits for ease of riding. It was always the outermost and most visible garment of court dress.

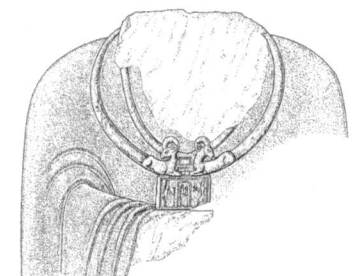

Figure 6.2 Detail from a fragmentary Egyptian statue of the Achaemenid period; an official is depicted wearing a golden Persian-style torc.

Each of these markers are qualified by Gordon as the non-negotiable and absolute features of a *khal'at*-style investiture. Interestingly, they are all comfortably located in the Achaemenid-era evidence, so much so, in fact, that it becomes clear that the Achaemenids should take their rightful place in the early, indeed formative, period of *khal'at*-history. In the case of Mordecai, details of his *khal'at*-honour are expanded on at Est. 8:15: **When Mordecai left the king's presence, he was wearing royal garments of blue and white, a large crown of gold and a purple robe of fine linen**. Taken in combination, then, Mordecai receives a robe of honour (classified as purple; see further Xen. *Cyrop.* 8.3.13), a gold crown and horse with a (gold?) ornamented bridle and headpiece. It is profitable to compare Mordecai's gifts with those bestowed by Cyrus the Great on Artapates, his loyal sceptre-bearer: 'he had a gold dagger, and wore a necklace and bracelets and all manner of ornaments which noble Persians put on; for he was honoured by Cyrus because of his affection and steadfastness' (Xen. *Anab.* 1.8.29). The Apocryphal 1 Esdras (3:5-7) gives us another example of Persian-style *khal'at*:

> Let each of us state what one thing is strongest; and to the one whose statement seems the wisest, King Darius will give rich gifts and great honours of victory. He shall be clothed in purple, and drink from gold cups, and sleep on a gold bed, and have a chariot with gold bridles, and a turban of fine linen, and a necklace around his neck; and because of his wisdom he shall sit next to Darius and shall be called Kinsman of Darius.

The honours bestowed on Joseph as pharaoh's favourite in the Genesis story (41:45) have a strikingly Persian feel to them, suggesting that the story, although set in the distant past in Egypt, came into its final form in the Achaemenid era:

> And Pharaoh said to Joseph, 'See I have set you over all the land of Egypt.' Removing his signet ring from his hand, Pharaoh put it on Joseph's hand; he arrayed him in garments of fine linen and put a gold chain around his neck. He had him ride in the chariot of his second-in-command; and they cried out in front of him, 'Bow the knee!'

(iii) Robe of Honour: the **gaunaka*

Garments played an important part in the wider culture of court society and have a very ancient pedigree in the Near East and this passage in Esther finds ready parallels in other biblical books in which garments become the focus of the transfer of power (whether authorized or not; see Num. 20:25-8; 2 Kgs 2:13-15; 1 Sam. 24:4; 1 Kgs 1:32-49). Isaiah records the promotion of a man named Elyakim to the position of Master of the Jerusalem Palace and notes how he was clothed by the king with a robe and a sash as a signal of his new authority over the royal household (Isa. 22:20). When Prince Jonathan, the son and heir of King Saul, gifted David his robe and belt he was effectively relinquishing his claim to the throne and announcing David as a more fitting (God-chosen) successor to Saul (1 Sam. 18:1-4). Most famous is the story of Joseph (a Persian-period text) and

Figure 6.3 A Persian magus depicted on a stone stela from northern Anatolia.

the gift his father, the tribal leader, made him of a well-dyed multi-coloured coat as a sign of favour in Gen. 37.

Besides the 'court robe' (**Figure 1.52**) discussed above, we have noted that the Persians also wore a riding habit (**Figure 1.51**; see comments on **1:4 the splendour and glory of his majesty**. See further Vogelsang 1992 and 2010), a distinctive part of which was a long-sleeved coat which reached well past the knees, sometimes to the floor (**Figures 6.3, 6.4**). It was known in OP. as a **gaunaka* (from OIr. **gau-na-ka* 'hairy, shaggy'; compare Elam. *kam-na-ak-ka*; Avest. *gaona*; Gk. *kandys*. See Thompson 1965 and Widengren 1956 and 1959). It is this garment which was bestowed

Figure 6.4 A Persian nobleman and his wife (?); from Persian-occupied Asia Minor.

Figure 6.6 Persian nobleman wearing the riding habit; from a sculpted relief panel at Persepolis.

on an honorand as a royal gift. Irene Good (2010) sensibly suggests that it was a kind of overcoat with wide, often over-long, sleeves and that it was usually

Figure 6.5 Bronze statuette of a Persian nobleman in a riding outfit; from the area of the Oxus River.

worn hanging from the shoulders (**Figures 6.5, 6.6**). The coat itself was ultimately derived from a very ancient rectangular-shaped garment shaped on the loom and known as the *chapan*; it is distinctly Central Asian in style (the same coat style is found in early China and has a common origin; see Knauer 1985 and 2003). A garment of considerable cost and a clear indicator of wealth and status, it was worn exclusively by the elite. In fact, the Persepolis reliefs show it worn only by the nobility; food-bearing servants wear just the long-sleeved tunic with trousers.

It becomes clear from the Greek literary sources that the coat played an important role in court etiquette and that the garment was loaded with ceremonial symbolism.

The ultra-long sleeves were supposed to be used in the presence of the Great King and any suppliant before the throne was expected to place his arms into them and allow the excess fabric to fall over his hands, thereby rendering them harmless (since they could not grip weapons). Failure to do this was read as an insult to the monarch or his representative, and Cyrus the Younger, Xenophon insists (*Hel.* 2.1.8.), used such an affront as an excuse to execute two of his powerful – and potentially troublesome – kinsmen:

> In this year, Cyrus executed Autoboisakes and Mitraios, the sons of (Darius II's) sister because, when they met with him, they did not put their hands into their long sleeves. Now, the Persians do this only as a mark of respect for the king; this type of sleeve is longer than a normal sleeve so when one puts a hand into it, the hand is rendered harmless.

No doubt jobs at court endowed a courtier the right (and probably the obligation) to wear special *gaunaka as a kind of royal livery and courtiers took their right to wear *khal'at* garments seriously. The eunuch Mithradates, rewarded by Artaxerxes II for his services during the Battle of Cunaxa in 401 BCE, never failed to appear in public without his royal coat and his gifted jewellery (Plut. *Art.* 15.2.).

Further understanding of the nature of *khal'at* emerges when we focus again on the wording of Est. 6:8 – Haman declares that **a royal robe the king has worn** should be brought and gifted to the worthy recipient. This is an important detail. The highest level of *khal'at*, it appears, was to receive a robe from the royal wardrobe which had been worn by the king himself. Not all courtiers were guaranteed this privilege. It meant that the chosen recipients were quite literally touched by, and with, majesty – that special, sacred charisma which oozes into and out of the body of the king. The ancient Iranian concept of a demi-mythical force bestowed upon the kings of Iran a mystical light (NP *farr-ī īzadī*) that legitimized their rule was so strong that it can be thought of as emanating from the royal body, permeating his garments, and making them hallowed (for a full discussion see Llewellyn-Jones 2020c). From the moment a man donned the royal robe he shared a union with the Great Kings of Persia; he became part of an exclusive group. It is in this context that we need to understand the true value of Mordecai's royal gift. Mordecai, the outsider-Jew, was honoured with a public ceremonial making him an influential insider, a pseudo-Persian, the bearer of the monarch's own aura, the royal charisma. This, in turn, bestowed upon Mordecai, as the wearer of the robe, a particular protection, so that to harm, hurt or even insult a man wearing the king's garment was a significant act of *lèse-majesté*. Therefore, when Haman ignored this Achaemenid axiom, he rightly paid for it with his life.

(iv) Horse

The type of privilege afforded Mordecai, who rides on the king's own horse, is attested in other sources. Xenophon (*Cyr.* 8.3.23) for instance records that Cyrus II rewarded an officer by giving him a horse which the monarch had previously ridden in a royal procession. The officer's public status increased exponentially as he was seen riding the king's steed.

For a nomadic people like the Achaemenid Persians, the horse had a significant practical and symbolic purpose and the importance of horses among the ancient Iranian nobility is evidenced by the fact that many of them bore names compounded with the Old Persian word *aspa* – 'horse'. Several of Darius I's inscriptions note that Persia was a land containing both good men and good horses (DZe §1; DPd §2; **Figure 6.7**) and Herodotus famously states that Persian fathers were intent on teaching their sons 'to ride, to draw the bow, and to speak the truth' (1.136; see also Str. 15.3.18). The Persian fondness for the horse is evident in a cylinder

Figure 6.7 Cylinder seal impression from Persian-occupied Egypt depicting a Persian warrior and his horse; official seal of the Egyptian satrap Aršama.

seal image from Persepolis (**Figure 6.8**) where here the common Mesopotamian motif of a cow suckling its calf is re-worked to show a mare and its offspring, protected beneath the wings of a sun-disk (perhaps the symbol of Ahuramazda; the falcon has no direct known correlation to the scene). Mare's milk was an important element of the Persian diet, and there can be little doubt that it was used in religious rituals, such as the initiation of kings at the ceremony of enthronement at Parsagade: 'The initiate must enter this, take off his own clothes and put on those worn by Cyrus the Elder before he became king; he must eat some fig-cake, chew some terebinth-wood and drink a cup of sour milk' (Ctesias F17 3.2). It is reasonable to assume, given the importance of the horse to Achaemenid culture, that the sour milk ingested by monarchs was taken from a mare.

Figure 6.8 Achaemenid cylinder seal showing a mare suckling her foal.

A companion to humans in life, the horse also played its role in the ceremonies of death and with the passing of a king or noble, his horse was included in the mourning procession with its mane cropped short (Hdt. 9.24; **Figure 6.9**). The horse played a noteworthy role in Achaemenid rituals and beliefs and just as kings were mounted high on horse-drawn chariots (**Figures 6.10,**

Figure 6.9 Achaemenid stamp seal impression depicting a seated Persian wearing the riding habit in the company of his horse.

Figure 6.10 Silver coin from Tyre depicting the Persian Great King riding in a chariot.

6.11; sometimes chariots were pulled by camels, see **Figure 6.12**), so Ahuramazda and other deities had similar modes of transportation (Hdt. 7.40; Arr. *Anab.* 2.11, III.15; Xen. *Cyrop.* 8.3.12). Moreover, just as the finest present to give a Persian was a horse (Xen. *Anab.* 1.2.27), so were the gods honoured with equine gifts such as the white horses which were sacrificed to the sun and to the waters (Hdt. 1.216, 7.113; 1.189; Xen. *Cyr.* 8.3.11–12; *Anab.* 4.5.35), both rituals being widely practised amongst Indo-European peoples (Clutton-Brock 1992; Kelekna 2009). As founder of the Empire, Cyrus II was honoured with a horse sacrificed to his soul every month. Moreover, the infamous tale recounted by Herodotus (3.85) of how Darius I acquired his kingdom through a trick involving the neighing of his horse is, in all probability, a Greek misunderstanding of the Iranian practice of hippomancy, or divination through the behaviour of horses (see also Ctesias F13 §17),

Figure 6.11 Miniature gold model of a royal chariot with four horses, a driver, and a seated dignitary. Found near the River Oxus.

Figure 6.12 Cylinder seal impression of the Great King's camel-drawn chariot. From Persepolis.

demonstrating the deep-seated importance of the horse in Iranian consciousness.

The premium Persian horses were bred in the alfalfa-rich plains of Media, and it was here that the main royal stud farms were located (Xen. *Anab.* 4.5.34, Str. *Geog.* 11.13.7, 14.9, Polyb. 10.70). Most prized of all were those steeds bred on the plains of Nisaea near Ecbatana and Bisitun, and Nisaean horses, with their distinctive rounded foreheads (**Figure 6.13**), became celebrated for their magnificence, fine proportions and swiftness (Hdt. 3.106, 7.40; Ar. *HA* 632a 30). Nisaea is said to have sustained 160,000 horses (Diod. 17.110), although stiff competition came from Media and Armenia which were also used for breeding good steeds (Str. *Geog.* 11.13.7,

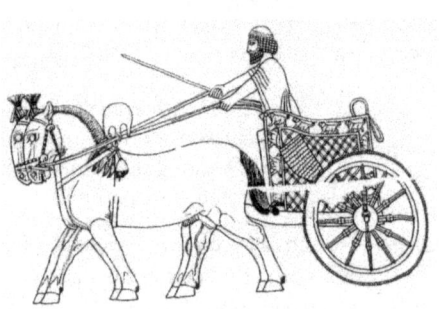

6.13 The royal chariot pulled by Nisaean horses, controlled by a charioteer; wall relief from the east staircase at Persepolis.

8; 14.9), as were the provinces of Babylonia (where one satrap possessed 800 stallions and 16,000 mares; Hdt. 1.192), Cilicia (which provided an annual tribute of 360 white horses; Hdt. 3.90), Chorasmia, Bactria, Sogdiana and lands of the Saka which provided the Empire with its cavalry (Tuplin 2010b). The Persepolis texts often speak of horses (as well as mules and donkeys), usually in the context of their food provisions and maintenance but also as property of the king or members of his family (PF 1668-9, 1675, 1793, PFa 24, 29; Azzoni and Dusinberre 2014). The texts also name individuals who safeguarded the welfare of the royal horses as well as groups of court officials serving as Masters of the Horse, as it were (PF 1942, 1943, 1947, 1948), and show that these men operated within a hierarchical system and could be paid well beyond the average ration-rate and could enjoy a diet of regular meat (Tuplin 2010b: 132-3). This suggests a high-rank at court for Masters of the Horse.

While there are no surviving monumental artistic representations of horses and riders in official Achaemenid art, textual evidence suggests that equine statues of horses with riders were commissioned for and by royalty and nobility (Hdt. 3.88). Small-scale representations of horses and cavalry figures survive in terracotta and metallic figurines (**Figure 6.14**), and representations on gems, coins and textiles (**Figure 6.15**). The Persepolis reliefs show riderless horses regularly: of the twenty-three tribute delegations appearing on the Apadana staircases, seven present horses as part of their gifts (Medes, Armenians, Cappadocians, two groups of Sakas, Sagartians and Thracians) and there are also depictions of horse-drawn chariots conveyed by Syrians and Libyans. In addition, the Great King's personal Nisaean mounts are depicted along with his chariot (and the chariot belonging to the Crown Prince; **Figure 6.13**). In the royal chariot the Great King obviously took on a majestic appearance, 'outstanding amongst the rest' (Curt. 4.1.1) but, as Briant makes clear, 'the royal horses and chariot do not appear

Figure 6.14 Small Achaemenid bronze figurine of a horse and its rider.

Figure 6.15 Detail taken from the 'Pazyrik Carpet' – a Persian horseman; from the Crimea.

on the Persepolis reliefs simply for decoration. The royal chariot obviously carried ideological weight and the vehicle was clearly part of the "royal insignia'" (Briant 2002: 224). As an obvious symbol of status and wealth, horses were closely connected to royal and courtly ideology and to the model warrior image (Hdt. 9.20, 22; DS 17.59.2; Ctesias F19 §1) but as a mark of conspicuous leisure, horses played a dominant role in the aristocratic pastimes of hunting and racing (Xen. Cyr. 8.3.25, 33; see further Hdt. 7.196). Women too rode horses, sometimes side-saddle (**Figure 6.16**). From all accounts, favourite horses could lead a pampered existence (Hdt. 9.70).

Figure 6.16 Women horse-riding; fragment of a relief sculpture from Persian-occupied Asia Minor.

(v) Horse trappings

Persian mounts and draught horses were controlled with bridles consisting of headstalls, reins, cheek-pieces and bits, examples of which survive in the archaeology of the Near East (Curtis and Tallis 2012: 110–15, 118–25; Drews 2004: 65–98). In addition to the guiding equipment, Persian horses, like those of Assyrian kings, were adorned with decorations attached to the headpieces of the bridles (**Figure 6.17**). They vary from splays of feathers to horsehair crests and cascades of tassels; sometimes sheets

Figure 6.17 Neo-Assyrian horse bridles and bits.

Figure 6.18 Parthian mounted warrior and his horse with rich trappings; from Persepolis.

of cut metal were used to emboss the leather harnesses. Bells of bronze or iron were also attached to the harnesses where they would give added weight to the feel of the reins and jingle to act as a kind of metronome, helping each horse to move in unison with others. Bells also served the purpose of drowning out the noise of battle and providing a familiar reassuring sound for the warhorse (O'Daniel Cantrell 2011: 21–2). Saddle cloths and other decorative paraphernalia made the horses of the king and his nobles a sight to behold (**Figures 6.18**, **6.19**, **6.20** and **6.21**).

Figure 6.19 Central Asian Late Antique wall painting depicting a horse with elaborate trappings. From Panjikent.

Figure 6.20 Brass figurine of a crowned man riding an elaborately canopied war horse; Late Sasanian or Early Islamic Iran.

Figure 6.21 Wall relief showing a Sasanian nobleman riding a richly decorated horse. From Taq-i Bustan, north-west Iran.

Chapter 7

1 So, the king and Haman went to Queen Esther's banquet, 2 and as they were drinking wine on the second day, the king again asked, 'Queen Esther, what is your request? It will be given you. What is your appeal? Even up to half the kingdom, it will be granted.'

3 Then Queen Esther answered, 'If I have found favour with you, Your Majesty, and if it pleases you, grant me my life – this is my petition - and spare my people – this is my request. 4 For I and my people have been sold to be destroyed, slaughtered, and annihilated. If we had merely been **sold as male and female slaves**, I would have kept silent, because no such suffering would justify distressing the king.'

5 King Xerxes asked Queen Esther, 'Who is he? Where is he – the man who has dared to do such a thing?' 6 Esther said, 'An opponent and an enemy! This hateful Haman!' Then Haman was panicked in front of the king and queen. 7 The king got up in wrath, left his wine and hastened outside, into the palace garden. But Haman, grasping that the king had already decided his fate, stayed behind to plead to Queen Esther for his life. 8 Just as the king returned from the palace garden to the banquet hall, **Haman was falling on the couch where Esther was reclining. The king exclaimed, 'Will he even molest the queen while she is with me in the house?'** As soon as the word left the king's mouth, **they covered Haman's face**. 9 Then Harbona, one of the eunuchs attending the king, said, 'A pole reaching to a height of fifty cubits stands by Haman's house. He had it set up for Mordecai, who spoke up to help the king.'

The king said, 'Impale him on it!' 10 So they impaled Haman on the pole he had set up for Mordecai. Then the king's rage diminished.

Commentary

7:4 sold as male and female slaves

Slavery was common throughout the ancient Near East (for an overview see Dandamanev 2008) At first, Persia did not have an extensive slave economy and in the early Achaemenid era there was only a small number of slaves in Persia, certainly in relation to the number of free persons even in the most developed countries of the empire. Slave labour was in no position to supplant the labour of free workers, but as a result of the far-flung conquests of the Great Kings, a dramatic change took place within Persian society. Soon after the consolidation of imperial power under Cyrus II and Cambyses II, Achaemenid nobles became the owners of very large numbers of slaves (Dandamanev and Lukonin 1989). Information on privately owned slaves in Persia is scanty, but a substantial number of slaves performed domestic work for the Achaemenids and the Persian nobility as bakers, cooks, cupbearers, entertainers and perfumiers. The archaeological evidence also testifies to the mass presence of unskilled labourers in the Persian heartlands.

In the cuneiform sources an Elamite term *kurtaš* (OP *māniya*) was used, very homogeneously, to agricultural labourers, artisans and construction workers. The term offers little specificity as to the actual jobs undertaken. The Persepolis tablets tell of how *kurtaš* received rations of food and drink at certain localities in and around Fars. *Kurtaš* were generically identified as 'workers of all trades' or 'workers at any task'. Some tablets recorded the transportation to Persepolis of grain, flour and wine intended as rations for specialist master craftsmen such as sculptors in stone, goldsmiths, master woodworkers, metal workers and skilled quarrymen. The *kurtaš* found in the Persepolis tablets were foreigners – Ionians, Sardians, Egyptians, Carians, Bactrians, Elamites, Babylonians – who found themselves at the imperial core working on the building projects of the Great King (Henkelman and Stolper 2009).

What was it that brought foreigners to Persepolis in the first place? A small percentage of foreigners were master craftsmen, brought into Persia on work contracts. This policy might have been in operation since Cyrus the Great's day when craftsmen from Lydia and Ionia had been brought to Pasargadae to help build the palace-pavilions. Cambyses too took craftsmen from Egypt and sent them to Persia. It is tempting to think that these master craftsmen and artisans might have come to Susa and Persepolis not because they were forced to but because they were requested by Persian officials. As such they participated in a kind of up-market corvée labour system. At the end of their term of employment they were free to return home or seek another contract. But this is merely a hypothesis and even if it could be proved then it certainly would not have applied to the many thousands of unskilled workers repetitively carrying out mundane manual labour. It has been estimated that in 500 BCE some 10,000–15,000 individuals made up the workforce of Persepolis. Often divided up into subgroups of work-gangs, classified by ethnicity, the Persepolis tablets show that, for instance, there were gangs of 300 Lycians, 150 Thracians, 547 Egyptians and 980 Cappadocians. All in all twenty-seven ethnic groups of *kurtaš* are attested at Persepolis.

It is doubtful that all of these people entered Persia as economic migrants seeking wages. The Persepolis Fortification tablets do not support that view. They clearly reveal that the food rations *kurtaš* received from the administration were enough only for survival and nothing more. In fact, the food doled out to the *kurtaš* was only distributed at a subsistence level. For the workers, the risk of starvation was never far away. The *kurtaš* of the Fortification Tablets were not in Persia of their own free will to earn a wage. They had been brought there forcibly, in very large numbers, and were exploited by the Persians through direct coercion regardless of whether they were only temporarily located there or were settled in Persia for life. Usually *kurtaš* were prisoners of war (the 'booty of the bow', as they were termed) recruited from those who had rebelled against Persian rule or had put up resistance to the Persian army. The Persepolis tablets make clear that for the majority of the workers, their placement in Persia was permanent and that they had been uprooted from their homelands and deported there specifically to create an enslaved labour force. Babylonia alone was obliged to supply the Persian king for these purposes an annual tribute of 500 castrated boys. These lads were taken from their families and transported east to Persia.

The policy of deportation of conquered populations was commonplace in the ancient Near East and in the Assyrian and Neo-Babylonian periods the practice had flourished (Oded 1979). During the nearly three hundred years of Assyria's hegemony over the Near East, the state deported approximately four and a half million people whose relocation in diverse areas of the Assyrian empire was carefully planned and organized. The Babylonians worked along the same guidelines, but on a more modest scale: some 4,600 persons in all were taken from Judah and led into captivity in Mesopotamia. The practice of uprooting whole communities and transplanting them in distant lands is equally well attested for the Persians too (Izdimirski 2018; Matarese 2021). Following the destruction of the city of Sidon by King Artaxerxes III, for instance, men and women of the city were led captive into the Persian heartlands. The Milesians too were victims of Persian deportation, as were the Paeonians of Thrace, the Barcaeans, Eretrians, Boeotians and the Carians. Deported populations often remained in Persia for many generations. A remarkable incident recorded by Diodorus Siculus (5.5.5) occurred to Alexander of Macedon as he marched towards Persepolis during his invasion of central Persia:

> At this point in his advance the King was confronted by a strange and dreadful sight, one to provoke indignation against the perpetrators and sympathetic pity for the unfortunate victims. He was met by Greeks bearing branches of supplication. They had been carried away from their homes by previous Kings of Persia and were about eight hundred in number, most of them elderly. All had been mutilated, some lacking hands, some feet, and some ears and noses. They were persons who had acquired skills or crafts and had made good progress in their instruction; then their other extremities had been amputated and they were left only those which were vital to their profession. All the soldiers, seeing their venerable years and the losses which their bodies had suffered, pitied the lot of the wretches. Alexander most of all was affected by them and was unable to restrain his tears.

It is clear that these old Greeks, ripped from their homes many decades before, were *kurtaš*. Even with some possible exaggeration about the rate of the mutilations they had been subject to, the story does provide a very grim perspective on Persia's labour system. The story's emotional pull stands in stark contrast with the Persepolis tablets' clinically cold administrative language. It would be too simple to dismiss Diodorus' narrative as anti-Persian propaganda. What we read here is an eye-opening account of the traumatic world of the *kurtaš* and the fact that for many enslaved war captives, brutally and cruelty was part of life (see further Miles 2003).

The Fortification Tablets reveal that there was an enormous bureaucratic push on the part of the Persians to micro-manage their huge foreign workforce. This was achieved through the careful rationing of a subsistence-only supply of food and drink. The rations were first given to various 'Heads of *kurtaš*' (Elam. *kurdabattish*) – overseers – who acted as distributors and doled out the rations to the work teams they supervised. Rations in kind – grain, barley, beer, oil, sometimes meat and vegetables – were distributed unequally according to gender and age. Men, boys, women and girls were provided with different amounts of food.

There were many female workers at Persepolis. They were usually engaged in textile production and weaving as well as rope-making. Some of these women had no doubt arrived in Persia alongside their husbands or fathers, and had been captured as a discrete family unit, but others were single women, war captives who lacked any familial ties. For those women who accompanied husbands or fathers into slavery, there was little hope that they could stay in family groups since the Persian administration tended to break apart families and deploy individual workers wherever they were most needed. It was unlikely that any family newly brought to Persia would stay together for long. Nevertheless, unrelated male and female *kurtaš* working on communal projects tended to group together to share food and, it is to be assumed, accommodation. Inevitably sexual (and perhaps emotional) bonds were made between workers. The Persians encouraged this. They even gave incentives to boost reproduction among the *kurtaš* population. The Fortification texts tell of a disconcertingly uncomfortable tale of a large-scale *kurtaš* breeding-programme throughout central Persia. The records kept a register of the number of pregnant women and show that their health was maintained through the provision of special rations. Post-partum women were also given 'feeding' rations, as one text (PF 1224) specifies:

> 32 BAN of grain, supplied by Ashbashupish. Shedda, a priest at Persepolis ... gave it as a bonus to Ionian women after giving birth at Persepolis, to the spinning-women, whose rations are set. Nine women who bore male children received two BAN and fourteen women who bore girls received one BAN.

Another cuneiform document (PF NN-258) records that,

> Lanunu, a woman who bore a male baby, received 10 quarts of wine, supplied by Irkezza.
> Parrkkuzzish, a woman who bore a female baby received 5 quarts of wine.
> They were given to a total of two post-partum women.
> Manzaturrush and his companions received it and gave it to them. Year 23, month 4 (of Darius I). (At) Tikrakkash.

These postnatal grain rations were provided over and above the normal subsistence rations. They were a reward, as it were, for successful reproduction. The food bonuses must have been welcomed by the new mothers though, since the extra calories allowed them to recuperate from the birth and gave them a rare opportunity to gain some weight. In this way they might produce healthy and nourishing breastmilk which would help an infant survive the perilous first months of life. The mother's food ration was doubled in the event of the birth of a boy, a detail that tells us much about the Persian perception of the hierarchies of gender. In the three-year period 500–497 BCE alone, the Fortification Tablets record there were 449 live births at Persepolis; 247 of them were boys, who made up 55 per cent of all children born at that time. Oddly there are no examples of twins. A statistical analysis of the Persepolis tablets reveals that the fertility rate in *kurtaš* communities was alarmingly low. Even allowing for the high infant mortality rate which can found in any ancient society, poor health and limited access to food took its toll on fertility. Moreover, many *kurtaš* groups did not have equal numbers of men and women. The Persepolis tablets indicate that the administration assiduously tried to bring more women into the labour force so as to increase the working population and it can be ascertained that between 502 and 499 BCE, the number of *kurtaš* children born in and around Persepolis increased from 16 to 99 – a very successful outcome. However, it is important to note that in order to increase work productivity, the Persian administration actively broke apart family units or simply forbade their creation. It is doubtful that *kurtaš* marriages were ever recognized by the Persians. 'Husbands' and 'wives' are never mentioned in the texts. The tablets also show that the bond between mother and child was not permanent either: mothers kept their children close at hand for the first few years of life, after which the children or youths were taken to different groups and started their working lives amidst other *kurtaš* communities.

The presence of enforced labour from captured peoples, an active breeding-programme, the routine relocation of individuals, the breakdown of family bonds and the control of bodies through the rationing of food, all contribute to the interpretation that the *kurtaš* were slaves. It was slave labour that lay behind the hallmarks of the physical presence of Persia's empire. Achaemenid Persia was not a slave society in the way that the Roman empire was, given that Rome's expansion was based on a very simple formula: peasants became soldiers who captured enemies to enslave for the purpose of replacing the labour lost on the farm to the war. But it must be conceded that as Persia grew in power and status, it exponentially required and desired slaves to make the imperial system work. Enough information exists to convince us that Persia was a slave-owning society and that the Achaemenid empire benefited from slavery.

7:8 Haman was falling on the couch where Esther was reclining. The king exclaimed, 'Will he even molest the queen while she is with me in the house?'

Persian nobility did not always sit upright to eat and drink, often they reclined on couches. Sometimes these were shared by two people, but very often each couch was occupied by one individual whose status was emphasized by the decoration and quality of the couch itself (Briant 2002: 279; Boardman 2000: 199–200). Of course,

Figure 7.1 Clay plaque depicting love making on a couch; Sumerian.

couches were also used for sleeping and for sex (**Figure 7.1** and **7.2**). The melodrama that unfolds is played out around Esther's couch. It appears that Haman threw himself at Esther's couch as a supplicant, to beg the queen to intercede with Xerxes and to save his life. He attempted, perhaps, to clutch or kiss her feet. This was an egregious error since Xerxes saw things very differently: in his eyes, Haman was making a sexual advance on the queen and his proximity to her couch meant only one thing. According to Plutarch (*Them.* 26.5), the Persians were 'extremely jealous of their wives ... Not only their wives but also the female slaves and concubines were rigorously watched.' Moreover, he observes (*Art.* 27.1), they were 'very jealous ... about anything pertaining to their love-lives, so that it is death for anyone merely approaching and touching a royal concubine'. Touching a queen-consort must have been tantamount to treason.

A series of Assyrian royal harem edicts (they are in fact instructions for conduct in the harem of the palace) stresses the physical distance which must be maintained between royal women and courtiers (Roth 1995: 195–209). Infringing these regulations incurred severe punishment, including the death penalty, while corporal punishment could amount to mutilation. It appears that protocol in the harem was the subject of countless regulations and instructions. Curses uttered whilst quarrelling with someone were severely punished (edicts 10–15; §911–12) and witnesses to these scenes were obliged to tell the supervisors of the harem (edict 21; §189, 192). Eunuchs who were permitted entrance to the apartments of the women were unable to speak with them, in the course of duty, unless under the

Figure 7.2 Clay moulded figurine representing a couple lying together on a couch; from Babylonia.

supervision of the head of the palace (edict 9; §906–10). That could only take place at a distance of seven paces from the woman they were talking to, who had to be suitably dressed (edict 21; §191). Culpable relations with a woman from the harem would lead to the punishment of the guilty party and his helpers (edict 19; §989). The women of the palace were forbidden to give their slaves gold, silver or precious stones (edict 5; §682–3). The wives were allowed to punish their servants, but this freedom, under the supervision of the king, did not extend to granting life or condemning to death (edict 18; §928). Married women in the service of the palace could not leave the building, not even on their days off, without the permission of the king (edict 3; §517). A typical selection of edicts read thus:

> Tiglath-pileser, king of the universe, King of Assyria, ... declares to the men, to the courtiers: If a woman of the palace sings or quarrels with another of her rank, and one of the royal eunuchs, courtiers or servants stands listening, he will be beaten one hundred times; one of his ears will be cut off. If a woman of the palace calls to a courtier while her hips are bare, not covered with a loin cloth, ... he will be beaten one hundred times. If a courtier wishes to speak to a woman of the palace, he may not approach her more than seven paces. If someone violates this decree and the one in charge of the palace hears of it but does not punish him, the one in charge of the palace will bear the punishment ... If the officials of the one in charge of the palace have not kept watch over the palace precincts, not reported offences to him and later the king has heard of the offence, the one in charge of the palace will bear responsibility for all offences. If officials have a commission to perform within the palace and the women of the palace stand at the entrance to their quarters, it must be reported to the one in charge of the palace, so that he might clear them away from the entrance to their quarters.

It is probable that the Achaemenid harem followed similar rules and that Haman's physical approach on Esther would have been in contravention of all rules of decorum. But there is more going on here than first meets the eye. Xerxes regards Haman's 'assault' on the queen as evidence of his desire to seize the throne. After all, in the ancient Near East, the possession of a predecessor's harem of women ensured the successor's hold on the throne and the control of the harem gave a new ruler the potential to legitimize his reign through the physical possession of a former monarch's household. Darius the Great had capitalized on this when in his bid for power he had married all the available royal women of the line of Cyrus II – the former wives and/or sisters of Cambyses II and Bardiya – whereupon he incorporated them into his harem and established them as the most-high ranking of all his existing wives. He quickly fathered children by his new acquisitions and promoted his sons born in the purple above those born before his accession (Brosius 1996: 47–64). Alexander of Macedon's acquisition of Darius III's harem *en masse* in 333 BCE and the appropriation of the royal wives and concubines heralded that Darius' days were numbered (Llewellyn-Jones 2002: 362–5). Upon his military victory and subsequent accession to the throne of Israel, David claimed the female harem of Saul; later a challenge came to both David and Solomon in the form of rebellions within the royal house when two of David's son's, Absalom and Adonijah, rebelled against the Israelite kings and attempted to win the royal concubines and incorporate them in rival royal harems (2 Sam. 15:16; 16:21-2; 20:3; 1 Kgs 2:13-25).

7:8 they covered Haman's face

The precise reason for this is unknown. Both the Greeks and Romans routinely covered the faces of individuals sentenced to death (Moore 1971: 72), but there is no solid evidence for this in Near Eastern practice. It was, of course, both a privilege and honour to look upon the face of a king (see comments on **1: 13 it was customary for the king to consult experts in matters of law and justice**), and so the enforced denial of the ability to look upon the monarch was a mark of shame and, indeed, desperation.

Chapter 8

1 That same day King Xerxes gave Queen Esther the estate of Haman, the enemy of the Jews. And Mordecai came into the presence of the king, for Esther had told how he was related to her. 2 The king took off his signet ring, which he had reclaimed from Haman, and presented it to Mordecai. And Esther appointed him over Haman's estate. 3 Esther again pleaded with the king, falling at his feet and lamenting. She implored him to put an end to the malicious plan of Haman the Agagite, which he had devised against the Jews. 4 Then the king extended the gold sceptre to Esther and she arose and stood before him. 5 'If it pleases the king,' she said, 'and if he regards me with favour and thinks it the right thing to do, and if he is pleased with me, let an order be written superseding the communications that Haman son of Hammedatha, the Agagite, devised and wrote to destroy the Jews in all the king's provinces. 6 For how can I bear to see tragedy fall on my people? How can I bear to see the destruction of my family?'

7 King Xerxes replied to Queen Esther and to Mordecai the Jew, 'Because Haman attacked the Jews, I have given his estate to Esther, and they have impaled him on the pole he set up. 8 Now write another decree in the king's name in behalf of the Jews as seems best to you, and seal it with the king's signet ring – for no document written in the king's name and sealed with his ring can be revoked.'

9 At once the royal scribed were mustered – on the twenty-third day of the third month, the month of Sivan. They wrote out all Mordecai's orders to the Jews, and to the satraps, governors and nobles of the 127 provinces stretching from India to Cush. These orders were written in the script of each province and the language of each people and also to the Jews in their own script and language. 10 Mordecai wrote in the name of King Xerxes, sealed the dispatches with the king's signet ring, and sent them by **mounted couriers, who rode fast horses especially bred for the king.**

11 The king's edict granted the Jews in every city the right to amass and defend themselves; to destroy, kill and annihilate the armed men of any race or province who might attack them and their women and children, and to plunder the property of their enemies. 12 The day appointed for the Jews to do this in all the provinces of King Xerxes was the thirteenth day of the twelfth month, the month of Adar. 13 A copy of the text of the edict was to be issued as law in every province and made known to the people of every race so that the Jews would be ready on that day to avenge themselves on their enemies. 14 The couriers, riding the royal horses, went out, spurred on by the king's command, and the edict was issued in the citadel of Susa.

15 When Mordecai left the king's presence, **he was wearing royal garments of blue and white, a large crown of gold and a purple robe of fine linen.** And the city of Susa held a joyous celebration. 16 For the Jews it was a time of exhilaration and joy, cheerfulness and honour. 17 In every province and in every city to which the edict of the king came, there was joy and gladness among the Jews, with feasting and celebrating. And many people of other races became Jews because trepidation about the Jews had come over them.

Commentary

8:1, 8:2 King Xerxes gave Queen Esther the estate of Haman, the enemy of the Jews. And Mordecai came into the presence of the king, for Esther had told how he was related to her. The king took off his signet ring, which he had reclaimed from Haman, and presented it to Mordecai. And Esther appointed him over Haman's estate

This is a perfectly feasible scenario. Achaemenid royal women enjoyed independent economic prosperity. Without any doubt, Darius I's mother, Irdabama was the wealthiest woman of her age, a significant presence at the royal court and an economic powerhouse in her own right. Irdabama enjoyed the privilege of ruling over an estate and a court of her own. She was responsible for its upkeep and maintenance, and for the feeding of her servants. The quantities of cereals, meat, wine and beer consumed and poured 'before Irdabama', as the Persepolis tablets put it, are substantial and add up to roughly one tenth of the amount consumed at the king's own court. One of the Persepolis administrative tablets (PF 1028) enumerates the sheer quantity of supplies and workers to be found at one of Irdabama's estates:

> 11,100 quarts of grain supplied by Kuntukka, workers of Irdabama received as rations, at Shiraz, their appointments being set by Rashda. Month 6 Year 22 (of Darius). 62 men 30 (quarts each), 8 boys 25, 34 boys 20, 26 boys 15, 19 boys 10, 22 boys 5, 190 women 30, 32 women 20, 11 girls 25, 20 girls 20, 24 girls 15, 17 girls 10, 25 girls 5. Total 490 workers.

Parysatis (Akkad. Purrushatu), the influential sister wife of Darius II (see Llewellyn-Jones 2022: 292–334), is known to have had enormous private estates throughout Babylonia. Her administrative personnel were none other than the Babylon-based bankers known as the Murashu. They leased the queen's lands and collected the rent for her. A typical document (Cardascia 1951: 95–6) reads:

> 317 *kur*, 2 PI, 3 *shatu* of barley, 5 *kur*, 2 PI, 3 *shatu* of wheat, (as) tax, part of the land of Parysatis and of the private domain of Ea-bullitsu, the administrator of

Parysatis, (part) of Year 4 of Darius (II) the king, who is at the service of Rimut-Ninurta, son of Murashu. Concerning the barley, 317 *kur*, 2 PI, 3 *shatu*, concerning the wheat, 5 *kur*, 2 PI, 3 *shatu*, (as) tax, part of the lands of Year 4 of Darius (the) king, Nabu-iddin son of Bel-erib, and Ea-bullitsu, slave of Ea-bullitsu on the order of Ea-bullitsu, administer of Parysatis, (from) the hands of Rimut-Ninurta son of Murashu, have been received. They have been paid. Nabu-iddin and Bel-amat-usur shall draw up (the receipt) and, coming from Ea-bullitsu, administrator of Parysatis, to Rimut-Nmuimey they give (it). (Written) in the presence of Ishtabuzana, judge of the Sin canal. (Written) in the presence of Nabu-mit-uballit, judge of the house of Parysatis, son of Mukin-apli,
(List of six witnesses follows.)
Nippur, day 11, month 6, Year 4 of Darius (II).

Xenophon also knew of villages which were owned by Parysatis near the Chalus River in western Mesopotamia, which had been given to her as a dowry, and notes too that she also owned villages in Media which had an abundance of 'grain, cattle and other unspecified property.' (Xen. *Anab*.1.4.9).

Persian queens also profited from the largesse of kings. Darius I's most prominent consort, Irtaštuna (Gk. Artystone), appears over thirty times in the Persepolis tablets. Some of the texts show the financial care which Darius lavished on her. One (PF 0723) is an order sent by Darius directly to Parnaka, the chief administrator at Persepolis, to ensure that Irtaštuna had good wine to drink:

Tell Yamakšedda the wine-bearer, Parnaka spoke as follows: 200 *marrish* (quarts) of wine are to be issued to the *dukšiš* (royal woman) Irtaštuna. It was ordered by the king. First month, year 9. Ansukka wrote (the text); Maraza communicated the contents.

Another (PF 6764) reveals how the king ordered a hundred sheep to be taken from his personal flock and given to his wife for her own estate:

Say to Harrena the overseer of livestock, Parnaka spoke thus: 'Darius the king ordered me, saying, "100 sheep from my estate are to be issued to the *dukšiš* Irtaštuna."' And now Parnaka says: 'As the King ordered me, so I am ordering you. Now you are to issue 100 sheep to the *dukšiš* Irtaštuna, as was commanded by the king'. First month, year 19. Ansukka wrote (the text); Maraza communicated the contents.

More importantly, the Persepolis texts actually preserve for us the personal 'voice' of the queen since several of the cuneiform tablets are commands issued directly from Irtaštuna herself:

Tell Datukka, Irtaštuna spoke as follows: '100 litres of wine to Ankanna; issue it from my estate at Mirandu ... and from my estate at Kukake.'

(PF 1835)

The queen dictated her own letters to scribes, who diligently dashed them off in wet clay. She wrote frequently to one of her principal servants, a Semite named Šalamana, her chief Chamberlain. Her instructions to him were always curt and to the point:

> Tell Šalamana, Irtaštuna spoke as follows: '200 litres of wine to Darizza. Issue it!'
> Tell Šalamana, Irtaštuna spoke as follows: '500 litres of wine to Mitranka and his companions. Issue it!'.
>
> (PF 1837)

Šalamana's personal seal has been identified – and its design says much about him (**Figure 8.1**). It cannot be taken as a 'portrait' of Šalamana and his royal mistress, but it is certainly a representation of his office, which is why, no doubt, he chose that particular image for his personal seal. It demonstrates the social context of Šalamana's life and his place within Achaemenid society.

All in all, four women of the Persian royal family are shown to have owned palaces with landed estates. Their expenses for food and wine provided for their official journeys are logged in the Persepolis archive. On one occasion expenses were incurred for a reception for 2,000 guests (Koch 1994). The income to defray these outgoings came from the royal revenues (Tolini 2013).

Figure 8.1 Seal of the steward Šalamana (PFS 535) from Persepolis.

8:10 mounted couriers, who rode fast horses especially bred for the king

See comments on **1:22 dispatches to all parts of the kingdom**

8:15 he was wearing royal garments of blue and white, a large crown of gold and a purple robe of fine linen

See comments on **6:8**

Chapter 9

[1 On the thirteenth day of the twelfth month, the month of Adar, the edict commanded by the king was to be carried out. On this day the enemies of the Jews had hoped to overpower them, but now the tables were turned and the Jews got the upper hand over those who hated them. 2 The Jews assembled in their cities in all the provinces of King Xerxes to attack those determined to destroy them. No one could stand against them, because the people of all the other nationalities were afraid of them. 3 And all the nobles of the provinces, the satraps, the governors and the king's administrators helped the Jews, because fear of Mordecai had seized them. 4 Mordecai was prominent in the palace; his reputation spread throughout the provinces, and he became more and more powerful.

5 The Jews struck down all their enemies with the sword, killing and destroying them, and they did what they pleased to those who hated them. 6 In the citadel of Susa, the Jews killed and destroyed five hundred men. 7 They also killed Parshandatha, Dalphon, Aspatha, 8 Poratha, Adalia, Aridatha, 9 Parmashta, Arisai, Aridai and Vaizatha, 10 the ten sons of Haman son of Hammedatha, the enemy of the Jews. But they did not lay their hands on the plunder.

11 The number of those killed in the citadel of Susa was reported to the king that same day. 12 The king said to Queen Esther, 'The Jews have killed and destroyed five hundred men and the ten sons of Haman in the citadel of Susa. What have they done in the rest of the king's provinces? Now what is your petition? It will be given you. What is your request? It will also be granted.'

13 'If it pleases the king,' Esther answered, 'give the Jews in Susa permission to carry out this day's edict tomorrow also, and let Haman's ten sons be impaled on poles.'

14 So the king commanded that this be done. An edict was issued in Susa, and they impaled the ten sons of Haman. 15 The Jews in Susa came together on the fourteenth day of the month of Adar, and they put to death in Susa three hundred men, but they did not lay their hands on the plunder.

16 Meanwhile, the remainder of the Jews who were in the king's provinces also assembled to protect themselves and get relief from their enemies. They killed seventy-five thousand of them but did not lay their hands on the plunder. 17 This happened on the thirteenth day of the month of Adar, and on the fourteenth they rested and made it a day of feasting and joy.

18 The Jews in Susa, however, had assembled on the thirteenth and fourteenth, and then on the fifteenth they rested and made it a day of feasting and joy.

19 That is why rural Jews – those living in villages – observe the fourteenth of the month of Adar as a day of joy and feasting, a day for giving presents to each other.

20 Mordecai recorded these events, and he sent letters to all the Jews throughout the provinces of King Xerxes, near and far, 21 to have them celebrate annually the fourteenth and fifteenth days of the month of Adar 22 as the time when the Jews got relief from their enemies, and as the month when their sorrow was turned into joy and their mourning into a day of celebration. He wrote them to observe the days as days of feasting and joy and giving presents of food to one another and gifts to the poor.

23 So the Jews agreed to continue the celebration they had begun, doing what Mordecai had written to them. 24 For Haman son of Hammedatha, the Agagite, the enemy of all the Jews, had plotted against the Jews to destroy them and had cast the pur (that is, the lot) for their ruin and destruction. 25 But when the plot came to the king's attention,[a] he issued written orders that the evil scheme Haman had devised against the Jews should come back onto his own head, and that he and his sons should be impaled on poles. 26 (Therefore these days were called Purim, from the word pur.) Because of everything written in this letter and because of what they had seen and what had happened to them, 27 the Jews took it on themselves to establish the custom that they and their descendants and all who join them should without fail observe these two days every year, in the way prescribed and at the time appointed. 28 These days should be remembered and observed in every generation by every family, and in every province and in every city. And these days of Purim should never fail to be celebrated by the Jews – nor should the memory of these days die out among their descendants.

29 So Queen Esther, daughter of Abihail, along with Mordecai the Jew, wrote with full authority to confirm this second letter concerning Purim. 30 And Mordecai sent letters to all the Jews in the 127 provinces of Xerxes' kingdom – words of goodwill and assurance – 31 to establish these days of Purim at their designated times, as Mordecai the Jew and Queen Esther had decreed for them, and as they had established for themselves and their descendants in regard to their times of fasting and lamentation. 32 Esther's decree confirmed these regulations about Purim, and it was written down in the records.]

Chapter 10

[1 King Xerxes imposed taxation throughout the empire, to its furthest shores. 2 And all his acts of power and might, together with a full account of the greatness of Mordecai, whom the king had promoted, are they not set out in the book of the annals of the kings of Media and Persia? 3 Mordecai the Jew was second in rank to King Xerxes, preeminent among the Jews, and held in highest authority by his many fellow Jews, because he worked for the good of his people and spoke up for the happiness of all the Jews.]

Concluding thoughts: The hidden Persian kings in the Hebrew Bible

The Book of Esther is not history, but like all the best historical novels, it is rich in historical detail. Written around a century after the time in which the action is set (the reign of Xerxes), Esther is nevertheless still a literary product of the Achaemenid period and, as such, it provides a persuasive, immersive experience for readers, leading them deep into the heart of the Persian royal court. The *realia* of palace life is all there in the details which the unknown author provides about eating and drinking, protocol and ceremony, hierarchy and competition, and gender ideology. Given that the author adds a liberal dose of hyperbole to the mix, Esther nevertheless submerges its readers in the historical milieu of the Persians. In this book I have attempted to encourage historians of the Persian empire to feel emboldened enough to investigate the text of Esther more thoroughly than they are currently inclined to do, if for no other reason than the fact that Esther provides us with a rich representation of the Persian court from the view-point of non-Persians. Unlike the majority of pejorative and hostile Greek accounts, Esther's Jewish author, very much at home among the elite of diaspora Susa, I suggest, is far more willing to picture the Persians in a positive light (by and large). For scholars and students of the Hebrew Bible, understanding the context of the Persian world of the Esther-story provides an important hook for any interpretation of the text. Understanding the Persian content of Esther deepens our appreciation of the story and its many intriguing details.

A similar approach to that which I have undertaken with Esther might be taken with Ezra and Nehemiah, Haggai, Zachariah and Malachi too, as those books are rich in detail about Achaemenid culture in Yehud and beyond. Indeed, given the undeniable significance of the Persian period in the formation and redaction of most of the biblical texts which make up the Hebrew Bible, I suggest that 'Persianisms' are intertwined throughout much of the story of YHWH's people. This should not come as a surprise. Whether working in the heartlands of the Persian empire (Babylonia, Elam or Persia) or far away from the imperial centre in Yehud or Jerusalem itself, Jewish scribes drew on the dominant culture around them for inspiration and as a consequence, the world of Persia permeates considerable portions of the Hebrew Bible.

The depiction in 1 Kings and 1 Chronicles of the glorious reign of King Solomon makes for an interesting case study. Attempting to verify the existence of Solomon is, at very best, a challenge. After all, the biblical accounts of the successes of biblical monarchs more generally rest upon a presupposition of supernatural realities and although there is archaeological and epigraphical evidence to substantiate the possibility of some (non-supernatural) scriptural assertions, archaeological finds to date have provided mostly indirect affirmation. When it comes to Solomon more specifically, the huge gaps in archaeological evidence make it difficult to empirically prove or disprove his existence at all. But in the biblical literary tradition he nonetheless looms large as the most splendid of Israel's kings. The literary depiction of Solomon's grandeur is based, I propose, on the model of Achaemenid kingship. The Chronicler's portrayal of Solomon as the king of peace (1 Chron. 22 and 28–9), for instance, is modelled on the figure of the Persian Great King who, in theory if not in practice, eagerly promoted the idea of a *Pax Achaemenidica*. The very *idea* of such a peace (and its physical manifestations in Persian art and epigraphy) can reasonably be assumed to have been known throughout the Achaemenid empire of the fifth and fourth centuries BCE, an empire of which Yehud was (albeit a tiny) part. The Deuteronomistic History version of Solomon's narrative was mostly composed in the fifth century BCE. That dating is not very controversial. However, many scholars believe that 1 Kings is based on much earlier sources, some dating to the reign of Solomon himself, conventionally placed *c*. 970–930 BCE. Some believe that the Temple description is taken from a 'document' contemporary with the original building. If that is so, then why is the extent of Solomon's realm as described in the bible reflective the political layout of the world in the late sixth and early fifth centuries BCE? If early (ninth century) 'Solomonic' sources were used, then how can Solomon be described as having traded through Ezion-geber (not built until late in the eighth century BCE), as having trade relations with Sheba (not active in long distance trade until the seventh century BCE), and as employing ships of Tarshish, which were active in trade between the eighth and sixth centuries BCE? The Book of Kings is evidence for what a fifth-century author believed about Tarshish, Sheba and Solomon's other international relations. It is as a fifth-century text that we must read Kings. The Achaemenid Great Kings provide a model for Solomon, and in both Kings and Chronicles, Solomon was elevated to the highest power imaginable in the cultural milieu of the fifth century – the power of the Persian Great King himself. But in the biblical literary tradition, Solomon's glory outshines even that of the Persian monarch: the description of the Temple and the adjacent palace (1 Kgs 6–7; 2 Chron. 3–4) is so detailed and yet so fantastic that the buildings are imagined as outstripping the Apadanas of Susa or Persepolis in scale and splendour. The boast that 'Silver and gold [was] as common in Jerusalem as stones, and cedar as plentiful as sycamore-fig trees in the foothills' (2 Chron. 1:14) echo the Susa Charters of Darius I, but easily tops them, and the number of stallions and mares in Solomon's stables, numbering 12,000, all specially imported from Egypt and Kush, were greater in number than those owned by Darius, Xerxes or any other Persian potentate. And if the Great King of Persia had some 360 women in his harem, then Solomon of Israel could boast of having no less than 700 consorts of royal birth (including a pharaoh's daughter) and 300 concubines in his (1 Kgs 11:1-3). 'Solomon's daily provisions were thirty cors of the finest flour', we are informed (1 Kgs 4:22) 'and sixty cors of meal, 23 ten head of stall-fed cattle, twenty of pasture-fed cattle and a hundred sheep and goats, as well as deer, gazelles, roebucks and choice fowl' – a menu (and a quantity of food) on par with the Great King's table. All in all, 'King Solomon was greater in riches and wisdom than all the other kings of the earth ... Year after year, everyone who came brought a gift – articles of silver and gold, robes, weapons and spices, and horses and mules', a ceremony on a scale, it would seem, that rivalled the great annual gift-giving ritual at Persepolis.

The cultural exchange between Persians and Jews was maintained throughout the Achaemenid period and is reflected in the biblical texts. We see it reflected best in the details: incense, for instance, which was much valued in Persian ceremony, had hitherto been of little importance in biblical texts but suddenly, in the Persian period, incense became prominent in the laws and psalms, just as incense altars appear in the archaeology of the time. Exchange of ideas also occurred. Second Isaiah (the author of Isa. 40–54) used some important Persian material. Isaiah 41:2-3; 42:1-7; 43:14; 44:28; 45:1-5, 13-14 and 48:14-15 parallel the Cyrus Cylinder so closely that both must have had a common source, which must have been the Persian propaganda which represented Cyrus to the Babylonians as chosen by the god Marduk, to the Jews as chosen by YHWH.

Beyond this, ensconced within the pages of the Hebrew Bible lie the shadowy forms of Persian kings, of the imperial Persian institutions and ideologies they created, and of the courtly life and society they ruled over. Searching them out might prove profitable in our understanding of the nature of the composition of select books and certain passages of the Hebrew Bible and inform us about the socio-cultural and political world of the Achaemenids in which they were created. The Book of Esther has been, for me, an obvious place to begin such an investigation, but the Hebrew bible contains so many more Persian reflections that need investigation; I predict that it will prove to be a profitable enterprise.

Bibliography

Abdi, K. (2010), 'The Passing of the Throne from Xerxes to Artaxerxes', in J. Curtis and S. Simpson (eds), *The World of Achaemenid Persia*, 275–84, London: I.B. Tauris.
Agostini, D. (2010), 'Encountering a Beautiful Maiden: On Zoroastrian *dēn* in Comparison with Dante's Beatrice', *Bulletin of the Asia Institute* 24: 15–23.
Albright, W.F. (1982), 'The Lachish Cosmetic Burner and Esther 2.12', in C.A. Moore (ed.), *Studies in the Book of Esther*, 261–8, New York: KATV Publishing House.
Allen, L. (2005a), *The Persian Empire*, London: University of Chicago Press.
Allen, L. (2005b), 'Le Roi Imaginaire: An Audience with the Achaemenid King', in O. Hekster and R. Fowler (eds), *Imaginary Kings. Royal Images in the Ancient Near East, Greece and Rome*, 39–62, Stuttgart: Franz Steiner Verlag.
Allen, L. (2007), '"Chilminarolim Persepolis": European Reception of a Persian Ruin', in C. Tuplin (ed.), *Persian Responses. Political and Cultural Interaction with(in) the Achaemenid Empire*, 313–42, Swansea: Classical Press of Wales.
Allsen, T.T. (2006), *The Royal Hunt in Eurasian History*, Philadelphia: University of Pennsylvania Press.
Almagor, E. (2020), 'The Royal Road from Herodotus to Xenophon (via Ctesias)', in C.J. Tuplin and J. Ma (eds), *Aršama and his World: The Bodleian Letters in Context. Vol. III. Aršama's World*, 147–85, Oxford: Oxford University Press.
Alster, B. (1997), *Proverbs of Ancient Sumer: The World's Earliest Proverb Collection*, Bethesda: CDL Press.
Alstola, T. (2020), *Judeans in Babylonia: A Study of Deportees in the Sixth and Fifth Centuries BCE*, Leiden: Brill.
Alter, R. (2015), *Strong as Death is Love. The Song of Songs, Ruth, Esther, Jonah, Daniel. A Translation with Commentary*, New York and London: W.W. Norton.
Álvarez-Mon, J. (2009), 'Notes on the "Elamite" Garment of Cyrus the Great', *The Antiquaries Journal*, 89: 21–33.
Álvarez-Mon, J. and Garrison, M.B., eds (2012), *Elam and Persia*, Winona Lake: Eisenbrauns.
Álvarez-Mon, J. (2015), 'The Introduction of Cotton in the Near East: A View from Elam', *IJSOIA (International Journal of the Society of Iranian Archaeologists)*, 1 (2): 41–52.
Ambrose, T. (2008), *The Nature of Despotism. From Caligula to Mugabe, the Making of Tyrants*, London: New Holland.
Anderson, G. (2000), *Fairy-tale in the Ancient World*, London: Routledge.
Anderson, M. (1990), *Hidden Power: The Palace Eunuchs of Imperial China*, Buffalo: Prometheus Books.
Aperghis, G.C. (1998), 'The Persepolis Fortification Texts – Another Look', in M. Brosius and A. Kuhrt (eds), *Studies in Persian History: Essays in Memory of David M. Lewis*, 35–62, Leiden: Nederlands Instituut Voor Het Nabije Oosten.
Arfaee, A. (2008), 'The Geographical Background of the Persepolis Tablets', PhD thesis, University of Chicago.

Arfa'i, A. (1999), 'La grande route Persépolis-Suse: Une lecture des tablettes provenant des Fortifications de Persépolis', *Topoi*, 9: 33–45.

Arnold, D. (2000), *Esther. Survivre dans un monde hostile*, Paris: Emmaus.

Asheri, D., Lloyd, A. and Corcella, A. (2007), *A Commentary on Herodotus Books I–IV*, Oxford: Oxford University Press.

Aster, S.Z. (2015), 'Ezekiel's Adaptation of Mesopotamian "Melammu"', *Die Welt Des Orients*, 45 (1): 10–21.

Axworthy, M. (2007), *Iran. Empire of the Mind. A History from Zoroaster to the Present Day*, London: Penguin.

Azarpay, G. (1972), 'Crowns and Some Royal Insignia in Early Iran', *Iranica Antiqua*, 9: 108–15.

Azzoni, A. and Dusinberre, E.R.M. (2014), 'Persepolis Fortification Aramaic Tablet Seal 0002 and the Keeping of Horses', in M. Kozuh, W.F.M. Henkelman, C.E. Jones and C. Woods (eds)

Bahrani, Z. (2001), *Women of Babylon. Gender and Representation in Mesopotamia*, London and New York: Routledge.

Bahrani, Z. (2003), *The Graven Image. Representation in Babylonia and Assyria*, Philadelphia: University of Pennsylvania Press.

Baker, P.L. (2010), 'Wrought of Gold or Silver. Honorific Garments in Seventeenth Century Iran', in J. Thompson, D. Shaffer and P. Mildh (eds), *Carpets and Textiles in the Iranian World 1400–1700*, 158–67, Oxford: May Beattie Archive, Ashmolean Museum, University of Oxford.

Baker, S.W. (1868) *The Nile Tributaries of Abyssinia*, London: Macmillan and Co.

Balcer, J.M. (1987), *Herodotus and Bisitun. Problems in Ancient Persian Historiography*, Stuttgart: Franz Steiner.

Balcer, J.M. (1993), *A Prosopographical Study of the Ancient Persians Royal and Noble, c. 550–450 BC*, Lampeter: Edwin Mellen Press.

Baldwin, J.G. (1984), *Esther. An Introduction and Commentary*, Leicester: Intervarsity Press.

Bardtke, H. (1963), *Das Buch Ester*, Gütersloh.

Barjamovic, G. (2011), 'Pride, Pomp and Circumstance: Palace, Court and Household in Assyria 879–612 BCE', in J. Duindam, T. Artan and M. Kunt (eds), *Royal Courts in Dynastic States. A Global Perspective*, 27–61, Leiden: Brill.

Batmanglij, N. (2008), *From Persia to Napa. Wine at the Persian Table*, Los Angeles.

Batmanglij, N. 2020. *Food of Life. Ancient Persian and Modern Iranian Cooking and Ceremonies*, Washington DC: Mage Publishers.

Battesti, T. (2011), 'Lumière de gloire et royauté en Iran', in Y. Vadé and B. Dupaigne (eds), *Regalia. Emblèmes et rites du pouvoir*, 165–86, Paris: L'Harmattan.

Beal, T.K. (1997), *The Book of Hiding. Gender, Ethnicity, Annihilation, and Esther*, London: Routledge.

Beaulieu, P-A. (2007), 'Late Babylonian Intellectual Life', in G. Leick (ed.), *The Babylonian World*, 473–84, London: Routledge.

Beck, P. (1972), 'A Note on the Reconstruction of the Achaemenid Robe', *Iranica Antiqua*, 9: 116–22.

Ben-Barak, Z. 1986, *Inheritance by Daughters in Israel and the Ancient Near East: A Social, Legal and Ideological Revolution*, Jaffa: Archaeological Center Publications.

Berg, S.B. (1979), *The Book of Esther. Motifs, Themes and Structure*, Missoula, MT: Scholars Press.

Berghe, L.V. (1993), 'De Skulpture', in F. van Norten (ed.), *Hofkunst van de Sassanieden*, 71–88, Brussels: Koninklijke Musea voor Kunst en Geschiedenis.
Berlin, A. (2001), *The JPS Bible Commentary: Esther*, Philadelphia: The Jewish Publication Society.
Bertelli, R. (2001), *The King's Body*, University Park: Penn State University Press.
Betzig, L. (1986), *Despotism and Differential Reproduction. A Darwinian View of History*, New York: Aldine Publishing Co.
Bickerman, E.J. (1938), *Institutions des Seléucides*, Paris: P. Geuthner.
Bickerman, E.J. (1967), *Four Strange Books of the Bible. Jonah, Daniel, Koheleth, Esther*, New York: Schocken Books.
Binder, C. (2008), *Plutarchs Vita des Artaxerxes. Ein historischer kommentar*, Berlin: de Gruyter.
Binder, C. (2010), 'Das Krönungszeremonial der Achaimeniden', in B. Jacobs and R. Rollinger (eds), *Der Achämenidenhof/The Achaemenid Court*, 473–97, Wiesbaden: Harrassowitz Verlag.
Bishop, T. (1998), 'The Gingerbread Host: Tradition and Novelty in the Jacobean Masque', in D. Bevington and P. Holbrook (eds), *The Politics of the Stuart Court Masque*, 88–120, Cambridge: Cambridge University Press.
Blair, S.S. (1995), *A Compendium of Chronicles. Rashid al-Din's Illustrated History of the World*, Oxford: Nour Foundation in association with Azimuth Editions and Oxford University Press.
Boardman, J. (1970), *Greek Gems and Finger Rings. Early Bronze Age to Late Classical*, London: Thames and Hudson.
Boardman, J. (2000), *Persia and the West. An Archaeological Investigation of the Genesis of Achaemenid Art*, London: Thames and Hudson.
Bonfiglio, R.P. (2021), 'The Art of Control: Iconography of the Early Achaemenid Empire', in P. Barmash and M.W. Hamilton (eds), *In the Shadow of Empire. Israel and Judah in the Long Sixth Century BCE*, 35–60, Atlanta: SBL Press.
Booth, C. (2015), *In Bed with the Ancient Egyptians*, Stroud: Amberley Publishing.
Booth, M., ed., (1996), *Harem Histories: Envisioning Places and Living Spaces*, Durham, NC: Duke University Press.
Borchhardt, J. 1976. *Die Bauskulptur des Heroons von Limyra: Das Grabmal des lykischen Königs Perikles*, Berlin: Gebr. Mann.
Bottéro, J. (2004), *The Oldest Cuisine in the World: Cooking in Mesopotamia*, trans. T. Lavender Fagan, Chicago: University of Chicago Press.
Boucharlat, R. (1985), 'Suse, marché agricole ou relais du grand commerce? Suse et la Susiane à l'époque des grands empires', *Paléorient*, 11 (2): 71–81.
Boucharlat, R. (1997), 'Susa Under Achaemenid Rule', in J. Curtis (ed.), *Mesopotamia and Iran in the Persian Period: Conquest and Imperialism 559–331 BC*, 54–67, London: British Museum Press.
Boyce, M. (1983), 'Iranian Festivals', in E. Yarshater (ed.), *The Cambridge History of Iran* III/2: *The Seleucid, Parthian and Sasanian Periods*, 792–815, Cambridge: Cambridge University Press.
Breasted, J.H. (1906), *Ancient Records of Egypt: Historical Documents from the Earliest Times to the Persian Conquest*, 5 vols, Chicago: University of Chicago Press.
Bremmer, J. (2008), *Greek Religion and Culture, the Bible and the Ancient Near East*, Leiden: Brill.
Brenner, A. (1994), 'Who's Afraid of Feminist Criticism? Who's Afraid of Biblical Humour? The Case of the Obtuse Foreign Ruler in the Hebrew Bible', *Journal for the Study of the Old Testament*, 19 (63): 38–55.

Brettler, M.Z. (1989), *God is King. Understanding an Israelite Metaphor*, Sheffield: JSOT Press.
Briant, P. (1982), *Etat et pasteurs au Moyen-Orient ancient*, Paris and Cambridge: Cambridge University Press.
Briant, P. (1988), 'Le nomadisme du Grand Roi', *Iranica Antiqua*, 23: 253–73.
Briant, P. (2002), *From Cyrus to Alexander. A History of the Persian Empire*, Winona Lake: Eisenbrauns.
Briant, P. (2003), 'À propos du roi-jardinier: Remarques sur l'histoire d'un dossier documentaire', in W. Henkelman and A. Kuhrt (eds), *A Persian Perspective. Essays in Memory of Heleen Sancisi-Weerdenburg, Achaemenid History XIII*, 33–49, Leiden: Nederlands Instituut voor het Nabije Oosten.
Briant, P. and Chauveau, M., eds (2009), *Organisation des pouvoirs et contacts culturels dans les pays de l'empire achéménide*, Paris.
Briant, P., Henkelman, W. and Stolper, M., eds, (2008), *L'archive des Fortifications de Persépolis*. Paris: De Boccard.
Bridges, E. (2014), *Imagining Xerxes: Ancient Perspectives on a Persian King*, London: Bloomsbury.
Brisch, N. (2008), *Religion and Power. Divine Kingship in the Ancient World and Beyond*, Chicago: Oriental Institute of the University of Chicago.
Brosius, M. (1996), *Women in Ancient Persia (559-331 BC)*, Oxford: Clarendon Press.
Brosius, M. (2000), *The Persian Empire from Cyrus II to Artaxerxes I*, Lactor, 16, London: London Association of Classical Teachers.
Brosius, M. (2003), (ed.). *Ancient Archives and Archival Traditions: Concepts of Record-Keeping in the Ancient World*, Oxford.
Brosius, M. (2006), *The Persians. An Introduction*, London: Routledge.
Brosius, M. (2007), 'Old Out of New? Court and Court Ceremonies in Achaemenid Persia', in A.J.S. Spawforth (ed.), *The Court and Court Society in Ancient Monarchies*, 17–57, Cambridge: Cambridge University Press.
Brosius, M. (2010a), 'The Royal Audience Scene Reconsidered', in J. Curtis and S. Simpson (eds), *The World of Achaemenid Persia*, 141–52, London: I.B. Tauris.
Brosius, M. (2010b), 'Das Hofzeremoniell', in B. Jacobs and R. Rollinger (eds), *Der Achämenidenhof/The Achaemenid Court*, 459–71, Wiesbaden: Harrassowitz Verlag.
Brosius, M. (2011), 'Greeks at the Persian Court', in J. Wiesehöfer, R. Rollinger and G. Lanfranchi (eds), *Ktesias' Welt/Ctesias' World*, 69–80, Wiesbaden: Harrassowitz Verlag.
Brosius, M. (2015), 'From Fact to Fiction: Persian History and the Book of Esther', in A. Fitzpatrick-Kinley (ed.), *Assessing Biblical and Classical Sources for the Reconstruction of Persian Influence, History, and Culture*, 193–202, Wiesbaden: Harrassowitz Verlag.
Brosius, M. (2021), *A History of Ancient Persia*, Oxford: Wiley-Blackwell.
Brown, J.P. (2001), *Israel and Hellas. Volume III: The Legacy of Iranian Imperialism and the Individual*, Berlin: De Gruyter.
Brown, W.P. (1996), *Seeing the Psalms. A Theology of Metaphor*, Louisville and London: Westminster/John Knox Press.
Brulé, P. (2003), *Women of Ancient Greece*, Edinburgh: Edinburgh University Press.
Budin, S.L. (2011), *Images of Woman and Child from the Bronze Age. Reconsidering Fertility, Maternity, and Gender in the Ancient World*, Cambridge: Cambridge University Press.
Bulliet, R.W. (1975), *The Camel and the Wheel*, Cambridge, MA: Harvard University Press.
Bullough, V.L. (2002), 'Eunuchs in History and Society', in S. Tougher (ed.), *Eunuchs in Antiquity and Beyond*, 1–17, Swansea and London: Classical Press of Wales.

Burke, P. (1994), *The Fabrication of Louis XIV*, New Haven: Yale University Press.
Calmeyer, P. (1976), 'Zur Genese Altiranischer Motive, V: Synarchie', *Archäologische Mitteilungen aus Iran*, 9: 63–95.
Calmeyer, P. (1996), 'Achaimenidische Möbel', in G. Herrmann (ed.), *The Furniture of Western Asia. Ancient and Traditional*, 224–31, Mainz: Philipp von Zabern.
Cardascia, G. (1951), *Les archives des Murašû*, Paris: Imprimerie Nationale.
Carney, E.D. (2000), *Women and Monarchy in Macedonia*, Norman: University of Oklahoma Press.
Carr, D.M. (2011), *The Formation of the Hebrew Bible. A New Reconsideration*, Oxford: Oxford University Press.
Carruthers, J. (2008), *Esther Through the Centuries*, Oxford: Wiley-Blackwell.
Cartmill, M. (1995), 'Hunting and Humanity in Western Thought', *Social Research*, 62 (3): 773–86.
Cassin, E. (1968), *La splendeur divine: Introduction à l'étude de la mentalité mésopotamienne*, Paris: De Gruyter.
Casson, L. (2001), *Libraries in the Ancient World*, New Haven: Yale University Press.
Chamberlin, J.E. (2006), *Horse. How the Horse has Changed Civilizations*, Oxford: Signal Books.
Chang, M.G. (2007), *A Court on Horseback. Imperial Touring and the Construction of Qing Rule, 1680–1785*, Cambridge, MA: Harvard University Asia Center.
Charles-Gaffiot, J. (2011), *Trônes en majesté. L'autorité et son symbole*, Paris: Cerf.
Choksy, J.K. (1988), 'Sacral Kingship in Sasanian Iran', *Bulletin of the Asia Institute*, 2: 35–52.
Christensen, A.E. (1936), *Les Gestes des rois dans les traditions de l'Iran antique*, Paris: Librairie orientaliste Paul Geuthner.
Chyutin, M. (2011), *Tendentious Hagiographies. Jewish Propagandist Fiction BCE*, London: Bloomsbury.
Cleland, L., Davies, G. and Llewellyn-Jones, L. (2007), *Greek and Roman Dress. From A–Z*, London: Routledge.
Clines, D.A.J. (1984), *The Esther Scroll: The Story of the Story*, JSOTSup 30, Sheffield: JSOT Press.
Clines, D.A.J. (1991), 'In Quest of the Historical Mordecai', *Vetus Testamentum*, 41: 129–36.
Clutton-Brock, J. (1992), *Horse Power: A History of the Horse and the Donkey in Human Societies*, Cambridge, MA: Harvard University Press.
Collon, D. (1987), *First Impressions. Cylinder Seals in the Ancient Near East*, London: British Museum Press.
Cook, J.M. (1983), *The Persian Empire*, London: Dent.
Cooper, J.S. (1982), 'Virginity in Ancient Mesopotamia', *CRRAI*, 47 (1): 91–112.
Cottrell, A. (2004), *Chariot. The Astounding Rise and Fall of the World's First War Machine*, London: Pimlico.
Cumming, C.G. (1934), *The Assyrian and Hebrew Hymns of Praise*, New York: Columbia University Press.
Curtis, J. (1996), 'Assyrian Furniture: The Archaeological Evidence', in G. Herrmann (ed.), *The Furniture of Western Asia. Ancient and Traditional*, 167–80, Mainz: Philipp von Zabern.
Curtis, J. and Simpson, S., eds (2010), *The World of Achaemenid Persia*, London: I.B. Tauris.
Curtis, J. and Tallis, N., eds (2005), *Forgotten Empire. The World of Ancient Persia*, London: British Museum Press.

Curtis, J. and Tallis, N. (2012), *The Horse. From Arabia to Royal Ascot*, London: British Museum Press.
Curtis, V.S. (1993), *Persian Myths*, London: British Museum Press.
Daems, A. (2018), 'Women of Elam', in J. Álvarez-Mon, G. Pietro Basello and Y. Wicks (eds), *The Elamite World*, 763–80, London and New York: Routledge.
Dahlén, A.P. (2020), 'Living the Iranian *Dolce Vita*: Herodotus on Wine Drinking and Luxury among the Persians', in A.P. Dahlén (ed.), *Achaemenid Anatolia: Persian Presence and Impact in the Western Satrapies 546–330 BC. Proceedings of an International Symposium at the Swedish Research Institute in Istanbul, 7–8 September 2017*, 99–126, Uppsala: Acta Universitatis Upsaliensis.
Dalley, S. (2007), *Esther's Revenge at Susa. From Sennacherib to Ahasuerus*, Oxford: Oxford University Press.
Dandamanev, M.A. (1984), 'Royal *Paradeisoi* in Babylonia', *Acta Iranica*, 23: 113–17.
Dandamanev, M.A. (1989), *A Political History of the Achaemenid Empire*, Leiden: Brill.
Dandamanev, M.A. (2008), *Slavery in Babylonia: From Nabopolassar to Alexander the Great (626–331 B.C.)*, DeKalb: Northern Illinois University Press.
Dandamanev, M.A. and Lukonin, V.G. (1989), *The Culture and Social Institutions of Ancient Iran*, Cambridge: Cambridge University Press.
Davaran, F. (2010), *Continuity in Iranian Identity*, London: Routledge.
Davidovich, T. (2007), *The Mystery of the House of Royal Women. Royal Pīlagšīm as Secondary Wives in the Old Testament*, Uppsala: Uppsala Universitet.
Davidson, J. (2006), 'The Greek Courtesan and the Art of the Present', in M. Feldman and B. Gordon (eds), *The Courtesan's Arts. Cross-Cultural Perspectives*, 29–51, Oxford: Oxford University Press.
Davidson, R.M. (2007), *Flame of Yahweh. Sexuality in the Old Testament*, Peabody, MA: Hendrickson.
Davies, N. G. (1908), *The Rock Tombs of El-'Amarna VI: The Tombs of Parennefer, Tutu and Aÿ. Archaeological Survey of Egypt 18th Memoir*, London: Egypt Exploration Fund.
Davis, D. (2006), *Shahnameh: The Persian Book of Kings*, New York: Penguin.
Day, L. (1995), *Three Faces of a Queen. Characterization in the Book of Esther*, Sheffield: Sheffield Academic Press.
Day, L. (2005), *Esther (Abingdon New Testament Commentaries)*, Nashville: Abingdon Press.
Dayagi-Mendels, M. (1989), *Perfumes and Cosmetics in the Ancient World*, Jerusalem: Israel Museum.
Dayagi-Mendels, M. and Rozenberg, S. (eds) (2010), *Chronicles of the Land. Archaeology in the Israel Museum, Jerusalem*, Jerusalem: Israel Museum.
de Goeje, M.J. (1888), 'Thousand and One Nights', *Encyclopaedia Britannica*, 9th edn, 316–18, London.
de Hulster, I.J. and Lemon, J.M. (eds) (2014), *Image, Text, Exegesis. Iconographic Interpretation and the Hebrew Bible*, London and New York: Bloomsbury.
de Hulster, I.J., Strawn, B.A. and Bonfiglio, R.P., eds (2015), *Iconographic Exegesis of the Hebrew Bible/Old Testament. An Introduction to its Methods and Practice*, Göttingen: Vandenhoeck & Ruprecht.
de Jong, A. (2010), 'Religion at the Achaemenid Court', in B. Jacobs and R. Rollinger (eds), *Der Achämenidenhof/The Achaemenid Court*, 533–58, Wiesbaden: Harrassowitz Verlag.
Deller, K. (1999), 'The Assyrian Eunuchs and their Predecessors', in K. Watanabe (ed.), *Priests and Officials in the Ancient Near East*, 303–11, Heidelberg: Universitätsverlag C. Winter.

De Morgan, J. (1905), *Memoirs Publiés sur la Direction de M. J De Morgan. Tomme VIII*, Paris.

Dentzer, J.-M. (1971), 'Aux origines de l'iconographie du banquet couché', *Revue Archéologique*, 2, 215–58.

Dieulafoy, M. (1888), 'L'harem a Suse', *Revue des études juives*, 8: 255–6.

Dieulafoy, M. (1890–2), *L'acropole de Suse*, 4 vols, Paris.

Degeorge, G. and Okada, A. (2013), *Hoysala. Dieux de l'Inde et beautés célestes*, Arles: Actes Sud.

DelPlato, J. (2002), *Multiple Wives, Multiple Pleasures. Representing the Harem, 1800–1875*, London: Fairleigh Dickinson University Press.

Desroches Noblecourt, C. (2007), *Gifts from the Pharaohs*, London: Flammarion.

De Troyer, K. (1995), 'An Oriental Beauty Parlour: An Analysis of Esther 2. 2-18 in the Hebrew, the Septuagint, and the Second Greek Text', in A. Brenner (ed.), *A Feminist Companion to Esther, Judith and Susanna*, 47–70, Sheffield: Sheffield Academic Press.

de Vaux, R. (1961), *Ancient Israel. Its Life and Institutions*, London: McGraw-Hill.

Dickson, C.R. and Botha, P.J. (2000), 'The Role and Portrayal of the King in Esther', *Old Testament Essays*, 13 (2): 156–73.

Dodson, A. and Hilton, D. (2005), *The Complete Royal Families of Ancient Egypt*, London: Thames and Hudson.

Drews, R. (2004), *Early Riders: The Beginnings of Mounted Warfare in Asia and Europe*, New York: Routledge.

Driver, G.R. (1956), *Aramaic Documents of the Fifth Century BC*, Oxford: Clarendon Press.

Duchesne-Guillemin, J. (1953), 'Les Noms des Eunuques d'Assuerus', *Mus*, 66: 105–8.

Duindam, J. (2003), *Vienna and Versailles: The Courts of Europe's Dynastic Rivals, 1550–1780*, Cambridge: Cambridge University Press.

Duindam, J. (2016), *Dynasties: A Global History of Power, 1300–1800*, Cambridge: Cambridge University Press.

Duindam, J., Artan, T., and Kunt, M. eds, (2011), *Royal Courts in Dynastic States. A Global Perspective*, Leiden: Brill.

Dunbar, E.S. (2022), *Trafficking Hadassah. Collective Trauma, Cultural Memory, and Identity in the Book of Esther and the African Diaspora*, London: Routledge.

Dusinberre, E.R.M. (2003), *Aspects of Empire in Achaemenid Sardis*, Cambridge: Cambridge University Press.

Dusinberre, E.R.M. (2005), 'Herzfeld in Persepolis', in A.C. Gunter and S.P. Hauser (eds), *Ernst Herzfeld and the Development of Near Eastern Studies 1900–1950*, 137–80, Leiden: Brill.

Dutz, W.F. (1977), *Persepolis and Archaeological Sites in Fars*, Tehran.

Dutz, W.F. and Matheson, S.A. 2001. *Parsa-Persepolis*, Tehran: Yassavoli Publications.

Edelman, D.V. (2015), 'What is Persian about the Book of Genesis?', in A. Fitzpatrick-Kinley (ed.), *Assessing Biblical and Classical Sources for the Reconstruction of Persian Influence, History, and Culture*, 149–81, Wiesbaden: Harrassowitz Verlag.

Edelman, D.V. and Ben Zvi, E. (eds) (2013), *Remembering Biblical Figures in the Late Persian and Early Hellenistic Periods*, Oxford: Oxford University Press.

Eicher, J. B. and Evensen, S.L. (2015), *The Visible Self. Global Perspectives on Dress, Culture, and Society*, New York and London: Bloomsbury.

Elias, N. (1983), *The Court Society*, Oxford: Basil Blackwell.

Elias, N. (1994), *The Civilizing Process*, Oxford: Wiley-Blackwell.

Ermidoro, S. (2015), *Commensality and Ceremonial Meals in the Neo-Assyrian Period*, Venice: Ca' Foscari.

Erskine, A., Llewellyn-Jones, L., and Wallace, S., eds (2013), *The Hellenistic Court*, Swansea: Classical Press of Wales.
Fales, F.M. (1994), 'A Fresh Look at the Nimrud Wine Lists', in L. Milano (ed.), *Drinking in Ancient Societies: History and Culture of Drinks in the Ancient Near East*, 361–80, Padua: Sargon.
Fales, F.M. and Postgate, N. (1992), *Imperial Administrative Records. Part 2. State Archives of Assyria*, Helsinki: Helsinki University Press.
Finkel, I.L. (2014), *The Ark Before Noah: Decoding the Story of the Flood*, London: Hodder and Stoughton.
Finkel, I.L. and Seymour, M.J., eds (2008), *Babylon*, London: British Museum Press.
Foster, B.R. (2005), *Before the Muses. An Anthology of Akkadian Literature*, Bethesda: CDL Press.
Fowler, M.A. and Marincola, J., eds (2002), *Herodotus. Histories Book IX*, Cambridge: Cambridge University Press.
Fox, M.V. (1985), *The Song of Songs and the Ancient Egyptian Love Songs*, Madison: University of Wisconsin Press.
Fox, M.V. (1991), *Character and Ideology in the Book of Esther*, Columbia: University of South Carolina Press.
Frankfort, H. (1944), *Kingship and the Gods*, Chicago: University of Chicago Press.
Frankfort, H. (1954), *The Art and Architecture of the Ancient Orient*, New Haven and London: Yale University Press.
Frazer, J. (1911), *The Magic Art. Volume I*. London: Macmillan.
Fredricksmeyer, E.A. (1997), 'The Origin of Alexander's Royal Insignia', *Transactions and Proceedings of the American Philological Association*, 127: 97–109.
Fredricksmeyer, E.A. (2000), 'Alexander the Great and the Kingship of Asia', in A.B. Bosworth and E.J. Baynham (eds), *Alexander the Great in Fact and Fiction*, 136–66, Oxford: Oxford University Press.
Frese, D.A. (2020), *The City Gate in Ancient Israel and Her Neighbors*, Leiden: Brill.
Frye, R.N. (1962), *The Heritage of Persia*, London: Weidenfeld and Nicholson.
Frye, R.N. (1972), 'Gestures of Deference to Royalty in Ancient Iran', *Iranica Antiqua*, 9: 102–7.
Frye, R.N. (1996), *The Golden Age of Persia*, New York: Barnes and Noble.
Gaca, K.L. (2011), 'Girls, Women, and the Significance of Sexual Violence in Ancient Warfare', in E.D. Heineman (ed.), *Sexual Violence in Conflict Zones*, 73–88, Philadelphia: University of Pennsylvania Press.
Gansell, A.R. (2014a), 'Images and Conceptions of Ideal Feminine Beauty in Neo-Assyrian Royal Contexts, c. 883–672 BCE', in B.A. Brown and M.H. Feldman (eds), *Critical Approaches to Ancient Near Eastern Art*, 391–420, Berlin: De Gruyter.
Gansell, A.R. (2014b), 'The Iconography of Ideal Female Beauty Represented in the Hebrew Bible and Iron Age Levantine Ivory Sculpture', in I.J. de Hulster and J.M. Lemon (eds), *Image, Text, Exegesis. Iconographic Interpretation and the Hebrew Bible*, 232–50, London and New York: Bloomsbury.
Gardiner, A.H. (1931), *The Library of A. Chester Beatty: Love Songs and Other Miscellaneous Texts*, London: Emery Walker.
Garrison, M.B. (2021), 'Seals and Sealing', in B. Jacobs and R. Rollinger (eds), *A Companion to the Achaemenid Persian Empire*, 769–91, Oxford: Wiley Blackwell.
Garthwaite, G.R. (2005), *The Persians*, Oxford: Blackwell Publishing.
Garvie, A.F. (2009), *Aeschylus: Persae: with Introduction and Commentary*, Oxford: Oxford University Press.

Geertz, C. (1983), *Local Knowledge: Further Essays in Interpretive Anthropology*, New York: Basic Books.
Gehman, H.S. (1924), 'Notes on the Persian Words in the Book of Esther', *JBL*, 43: 321–8.
Gerleman, G. (1966), *Studien zur Esther. Stoff – Struktur – Stil – Sinn*, Neukirchen-Vlyun: Neukirchener Verlag.
Gershevitch, I. (1985), *The Cambridge History of Iran. Volume 2. The Median and Achaemenian Periods*, Cambridge: Cambridge University Press.
Gerstenberger, E.S. (2011), *Israel in the Persian Period. The Fifth and Fourth Centuries BCE*, Atlanta: SBL Press.
Gertoux, G. (2015), *Queen Esther, Wife of Xerxes. Chronological, Historical and Archaeological Evidence*, Privately Published.
Gharipour, M. (2013), *Persian Gardens and Pavilions. Reflections in History and the Arts*, New York and London: I.B. Tauris.
Ghirshman, R. (1964), *Persia. From the Origins to Alexander the Great*, London: Thames and Hudson.
Ghirshman, R. and Herzfeld, E. (2000), *Persepolis. The Achaemenians' Capital*, Tehran: Mirdashti Farhangsara Book.
Gindin, T.E. (2016), *The Book of Esther Unmasked*, Los Angeles: Zeresh Books.
Glassner, J.J. (2004), *Mesopotamian Chronicles*, Atlanta: Society of Biblical Literature.
Gnoli, G. (1974a), 'Politica religiosa e concezione della regalità sotto gli Achemenidi', in *Gururājamañjarikā: Studi in onore di Giuseppe Tucci* vol. I, 23–88, Naples: Istituto Universitario Orientale.
Gnoli, G. (1974b), 'Politique religieuse et conception de la royauté sous les Achéménides', in J. Duchesne-Guillemin and P. Lecoq (eds), *Commémoration Cyrus: actes du congrès de Shiraz 1971 et autres études, rédigées à l'occasion du 2500e anniversaire de la fondation de l'empire perse* (vol. 2; Acta Iranica 2), 117–90, Leiden: E.J. Brill.
Goffman, E. (1956a), *The Presentation of Self in Daily Life*, New York: Doubleday.
Goffman, E. (1956b), 'The Nature of Deference and Demeanour', *American Anthropologist*, 58: 473–502.
Goldman, B. (1964), 'Origin of the Persian Robe', *Iranica Antiqua*, 4: 133–52.
Goldman, B. (1991), 'Women's Robes: The Achaemenid Era', *Bulletin of the Asia Institute*, 5: 83–103.
Good, I. (2010), 'Early Islamic Textiles and their Influence on Pre-Islamic Dress', in G. Vogelsang-Eastwood (ed.), *Berg Encyclopedia of World Dress and Fashion, Volume 5: Central and Southwest Asia*, 282–7, Oxford: Berg.
Gordis, R. (1974), *Megillat Esther: The Masoretic Hebrew Text*, New York: Rabbinical Assembly.
Gordis, R. (1981), 'Religion, Wisdom and History in the Book of Esther – A New Solution to an Ancient Crux', *JBL*, 100: 359–88.
Gordon, S. (2001), 'A World of Investiture', in S. Gordon (ed.), *Robes and Honor. The Medieval World of Investiture*, 1–22, New York: Palgrave Macmillan.
Gordon, S. (2003), *Robes of Honour. Khil'at in Pre-Colonial and Colonial India*, Delhi: Oxford University Press.
Gordon, S. (2010), 'Khil'at: Clothing to Honour a Person or Situation', in G. Vogelsang-Eastwood (ed.), *Berg Encyclopaedia of World Dress and Fashion. Volume 5: Central and Southwest Asia*, 462–7, Oxford: Berg.
Grabbe, L.L., Boccaccini, G. and Zurawski, J.M., eds (2016), *The Seleucid and Hasmonean Periods and the Apocalyptic World View*, London: Bloomsbury.

Grayson, A.K. (1972), *Assyrian Royal Inscriptions*, 2 vols, Wiesbaden: Otto Harrassowitz Verlag.
Grayson, A.K. (1975), *Babylonian Historical-Literary Texts*, Toronto: University of Toronto Press.
Grayson, A.K. (1995), 'Eunuchs in Power', in M. Dietrich and O. Loretz (eds), *Vom Alten Orient zum Alten Testament. Festschrift W. v. Soden*, 85–98, Neukirchen-Vluyn: Verlag Butzon & Bercker; Neukirchener Verlag.
Grayson, A.K. (1996), *Assyrian Rulers of the Early First Millennium BC (858–745 BC). Royal Inscriptions of Mesopotamia Assyrian Periods, Volume 3*, Toronto, Buffalo and London: University of Toronto Press.
Green, J.D.M. (2019), 'Gender and Sexuality', in A.C. Gunther (ed.), *A Companion to Ancient Near Eastern Art*, 179–207, Oxford: Wiley Blackwell.
Gressmann, H. (1929), *Der Messias*, Göttingen: Vandenhoeck & Ruprecht.
Griffiths, A. (1987), 'Democedes of Croton. A Greek Doctor at the Court of Darius', in H. Sancisi-Weerdenburg and A. Kuhrt (eds), *Achaemenid History Vol. II. The Greek Sources*, 37–51, Leiden: Nederlands Instituut voor het Nabije Oosten.
Grossman, J. (2011), *Esther. The Outer Narrative and the Hidden Meaning*, Winona Lake: Eisenbrauns.
Groß, M.M. (2020), *At the Heart of Empire. The Royal Household in the Neo-Assyrian Period*, Leuven: Peeters.
Groves, E. (2003), 'Double Take: Another Look at the Second Gathering of the Virgins in Esther 2.19A', in S.W. Crawford and L.J. Greenspoon (eds), *The Book of Esther in Modern Research*, 91–110, London and New York: T & T Clark.
Gruber, M.I. (1980), *Aspects of Non-Verbal Communication in the Ancient Near East*, 2 vols. Rome: Biblical Institute Press.
Gunter, A.C. and Hauser, S.R., eds (2005), *Ernst Herzfeld and the Development of Near Eastern Studies, 1900–1950*, Leiden: Brill.
Guterbock, H.G. and van Hout, T. (1991), *The Hittite Instruction for the Royal Bodyguard*, Chicago: The Oriental Institute.
Guyot, P. (1980), *Eunuchen als Sklaven und Freigelassene in der griechisch-römichen Antike*, Stuttgart: Klett-Cotta.
Gzella, H. (2021), *Aramaic: A History of the First World Language*, Grand Rapids: William B. Eerdmans Publishing Co.
Hackl, J. and Ruffing, K. (2021), 'Taxes and Tributes', in B. Jacobs and R. Rollinger (eds), *Blackwell Companion to the Achaemenid Persian Empire*, 967–97, Oxford: Wiley-Blackwell.
Hakohen, M. (1961), '[Ahasuerus' Characterization in the Legends of the Sages (Heb.)]', *Mahanayim*, 54: 33–8.
Hallo, W.W. (1983), 'The First Purim', *Biblical Archaeology*, 46: 19–26.
Hallo, W.W., ed. (1997), *The Context of Scripture. Canonical Compositions from the Biblical World*, 4 vols, Leiden: Brill.
Hallock, R.T. (1969), *Persepolis Fortification Tablets*, Chicago: University of Chicago Press.
Hallock, R.T. (1978), 'Selected Fortification Texts', *Cahiers de la Délégation Française en Iran*, 8: 109–36.
Hallock, R.T. (1985), 'The Evidence of the Persepolis Tablets', in I. Gershevitch (ed.), *The Cambridge History of Iran. Volume 2. The Median and Achaemedian Periods*, 588–609, Cambridge: Cambridge University Press.
Hamilton, M.W. (2005), *The Royal Body. The Social Poetics of Kingship in Ancient Israel*, Atlanta: Society of Biblical Literature.

Hancock, R.S. (2013), *Esther and the Politics of Negotiation. Public and Private Spaces and the Figure of the Royal Counsellor*, Minneapolis: Fortress Press.

Harper, P.O., Aruz, J. and Tallon, F., eds (1992), *The Royal City of Susa. Ancient Near Eastern Treasures in the Louvre*, New York: Metropolitan Museum of Art.

Harvey, C.D. (2003), *Finding Morality in the Diaspora? Moral Ambiguity and Transformed Morality in the Book of Esther*, Berlin and New York: De Gruyter.

Hazewindus, M.W. (2004), *When Women Interfere. Studies in the Role of Women in Herodotus' Histories*, Amsterdam: Brill.

Head, D. (1992), *The Achaemenid Persian Army*, Stockport: Montvert Publications.

Henkelman, W.F.M. (1995-6), 'The Royal Achaemenid Crown', *Archäologische Mitteilungen aus Iran*, 28: 275-93.

Henkelman, W.F.M. (2003a), 'An Elamite Memorial: The Šumar of Cambyses and Hystaspes', in W. Henkelman and A. Kuhrt (eds), *A Persian Perspective. Essays in Memory of Heleen Sancisi-Weerdenburg, Achaemenid History XIII*, 101-72, Leiden: Nederlands Instituut voor het Nabije Oosten.

Henkelman, W.F.M. (2003b), 'Persians, Medes and Elamites: Acculturation in the Neo-Elamite Period', in G.B. Lanfranchi, M. Roaf and R. Rollinger (eds), *Continuity of Empire (?) Assyria, Media, Persia*, 181-231, Padua: S.a.r.g.o.n.

Henkelman, W.F.M. (2008), *The Other Gods Who Are. Studies in Elamite-Iranian Acculturation Based on the Persepolis Fortification Texts. Achaemenid History XIV*, Leiden: Nederlands Instituut voor het Nabije Oosten.

Henkelman, W.F.M. (2010a), 'Consumed Before the King. The Table of Darius, Irdabama and Irtaštuna and That of his Satrap, Karkiš', in B. Jacobs and R. Rollinger (eds), *Der Achämenidenhof/The Achaemenid Court*, 667-775, Wiesbaden: Harrassowitz Verlag.

Henkelman, W.F.M. (2010b), 'Xerxes, Atossa, and the Persepolis Fortification Archive', *The Netherlands Institute for the Near East Leiden/The Netherlands Institute in Turkey Istanbul. Annual Report*, 26-33.

Henkelman, W.F.M. (2011a), 'Cyrus the Persian and Darius the Elamite: A Case of Mistaken Identity', in R. Rollinger, B. Truschnegg and R. Bichler (eds), *Herodot und das Persische Weltreich/Herodotus and the Persian Empire*, 577-634, Wiesbaden: Harrassowitz Verlag.

Henkelman, W.F.M. (2011b), 'Parnaka's Feast: Šip in Pārsa and Elam', in J. Álvarez-Mon and M.B. Garrison (eds), *Elam and Persia*, 89-166, Winona Lake: Eisenbrauns.

Henkelman, W.F.M. and Jacobs, B. (2021), 'Roads and Communication', in B. Jacobs and R. Rollinger (eds), *Blackwell Companion to the Achaemenid Persian Empire*, 719-35, Oxford: Wiley-Blackwell.

Henkelman, W.F.M. and Stolper, M.W. (2009), 'Ethnic Identity and Ethnic Labelling at Persepolis: The Case of the Skudrians', in P. Briant and M. Chauveau (eds), *Organisation des pouvoirs et contacts culturels dans les pays de l'empire achéménide*, 271-329, Paris: De Boccard.

Herzfeld, E. (1941), *Iran in the Ancient East*, London: Oxford University Press.

Herzfeld, E. (1968), *The Persian Empire: Studies in Geography and Ethnography of the Ancient Near East*, Wiesbaden: F. Steiner.

Hesker, O. and Fowler, R. eds (2005), *Imaginary Kings. Royal Images in the Ancient Near East, Greece and Rome*, Munich: Franz Steiner Verlag.

Hill, A. (2006), 'On David's "Taking" and "Leaving" Concubines (2 Samuel 5:13; 15:16)', *JBL*, 125 (1): 129-50.

Hobhouse, P. (2003), *The Gardens of Persia*, London: Cassell Illustrated.

Holm, T.L. (2013), *Of Courtiers and Kings. The Biblical Daniel Narratives and Ancient Story Collections*, Winona Lake: Eisenbrauns.
Holt, E.K. (2021), *Narrative and Other Readings in the Book of Esther*, London: T&T Clark.
Homan, M.M. (2002), *To Your Tents, O Israel! The Terminology, Form and Symbolism of Tents in the Hebrew Bible and the Ancient Near East*, Leiden: Brill.
Hopkins, K. (1963), 'Eunuchs in Politics in the Later Roman Empire', *Proceedings of the Cambridge Philological Society*, 189: 62–80.
Hornblower, S. (2003), 'Panionios of Chios and Hermotimos of Pedasa (Hdt. 8.104-106)', in P. Derow and R. Parker (eds), *Herodotus and his World. Essays from a Conference in Memory of George Forrest*, 37–57, Oxford: Oxford University Press.
How, W.W. and Wells, J. (1912), *A Commentary on Herodotus. Volume II: Books VI–IX*, Oxford: Oxford University Press.
Huff, D. (2005), 'From Median to Achaemenian Palace Architecture', *Iranica Antiqua*, 40: 371–95.
Huff, D. (2010), 'Überlegungen zu Funktion, Genese und Nachfolge des Apadana', in B. Jacobs and R. Rollinger (eds), *Der Achämenidenhof/The Achaemenid Court*, 311–74, Wiesbaden: Harrassowitz Verlag.
Hughes, J.R. (2016), 'Which Persian Monarch was the Ahasuerus of the Book of Esther?', *Journal of Creation*, 3 (3): 74–7.
Hyland, J.O. (2019), 'The Achaemenid Messenger Service and the Ionian Revolt. New Evidence from the Persepolis Fortification Archive', *Historia*, 68: 150–69.
Izdimirski, (2018), 'Deportation of *Kurtaš* Workers in the Achaemenid Empire According to the Classical Literary Tradition', *Živa Antika*, 68: 5–17.
Jacobs, B. (2009), 'Grausame Hinrichtungen – friedliche Bilder. Zum Verhältnis der politischen Realität zu den Darstellungsszenarien der achämenidischen Kunst', in M. Zimmermann (ed.), *Extreme Formen von Gewalt in Bild und Text des Altertums, Münchner Studien zur Alten Welt 5*, 121–53, Munich: Herbert Utz Verlag.
Jacobs, B. (2010), 'Höfischer Lebensstil und materielle Prachtenfaltung', in B. Jacobs and R. Rollinger (eds), *Der Achämenidenhof/The Achaemenid Court*, 377–409, Wiesbaden: Harrassowitz Verlag.
Jacobs, B. and Rollinger, R., eds (2010), *Der Achämenidenhof/The Achaemenid Court*, Wiesbaden: Harrassowitz Verlag.
Jacobs, B. and Rollinger, R., eds (2021), *The Blackwell Companion to the Achaemenid Persian Empire*, 2 vols, Oxford: Wiley Blackwell.
Jamzadeh, P. (1996), 'The Achaemenid Throne-Leg Design', *Iranica Antiqua*, 31: 101–46.
Janković, B. (2008), 'Travel Provisions in Babylonia in the First Millennium BC', in P. Briant, W. Henkelman and M. Stolper (eds), *L'archive des Fortifications de Persépolis*, 429–64, Paris: De Boccard.
Jidejian, N. (2006), *Sidon Through the Ages*, Beirut: Aleph.
Jigoulov, V.S. (2010), *The Social History of Achaemenid Phoenicia*, London: Equinox.
Joannes, F. (2004), *The Age of Empires. Mesopotamia in the First Millennium BC*, Edinburgh: Edinburgh University Press.
Johnson, J. (1974), 'The Demotic Chronicle as an Historical Source', *Enchoria*, 4: 1–17.
Jones, B.W. (1977), 'Two Misconceptions re the Book of Esther', *Catholic Biblical Quarterly*, 39: 172–7.
Jones, G.H. (1989), 'The Concept of Holy War', in R.E. Clements (ed.), *The World of Ancient Israel*, 299–322, Cambridge: Cambridge University Press.
Jursa, M. (2008), 'On the Initiation of Babylonian Priests', *Zeitschrift für Altorientalische und Biblische Rechtsgeschichte*, 14: 1–38.

Jursa, M. (2011), 'Höflinge (*ša rēši, ša rēš šarru, ustarbaru*) in babylonischen Quellen der ersten Jahrtausends', in J. Wiesehöfer, R. Rollinger and G. Lanfranchi (eds), *Ktesias' Welt/Ctesias' World*, 159–74, Wiesbaden: Harrassowitz Verlag.

Kahana, H. (2005), *Esther. Juxtaposition of the Septuagint Translation with the Hebrew Text*, Leuven: Peeters.

Kantorowicz, E.H. (1957), *The King's Two Bodies. A Study in Medieval Political Theology*, Princeton: Princeton University Press.

Kaplan, F.E.S. (2008), 'Politics in an African Royal Harem: Women and Seclusion at the Royal Court of Benin, Nigeria', in A. Walthall (ed.), *Servants of the Dynasty. Palace Women in World History*, 115–36, Berkeley: University of California Press.

Kaptan, D. (2002), *The Daskyleion Bullae: Seal Images from the Western Achaemenid Empire*, 2 vols, Leiden: Nederlands Instituut Voor Het Nabije Oosten.

Karlsson, M. (2016), *Relations of Power in Early Neo-Assyrian State Ideology*, Studies in Ancient Near Eastern Records 10, Boston and Berlin: De Gruyter.

Karlsson, M. (n.d.), 'The Expression "Non-Lord of a Throne" in Assyrian Royal Inscriptions', online https://www.academia.edu/24203164/The_Expression_Non_Lord_of_a_Throne_in_Assyrian_Royal_Inscriptions (accessed 26/10/2020).

Keaveney, A. (1998), 'Xerxes' New Suit: Aeschylus' Persae 845–851', *Giornale-Italiano di Filologia*, 15, November: 239–41.

Keaveney, A. (2003), *The Life and Journey of the Athenian Statesman Themistocles (524–460 BC?) as a Refugee in Persia*, Lampeter: Edwin Mellen Press.

Keaveney, A. (2010), 'The Chiliarch and the Person of the King', in B. Jacobs and R. Rollinger (eds), *Der Achämenidenhof/The Achaemenid Court*, 499–508, Wiesbaden: Harrassowitz Verlag.

Keel, O. (1978), *The Symbolism of the Biblical World. Ancient Near Eastern Iconography and the Book of Psalms*, New York: The Seabury Press.

Keel, O. (1994), *The Song of Songs. A Continental Commentary*, Minneapolis: Fortress Press.

Keel, O. (2012), 'Paraphernalia of Jerusalem Sanctuaries and Their Relation to Deities Worshiped Therein during the Iron Age IIA–C', in J. Kamlah and H. Michelau (eds), *Temple Building and Temple Cult. Architecture and Cultic Paraphernalia of Temples in the Levant (2.–1. Mill. B.C.E.), Proceedings of a Conference on the Occasion of the 50th Anniversary of the Institute of Biblical Archaeology at the University of Tübingen (28–30 May 2010) (ADPV 41)*, 317–42, Wiesbaden: Harrassowitz Verlag.

Keel, O. and Uehlinger, C. (1998), *Gods, Goddesses, and Images of God in Ancient Israel*, Minneapolis: Fortress Press.

Kelekna, P. (2009), *The Horse in Human History*, Cambridge: Cambridge University Press.

Khalil, L.A. (1986), 'A Bronze Caryatid Censor from Amman', *The Journal of the Council for British Research in the Levant*, 18: 103–10.

Khatchadourian, L. (2016), *Imperial Matter: Ancient Persia and the Archaeology of Empires*, Oakland: University of California Press.

Kinnier Wilson, J.V. (1972), *The Nimrud Wine Lists: A Study of Men and Administration at the Assyrian Capital in the Eighth Century BC*, London: British School of Archaeology in Iraq.

Kitz, A.M. (2000), 'The Hebrew Terminology of Lot Casting and its Near Eastern Context', *Catholic Biblical Quarterly*, 62: 207–14.

Kleber, K. ed. (2021), *Taxation in the Achaemenid Empire*, Wiesbaden: Harrassowitz.

Klein, L.R. (1995), 'Honor and Shame in Esther', in A. Brenner (ed.), *A Feminist Companion to Esther, Judith, and Susanna*, The Feminist Companion to the Bible 7, 149–75, Sheffield: Sheffield Academic Press.

Knauer, E.R. (1985), 'Towards a History of the Sleeved Coat: A Study of the Impact of an Ancient Eastern Garment on the West', *Expedition*, 21 (1): 18-36.
Knauer, E.R. (2003), 'A Quest for the Origins of the Persian Riding Coats: Sleeved Garments with Underarm Openings', in C. Fluck and G. Vogelsang-Eastwood (eds), *Riding Costume in Egypt. Origin and Appearance*, 7-28, Leiden: Brill.
Knight, D.A. and Levine, A.-J. (2011), *The Meaning of the Bible*, New York: HarperCollins.
Koch, H. (1994), 'Frauen im Achämenidenreich', in P. Vavroušek (ed.), *Iranian and Indo-European Studies. Memorial Volume of Otakar Klíma*, 125-41, Prague: Enigma Corporation.
Koch, H. (2001), *Persepolis*, Mainz Am Rhein: Philipp von Zabern.
Köhlmoos, M. (2019), 'Tearing One's Clothes and Rites of Mouring', in C. Berner, M. Schaffer, M. Schott, S. Schulz, and M. Weingartner (eds), *Clothing and Nudity in the Hebrew Bible*, 303-13, London: Bloomsbury.
Koller, A. (2020), 'Thrones and Crowns: On the Regalia of the West Semitic Monarchy', in L. Naeh and D. Brostowsky Gilboa (eds), *The Ancient Throne: The Mediterranean, Near East, and Beyond, from the 3rd Millennium BCE to the 14th Century CE*, 123-34, Vienna: Austrian Academy of Sciences Press.
Komaroff, L., ed. (2011), *Gifts of the Sultan: The Arts of Giving at the Islamic Courts*, Los Angeles: Los Angeles County Museum of Art.
Krefter, F. (1971), *Persepolis. Rekonstruktionen*, Berlin: Gebr. Mann.
Kugel, J. (2007), *How to Read the Bible*, New York: The Free Press.
Kuhrt, A. (1988), 'Earth and Water', in A. Kuhrt and H. Sancisi-Weerdenburg (eds), *Achaemenid History III. Method and Theory*, 87-99, Leiden: Nederlands Instituut voor het Nabije Oosten.
Kuhrt, A. (1995), *The Ancient Near East c. 3000-330 BC*, 2 vols, London: Routledge.
Kuhrt, A. (2001a), 'The Achaemenid Persian Empire (c. 550-c. 330 BCE): Continuities, Adaptations, Transformations', in S.E. Alcock, T.N. D'Altroy, K.D. Morrison, and C.M. Sinopoli (eds), *Empires. Perspectives from Archaeology and History*, 93-123, Cambridge: Cambridge University Press.
Kuhrt, A. (2001b), 'Women and War', *Journal of Gender Studies in Antiquity*, 2: 1-25.
Kuhrt, A. (2002), *'Greece' and 'Greeks' in Mesopotamian and Persian Perspectives*, The 21st J.L. Myres Memorial Lecture, Oxford: Myres Memorial Lectures.
Kuhrt, A. (2007), *The Persian Empire. A Corpus of Sources from the Achaemenid Period*, 2 vols, London: Routledge.
Kuhrt, A. (2010), 'Der Hof der Achämeniden: Concluding Remarks', in B. Jacobs and R. Rollinger (eds), *Der Achämenidenhof/The Achaemenid Court*, 901-12, Wiesbaden: Harrassowitz Verlag.
Kwasman, T. and Parpola, S. (1991), *Legal Transactions of the Royal Court at Nineveh, Part I: Tiglath-Pileser III through Esarhaddon*, State Archives of Assyria 6, Helsinki: Helsinki University Press.
Lal, K.S. (1988), *The Mughal Harem*, Delhi: Aditya Prakashan.
Lal, R. (2005), *Domesticity and Power in the Early Mughal World*, Cambridge: Cambridge University Press.
Landy, Y. (2010), *Purim and the Persian Empire. A Historical, Archaeological and Geographical Perspective*, Jerusalem: Feldheim Publishers.
Lanfranchi, G.B. (2010), 'Greek Historians and the Memory of the Assyrian Court', in B. Jacobs and R. Rollinger (eds), *Der Achämenidenhof/The Achaemenid Court*, 39-65, Wiesbaden: Harrassowitz Verlag.

Lanfranchi, G.B. and Rollinger, R., eds (2010), *Concepts of Kingship in Antiquity*, Padua: S.a.r.g.o.n.
Laniak, T.S. (1998), *Shame and Honor in the Book of Esther*, Atlanta: Scholars Press.
Leick, G. (1994), *Sex and Eroticism in Mesopotamian Literature*, London: Routledge.
Lecoq, P. (1997), *Les inscriptions de la Perse achéménide*, Paris: Gallimard.
Lenfant, D. (2004), *Ctésias de Cnide. La Perse, L'Inde, autre fragments*, Paris: Les Belles Lettres.
Lenfant, D. (2007a), 'Greek Historians of Persia', in J. Marincola (ed.), *A Companion to Greek and Roman Historiography*, Vol. I, 201–9, Oxford: Blackwell Publishing.
Lenfant, D. (2007b), 'On Persian *Tryphē* in Athenaeus', in C. Tuplin (ed.), *Persian Responses. Political and Cultural Interaction With(in) the Achaemenid Empire*, 51–65, Swansea: Classical Press of Wales.
Lenfant, D. (2009), *Les Histoires perses de Deinon et d'Héraclide. Fragments édités, traduits et commentés*, Paris: De Boccard.
Lenfant, D. (2012), 'Ctesias and his Eunuchs. A Challenge for Modern Historians', *Histos*, 6: 257–97.
Lenfant, D. (2019), 'Polygamy in Greek Views of Persians', *Greek, Roman, and Byzantine Studies*, 59: 15–37.
Leonowens, A.H. (1873), *The Romance of the Harem*, Boston: J.R. Osgood and Co.
Lerner, J.A. (2010), 'An Achaemenid Cylinder Seal of a Woman Enthroned', in J. Curtis and S. Simpson (eds), *The World of Achaemenid Persia*, 153–64, London: I.B. Tauris.
Levenson, J.D. (1997), *Esther*, Louisville: Westminster/John Knox Press.
Levit-Tawil, L. (1983), 'The Enthroned King Ahasuerus at Dura in Light of the Iconography of Kingship in Iran', *Bulletin of the American Schools of Oriental Research*, 250: 57–78.
Levy, J. (2011), *Poison. A Social History*, Stroud: History Press.
Lewis, D.M. (1977), *Sparta and Persia. Lectures Delivered at the University of Cincinnati, Autumn 1976, in Memory of Donald W. Bradeen [by] David M. Lewis*, Leiden.
Lewis, D.M. (1997a), 'The Persepolis Fortification Texts', in P.J. Rhodes (ed.), *Selected Papers in Greek and Near Eastern History by David M. Lewis*, 325–31, Cambridge: Cambridge University Press.
Lewis, D.M. (1997b), 'The King's Dinner', in P.J. Rhodes (ed.), *Selected Papers in Greek and Near Eastern History by David M. Lewis*, 332–41, Cambridge: Cambridge University Press.
Lewis, R. (2000), 'Harems and Hotels: Segregated City Spaces and Narratives of Identity in the Work of Oriental Women Writers', in L. Durning and R. Wrigley (eds), *Gender and Architecture*, 171–87, Chichester: Wiley.
Lewis, R. (2004), *Rethinking Orientalism. Women, Travel and the Ottoman Harem*, New York: Rutgers University Press.
Lichtheim, M. (1980), *Ancient Egyptian Literature. Volume III: The Late Period*, Berkeley: University of California Press.
Linafelt, T. (1992), 'Taking Women in Samuel: Readers/Responses/Responsibility', in D.N. Fewell (ed.), *Reading Between Texts: Intertextuality and the Hebrew Bible*, 99–113, Louisville: Westminster/John Knox Press.
Lincoln, B. (2007), *Religion, Empire and Torture. The Case of Achaemenid Persia, with a Postscript on Abu Ghraib*, Chicago: University of Chicago Press.
Lindenberger, J.M. (2003), *Ancient Aramaic and Hebrew Letters*, Atlanta: Society of Biblical Literature.

Livingstone, A. (1989), *Court Poetry and Historical Miscellanea*, State Archives of Assyria 3, Helsinki: Helsinki University Press.
Llewellyn-Jones, L. (2002), 'Eunuchs and the Royal Harem in Achaemenid Persia (559-331 BC)', in S. Tougher (ed.), *Eunuchs in Antiquity and Beyond*, 19-49, Swansea: Classical Press of Wales.
Llewellyn-Jones, L. (2003), *Aphrodite's Tortoise. The Veiled Woman of Ancient Greece*, Swansea and London: Classical Press of Wales.
Llewellyn-Jones, L. (2008), 'Achaemenid Persia', in S. Bourke (ed.), *The Middle East. The Cradle of Civilization Revealed*, 216-45, London: Thames and Hudson.
Llewellyn-Jones, L. (2009a), 'Ethnic Conceptions of Beauty in Achaemenid Period Seals and Gemstones', in S. Hales and T. Hodos (eds), *Local and Global Identities: Rethinking Identity, Material and Visual Cultures in the Ancient World*, 171-200, Cambridge: Cambridge University Press.
Llewellyn-Jones, L. (2009b), '"Help me Aphrodite!" Representing the Royal Women of Persia in Oliver Stone's *Alexander*', in F. Greenland and P. Cartledge (eds), *Responses to Oliver Stone's Alexander*, 150-97, Madison: University of Wisconsin Press.
Llewellyn-Jones, L. (2009c), 'The First Persian Empire', in T. Harrison (ed.), *The Great Empires of the Ancient World*, 65-95, London: Thames and Hudson.
Llewellyn-Jones, L. (2010a), 'The Big and Beautiful Women of Asia: Picturing Female Sexuality in Greco-Persian Seals', in J. Curtis and S. Simpson (eds), *The World of Achaemenid Persia*, 165-76, London: I.B. Tauris.
Llewellyn-Jones, L. (2010b), 'Pre-Islamic Dress Codes in the Eastern Mediterranean and Southwest Asia', in G. Vogelsang-Eastwood (ed.), *Berg Encyclopaedia of World Dress and Fashion. Volume 5: Central and Southwest Asia*, 24-30. Oxford: Berg.
Llewellyn-Jones, L. (2011), 'Hair', in M. Finkelberg (ed.), *The Homer Encyclopaedia. Volume II*, 327-8, Oxford: Blackwell Publishing.
Llewellyn-Jones, L. (2012), 'The Great Kings of the Fourth Century and the Greek Memory of the Persian Past', in J. Marincola, L. Llewellyn-Jones and C. Maciver (eds), *Greek Notions of the Past in the Archaic and Classical* Eras. *History Without Historians*, 317-46, Edinburgh: Edinburgh University Press.
Llewellyn-Jones, L. (2013a), *King and Court in Ancient Persia, 559-331 BC*, Edinburgh: Edinburgh University Press.
Llewellyn-Jones, L. (2013b), 'Empire of the Gaze: Seraglio Fantasies *à la greque* in Chariton's *Callirhoe*', in S. Blundell, D. Cairns and N. Rabinowitz (eds), *Vision and Viewing in Ancient Greece. Helios* (special edition), 167-91.
Llewellyn-Jones, L. (2015), 'Beautiful to Behold is the King: The Body of the Achaemenid Monarch', in F. Wascheck and A. Shapiro (eds), *Fluide Körper-Bodies in Transition*, 211-48, Cologne: Wilhelm Fink.
Llewellyn-Jones, L. (2017), 'The Achaemenids', in T. Daryaee (ed.), *King of the Seven Climes: A History of Ancient Iran*, 50-92, Irvine, CA: UCI Jordan Center for Persian Studies.
Llewellyn-Jones, L. (2019), 'Harem Politics: Royal Women and Succession Crises in the Ancient Near East (c. 1400-300 BCE)', in E. Woodacre (ed.), *History of Monarchy*, 534-50, London: Routledge.
Llewellyn-Jones, L. (2020a), 'Violence and the Mutilated Body in Achaemenid Iran', in L. Fibiger, G.G. Fagan and M. Hudson (eds), *The Cambridge History of Violence. Volume 1 – The Prehistoric and Ancient Worlds*, 360-79, Cambridge: Cambridge University Press.

Llewellyn-Jones, L. (2020b), 'The Court', in B. Jacobs and R. Rollinger (eds), *The Blackwell Companion to the Achaemenid Persian Empire*, II, 1035–46, Oxford: Wiley Blackwell.

Llewellyn-Jones, L. (2020c), 'The Royal *Gaunaka: Dress, Identity, Status and Ceremony in Achaemenid Iran', in S.-J. Simpson and S. Pankova (eds), *Masters of the Steppe: The Impact of the Scythians and Later Nomad Societies of Eurasia*, 248–57, Oxford: Archaeopress.

Llewellyn-Jones, L. (2022), *Persians. The Age of the Great Kings*, London and New York: Wildfire.

Llewellyn-Jones, L. and Robson, J. (2010), *Ctesias' History of Persia. Tales of the Orient*, London: Routledge.

L'Orange, H.P. (1953), *Studies in the Iconography of Cosmic Kingship*, Oslo: Aschehoug.

Macchi, J-D. (2018), *Esther (International Exegetical Commentary on the Old Testament)*, Stuttgart: Kohlhammer.

Macgregor, S.L. (2017), *Beyond Hearth and Home. Women in the Public Sphere in Neo-Assyrian Society*, Helsinki: Neo-Assyrian Text Corpus Project, Institute for Asian and African Studies, University of Helsinki.

Mackey, S. (1996), *The Iranians. Persia, Islam and the Soul of a Nation*, New York: Dutton.

Madhloom, T.A. (1970), *The Chronology of Neo-Assyrian Art*, London: The Athlone Press.

Magdalene, F.R. (2007), *On the Scales of Righteousness: Neo-Babylonian Trial Law and the Book of Job*, Brown Judaic Studies 348, Providence, RI: Brown Judaic Studies.

Maguire, H. (2004), *Byzantine Court Culture from 829 to 1204*, Cambridge, MA: Harvard University Press.

Mahmoudi Farahani, L., Motamed, B. and Jamei, E. (2016), 'Persian Gardens: Meanings, Symbolism, and Design', *LANDSCAPE ONLINE*, 46: 1–19, DOI 10.3097/LO.201646.

Manniche, L. (1999), *Sacred Luxuries. Fragrance, Aromatherapy, and Cosmetics in Ancient Egypt*, London: Opus Publishing.

Mapfeka, T.K. (2020), 'Esther 9 Through the Lens of Diaspora: The Exegetical and Ethical Dilemmas of the Massacres in Susa and Beyond', in J. van Ruiten and K. van Bekkum (eds), *Violence in the Hebrew Bible. Between Text and Reception*, 398–414, Leiden and Boston: Brill.

Marr, J.L. (1998), *Plutarch. Life of Themistocles*, Warminster: Aris & Phillips.

Marsman, H.J. (2003), *Women in Ugarit and Israel. Their Social and Religious Positions in the Context of the Ancient Near East*, Leiden: Brill.

Matarese, C. (2021), *Deportationen im Perserreich in Teispidisch-Achaimenidischer Zeit*, Wisbaden: Harrassowitz Verlag.

Matheson, S.A. (1972), *Persia. An Archaeological Guide*, London: Faber & Faber.

May, N. (2014), 'Gates and their Functions in Mesopotamia and Ancient Israel', in N. May and U. Steinert (eds), *The Fabric of Cities. Aspects of Urbanism, Urban Topography and Society in Mesopotamia, Greece and Rome*, 77–121, Leiden: Brill.

Mayrhofer, M. (1973), *Onomastica Persepolitana*, Vienna: Verlag der Osterreichischen Akademie Der Wissenschaften.

McGovern, P.E. (2009), *Uncorking the Past. The Quest for Beer and Other Alcoholic Beverages*, Berkeley: University of California Press.

Meiggs, R. and Lewis, D.M. (1988), *A Selection of Greek Historical Inscriptions to the End of the Fifth Century BC*, Oxford: Clarendon Press.

Meinhold, A. (1976), 'Die Gattung des Josephsgeschichte und des Estherbuches: Diasporanovelle, II', *ZAW*, 88: 72–93.

Melville, S.C. (1999), *The Role of Naqia/Zakutu in Sargonid Politics*, Helsinki: Neo-Assyrian Text Corpus Project.

Melville, S.C. (2006), 'Eponym Lists', in M.W. Chavalas (ed.), *The Ancient Near East*, 293–8, Oxford: Wiley-Blackwell.

Middlemas, J. (2019), 'Dating Esther. Historicity and Provenance of Masoretic Esther', in R.J. Bautch and M. Lackowski (eds), *On Dating Biblical Texts to the Persian Period*, 149–68, Tübingen: Mohr Siebeck.

Mikasa, T. (ed.) (1984), *Monarchies and Socio-Religious Traditions in the Ancient Near East: Papers Read at the 31st International Congress of Human Sciences in Asia and North Africa*, Wiesbaden: Otto Harrassowitz.

Miles, J. (2015), 'Reading Esther as Heroine: Persian Banquets, Ethnic Cleansing, and Identity Crisis', *Theology Bulletin*, 45 (3): 131–43.

Miles, M. (2003), 'Segregated We Stand? The Mutilated Greeks' Debate at Persepolis, 330 BC', available at: https://www.independentliving.org/docs7/miles2003.html (accessed 13 January 2022).

Millard, A. (1980), 'Review of *Assyrian and Babylonian Chronicles*. A. K. Grayson', *JAOS*, 100 (3): 364.

Miller, M. (1997), *Athens and Persia in the Fifth Century BC. A Study in Cultural Receptivity*, Cambridge: Cambridge University Press.

Montero Fenollòs, J.L. (2006), 'La "maison de succession" à l'époque néoassyriene', in V.A. Troncoso (ed.), *Diodokhos tēs Basileias: La figura del sucesor en la realeza helenística, Anejo IX*, 205–22, Madrid: Servicio de Publicaciones, Universidad Complutense.

Moore, C.A. (1971), *The Anchor Yale Bible: Esther. A New Translation with Introduction and Commentary*, New Haven: Yale University Press.

Moorey, P.R.S. (1980), 'Metal Wine-Sets in the Ancient Near East', *Iranica Antiqua*, 15: 182–97.

Moorey, P.R.S. (2002), 'Novelty and Tradition in Achaemenid Syria. The Case of the Clay Astarte Plaques', *Iranica Antiqua*, 37: 203–18.

Moran, W.L. (1992), *The Amarna Letters*, Baltimore and London: The Johns Hopkins University Press.

Mousavi, A. (2012), *Persepolis. Discovery and Afterlife of a World Wonder*, Berlin: De Gruyter.

Murray, D. (2015), 'The Waters at the End of the World. Herodotus and Mesopotamian Cosmic Geography', in E. Barker, S. Bouzarovski, C. Pelling and L. Isaksen (eds), *New Worlds from Old Texts*, 12–27, Oxford: Oxford University Press.

Nashat, G. (2003), 'Women in Pre-Islamic and Early Islamic Iran', in G. Nashat and L. Beck (eds), *Women in Iran. From the Rise of Islam to 1800*, 11–47, Urbana and Chicago: University of Illinois Press.

Nelson, S.M. (2003), *Ancient Queens*, Walnut Creek: Altamira Press.

Niditch, S. (1987), *A Prelude to Biblical Folklore. Underdogs and Tricksters*, Chicago: University of Illinois Press.

Niditch, S. (2008), *'My Brother Esau is a Hairy Man'. Hair and Identity in Ancient Israel*, Oxford: Oxford University Press.

Nielsen, I. (1999), *Hellenistic Palaces*, Aarhus.

Nielsen, I., ed. (2001), *The Royal Palace Institution in the First Millennium BC. Regional Development and Cultural Interchange between East and West*, Aarhus: Aarhus University Press.

Noonan, B.J. (2021), *Non-Semitic Loanwords in the Hebrew Bible. A Lexicon of Language Contact*, Winona Lake: Eisenbrauns.

Novak, M. (2002), 'The Artificial Paradise: Programme and Ideology of Royal Gardens', in S. Parpola and R. M. Whiting (eds), *Sex and Gender in Ancient Near East*, 443–60, Helsinki: Neo-Assyrian Text Corpus Project.

Novotny, J.R. (2001), 'Daughters and Sisters of Neo-Hittite and Aramaean Rulers in the Assyrian Harem', *The Canadian Society for Mesopotamian Studies*, 36: 174–84.

Novotny, J.R. and Singletary, J. (2009), 'Family Ties: Assurbanipal's Family Revisited', in M. Luukko, S. Svärd and R. Mattila (eds), *Of God(s), Trees, Kings, and Scholars. Neo-Assyrian and Related Studies in Honour of Simo Parpola*, 167–77, Helsinki: Finnish Oriental Society.

Oakley, F. (2006), *Kingship*, Oxford: Blackwell Publishing.

Oates, J. and Oates, D. (2001), *Nimrud. An Assyrian Imperial City Revealed*, London: British School of Archaeology in Iraq.

O'Daniel Cantrell, D. (2011), *The Horsemen of Israel. Horses and Chariotry in Monarchic Israel (Ninth- Eighth Centuries BCE)*, Winona Lake: Eisenbrauns.

Oded, B. (1979), *Mass Deportations and Deportees in the Neo-Babylonian Empire*, Wiesbaden: Reichert.

Ogden, D. (1999), *Polygamy, Prostitutes and Death. The Hellenistic Dynasties*, London: Duckworth with the Classical Press of Wales.

Olmstead, A.T. (1948), *History of the Persian Empire*, Chicago: University of Chicago Press.

Oost, S.I. (1977/8), 'Xenophon's Attitude toward Women', *The Classical World*, 71 (4): 225–36.

Omanson, R.L. and Noss, P.A. (1997), *The Book of Esther. The Hebrew and Greek Texts*, Stuttgart and New York: American Bible Society.

Oppenheim, A.L. (1964), *Ancient Mesopotamia*, Chicago: University of Chicago Press.

Oppenheim, A.L. (1967), *Letters from Mesopotamia*, Chicago: University of Chicago Press.

Oppenheim, A.L. (1973), 'Note on *ša rēši*', *Journal of the Ancient Near Eastern Society*, 6: 325–34.

Ornan, T. (2019), 'The Throne and the Enthroned: On the Conceived Human Image of Yahweh in Iron II Jerusalem', *TEL AVIV*, 46: 198–210.

Oswalt, J.N. (1996), *The Book of Isaiah: Chapters 1–39*, Grand Rapids: William B. Eerdmans Publishing Co.

Palagia, O. (2018), 'Alexander the Great, the Royal Throne and the Funerary Thrones of Macedonia', *Karanos*, 1: 23–34.

Parker, S.B. (1997), *Ugaritic Narrative Poetry*, Atlanta: Scholars Press.

Parkinson, R.B. (1999), *The Tale of Sinuhe and Other Ancient Egyptian Poems, 1940–1640 BC*, Oxford: Oxford University Press.

Parpola, S. (1970), *Letters from Assyrian Scholars to Kings Esarhaddon and Assurbanipal. Vol. I: Texts*, Neukirchen: Butzon and Bercker.

Parpola, S. and Watanabe, K. (1988), *Neo-Assyrian Treaties and Loyalty Oaths. State Archives of Assyria*, Vol. II, Helsinki: Helsinki University Press.

Paspalas, S.A. (2000), 'On Persian-Type Furniture in Macedonia: The Recognition and Transmission of Forms', *American Journal of Archaeology*, 104 (3): 531–60.

Patterson, J. (2007), 'Friends in High Places: The Creation of the Court of the Roman Emperor' in A.J.S. Spawforth (ed.), *The Court and Court Society in Ancient Monarchies*, 121–56, Cambridge: Cambridge University Press.

Peirce, L. (1993), *The Imperial Harem. Women and Sovereignty in the Ottoman Empire*, Oxford: Oxford University Press.

Peirce, L. (2008), 'Beyond Harem Walls: Ottoman Royal Women and the Exercise of Power', in A. Walthall (ed.), *Servants of the Dynasty. Palace Women in World History*, 81-94, Berkeley: University of California Press.

Penzer, N.M. (1936), *The Ḥarēm. An Account of the Institution as it Existed in the Palace of the Turkish Sultans, with a History of the Grand Seraglio from its Foundation to Modern Times*, London: G.G. Harrap.

Perrot, J. (1974), 'Historique des rescherches', *Cahiers de la délégation archéologique française en Iran*, 4: 15-20.

Perrot, J. (1981), 'L'architecture militaire et palatiale des Achéménides à Suse', in *150 Jahre Deutsches Archäologisches Institut, 1829-1979. Internationale Kolloquium*, 90-134, Mainz: Philipp von Zabern.

Perrot, J. (1996), 'The Palace of Susa', in J. Goonick Westenholz (ed.), *Royal Cities of the Biblical World*, 53-60, Jerusalem: Bible Lands Museum.

Perrot, J. (2010), *Le palais de Darius à Suse. Une résidence royale sur la route de Persépolis à Babylone*, Paris: Presses de l'Université Paris-Sorbonne.

Pham, X.H.T. (2000), *Mourning in the Ancient Near East and the Hebrew Bible*, Sheffield: Sheffield Academic Press.

Pinnock, F. (2018), 'A City of Gold for the Queen: Some Thoughts about the Mural Crown of Assyrian Queens', in M. Cavalieri and C. Boschetti (eds), *MVLTA PER ÆQVORA Il polisemico significato della moderna ricerca archeologica. Omaggio a Sara Santoro*. Volume 2, 731-50, Louvain: Presses Universitaires de Louvain.

Pirngruber, R. (2011), 'Eunuchen am Königshof. Ktesias und die altorientalische Evidenz', in J. Wiesehöfer, R. Rollinger and G. Lanfranchi (eds), *Ktesias' Welt/Ctesias' World*, 279-312, Wiesbaden: Harrassowitz Verlag.

Porten, B. and Yardeni, A. (1987-99), *Textbook of Aramaic Documents from Ancient Egypt*, Jerusalem: Hebrew University.

Porter, Y. (2003), *Palaces and Gardens of Persia*, Paris: Flammarion.

Portnoy Marshall, A. (1989), 'Ahasuerus is the Villain', *Jewish Bible Quarterly*, 18 (3): 187-9.

Portuese, L. (2020), *Life at Court. Ideology and Audience in the Late Assyrian Palace*, Münster: Zaphon.

Potts, D.T. (1999), *The Archaeology of Elam. Formation and Transformation of an Ancient Iranian State*, Cambridge: Cambridge University Press.

Potts, D.T. (2008), 'The Persepolis Fortification Texts and the Royal Road: Another Look at the Fahliyan Area', in P. Briant, W. Henkelman and M. Stolper (eds), *L'archive des Fortifications de Persépolis*, 275-302, Paris: De Boccard.

Potts, D.T. (2010), 'Monarchy, Factionalism and Warlordism: Reflections on Neo-Elamite Courts', in B. Jacobs and R. Rollinger (eds), *Der Achämenidenhof/The Achaemenid Court*, 107-37, Wiesbaden: Harrassowitz Verlag.

Potts, D.T. (2011), 'The Elamites', in T. Daryaee (ed.), *The Oxford Handbook of Iranian History*, 37-56, Oxford: Oxford University Press.

Pritchard, J.B. (1969), *Ancient Near Eastern Texts Relating to the Old Testament. Third Edition with Supplement*, Princeton: Princeton University Press.

Queen-Sutherland, K. (2016), *Ruth and Esther*, Macon, GA: Smyth & Helwys Publishing.

Quick, L. (2021), *Dress, Adornment, and the Body in the Hebrew Bible*, Oxford: Oxford University Press.

Radner, K. (2015), 'High Visibility Punishment and Deterrent: Impalement in Assyrian Warfare and Legal Practice', in H. von Reinhard Achenbach, H. Neumann and E. Otto (eds), *Zeitschrift für Altorientalische und Biblische Rechtsgeschichte. Journal for Ancient Near Eastern and Biblical Law*, 21, 103-28, Wiesbaden: Harrassowitz Verlag.

Rawski, E.S. (1998), *The Last Emperors: A Social History of Qing Imperial Institutions*, Berkeley: University of California Press.

Redford, S. (2002), *The Harem Conspiracy. The Murder of Ramesses III*, DeKalb: Northern Illinois University Press.

Rehm, E. et al. (2006), *Pracht und Prunk der Großkönige – Das persische Weltreich*, Stuttgart: Konrad Theiss.

Reinhold, M. (1970), 'History of Purple as a Status Symbol in Antiquity', *Latomus*, 116: 37–47.

Ringgren, H. (1981), 'Skonhetsavlingen I esters bok', *SEÅ*, 46: 69–73.

Robins, G. (1993), *Women in Ancient Egypt*, London: British Museum Press.

Rollinger, R. (2004), 'Herodotus, Human Violence and the Ancient Near East', in V. Karageorghis and I. Taifacos (eds), *The World of Herodotus*, 121–50, Nicosia: Foundation Anastasios G. Leventis.

Rollinger, R. (2010), 'Extreme Gewalt und Srtafgericht. Ktesias und Herodot als Zeugnisse für den Achaemenidenhof', in B. Jacobs and R. Rollinger (eds), *Der Achämenidenhof/ The Achaemenid Court*, 557–666, Wiesbaden: Harrassowitz Verlag.

Root, M.C. (1979), *The King and Kingship in Achaemenid Art: Essays on the Creation of an Iconography of Empire*, Leiden: E.J. Brill.

Root, M.C. (1990), *Crowning Glories. Persian Kingship and the Power of Creative Continuity*, Ann Arbor: Kelsey Museum of Archaeology.

Root, M.C. (2003), 'The Lioness of Elam: Politics and Dynastic Fecundity at Persepolis', in W. Henkelman and A. Kuhrt (eds), *A Persian Perspective. Essays in Memory of Heleen Sancisi-Weerdenburg, Achaemenid History XIII*, 9–32, Leiden: Nederlands Instituut voor het Nabije Oosten.

Root, M.C. (2011), 'Elam in the Imperial Imagination: From Nineveh to Persepolis', in J. Álvarez-Mon and M.B. Garrison (eds), *Elam and Persia*, 419–74, Winona Lake: Eisenbrauns.

Rose, J. (2001), 'Sasanian Splendor: The Appurtenances of Royalty', in S. Gordon (ed.), *Robes and Honor. The Medieval World of Investiture*, 35–58, New York: Palgrave Macmillan.

Roth, M. (1995), *Law Collections from Mesopotamia and Asia Minor*, Atlanta: Scholars Press.

Roth, S. (2012), 'Harem', in E. Frood and W. Wendrich (eds), *UCLA Encyclopedia of Egyptology*, Los Angeles. http://digital2.library.ucla.edu/viewItem.do?ark=21198/ zz002bqmpp (accessed 12 November 2021).

Rubinson, K.S. (1990), 'The Textiles from Pazyryk: A Study in the Transfer and Transformation of Artistic Motifs', *Expedition*, 32 (1): 49–61.

Rudenko, S.I. (1970), *Frozen Tombs of Siberia: The Pazyrik Burials of Iron-Age Horsemen*, London: Dent.

Ruiz-Ortiz, F-J. (2017), *The Dynamics of Violence and Revenge in the Hebrew Book of Esther*, Leiden and Boston: Brill.

Russell, J.M. (1991), *Sennacherib's Palace Without Rival at Nineveh*, London and Chicago: University of Chicago Press.

Saïd, E.W. (1978), *Orientalism*, London: Routledge and Kegan Paul.

Salvesen, A. (1998), 'Trappings of Royalty in Ancient Israel', in J. Day (ed.), *King and Messiah in Israel and the Ancient Near East*, 119–41, Sheffield: Sheffield Academic Press.

Samet, N. (2021), '*Ben Bayit*: New Light on an Overlooked Biblical Administrative Term and Its Historical Setting', in P. Machinist, R.A. Harris, J.A. Berman, N. Samet, and

N. Ayali-Darshan (eds), *Ve-'Ed Ya'aleh (Gen 2:6): Essays in Biblical and Ancient Near Eastern Studies Presented to Edward L. Greenstein*, 375–92, Atlanta: SBL Press.

Samuel, M. (1955), *Certain People of the Book*, New York: Knopf.

Sánchez, M.G. (2006), 'La figura del sucesor del Gran Rey en la Persia aqueménida', in V.A. Troncoso (ed.), *Diodokhos tēs Basileias: La figura del sucesor en la realeza helenística. Anejo IX*, 223–39, Madrid: Servicio de Publicaciones, Universidad Complutense.

Sánchez, M.G. (2009), *El Gran Rey de Persia: Formas de Representación de la Alteridad Persa en el Imaginario Griego*, Barcelona: Universitat de Barcelona.

Sancisi-Weerdenburg, H. (1983), 'Exit Atossa: Images of Women in Greek Historiography on Persia', in A. Cameron and A. Kuhrt (eds), *Images of Women in Antiquity*, 20–33, London: Croom Helm.

Sancisi-Weerdenburg, H. (1987a), 'Decadence in the Empire or Decadence in the Sources? From Source to Synthesis: Ctesias', in H. Sancisi-Weerdenburg (ed.), *Achaemenid History I. Sources, Structures and Synthesis*, 33–45, Leiden: Nederlands Instituut Voor Het Nabije Oosten.

Sancisi-Weerdenburg, H. (1987b), 'The Fifth Oriental Monarchy and Hellenocentrism', in H. Sancisi-Weerdenburg and A. Kuhrt (eds), *Achaemenid History II. The Greek Sources*, 117–31, Leiden: Nederlands Instituut Voor Het Nabije Oosten.

Sancisi-Weerdenburg, H. (1989), 'Gifts in the Persian Empire', in P. Briant and C. Herrenschmidt (eds), *Les tributes dans l'empire perse. Actes de la Table Ronde de Paris 12–13 décembre 1986*, 129–46, Paris: Peeters.

Sancisi-Weerdenburg, H. (1995), 'Persian Food: Stereotypes and Political Identity', in J. Wilkins et al. (eds), *Food in Antiquity*, 286–302, Exeter: University of Exeter Press.

Sancisi-Weerdenburg, H. (1997), 'Crumbs from the Royal Table', *Topoi*. Supplement, 1: 332–42.

Sancisi-Weerdenburg, H. (1998), 'Bāji', in M. Brosius and A. Kuhrt (eds), *Studies in Persian History: Essays in Memory of David M. Lewis*, 23–34, Leiden: Nederlands Instituut Voor Het Nabije Oosten.

Sarkhosh Curtis, V. (1996), 'Parthian and Sasanian Furniture', in G. Herrmann (ed.), *The Furniture of Western Asia. Ancient and Traditional*, 233–44, Mainz: Philipp von Zabern.

Scarce, J. (1987), *Women's Costume of the Near and Middle East*, London: Unwin Hyman.

Schaudig, H. (2001), *Die Inschriften Nabonids von Babylon und Kyros' des Großen*, Münster: Ugarit-Verlag.

Scheidel, W. (2009), 'Sex and Empire. A Darwinian Perspective', in I. Morris and W. Scheidel (eds), *The Dynamics of Ancient Empires. State Power from Assyria to Byzantium*, 255–324, Oxford: Oxford University Press.

Schimmel, A. (2004), *The Empire of the Great Mughals. History, Art and Culture*, London: Reaktion Books.

Schlumberger, D. (1971), 'La coiffure du grand roi', *Syria*, 48: 375–83.

Schmandt-Besserat, D. (1978), *Ancient Persia. The Art of Empire*, Austin: University of Texas at Austin.

Schmidt, E.F. (1953), *Persepolis I*, Chicago: University of Chicago Press.

Schmidt, E.F. (1957), *Persepolis II, Contents of the Treasury and Other Discoveries*, Chicago: University of Chicago Press.

Schmidt, E.F. (1970), *Persepolis III, The Royal Tombs and Other Monuments*, Chicago: University of Chicago Press.

Schmitt, R. (1977a), 'Königtum im Alten Iran', *Saeculum*, 28: 384–95.

Schmitt, R. (1977b), 'Thronnamen bei den Achaimeniden', *Beiträge zur Namenforschung*, 12: 422–5.
Scholz, P.O. (1999), *Eunuchs and Castrati. A Cultural History*, Princeton: Markus Wiener Publishers.
Scott, B.Y. (1958), 'The Hebrew Cubit', *Journal of Biblical Literature*, 77: 205–14.
Secunda, S. (2020), *The Talmud's Red Fence: Menstrual Impurity and Difference in Babylonian Judaism and its Sasanian Context*, Oxford: Oxford University Press.
Seidler, A. (2019), '"Fasting," "Sackcloth," and "Ashes"—From Nineveh to Shushan', *Vetus Testamentum*, 69: 117–34.
Sekunda, N.V. (2010), 'Changes in Achaemenid Royal Dress', in J. Curtis and S. Simpson (eds), *The World of Achaemenid Persia*, 256–72, London: I.B. Tauris.
Sekunda, N.V. and Chew, S. (1992), *The Persian Army*, Oxford: Osprey Publishing.
Shahbazi, A.S. (2004), *The Authoritative Guide to Persepolis*, Tehran: Safir.
Shahbazi, A.S. (2009), s.v. 'Persepolis', in *Encyclopaedia Iranica*, New York.
Shaked, S. (2004), *Le satrape de Bactriane et son gouverneur. Documents araméens du IVe avant notre ère provenant de Bactriane*, Paris: De Boccard.
Shea, W.H. (1987), 'Esther and History', *Concordia Journal*, July: 234–48.
Silverman, J.M. (2012), *Persepolis and Jerusalem: Iranian Influence on the Apocalyptic Hermeneutic*, London: T & T Clark.
Silverman, J.M. (2020), *Persian Royal Judaean Elite Engagements in the Early Teispid and Achaemenid Empire: The King's Acolytes*, London: T & T Clark.
Silverman, J.M. and Waerzeggers, C. (eds) (2015), *Political Memory in and After the Persian Empire*, Atlanta: SBL Press.
Silverstein, A. (2018), *Veiling Esther, Unveiling Her Story. The Reception of a Biblical Book in Islamic Lands*, Oxford: Oxford University Press.
Simpson, St J. (1998), 'Late Achaemenid Silver Bowl from Mazanderan', *British Museum Magazine*, 32: 32.
Sissom, D. (2019), *The Bridge to the New Testament. A Comprehensive Guide to the Forgotten Years of the Inter-Testament Period*, Huntsville: Testament Press.
Solvang, E.K. (2003), *A Woman's Place is in the House. Royal Women of Judah and their Involvement in the House of David*, Sheffield: Sheffield Academic Press.
Sommer, B.D. (2009), *The Bodies of God and the World of Ancient Israel*, Cambridge: Cambridge University Press.
Soudavar, A. (2003), *The Aura of Kings. Legitimacy and Divine Sanction in Iranian Kingship*, Costa Mesa: Mazda Publishers.
Spawforth, A.J.S. (2007a), 'The Court of Alexander the Great', in A.J.S. Spawforth (ed.), *The Court and Court Society in Ancient Monarchies*, 82–120, Cambridge: Cambridge University Press.
Spawforth, A.J.S. ed. (2007b), *The Court and Court Society in Ancient Monarchies*, Cambridge: Cambridge University Press.
Spence, K. (2007), 'Court and Palace in Ancient Egypt: The Amarna Period and the Later Eighteenth Dynasty', in A.J.S. Spawforth (ed.), *The Court and Court Society in Ancient Monarchies*, 267–328, Cambridge: Cambridge University Press.
Spence, K. (2009), 'The Palaces of el-Amarna: Towards an Architectural Analysis', in R. Gundlach, and J. Taylor (eds), *Egyptian Royal Residences: 4th Symposium on Egyptian Royal Ideology, London, June 1st–5th, 2004, Königtum, Staat und Gesellschaft früher Hochkulturen 4, 1: Beiträge zur altägyptischen Königsideologie*, 165–87, Wiesbaden: Harrassowitz Verlag.

Stevens, A. (1995), *Private Myths: Dreams and Dreaming*, Cambridge, MA: Harvard University Press.
Stevenson, R.B. (1987), 'Lies and Invention in Deinon's *Persica*', in H. Sancisi-Weerdenburg and A. Kuhrt (eds), *Achaemenid History II. The Greek Sources*, 27–35, Leiden: Nederlands Instituut Voor Het Nabije Oosten.
Stevenson, R.B. (1997), *Persica. Greek Writing about Persia in the Fourth Century BC*, Edinburgh: Scottish Academic Press.
Stol, M. (2016), *Women in the Ancient Near East*, Berlin: De Gruyter.
Stolper, M.W. (1985), *Entrepreneurs and Empire: The Murašû Archive, The Murašû Firm, and Persian Rule in Babylonia*, Uitgaven van het Nederlands Historisch-Archaeologisch Instituut te Istanbul 54, Leiden: Nederlands Instituut Voor Het Nabije Oosten.
Stoneman, R. (2015), *Xerxes: A Persian Life*, New Haven: Yale University Press.
Stronach, D. (1978), *Parsagade. A Report on the Excavations Conducted by the British Institute of Persian Studies from 1961 to 1963*, Oxford: Oxford University Press.
Stronach, D. (1989), 'The Royal Garden at Pasargadae: Evolution and Legacy', in L. Vanden Berghe, E. Haerinck and L. de Meyer (eds), *Archaeologica Iranica et Orientalis: Miscellanea in Honorem Louis Vanden Berghe*, 476–502, Ghent: Peeters Presse.
Stronach, D. (1997a), 'Darius as Parsagadae: A Neglected Source for the History of Early Persia', *Topoi*, Supplement 1: 351–63.
Stronach, D. (1997b), 'Anshan and Persia: Early Achaemenid History, Art and Architecture on the Iranian Plateau', in J. Curtis (ed.), *Mesopotamia and Iran in the Persian Period: Conquest and Imperialism 539–331 BC*, 35–53, London: British Museum Press.
Stronach, D. (2011), 'Court Dress and Riding Dress at Persepolis: New Approaches to Old Questions', in J. Álvarez-Mon and M.B. Garrison (eds), *Elam and Persia*, 475–87, Winona Lake: Eisenbrauns.
Stronk, J. (2004–5), 'Ctesias of Cnidus: From Physician to Author', *Talanta*, 36–7: 101–22.
Strootman, R. (2007), 'The Hellenistic Royal Court. Court Culture, Ceremonial and Ideology in Greece, Egypt and the Near East, 336–30 BCE', Unpublished Thesis, Utrecht.
Strootman, R. (2014), *Courts and Elites in the Hellenistic Empires: The Near East After the Achaemenids, c. 330 to 30 BCE*, Edinburgh: Edinburgh University Press.
Sumner, W.M. (1986), 'Achaemenid Settlement in the Persepolis Plain', *American Journal of Archaeology*, 90 (1): 3–31.
Svärd, S. (2016), 'Neo-Assyrian Elite Women', in S. Budin and J. Macintosh Turfa (eds), *Women in Antiquity. Real Women Across the Ancient World*, 126–37, London: Routledge.
Svärd, S. and Luukko, M. (2009), 'Who Were the "Ladies of the House" in the Assyrian Empire?', in M. Luukko, S. Svärd and R. Mattila (eds), *Of God(s), Trees, Kings, and Scholars. Neo-Assyrian and Related Studies in Honour of Simo Parpola*, 279–94, Helsinki: Finnish Oriental Society.
Tadmor, M. (1974), 'Fragments of an Achaemenid Throne from Samaria', *Israel Exploration Journal*, 24 (1): 37–43.
Talmon, S. (1963), 'Wisdom in the Book of Esther', *Vetus Testamentum*, 13: 445–64.
Tappy, R. E. (2001), *The Archaeology of Israelite Samaria, Vol. II: The Eighth Century BCE*, Winona Lake: Eisenbrauns.
Tavernier, J. (2007), *Iranica in the Achaemenid Period (ca. 550–330 BC). Lexicon of Old Iranian Proper Names and Loanwords attested in Non-Iranian Texts*, Leuven: Peeters.

Tavernier, J. (2010), 'Multilingualism in the Fortification and Treasury Archives', in P. Briant, W. Henkleman, W. and M. Stolper (eds), *L'archive des Fortifications de Persépolis*, 59–85, Paris: De Boccard.

Taylor, L.R. (1927), 'The *Proskynesis* and the Hellenistic Ruler Cult', *JHS*, 47: 53–62.

Taylor, M.A. (2020), *Ruth, Esther. The Story of God Bible Commentary*, Grand Rapids: Zondervan Academic.

Testen, D. (1998), 'Semitic Terms for "Myrtle": A Study in Covert Cognates', *Journal of Near Eastern Studies*, 57: 281–90.

Thompson, G. 1965, 'Iranian Dress in the Achaemenian Period. Problems Concerning the Kandys and other Garments', *Iran*, 3: 121–6.

Thompson, S. (1955–8), *The Motif-Index of Folk-Literature*, Bloomington: Indiana University Press.

Tilia, A.B. (1972), *Studies and Restorations at Persepolis and Other Sites of Fārs I*, Rome: IsMEO.

Tilia, A.B. (1978), *Studies and Restorations at Persepolis and Other Sites of Fārs II*, Rome: IsMEO.

Tolini, G. (2013), 'Les ressources de la Babylonie et la table de Darius le Grand (522–486)', in C. Grandjean (ed.), *Le banquet du monarque dans le monde antique*, 145–62, Rennes: Presses Universitaires de Rennes.

Tomes, R. (2005), '*I Have Written to My Lord the King*': *Secular Analogies for the Psalms*, Sheffield: Sheffield Phoenix Press.

Tougher, S. (2008), *The Eunuch in Byzantine History and Society*, London: Routledge.

Tsai, S-S.H. (1996), *The Eunuchs in the Ming Dynasty*, Albany, NY: Suny Press.

Tsai, S.-S.H. (2002), 'Eunuch Power in Imperial China', in S. Tougher (ed.), *Eunuchs in Antiquity and Beyond*, 221–33, London and Swansea: Classical Press of Wales.

Tuplin, C. (1987), 'The Administration of the Achaemenid Empire', in I. Carradice (ed.), *Coinage and Administration in the Athenian and Persian Empires*, BAR International Series, 34, 109–66, London: BAR Publishing.

Tuplin, C. (1996), *Achaemenid Studies*, Stuttgart: F. Steiner.

Tuplin, C. (1998a), 'Review: Women in Ancient Persia', *The Classical Review*, 48 (1): 104–6.

Tuplin, C. (1998b), 'The Seasonal Migration of Achaemenid Kings: A Report on Old and New Evidence', in M. Brosius and A. Kuhrt (eds), *Studies in Persian History: Essays in Memory of David M. Lewis*, 63–114, Leiden: Nederlands Instituut Voor Het Nabije Oosten.

Tuplin, C. (2004), 'The Persian Empire', in R. Lane Fox (ed.), *The Long March: Xenophon and the Ten Thousand*, 154–83, New Haven and London: Yale University Press.

Tuplin, C., ed. (2007a), *Persian Responses. Political and Cultural Interaction With(in) the Achaemenid Empire*, Swansea: Classical Press of Wales.

Tuplin, C. (2007b), 'Treacherous Hearts and Upright Tiaras: The Achaemenid King's Head-Dress', in C. Tuplin (ed.), *Persian Responses. Political and Cultural Interaction With(in) the Persian Empire*, 67–97, Swansea: Classical Press of Wales.

Tuplin, C. (2010a), 'All the King's Men', in J. Curtis and St. J. Simpson (eds), *The World of Achaemenid Persia*, 51–61, London: I.B. Tauris.

Tuplin, C. (2010b), 'All the King's Horses: In Search of Achaemenid Cavalry', in M. Trundle and G. Fagan (eds), *New Perspectives on Ancient Warfare*, 101–82, Leiden: Brill.

Tuplin, C. (2020), 'Sigilography and Soldiers: Cataloguing Military Activity on Achaemenid Period Seals', in E.R.M. Dusinberre, M.B. Garrison and W.F.M. Henkelman (eds), *The Art of Empire in Achaemenid Persia. Studies in Honour of Margaret Cool Root.*

Achaemenid History XVI, 329–459, Leiden and Leuven: Nederlands Instituut Voor Het Nabije Oosten.
Tuplin, C.J. and Ma, J., eds (2021), *Aršama and his World: The Bodleian Letters in Context*, 3 vols, Oxford: Oxford University Press.
Uchitel, A. (1997), 'Persian Paradise. Agricultural Texts in the Fortification Tablets', *Iranica Antiqua*, 32: 137–44.
Uehlinger, C. (1999), 'Powerful Persianisms in Glyptic Iconography of Persian Period Palestine', in B. Becking and M.C.A. Korpel (eds), *The Crisis of Israelite Religion*, 136–82, Leiden: Brill.
Uehlinger, C. and Müller Trufaut, S. (2001), 'Ezekiel 1, Babylonian Cosmological Scholarship and Iconography: Attempts at Further Refinement', *Theologische Zeitschrift*, 57: 140–71.
Vahman, F. (1985), 'A Beautiful Girl', *Acta Iranica*, 25 (2): 665–73.
Vale, M. (2001), *The Princely Courts. Mediaeval Courts and Culture in North-West Europe*, Oxford: Oxford University Press.
van de Mieroop, M. (1999), *Cuneiform Texts and the Writing of History*, London: Routledge.
van de Mieroop, M. (2004), *A History of the Ancient Near East*, Oxford: Wiley.
van Selms, A. (1957), 'The Origin of the Title "The Friend of the King"', *Journal of Near Eastern Studies*, 16: 118–23.
Vogelsang, W. (1992), *The Rise and Organisation of the Achaemenid Empire: The Eastern Evidence*, New York and Cologne: Brill.
Vogelsang, W. (2010), 'Trouser Wearing by Horse-Riding Nomads in Central Asia', in G. Vogelsang-Eastwood (ed.), *Berg Encyclopaedia of World Dress and Fashion. Volume 5: Central and Southwest Asia*, 349–54, Oxford: Berg.
Vogelstein, M. (1943), 'Bakshish for Bagoas?', *Jewish Quarterly Review*, 33: 89–92.
von Graeve, V. (1970), *Der Alexandersarhophag und seine Werkstatt*, Berlin: Gebr. Mann.
von Graeve, V. (1987), 'Eine Miszelle zur griechischen Malerei', *IstMitt*, 37: 131–44.
von Rad, G. (1991), *Holy War in Ancient Israel*, Michigan: William B. Eeerdmans Publishing Co.
Wadsworth, T. (1980), 'Is there a Hebrew Word for Virgin? Bethulah in the Old Testament', *ResQ*, 23: 161–71.
Wahl, H.M. (2009), *Das Buch Esther. Übersetzung und Kommentar*, Berlin: De Gruyter.
Walker, E. (2010), *Horse*, London: Reaktion.
Wasmuth, M. (2019), 'Transient or Eternal? Cross-regional Display Reconsidered: The Missing Head of the Statue of Darius I', *Journal of Ancient Egyptian Interconnections*, 24: 49–66.
Watanabe, C.E. (2002), *Animal Symbolism in Mesopotamia. A Contextual Approach*, Vienna: Institut für Orientalistik der Universität Wien.
Waters, M. (2014), *Ancient Persia: A Concise History of the Achaemenid Empire, 550-330 BCE*, Cambridge: Cambridge University Press.
Wechsler, M.G. (2000), 'Two Para-Biblical Novellae from Qumran Cave 4: A Reevaluation of 4Q550*', *Dead Sea Discoveries*, 7 (2): 130–72.
Weidner, E. (1954), 'Hof-und Harems-Erlasse assyrischer Könige aus dem 2. Jahrtausend', *Archiv für Orientforschung*, 17: 257–93.
Weisberg, D.B. (1967), *Guild Structure and Political Allegiance in Early Achaemenid Mesopotamia*, New Haven: Yale University Press.
Weltecke, D. (2000), 'Originality and Function of Formal Structures in the Chronicle of Michael the Great', *Hugoye: Journal of Syriac Studies*, 3 (2): 173–204.

Wenham, G.J. (1972), 'Bĕtûlâh, a Girl of Marriageable Age', *Vetus Testamentum*, 22: 236-48.
White Crawford, S. (1996), 'Has Esther Been Found at Qumran? 4QProto-Esther and the Esther Corpus', *Revue de Qumran*, 17: 307-25.
White Crawford, S. (2002), '4Q Tales of the Persian Court (4Q550 a-e) and its Relation to Biblical Royal Courtier Tales, Especially Esther, Daniel and Joseph', in E. Herbert and E. Tov (eds), *The Bible as Book: The Hebrew Bible and the Judaean Desert Discoveries*, 121-38, London: British Library.
Widengren, G. (1951), *The King and the Tree of Life in Ancient Near Eastern Religion*, Uppsala: Lundequistska bokhandeln.
Widengren, G. (1956), 'Some Remarks on Riding Costume and Articles of Dress Among Iranian Peoples in Antiquity', in A. Furumark (ed.), *Artica (Studia Ethnographica Upsaliensa XI)*, 228-76, Uppsala: Almqvist & Wiksell.
Widengren, G. (1959), 'The Sacral Kingship of Iran', *La regalita sacra, contributi alterna dell' VIII Congresso Internazionale de Storia delle Religioni (Roma, Aprile 1955)*, 242-57, Leiden: Brill.
Widengren, G. (1965), *Die Religionen Irans*, Stuttgart: Kohlhammer.
Widengren, G. (1968), *Les religions de l'Iran*, Paris: Payot.
Wiesehöfer, J. (1996), *Ancient Persia from 550 BC to 650 AD*, London and New York: I.B. Tauris.
Wiesehöfer, J. (2009), 'The Achaemenid Empire', in I. Morris and W. Scheidel (eds), *The Dynamics of Ancient Empires. State Power from Assyria to Byzantium*, 66-98, Oxford: Oxford University Press.
Wiesehöfer, J. (2010), 'Günstlinge und Privilegien am Achaimenidenhof', in B. Jacobs and R. Rollinger (eds), *Der Achämenidenhof/The Achaemenid Court*, 509-30, Wiesbaden: Harrassowitz Verlag.
Wiesehöfer, J., Rollinger, R. and Lanfranchi, G. eds (2011), *Ktesias' Welt/Ctesias' World*, Wiesbaden: Harrassowitz Verlag.
Wilber, D.N. (1962), *Persian Gardens and Garden Pavilions*, Tokyo: Charles E. Tuttle.
Wilber, D.N. (1969), *Persepolis. The Archaeology of Parsa, Seat of the Persian Kings*, Princeton: Darwin Press.
Wilcke, C. (1985), 'Familiengründung im Alten Babylonien', in E. Müller (ed.), *Geschlechtsreife und Legitimiation zur Zeugung*, 215-319, Munich: Alber.
Wilkinson, R.H. (1992), *Reading Egyptian Art*, London: Thames and Hudson.
Wills, L.M. (1990), *The Jew in the Court of the Foreign King*, Minneapolis: Fortress Press.
Wills, L.M. (1995), *The Jewish Novel in the Ancient World*, Ithaca and London: Cornell University Press.
Yamauchi, E.M. (1990), *Persia and the Bible*, Grand Rapids: Baker Book House.
Yamauchi, E.M. (1992), 'Mordecai of the Persepolis Tablets and the Susa Excavations', *Vetus Testamentum*, 42: 272-75.
Yeazell, R.B. (2000), *Harems of the Mind. Passages of Western Art and Literature*, New Haven and London: Yale University Press.
Young, I., and Rezetko, R. eds (2008), *Linguistic Dating of Biblical Texts*, 2 vols, London: Routledge.
Yoyotte, M. (2008), 'Le harem dans l'Égypte ancienne', in C. Ziegler (ed.), *Reines d'Égypte: D'Hétephérès à Cléopâtre*, 76-90, Monaco: Somogy.
Ziderman, I. (2004), 'Purple Dyeing in the Mediterranean World', in L. Cleland and K. Stears (eds), *Colour in the Ancient Mediterranean World*, 40-5, Oxford: Archaeopress.

Index

Achaemenid empire (see also Persian) 17, 23, 25, 32-33
Administration 122, 162-3, 172-3
Ahuramazda 18, 23-24, 26, 29, 32, 112, 156-58, 60, 66, 69, 175, 184, 205-6
Audience, royal 167-70, 177, 184, 191

Banquet, Achaemenid 50-54, 79
    Couches at 215-16
    in Esther 48-49, 92, 122, 153-4
    guests and seating at 15, 54-55, 82
    in the Near East 49-50
    wine at 49, 83-89, 122-3
    women at 91-93
Beauty
    in art 103
    beauty treatments 121, 140-4
    contests 125
    divine 102
    Esther's 121, 151
    Fertility and 104-6
    Ideals of 100-103, 108
    Men and 140
    products 142-44
    slaves 142
    women 142

Clothing 18, 63-64
    court robe 64-65, 71, 184, 203
    gaunaka 202-4
    Khal'at 200-2 (see also gift-giving)
    royal robe 63, 189-93, 197, 202, 220, 222
Communication 117-20, 222
Court
    Advisors at 110-11
    Assyrian 116-17
    Attendants at 123
    conduct at 166, 184
    courtiers 55-56, 84-85, 89, 111, 113
    in Esther 123-4
    gestures at 66-169
    Greek ideas of 166, 168
    inner and outer 123, 189, 193
    nomadic 79, 85 (see also royal tent)
    Persian 4, 55-57, 116-17, 166, 172
    at Susa 2-4
    tales and stories of 5-7, 9
Ctesias of Cnidus 4, 8, 17, 50-51, 55
Cyrus the Great 31

Darius the Great 17-18, 23, 26-27
Display 59, 69-70, 74, 181-2, 229

Esther, Book of
    authorship 3-5, 9, 11, 22-23, 227
    problematic chapter nine 9-11, 223-4
    Hasmonaean additions to 10-11
    date of composition 1-2, 4, 97
    lacking references to God and Jewish practices 2, 4, 30
    Hebrew version 2-3, 10, 16, 48, 139, 229
    Greek version 2-3, 16, 21, 138, 198
Esther (fictional character)
    Family of 121-2, 219, 224
    goddess Ishtar and 100, 139, 166
    marriage to Xerxes 90-91, 115-16, 122, 151-3, 188-9, 216
    meaning of name 121, 139
Eunuchs 94-7, 138, 146, 177, 181, 216

Gates, palace 155-9

Harem (see also Women) 134-7, 145
    conduct in 216-17
    Esther and 145, 217
    Greek and Roman views of 145-6
    household 29, 121, 123, 130
    iconography of 137-8
    ideology, and 131-2
    protocol, and 146-7

seclusion in 146
of Soloman 228
Herodotus 8, 25, 60, 122, 195–6, 206
Horses 206–7, 219

King of Persia 29–30, 30–33, 40–43, 61–62, 78, 97–98, 112, 115, 184, 190

Lamentation 179–80
Lots 165, 170–1

Mordecai (fictional character) 11, 47–48, 63, 121–2, 139, 155, 158, 189, 198–200, 202, 204

Numismatics 58–59

Palace and royal residence 69–79
Persepolis 18, 25–26
Persia, Persian (see also Achaemenid)
  empire 4, 22
  hero 18
  imperial titles 20–21, 24–25
  Medes and 58
  names, fake 3
Purim 3, 10–11

Seals 173–5, 219, 222
Slaves, slavery 211–15
Storytelling and folktales 124–5
Susa 44–47, 172–3

Tablets, cuneiform
  Hamadan 26
  Persepolis 26
  Persepolis Fortification 18, 29–30, 52, 84, 162
  Persepolis Treasury 18
Textiles
  materials and dying 80–81
  Pazyryk textile 39, 103
  royal tent 79, 82
  upholstery 38

tribute, royal
  as tax 59, 172, 225
  bribe 171–2
  from satraps 58
  gift 165, 199–200, 228
  Greek views of 199
  symbol of power 58

Vashti (fictional character)
  Banquet of 15–16, 92–93
  disobedience 107
  marriage to Xerxes 115–16, 152
  name of 89–90
  removal 109, 114, 117, 121–3
Violence 19, 122, 123, 160–2, 195

Women
  attendants 144–145
  concubines 90, 126–7, 146–51, 188
  crowns and veils of 97–100, 152, 190, 192
  Fertility of 82
  gestures of respect 169–70
  Greek view of 114, 122, 130, 145, 149–50, 216
  Hierarchy of 115–16
  Independence of 132–3, 220–2
  marriage and 152–3
  menstruation 188
  music and 148
  polygyny 90, 115, 130, 188
  rules and conduct for 217
  servants and 214–15, 217
  sex trafficking of 127–30
  virginity 126–7, 154
  visibility of 108–9
  wives 90–91, 115–16, 129–30, 133, 188, 217

Xerxes, king of Persia 16–19, 21–22, 28–29, 58, 159–60
Xerxes (semi-fictional literary character) 21–22, 30, 33, 63, 110, 115